Gardner History and Genealogy

GARDNER

HISTORY AND GENEALOGY

BY

LILLIAN MAY

AND

CHARLES MORRIS GARDNER

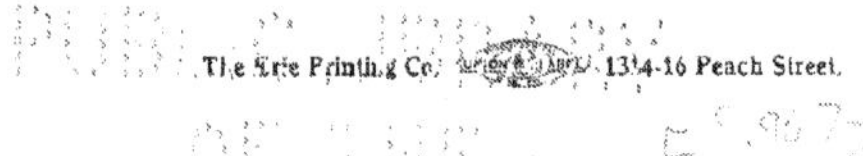

The Erie Printing Co. 1314-16 Peach Street.

PREFACE.

In the following history and genealogy we have not depended upon tradition, but have carefully gathered all written records, comparing and selecting what proved to be authentic. The early Rhode Island records were copied We present the early deeds, wills, and written records of births and deaths, we present the family records, which have been preserved as written and handed down from generation to generation

We wish to acknowledge our indebtedness to those who rendered assistance in collecting this information from the many families who are scattered over the entire country—the records loaned by Mrs Bates, of Rhode Island, Thomas Peirce, Stephen Reynolds, of Wickford, Alonzo J Gardiner, of Allenton, R. I., Rev A Gardner, West Willington, Conn, Mrs Lucy Gardner Moffitt, Stephentown, N Y, Rev William Gardner, Washington, D C. Burton J Gardner, Broadhead, Wis, Floyd Carter, Uniopolis, Ohio, Mrs. Eva L Bundy, Manchester, Ohio, Charles H Gardner, Cleveland, Ohio, and others, besides the kindness and courtesies of the many librarians

LILLIAN MAY and CHARLES MORRIS GARDNER.

Why I Wrote the History of the Gardner Family and Some Experiences in Travels.

The Gardner family had always been of great interest to the writer, being the youngest son of Abraham, Jr, and Harriet (Brentlinger) Gardner, born July 25, 1863, on a farm near Wapakoneta, Auglaize county, Ohio I well remember the aunts as they visited my parents or my parents visited them Father had but one brother, Benjamin, who went West before the writer was born. Grandfather Gardner had died before I was born. I did not see a Gardner by name other than father and the other children of this family As I grew up I learned that our relatives lived in Brown county, Ohio Father would frequently tell us about his father and mother coming to the new home in Allen county, now Auglaize county My parents lived about four miles west of the old homestead, and when we would visit our aunts we passed within sight of the Gardner farm. This would cause us children to make inquiry relative to the family When I was a boy about 12 years old, I remember on one Sabbath morning, father having breakfasted very early, he ordered the "gray mare" brought, as he wished to go several miles On his return that evening, he told us what had been read to him from a book, which has since proven to be the autobiography of Elder Matthew Gardner I remember father stating he desired to borrow the book, then to purchase it, but the owner would not permit him to take it in his hands The gentleman referred to was a member of the Christian Church, the denomination for which Elder Gardner preached, living on "Two Mile," Auglaize county, Ohio I remember distinctly many of the features of the life of Elder Gardner as narrated by my father, the relation he sustained to my grandfather and many of the circumstances When I grew to manhood I made a continuous effort to secure the book Whenever I met a preacher of that denomination I made diligent inquiry about the book The last preacher of that denomination I met was while I was teaching school in Hardin county, Ohio I offered to pay him $10 if he would secure a copy of the book for me. I did not get it at that price.

Not knowing the names of the relatives, I did not know when I did meet them, for I met a great many Gardners in my work.

While at Marietta, Ohio, about the year 1889, I attended an Annual Conference of the Methodist Episcopal Church, and they were electing delegates to the Ecumenical Conference at London, England Many of the members of the Conference were vigorously campaigning for Hon. Mills Gardner, of Washington C H, Ohio. There I learned the activity and great interest he took in the work of this demonstration.

I resolved when in that part of Ohio to call and see him, but it seemed I never would get to his city I was at Cincinnati later, and a gentleman said to me "Gardner, have you not relatives in Brown county? You resemble them" I had but limited time and could not visit them This man said he personally knew Matthew, Seth, Charlotte and many of the older ones A few years later I met a physician in Toledo Ohio, who said he personally knew Seth, Hank (Henry) and their children I began to learn their names in this manner While in Fort Wayne, Ind, in the spring of 1905, my cousin, Lewis Fairfield, spent a few hours with me, and discussing family relations, said "While my brother was at Washington C. H, Ohio, he called on a Mr Gardner there, ex-Congressman, and he is of our branch of the family"

In July, 1905, our business relation took us to Lima, Ohio, Allen county While there I secured a conveyance and drove to the "old farm" one Sabbath afternoon to see the graves of my grandparents Mr. George Connor, who now owns the farm, took me to the ground, and we found the fence in great need of repair The markers at the graves were either broken, had fallen or were about to fall Little attention had been given them by the relatives since grandmother had been buried in the year 1879 Mr Connor had carefully kept the ground from growing up with weeds and briars. I stated to him we would immediately place a fence of the best material he could purchase, and we proceeded to reset the markers by building a concrete base under all, and in a few days the little cemetery was made as new, and protected the graves of those buried

Mr. Connor said "Charley, if I was you I would invite the relatives in to see the new work which has been done and assist to pay for the repairs" With that suggestion there was announced a family reunion to be held August 29, 1905, on the old homestead The county papers announced it and a gathering of the friends resulted. The following publication appeared in each of the Wapakoneta papers announcing the gathering

THE GARDNER FAMILY REUNION.

"We have been requested to announce that a reunion of the Gardner family will be held on the old Gardner farm, now known as the George Connor farm, in this township, on the 29th day of August, and that all relatives are urged to attend"

FAMILY HISTORY

Abraham Gardner, Sr, the first settler in this county by that name, was born and reared in Brown county, this State, his grandfather having emigrated from Rhode Island to New York in 1765, his father then coming to Ohio. He had eight brothers and four sisters The many families who are descendants of this family are mostly residents of Southern Ohio. A distinguished member of the family is the Hon Mills Gardner of Washington C H, Ohio. Another who achieved distinction was Matthew Gardner, a brother of Abraham Gardner, Sr Matthew was the "John Wesley" of the Christian Church, having participated in the theological discussions in the early history of that denomination, and he preached to one congregation for 52 successive years

Abraham Gardner, Sr , bought 160 acres of land in this county (then Allen county) from the Government about the year 1835, and was therefore one of our earliest pioneers A part of this tract is now embraced in what is known as the George Connor farm, four miles northeast of Wapakoneta. He had ten children, eight daughters and two sons The two sons were Abraham and Benjamin Benjamin Gardner located in the State of Kansas away back in the sixties He died September, 1904, survived by a large family Abraham Gardner, Jr , who will be remembered by many of our readers, lived here till 1879, when he, too, struck out for the West, locating finally in California, where he accumulated a competence and where he died on the 21st of January, 1905. Abraham Gardner, Jr 's family consisted of his wife and four children, three sons and one daughter.

The daughter is now living at Duluth, Minn The eldest son, Horace W Gardner, is the electrician of the Santa Fe Railway system.

The youngest son, Charles M Gardner, is engaged in business at Toledo, Ohio The surviving daughters are Lucy, wife of Samuel Carter of Uniopolis; Sarah, widow of David Butler, late of Uniopolis, Caroline, wife of George Harshbarger of Moulton township, Clarissa, wife of George Fairfield, formerly of this county, but for the past 20 years a resident of Paulding, Paulding county, Ohio One of the deceased daughters married William Brentlinger, whose sons and daughter are well-known residents of this county On the old homestead is a cemetery, in which are buried the remains of Abraham Gardner, Sr , and other members of the Gardner family, and that has been kept in good repair by Mr George Connor, the present owner of the Gardner farm, and a life-long friend of the family

Mr Connor extends an earnest invitation to all friends and relatives of the family to attend the reunion on the 29th inst.

THE GARDNER REUNION

The first reunion of the Gardner family was held on the 29th of August on the old Gardner farm, now owned by Mr. George Connor. The writer visited the old homestead a few weeks since, when Mr Connor extended an invitation to the relatives and friends of Abraham Gardner, Sr , to visit the old homestead An informal gathering was the result, which was composed of many relatives and friends of the old pioneer The surviving members of the family of Abraham Gardner, Sr , composed of four sisters, were all present. It was indeed a pleasure to see these sisters meet again and recount the experiences of the many years past It was true with the expression of the poet

> "Backward, turn backward, oh ! time in thy flight,
> Make me a child again, just for tonight"

The old spring was visited, the old loghouse, erected by the hands of their father, a part of which still stands, a visit to the room in which the father died, and, last, a visit to the little graveyard, where rest the remains of the father and mother and the first wife of Abraham Gardner, Jr , and their infant daughter and two children of Benjamin Gardner

This little ground had just undergone a remarkable change in improvement at the hands of Mr. Connor, and the cherished desire of a quiet resting-place upon his own farm was carried out by these children in deference to the expressed wish of the old pioneer Eccentric as Mr Gardner may have been, exacting in his demands, although 50 years have passed, it is an inspiration to any person to visit this old farm and see the marked results of the exacting life-work of this man Represented by the children of the deceased members of this immediate family was the William Brentlinger children, Abram Brentlinger and family, Charles Brentlinger, Sarah Shaw, wife of John Shaw, Levi Brentlinger and family The mother of the Brentlinger children was Miranda Gardner Charles M Gardner of Toledo, son of Abraham Gardner, Jr, was the only one present bearing the family name

The serving of the dinner was a very happy occasion At the head of the table was seated Grandma Weaver, the oldest person present, being well advanced in 90 years, and who lacks only about 10 years of being as old as Mr Gardner Sr, were he living at this time Mrs. Weaver has lived upon this farm longer than was the privilege of its first owner

Following down the table was arranged the oldest of the Gardner family, and seated next was Mr and Mrs Connor In the afternoon George Fairfield, in a very interesting address, recounted the experiences and the pleasures of the early pioneer life and the pleasant visits to this farm. The historical features were discussed by Charles M Gardner. It was concluded to hold another reunion of the friends and relatives on the same day of the month in 1906

The writer desires to say, in behalf of the relatives, that no more cordial, hospitable treatment and kindness could be demonstrated than by Mr Connor, his good wife and children. On our arriving at the farm in the morning, Mr Connor said "The farm is yours today, do just as you wish"

While attending this reunion I decided to begin the research and write a history of the Gardner family As explanation for recording the articles published in the Wapakoneta papers and the letters that will follow is to show how little information any of the branches of the family possessed, until we had secured from all and verified with records possessed by the various branches of the family.

On going to my hotel the next day following the reunion, I wrote the Hon Mills Gardner a letter stating my relation to the family and purpose to secure data and write the history of the family As is characteristic of Mr Gardner, we received the very excellent letter, which we will give the reader.

Washington C H, Ohio, September 4, 1905

Mr. C M Gardner, Toledo, Ohio

My Dear Sir—I was very glad to receive your favor of August 31 and to hear from relatives whom I have never seen I, like you, know comparatively little about our family I personally knew but few of them. My grandfather was Benjamin Gardner He died in Brown county, near Russelville, in 1840, in his eightieth year His son, Seth Gardner, was my father I knew well Uncle Matthew the preacher I saw when a boy another son called Henry, generally called Hank. I knew a daughter Charlotte and visited her many years ago I understand grandfather had 10 children, but never knew but few of their names. I have heard of the name of Abraham, your grandfather, and a son, Benjamin I think there was a son, William, that lived in Clermont county, but of this I am not sure There is a William who lives near Williamsburg in Clermont county who is of the same family, but I have not met him and don't know how near related. My grandfather, Benjamin Gardner, as I said, died in 1840, and is buried on his old homestead in Brown county, near Russelville My father, who died in 1873, is buried in the same ground Uncle Matthew died also in 1873 in Brown county, and is buried in Union Church Cemetery, near Higginsport, Brown county, Ohio. Aunt Charlotte died near Sardina, Brown county, Ohio, but I do not know whether she is buried there or in the same cemetery as grandfather Grandfather was born in Rhode Island, moved when quite young to New York and came to Ohio as early as the year 1800 and settled in Brown county, I think, on the farm on which he died I was raised from two years' old in Highland county The family have no records Uncle Matthew wrote his life, but, unfortunately, he did not give much of the family history He did not name more than two or three of the children, and those only incidentally He gives the birthplace and residence and death of his father and mother, states grandfather was in the Revolutionary Army and was discharged at the close of the war, some of the incidents of his struggles to clear up a farm from a wilderness, and devotes all the balance of the book to his individual life as a preacher, and gives but very little family history I have two brothers—George B Gardner, who resides at Hillsboro, Ohio, and Thomas F. Gardner, who resides here. Uncle Matthew had a large family of boys and girls, several of whom are dead He has one son, John W, who lives in Ripley, Ohio I have met him once or twice, and the only living one that I know

I have a copy of Uncle Matthew's life I think I can procure another and will send it to you If I do not get it I will lend you the one I have for the purpose you want it I am sorry I know so little of the family history. The early settlers of this country kept but meager family records, and their children did not try to hunt them up, so it makes it difficult for this generation to do so.

I think my brother, George B Gardner, at Hillsboro, who is two years older than I, and is better acquainted with the family history, can give you more real information than I can He was my father's executor Anything I can do to assist you in your efforts I shall be pleased to do

Yours very truly,

MILLS GARDNER.

This letter was indeed a revelation and gave us material with which to operate. I immediately wrote John W Gardner, referred to, at Ripley, Ohio I am sorry I have not at command his reply This gave us so much record of the family I felt I possessed a new world I then proceeded to get data of all the relatives in Auglaize county, Ohio, and the last week of November, while at Springfield, Ohio, telephoned Washington C H and arranged for a visit to the home of Mr Gardner.

We took an early train on a new road, and after sitting for several hours in a cornfield waiting the clearing away of a wreck, we proceeded to our destination, reaching there about noon Miss Gertrude Gardner met us, the first Gardner, as a known relative, we had ever seen, save my own brothers and sister Soon Miss Edith and her father came To attempt to describe the cheerful welcome would be impossible. Reader, you cannot know till you do likewise We will never forget our visit to the home of Hon Mills Gardner We visited every moment of time till about 8 P M, and returned to Springfield The joy and gladness the visit brought to me is beyond expression I said "Have I been spending these 42 years so near to my kinsfolk and not mingling with them when there is so much happiness in doing so?" I secured the book written by Matthew Gardner, and I confess I did not eat or sleep as usual till I had learned what I could of the family to which I belong. I found therein the name of Orlando Rose casually mentioned, who lived at Stephentown, N. Y. I concluded to know more of the record than briefly recorded in Matthew Gardner's book. I wrote a letter to the postmaster at North Stephentown, N Y., and made inquiry for the Rose family or any relatives of the Gardners I received the following

North Stephentown, N. Y., April 7, 1906.

C M. Gardner, Esq, Detroit, Mich

Dear Sir—In reply to yours of recent date, you may hear something of interest to you by writing Mrs Rinaldo Shaw, South Berlin, N. Y; Mrs. Myra Bull, Stephentown, N. Y; Mrs J J. Moffitt, East Nassau, N Y, R. F D, daughters of Sylvester Gardner, deceased, Mr Orlando Rose dead 14 years I will hand your letter to John C. Gardner, this office, a nephew of Mr Orlando Rose

Yours truly, W A. GILE, P M

I wrote each one at the above addresses, and in due time received the following

South Berlin, N Y, April 12, 1906.

Mr Gardner

Dear Sir—I received your letter asking me to tell you what I know about the record of our family Matthew Gardner was an own cousin of my father and second cousin to Orlando Rose's wife. Her father and my father were brothers His name was Caleb They were sons of Caleb Gardner My grandfather had seven sons and one daughter Matthew Gardner left Stephentown in 1800. He was only 10 years old. I have heard of it a number of times When he visited Stephentown he always came to see us His father and my grandfather, Caleb Gardner, were brothers. Our family connections are very few in this country

Hastily yours,
MRS. RINALDO SHAW.

Garfield, N Y, April 12, 1906

Mr Gardner—Just received your letter of inquiry and will answer as well as I know I used to have many fine visits with cousin Matthew Gardner, but never knew any of the relations that lived West but him.

My grandfather's name was Caleb Gardner, brother to Matthew Gardner My father's name was Sylvester, born in 1801, seventh child of Caleb Gardner, and his father's name was Benjamin He, Benjamin and his wife are buried on the farm Rufus Sweet owns, just north of his house My grandfather was a large landowner, and I was born on the farm south of where Matthew's father lived when he went to Ohio My father owned the farm he left There has been large families raised on the Gardner farms at Stephentown, but the most are dead and moved away, only the cousins, which are few, are left. Mrs. Rose is a second cousin to Matthew Gardner She is a daughter to Caleb, Jr, first cousin of mine.

We were all born on the farm north of the turnpike and Stephentown depot Some live in Berlin, one is living at the depot and I live at South Stephentown, but our address is East Nassau, N Y I must tell you that cousin Matthew traced our genealogy to England, and wrote a book and had a great many printed, but I never had one, but have tried to get one, but failed Perhaps you could get one from Matthew's children. That would give you great information, besides getting our English coat-of-arms

They came from England and first settled in Rhode Island, then moved to Stephentown, N Y, and Hancock There were several families of them.

I cannot just tell you the particulars, as it is so long ago, and the forefathers are dead There are some of the cousins living in Michigan now, but probably they know nothing about the genealogy Hope this will help you along some. With many kind wishes to one of our kindred

MRS J. J. MOFFITT,

East Nassau, N. Y.

When I read the life of Matthew Gardner I felt the disappointment experienced by all readers of his book because of the lack of information of the family, which knowledge we know he possessed. When we received and read the letter from Mrs J J Moffitt it sent the blood tingling through our veins. We could scarcely believe that the great man he was had searched so diligently for our ancestors' record and history, secured the English coat-of-arms and utterly failed to record what he knew would be of such great interest to the family.

In conversation with Judge George B. Gardner of Hillsboro, Ohio, when we read him Mrs Moffitt's letter, he uttered an expression peculiar, it is said, to Mr. Gardner, that would express the feeling he had

We did not set out to write a criticism of any member of the family, but we cannot but note what seems to be gross neglect of duty to the family. Mr Walter L. Shinkle, grandson of Matthew Gardner, stated. "Once I thought I would go over to Uncle Wash's when grandfather came and ask him about the family record and possess what I knew he did know He turned and demanded. 'Why do you want to know?' It is of no importance, it will not benefit anyone, it is time lost, better do something to improve your time better." Mrs. Moffitt's letter clearly indicates a tendency to know for his own personal gratification We resolved if there was an extreme in the records we made, it would be too much record

After corresponding with all the branches of the family and securing all the information possible and where to go to secure information, we began our travels On May 4, 1906, we left Detroit, Mich, via Cincinnati, Ohio, for Brown county. We reached Ripley, Ohio, late in the afternoon, and was met by Stacy E Gardner, son of John W Gardner We were driven over the hill roads to the home of John W Gardner, some seven miles in the country It was just twilight when we arrived at the farm home We were met by Mr and Mrs. Gardner and their two daughters, Alice and Hattie We were very cordially received While waiting at Ripley for our carriage another son of Mr. Gardner, Louis Gardner, came to meet us. He said: "You will find one of the best fathers and a mighty good old mother, even though I do say it" So we did Mr John W. Gardner is certainly a type of the family. We were very tired, having been en route the day and night preceding.

The following morning Stacy E Gardner drove us to the old family homestead, and silently we stood at the graves of our departed dead A little more than 100 years the two, whose dust lies resting beneath the cased tombs, had come to that farm, a wilderness, and had reared a large family and sacrificed the comforts of an Eastern home, where all advantages could be had, that the following generations might have greater comforts and happiness We visited the old house, studied its architecture Nearly 100 years has passed since Mr Gardner erected this house The old crane is in as perfect condition as when placed there by him, and is in as good state of preservation and could perform its duty the same as a hundred years ago Could these old people have one glimpse of their once happy home and all the modern conveniences! The road that led to Ripley and Maysville was mud, and plenty of it The road is now one of the very best constructed of crushed limestone, and is only a little more than an hour's ride to what was then their market, and occupied a whole day to go and return

For three days we visited these relatives, and when the time came to depart we felt we had only begun to visit On preparing to leave our carriage was called and we were driven over roads through some of the most beautiful scenery. If the reader has never experienced the sights of the shores of the Ohio he knows not the pleasure of a 16-mile drive from our starting point to Aberdeen along the shores of the Ohio

We bade our good friends adieu and were away, to be entertained by his son, Charles W Gardner, and his good wife at Aberdeen We arrived at noon after a few hours of brisk driving over the hills on an early May day We had a very pleasant stay here.

Mr Gardner has been very successful in business and has a beautiful home in Aberdeen We cannot but record here that Aberdeen has become of world-wide renown

There lived an old 'squire," who had great interest in the successful termination of the affairs of Cupid Kentucky had its thousands of young, and even older, who desired a hasty termination of single-blessedness, and the boat with its oarsman was always ready when the sound of the hoofs of the rapid-advancing horse could be heard A race for the river, then a race for Massa Beasley's Once at Massa Beasley's it was a race to tie the nuptial knot before the opposing parents arrived It is said that Mr. Beasley never failed to have the "words' said when the parents entered. Kentucky had to pass special legislation to legalize these marriages Our hostess lives in this same house. We enjoyed the novelty of being in the house where 4,427 marriage ceremonies were performed by this venrable old man

The following day we crossed the river to Maysville, once known as Limestone Landing One hundred and six years before our great-grandparents landed here We stood where they stood; we crossed the river where they crossed.

We took our departure and floated down on the waters of the Ohio to the same landing where they disembarked, when they took all their earthly possessions and a family of 10 children to their wilderness home.

What a contrast! What an age in which we live! Will the next 100 years produce such wonderful changes? We proceeded to Higginsport and went to the home of William Gardner. We had a very pleasant time, and, like the other places, left before we had finished our visit Mr Gardner is a leader in his community and an agreeable entertainer, as well as his good wife and children

The carriage of John D Gardner came for us and we arrived at noon at this generous home Mr Gardner and family are of the younger families that we had visited. The same as all the other places, we had a royal welcome and entertainment We remained here for four days, visiting several other places, returning at night

The following day we spent with Walter L Shinkle's family. We secured a great amount of record here, and as he lives near Union Church, we went to the cemetery and secured data from the markers of the deceased members of the family buried there. The data secured enabled us to correct several errors, as we had not been certain of some, as we had no access to some records destroyed by fire These markers, as is true of all old ones, have the name, then following is son or daughter of the parents, as the case may be After visiting with Mr Shinkle's family and securing the valuable information, we returned to Mr. Gardner's home On the Sabbath we attended Union Church and addressed the congregation in the morning Mr John D Gardner possessed very valuable information As has been said in another section of this book, the family of Benjamin Gardner, Sr, had three groups in Brown county, and this was the community of the largest group of the boys Jeptha Gardner, the father of John D Gardner, had a disposition and temperament that any of the relatives would visit him, while that was not true with Matthew the preacher

Social visits were not a part of his program, and the result was his younger children knew but little of family history Jeptha Gardner, being one of the older sons of Matthew Gardner, they would visit frequently. We were able to secure from John D as much history as from all other places He had kept memoranda of many of the important features He was one of the most careful men in every respect we met in all our travels The carefulness of this man enabled us to arrange our records with accuracy

On Monday we took our departure for Georgetown, where we remained over night with Lewis G De Vore, grandson of Matthew Gardner We had a very pleasant visit here and availed ourselves of the records of the county We were then in possession of the names of several branches of the family, and searched diligently for what might be recorded. We searched the records of administration, executors and studied the wills We then turned to the marriage records The county was organized in 1818, being composed of parts of Clermont and Adams counties The first marriage recorded of a Gardner is Clarissa Gardner to Joseph Wright, married September 25, 1818; Henry Gardner to Rachael Newland (Book A, No 1, page 88), married March 1 1821, Abraham Gardner to Sarah Purcell (Book C, No 3, page 13), married November 10, 1823, Benjamin H Gardner to Theresa Devore (Book C, page 44); Benjamin H Gardner to Matilda Howells (Book D, page 34) This completed the record of the sons and daughters of Benjamin Gardner, Sr, in Brown county, the other members of the family having secured their licenses in Clermont, Adams and Highland counties before Brown county was organized.

We departed from Georgetown and stopped off at Sardina. Here we discovered what we were not expecting We had diligently searched for the Purcell family When we left the train we were in plain view of the old home of Squire Purcell, brother of Sarah (Purcell) Gardner, wife of Abraham Gardner, Sr We had discovered at the office of the Probate Court at Georgetown that Squire Purcell was one of the sureties on bond furnished by Clarissa (Gardner) Wright, executor of the estate of Joseph Wright

We continued our journey to Hillsboro, Ohio, where we were met by Judge George B. Gardner. Before we were off the train we recognized the Judge He is indeed a Gardner One must meet the Judge to fully appreciate his excellent qualities in every respect We were taken to his home and made to feel immediately that we were with our family

The time was spent in searching the records and studying history and connecting our data secured early in the research when the means were not as advantageous We will say more of the Judge in the family record

We departed for Washington C. H to visit the Hon. Mills Gardner and daughters We were met at the train by Mr. Gardner, who drove us to his home After refreshing ourselves, we proceeded to study family record

The letter of Mrs Moffitt became the main topic of interest, as it had revealed to the family so much that might be recovered Until a late hour we exchanged notes and reviewed memorandums We secured data and corrections that enabled us to shape our work The following day we returned home, arriving in Detroit late that evening, and the following day, May 17, 1906, began writing the history of the Gardner family It became necessary to immediately send out about 1 000 letters in all at that date. They were prepared and mailed that week and we began while many of the incidents were fresh in our mind. One letter was directed to Sir Henry Mortimer Durand, British Embassy, Washington, D C, to be directed by him how to proceed to secure information in connection with the coat-of-arms, etc The following letter was received

British Embassy, Washington, May 22, 1906

Sir—I am directed by H M Charge d-Affaires to acknowledge the receipt of your letter of May 19 and to advise you to consult the Herald's College, which deals with all matters concerning coats-of-arms, etc

The address of the College is Queen Victoria Street, London, E C.

I am, sir,

C M GARDNER Sec in H M Embassy

We have this date written the College for information regarding the coat-of-arms and record of the family there The following letter was received in reply ·

Herald's College, London, E C, 11 June, 1906.

Dear Sir—Thanks for your letter of the 24th ult To enable us to draw upon account of the family, together with the arms, it will be necessary first to make searches in local sources of information, as well as in the archives of the College.

These searches will entail a certain amount of expense, and if you wish to proceed I would ask you to favor me with a cheque of 50 pounds.

When writing, perhaps you would send me copies of any papers you possess bearing on your paternal descent

Yours faithfully,
H FARNHAM BURKE,
Summerset Herald and Registrar

C M Gardner, Detroit, Mich

We wrote the War Department, Washington, D C, to determine the record of Benjamin Gardner, Sr., and his service in the Revolution as far as possible. We desire, before giving the letter to call attention to the fact that Benjamin Gardner, Sr, and Jr, referred to in the letter are the father and son of Stephentown, the Jr being the Sr of Brown county, Ohio

The Military Secretary, War Department, Washington, D C '
War Department, the Military Secretary's Office Washington, D C
Respectfully return to C M Gardner Detroit, Mich :

It is shown by the records of this office that one Benjamin Gardner, rank not stated served in Captain James Denison's Company, Fourth Regiment (1776-1781) New York Militia, commanded by Col Killian Van Rensselaer, Revolutionary War A company payroll dated Albany, June 4, 1777, shows that the company was employed in quelling an insurrection in the northeast part of the Manor Rensselaerwick, and bears the following items concerning the soldier "Time of entering the service, April 17, 1777, time of leaving the service, April 24, ——, Number of days in service, 8.'

The record also shows that one Benjamin Gardner, Jr, rank not stated, served in the same regiment, but the period of service is not indicated.

His name appears on an undated receipt roll, which shows that certificate No 3 for 6 pounds, 5 shillings, issued by the Treasurer of the State of New York, pursuant to an Act of the Legislature passed April 27, 1784, was received for service performed by him in this regiment Nothing relative to the subject of inquiry has been found of record

F C,
The Military Secretary

It will be remembered that they did not have the methods of making and preserving records then that the Department has at present

We began the work of compiling from the written records of the Narragansett country, and from that have been able to secure the data of the early births, marriages and deaths of our forefathers.

After we had exhausted the records at Buffalo, N Y, we then turned our attention to the county in which they settled in Eastern New York and visited the various places

We arranged to see the former homes of these pioneer colonists, and on August 4, 1906, left Buffalo for Stephentown, N Y.

We were met by Mr John J Moffitt, who took us to his home where we saw the first relative of the East, and where they saw the second one of the line of descent of the old pioneer that left Stephentown in 1800

We remained with Mr and Mrs Moffitt for several days and there gathered much history We had a very delightful time and enjoyed ourselves very much with these newly found relatives.

The day following our arrival we drove to the old homestead of our grandparent that removed to Ohio in 1800, and there viewed what is remaining of the house. We cannot but recall the architectural plan of this building as it was before destroyed We remembered the plan of the new house erected after the farm was cleared in Ohio This building in New York was identical in plan, position and on the same side of the slope of the hill as that one erected in Ohio The old pioneer duplicated the New York building in the one he erected in Ohio

While there Mr William Cranston, with his family, came and we all spent the remainder of the afternoon pleasantly reviewing and recalling history.

A few days later we came to the home of Mr Cranston and spent several days Mr Cranston married a Miss Bull, whose mother was a daughter of Sylvester Gardner.

It is necessary to visit this home to understand the hospitality and generosity of the members of same

From Mr Cranston's we went to several homes and secured the records of the various families connected with the Gardner family

On Monday of the following week we all met at the home of Mr Rufus Sweet, who lives on the old homestead of Benjamin Gardner and owns same We repaired and reset the markers of the graves of those buried there More fortunately for Benjamin Gardner of this generation and his good wife, they are buried in the yard on Mr Sweet's farm and their graves have received the best of attention and care for nearly 100 years This graveyard was the third one of the generations deceased, back of the writer's own father's, that he assisted in repairing and with our own hands assisted in replacing the stones and placing the cement and concrete around the bases

While we were doing this work a statement made by Mr. Sweet's son impressed the writer as a very important one He said "I wonder if in 100 years some one will be digging around to repair our graves?"

As we live and teach our children the respect due parents so we believe will be the respect shown us by our descendants of the next centuries It has been indeed a great pleasure to be able to go to the graves of these forefathers for the past 300 years and repair the graves and reset and rebuild the markers

We left the homes of these good people and returned to Albany and took up the study of the records of all the surrounding country and States as on file in the great building of the State

Completing the work here, we returned to Buffalo and prepared for the reunion of the family in Ohio

On August 25, 1906, we left Buffalo via Detroit by steamer for Wapakoneta to attend the reunion

While at Wapakoneta, Ohio, attending the reunion, we met for the first time Mr Charles H Gardner, of Cleveland, Ohio, and on being urged to visit his home, we came to Buffalo via Cleveland and remained over night with Mr Gardner and his family in their palatial Euclid avenue home

We had been studying this branch of the family to connect them, and as far as they were concerned and knowledge of their ancestors, they were as the "two lost tribes"

We will refer the reader to the history of the grandparents of these children of which Mr Gardner is a member

It has been said that possibly the grandfather remembered that he purchased his time from his father so he could get married, and had not forgotten it Another suggestion was that no doubt there were so many of the family that the grandfather knew that if he kept in touch with them and they began to visit he would have to work much more than he did, and he worked all the time, except on the Sabbath, to maintain his family and clear his homestead and accumulate his fortune

We had not visited the childhood home of these sons, and a few days later we received an urgent request from Roscoe (Rock) to go to the old home town (Chagrin Falls) and see the place of their home We left for Cleveland and visited the home of the birth and childhood of these three generations of this branch of Gardners

Chagrin Falls is a beautiful little town of about 2,500 souls, located about an hour's ride southeast of Cleveland, Ohio

About 1820 there came into this place, a wilderness, two strong characters—Albon Crocker Gardner and Deacon Hervey White

The first a physical giant—a man of iron constitution and a will equally strong—a mathematical mind and an honest man

The second differed to this extent he was an artist and a manufacturer—a broad, noble character

Albon Crocker Gardner purchased much land and the opportunities for his growing family was without bound

About one mile south of the town is located a great farm, on which these children were reared The father devoted much of his early life in the manufacture of woolen goods, owning and operating a woolen mill

He would go to his mill and remain all the week, returning home very late on Saturday evening and be off again early Monday morning, and the family would see but little of him. His meals would be taken to him, and in this way Mr Gardner reared the family Is it any wonder his children did not know who his brothers and sisters were?

Northeast of the town is a narrow valley, and across the valley Deacon Hervey White threw a dam which retained the water for a great distance back and formed a great lake of water Below this was the great ax factory of Hervey White, known to all pioneers of Ohio From this factory went the axes that all our grandfathers of Ohio used to clear away the forests His attention was more closely given to his family and the result was the Whites are more generally known to the present members of the family

We were accompanied here by Charles H. Gardner, who directed us to the place, where this large family had been reared

Gardner habits are as old as time They will never break away from the idea of a graveyard on the farm On this farm is a cemetery More fortunate for this one than that of many, it has now become the cemetery of the entire town and surrounding community

We returned to our own city, to be away again for Eastern New York and attend the family reunion there, and then to Rhode Island to visit the homes of the people surviving and the graves of those who have gone before.

We received a mailing-list from our Mr Charles Shumway's daughters, in which was the name of Rev. William Gardner, Rio, Wis

We wrote the "Reverend," and in reply received what has proven to be one of the long-looked-for lines of descent.

Mr Gardner had visited Rhode Island a few years before and could direct us just where to go for valuable information and where to write We wrote a letter to Mrs Robinson, of Wakefield, R I, who had given years of study to the subject and had compiled much history and records

With this and much more we found on going there, we have secured much valuable record

We are very sorry to say here, in connection with Mrs Robinson, that she had died but a short time before we arrived at her place of abode

After returning from Ohio, the reunion of the Eastern branch of the family was held in Stephentown, N Y, where we went that we might become the better acquainted with those who might be present and gather more of the history of the family. We enjoyed the occasion very much and the meeting of new faces

It is with pleasure that we record the following

Mr Charles M Gardner—We, the descendants of the Eastern branch of the Gardner family in America, in reunion assembled, hereby desire to express to you our appreciation of your efforts toward making today's event possible

We feel gratified with the sturdy growth and useful position to which our family has attained, and for the record of its growth, the story of its struggles and the history of its origin to pass from recollection, with the passing of its founders, would indeed be an occasion for deep regret We also fully realize that after a comparatively few years of further growth and amalgamation with our common race the compilation of such a history would have become impossible

It is with sincere gratitude, therefore, that we are privileged to record that this story has been rescued and the history preserved by you, our friend and relative, before it has become too late We well know what it has meant for a business man to devote a year of busy life to the benefit of this cause, and this, too, we deeply appreciate

In testimony to the above, we have hereunto affixed our names

Done at Stephentown, Rensselaer county, New York, this fifteenth day of September, One Thousand Nine Hundred and Six

Kirk E Gardner,
Helen M. Gardner,
Elizabeth G Carpenter,
Daniel Shepardson,
Emma C Shepardson,
John J Moffitt,
Lucy Gardner Moffitt,
Ora M Ford,
Edward M Ford,
John H Gardner
Caroline M Gardner,
Fred G Gardner
Helen Marion Gardner,
Fred Elwood Gardner, age five
Adelaide Electa Wood Gardner,

Eunice M Sweet,
Mary E Sweet,
Mira Gardner Bull,
Charles Moffitt Ford,
Harriet Reynolds Ford,
Helen M G Shumway,
Charles F Shumway,
Mary J Shumway,
Nellie H. Shumway,
Michael Halpin,
Augusta L. Woodward
Carrie Gardner Chaloner,
Mary A Chaloner,
Rufus Sweet.

We proceeded to the city of New York, examining the records in the genealogical departments of the several libraries

Our great desire had been to stand where the forefathers had stood and view their former homes After a delightful ride on one of the palatial steamers, we awakened at Fall River, Mass., from which place we proceeded by trolley to the first American home of our first American father, Newport, R. I

After a delightful ride on a bright fall morning, we arrived at old Trinity Church The bells were calling the worshippers to the sanctuary We spent the next hour in this quaint old house of worship Our thoughts passed over the two and a half centuries to the founders and builders of this structure Our mind recalled the statement engraved upon the gravestone of him "who outlived all the other members of the vestry to see the church completed"

We stood at the graves of these early colonial fathers, and could but attempt to measure the achievements of the lives of those buried in that little cemetery For more than two centuries the songs that they sang have been sung, the Gospel that was preached to them has been preached to the many generations that have come and gone

Early in our American history is recorded the life of one who occupied so prominent and conspicuous a place—Caleb Gardner We visited the home and were curious to take the observation he did, looking over the bay as he did when he located the English fleet that had come to destroy the French fleet lying at anchor. By a careful study of the inlets of this bay, one could readily see, with the knowledge Mr Gardner possessed of these waters, how he guided the French fleet to a place of safety.

Our attention was next turned to that territory so fittingly described by the petitioners and termed King's country, Old Narragansett

We landed at Saunderstown, right upon the land owned by one of the second generation A ride down Boston Neck, crossing to the mainland, we were upon sacred ground In fact, there is not a particle of the old Pettaquamscutt purchase but what was the familiar home of some branch of this family.

The records of all the towns (townships) were diligently searched for every trace of record pertaining to this family from its origin.

We procured conveyance and drove over hill and vale searching the location as described by deed and will We drove to the old churchyard, where was erected the first Episcopal Church of that territory In the city of the dead we spent considerable time, living in memory with those who had laid the foundation, so deep and broad, for the Christian and intellectual development of this great family and its thousands who were to follow and become the standard-bearers of the principles advocated by these colonists in centuries to come

When one studies the lives of these great men and noble mothers and sees these principles reflected in the lives of our great men of this generation, there can be no question of doubt as to the blood that courses the veins, as it has come from generation to generation and is seen in the lives of the self-sacrificing, devout men who have pushed westward, until every State in the Union now claims some branch of the family that had its origin in old Pettaquamscutt.

Not all of the best of the lives were sent forth from these hills to open up the new territories, but Rhode Island has maintained the standard and has lifted it higher and higher, and has at all times and in all relations maintained the history of which she may well be proud

The old church in which the sainted Dr McSparren zealously proclaimed the Gospel in its simplicity has been removed for more than a century to the old town of Wickford, where it might be better preserved

Those who had departed and the body laid in this churchyard remain, and a beautiful monument has been erected to commemorate the final resting-place of the good Doctor and his early parishioners

Reader, there is one thing that we do believe should be done to commemorate and keep before the American people the name of the first and second generation of our family, that is, the erection in that cemetery of a monument sacred to the memory of those who were called upon to endure the early hardships of the American pioneer life

The purpose of the authors of this book has been as far as possible to preserve the history of this family, and we herewith urge you to become a contributor to a fund to erect such a monument to the memory of George Gardner, his two good wives and 14 children

RHODE ISLAND.

HISTORICAL

At the dawn of the seventeenth century the western shore of Narragansett bay was occupied by the Narragansett tribe of Indians, numbering 5,000 warriors, while the eastern shore and the country out to Massachusetts bay pertained to the Wamponoags, under the Sachem Massasoit

The first white settler was Roger Williams, a young clergyman who had been banished from Massachusetts for his "new and dangerous opinions" and ordered to be carried to England Escaping from his stern Puritan guards, he took refuge among the Indians, and in 1636, with five companions, he descended the Seekonk river in a canoe He landed at a favorable place near the head of Narragansett bay and named it Providence, in memory of "God s merciful providence to him in his distress" The domain was granted to him by Canonicus, the sachem of the Narragansetts, in acknowledgment of the minister's kindness Other bands of exiles from Massachusetts founded Portsmouth (in 1638) and Newport (in 1639), and in 1643 these three colonies were united under the title of "The Providence Plantations in the Narragansett Bay in New England" The new commonwealth sent as its ambassador to England the well-beloved Roger Williams, who secured for it, from the Earl of Warwick, a favorable colonial charter, which was supplanted in 1663 by a still more liberal charter from King Charles II

During King Philip's war, in 1675-76, the Indians burned Providence and otherwise ravaged the province An army of 1,000 New England soldiers stormed the tribal fortress of the Narragansetts, near Kingston, and slew 300 Indians and took 600 prisoners, losing in the attack 230 men

The first church was organized at Providence in 1638, and the first public school at Newport in 1640 In 1693 a postal route was established to Boston, and 15 years later the first colonial census showed a population of 7,181. Journalism began with the Rhode Island Gazette at Newport in 1732

During the Revolution the privateers of Narragansett bay swept the seas, and 3,000 Rhode Island troops served in the Continental line at one time Bristol and Warren were bombarded by the Britons, and Newport remained in their occupation from 1776 to 1779, when it was evacuated, almost in ruins

Rhode Island was the last of the 13 States to accept the Constitution of the United States During the confederation period Rhode Island's delegates had been obstructive on more than one occasion, and during the last supreme efforts to convert the alliance of States into a nation the Republic of Rhode Island was not even represented in the Constitutional Convention Thorny, resolute and independent, the little State stood out against the current of union until it began to be seriously proposed to blot out this "abominable" commonwealth and divide her territory between Massachusetts and Connecticut When President Washington made his grand tour throughout New England in 1789 he carefully avoided crossing the frontiers of Rhode Island In 1790 the Federal Constitution was at last ratified, and Little Rhody became a State of the Great Republic The Royal Charter remained in force until 1843, when it gave way to a new State Constitution In 1842 T W Dorr claimed to have been elected Governor, and his adherents rose in arms against the regular State officials and erected fortifications Upon the advance of the State troops, with other New England soldiers, the army of the Dorr rebellion melted away without fighting

Out of a population of 175,000, Rhode Island sent out to the war for the Union 22,236 soldiers, of whom 2,800 suffered death or wounds

The State is named from the island upon which Newport stands, and this in turn commemorates the Isle of Rhodes, in the Mediterranean sea, famous for its defense against the Saracens by the Knights of St John The Colonial Act of 1644 says· "The island of the Aquethneck shall be called the Isle of Rhodes"

The arms of Rhode Island consist of a golden anchor, representing hope, emblazoned on a shield of blue, typical of maritime activities and ambitions The motto of the State is included in the single word Hope

DESCRIPTIVE

Rhode Island is the smallest State in the Republic, its land surface being but little more than that of Delaware even and 1-240 of the area of Texas. The chief geographical feature is Narragansett bay, an arm of the sea entered between Point Judith and Saconnet Point, and reaching up for 30 miles, or nearly to Providence It covers 130 square miles, and has 10 harbors branching off and several islands Along the shores are many beaches and promontories, fully occupied as summer resorts with scores of hotels and thousands of cottages and villas Commodious steamboats ply along the bay and its inlets all summer long, bearing myriads of pleasure-seekers and leading to the scenes of the far-famed Rhode Island clambakes at Rocky Point and elsewhere The island known by the Indians as Aquidneck, and named by the colonists Rhode Island (whence the title of the State), covers 37 square miles, being 15 miles long and of varying widths This beautiful domain has been entitled "The Isle of Peace" and "The Eden of America," and consists of far-viewing hills, pastoral valleys and sequestered ponds fronting the blue outer waters with long sandy beaches and bold cliffs

A steam ferry runs from Rhode Island to Conanicut, an island of eight square miles, largely occupied by summer estates, villas and hotels Prudence Island, farther to the northward, covers four square miles, and has a number of farms and summer homes Patience, Hope, Despair and other smaller islets further adorn the surface of the bay Thirty miles southwest of Newport, in the Atlantic ocean, lies Block Island, the Indian Manisees, eight by three miles in area, with its surface divided between high bare hills, wind-swept downs and enclosed salt ponds It constitutes the town of New Shoreham, with 1,320 inhabitants, and has numerous summer hotels, with steamboats running to and from Providence, Newport and New London Narragansett Pier is another famous resort a few miles north of Point Judith and facing the Atlantic The bay is prolific in oysters and clams, lobsters and quahaugs and many varieties of food fish, in whose pursuit 1,400 men are engaged

Watch Hill, at the remote southwestern point of the State, is a bold promontory between Narragansett Beach and Napatree Beach, crowned with a group of hotels and summer cottages It looks out over the sea, and at night commands a view of 11 light-houses

The chief rivers are the Pawcatuck, navigable to Westerly, the Seekonk, to Pawtucket, and the Providence, a deep estuary eight miles long, from Nayatt Point to Providence Large sums have been expended by the National Government on the Providence river, which has been deepened by skillful engineering works from 4 feet to 25 feet, giving a commodious outlet for the large commerce of the Rhode Island metropolis West of the bay the country is diversified with many high hills and broad woodlands These lake-strewn forests of oak and walnut fall to the southward into pine plains and cedar swamps and then into broad and level salt marshes, which front the sea with wind-swept sand hills and long beaches, amid which salty lagoons enter from the outer main.

The climate is the most equable in New England, possibly on account of the divergence of a branch of the Gulf Stream into Narragansett bay, bringing with it an unusual warmth and moisture

Providence, the metropolis, and the second city of New England, stands on a group of hills at the head of the navigable waters connected with Narragansett bay, and is an enterprising and wealthy community with large manufacturing and financial interests and a profitable maritime trade Newport, at the head of a noble harbor on Rhode Island, is chiefly famous as a summer resort for wealthy New York and Boston families, whose beautiful estates extend from the old pre-Revolutionary town out to the sea bounds, and are adorned with magnificent cottages.

NARRAGANSETT PLANTERS.

By EDWARD CHANNING, Ph D

"In the southern corner of Rhode Island there lived in the middle of the eighteenth century a race of large landowners who have been called the Narragansett Planters Unlike the other New England aristocrats of their time, these people derived their wealth from the soil and not from their success in mercantile adventures They formed a landed aristocracy which had all the peculiarities of a landed aristocracy to as great extent as did that of the Southern colonies Nevertheless, the Narragansett magnates were not planters in the usual and commonly-accepted meaning of the word It is true enough that they lived on large, isolated farms, surrounded by all the pomp and apparent prosperity that a horde of slaves could supply, but if one looks under the surface he will find that the routine of their daily lives was entirely unlike that of the Virginia planters The Narragansett wealth was derived not so much from the cultivation of any staples, like tobacco or cotton, as from the product of their dairies, their flocks of sheep, and their droves of splendid horses, the once famous Narragansett pacers In fine, they were large, large for the place and epoch, stock farmers and dairymen

"Narragansett society was unlike that of the rest of New England It was anomaly in the institutional history of Rhode Island It has been claimed that the progenitors of the Narragansett farmers were superior in birth and breeding to the other New England colonists, and that to this the aristocratic frame of Narragansett society is due I do not find this to have been the case Nor do I believe the settlers of this particular portion of Rhode Island to have been one whit better born or bred than the founders of other Rhode Island, Massachusetts or Connecticut towns

"Slavery, both negro and Indian, reached a development in colonial Narragansett unusual in the colonies north of Mason and Dixon's line In 1730 South Kingstown contained 965 whites, 333 negroes and 223 Indians Eighteen years later the proportion was nearly the same—1,405 whites, 380 negroes and 195 Indians Undoubtedly a few of these Indians and negroes were free, but then the indented servants (practically slaves for a term of years), here reckoned among the whites, were probably sufficient in number to more than balance the free negroes and Indians The proportion then of slaves to free was between one-half and one-third, a proportion to be found nowhere else in New England

"Many persons, ignoring the early history of the Narragansett country, seem to take it for granted that the progenitors of the great families were Episcopalians Such, however, was not the case We are told, for instance, that the elder Richard Smith possessed a conscience too tender for the English Gloucestershire or the old colonial Taunton He sought refuge in the Narragansett wilderness, where he bought and hired large tracts of land from the natives and opened a trading-house for their convenience. His son, Major Richard Smith, who joined him in 1659, had served, if tradition is correct, as an officer in Cromwell's victorious army Assuredly neither of them was the man to entertain a kindly feeling toward Episcopacy. Their early neighbors and associates were either fellow-members of the Atherton Company or men sent out by it, and they hailed, almost to a man, from Massachusetts or Connecticut, where the English of the Restoration was regarded with almost as much horror as the 'Babylonian woe' itself

"Roger Williams preached to the assembled Indians and English, and other Godly men at one time or another ministered to the spiritual needs of the Narragansett people It was because the Episcopal form was one well suited to the time and the place that it became the established church of the country and added a pleasing color to the social life of the Narragansett farmers.

"To sum up, in colonial Narragansett the nature and constitution of the place, the extension of slavery, both in negroes and Indians, the mode of colination, the political predominance enjoyed by the freeholders in Rhode Island, were all favorable to the production of a state of society which has no parallel in New England. That these causes did not produce such a result no one, who has carefully studied the early records, can deny.

"Rhode Island Colony in general was a country for pasture, not for grain. Extending along the shore of the ocean and a great bay, the air softened by a sea vapor, and the winters were milder and shorter than up inland. In Narragansett resided the landed aristocracy of the colony. Their plantations were large, many containing thousands of acres, and noted for dairies and the production of cheese. The grass in the meadows was very thick and as high as the tops of the walls and fences. Two acres were sufficient for the annual food of each cow. One farm had 12 negro women as dairy women, each one of whom had a girl to assist her. Land was sold as high as $60 per acre, when money had double the value it has now. Large flocks of sheep were kept and the clothing was manufactured for the household, which sometimes exceeded 70 persons in parlor and kitchen. Grains were shipped to the West Indies. The labor was mostly performed by African slaves and Narragansett Indians.

"Ancient Narragansett was distinguished for its generous hospitality. Strangers and traveling gentlemen were always received and entertained as guests. An acquaintance with one family was an introduction to all their friends. Public houses were rare. The society was refined and well informed. Books were not so general as now, but the wealthy employed tutors for their children and completed their education by placing them in the families of learned clergymen.

"That the gentlemen of ancient Narragansett were well informed and possessed of intellectual taste, the remains of their libraries and paintings would be sufficient testimonials. Many of these paintings and libraries are now dispersed.

"This state of society, supported by slavery, would produce festivity and dissipation, the natural result of wealth and leisure. The great land proprietors indulged in these expensive festivities until the Revolution.

"At Christmas commenced the Holy Days. The work of the season was completed and the 12 days were devoted to festive associations. All connections by blood or affinity were entitled to respectful attention and were treated as welcome guests, as a matter of right on one side and courtesy on the other. Every gentleman of estate had his circle of connections, friends and acquaintances, and these were invited from one plantation to another. Every member of the family had his particular horse and servant, and rarely rode unattended by his servant, to open gates and to take charge of the horses, carriages were unknown. Pul[illegible]oads were few, there were driftways, with gates, from one plantation to another.

"In imitation of the whites, the negroes held a mock annual election of their Governor. When the slaves were numerous their election was held in each town. The annual festivity was looked for with great anxiety, and party-feeling was as violent as among the whites. The slaves assumed the ranks of their masters, whose reputation was degraded if the negroes appeared in inferior apparel or with less money than those of masters of equal wealth The horse of the wealthy land-holders were on this day all surrendered to the use of the slaves, who with cues, real or false, head pomatumed and powdered, cocked hat, mounted on the best Narragansett pacers, sometimes with their master's swords, with their ladies on pillions, pranced to election at ten o clock.

"It is years since the state of Narragansett society changed, and the revolution has been deep, effectual, complete The abolition of slavery, the repeal of the law of primogeniture, the division of estates equally among all, has divided and sub-divided inheritance into such small portions that the whole has disappeared from every branch of their families; and in most instances not a foot remains among them,—nay, not even 'the green graves of their sires'"

JOSEPH GARDNER.

A few persons have been disposed to treat our first American father as Joseph Gardner instead of George Gardner

The position taken has been most warmly championed by J Warren Gardner, Brewster, Nebraska Mr Gardner takes the position that there were two distinct families, the George Gardner family of Newport and the Joseph Gardner family of Narragansett

We propose to show by Mr Gardner's own statements wherein he is incorrect, and that the children who were the early inhabitants of Narragansett were the sons of George Gardner of Newport and that there was no Joseph Gardner of Narragansett as claimed by him.

In taking the position we do, it is not to defend the George Gardner theory, but because there is no foundation upon which to base the conclusion in favor of Joseph Gardner.

The following is the reproduction of a record made by William G Gardner, July 11, 1790, about one hundred and twenty years after the death of the first American father

Memoranda.

"Joseph Gardner, the youngest son of Sir Thomas Gardner, Knight, came over among the first settlers, and died in Kings County, Rhode Island, State, aged 78 years. Born A D. 1601 Died A D. 1679. Left six sons, viz Benoni, died 1731 aged 104 years, Henry, died 1737 aged 101 years, Wm , died at sea by pirates, George lived to see 94, Nicholas and Joseph lived also to a great age."

We desire to call the attention of the reader to the fact that this record was made more than one hundred years after this family had passed away and was the result of tradition If you have ever attempted to learn anything relative to a family by tradition for fifty years you would appreciate how utterly incompetent and erroneous such a record would be.

We desire to be fair with our opponents Mr J. Warren Gardner takes the position that Benony Gardner, twice took the oath before the Courts in which he said he was "upwards of ninety" was one of the evidences to substantiate the position that he could not be the son of George Gardner and Herodias Hicks, this date of age causing him to be born more than three years prior to the marriage of the parents, and about three years prior to the coming of the mother to Newport.

His second position that the Narragansett Gardners spelled the name with "i" while the Newport Gardners spelled it "Gardner" His third position was, that the Gardiners of Maine, being of the Narragansett family, spelling the name with the "i" did not accept George but Joseph

Wilkins Updike, apparently was the first to use the name Joseph, accepting the Bible record as authentic. We cannot accept the Bible record for the following reasons

First. There is not one public document of any character that mentions the name of Joseph Gardner until the year 1691, when a deed is signed by Joseph Gardner transferring certain land in which mention is made of George Gardner, the father of Joseph the signer The second record was in 1705 when Joseph Gardner was deputy for Newport

Second If the children of this Joseph Gardner were mentioned as becoming inhabitants of the Narragansett Country, why would not Joseph's name appeared? It was the custom then to officially recognize and admit them as inhabitants of those new colonies. Land transfers, wills, town-council meetings, all bore the names of those having any relation with same It must be remembered that there were very few people, and in some manner they were identified with the public records No Joseph Gardner appeared until Joseph Gardner, the son of George Gardner had attained the age when his signature appears in deeds, town-meetings, &c.

George Gardner's name appears as soon as he went to Rhode Island He was admitted an inhabitant of the Island of Aquidneck 1638 And the reader will observe the connections as history gives it down till the time of his death.

The Gardiners of Maine do accept and treat George Gardner as their first American father and no mention is made of Joseph Gardner

The only excuse for the position of Joseph Gardner was to evade the early marriage of the first wife of George Gardner This has been so expressed in correspondence with the Joseph Gardner advocates.

The spelling of the name with or without "i" has no significance as both methods are adopted by the same family

The errors are largely due to the careless methods adopted by many who have no particular interest in the family It did not concern the party when writing whether they stated one thing or another Mr. J Warren Gardner has studied very critically, records for more than forty years, but the burden of his work was to establish a Joseph line instead of George and we find his writings are full of errors

These records are the results of research of the original records of the families and public documents. If there are any errors the families and makers of the public records are responsible We have used all records thus obtainable and it establishes beyond doubt that our first American father was George Gardner'

ANOTHER GARDNER LINE.

Another Gardner Line Established about the Time of the Family, the Subject of this Work.

We introduce this to evidence the errors of many writers who have confused the two families. The relation prior to coming to America is very close but take us to the mother country for the same parentage

The writer found in the New England Genealogical Register in connection with the Vassal estate the following history, which determined the early settlements made by the family and the places selected by them

In the autobiography of Elder Matthew Gardner he states ' the family came from England in the year about 1685" We find in tracing the family records that have been compiled since the writing of the Matthew Gardner book that the family came to America nearly fifty years prior to the time designated by Mr. Gardner in his work

The past fifty years have been spent in research by the various members of the family, and records made of same are now preserved in book form, and access may be had to the records without having to go to the written records at the various churches, counties, &c, where they were, besides, the written records of the families have been compiled with the connections as will be seen in this family outline

ORIGIN OF NAME.

The name Gardner is undoubtedly of Latin origin In Latin it is Gordianus In Italian it is Gardena In Spain it is De Guarder In France Des Jardine, pronounced Zaar-din-nar In German it is Gaertner.

A knight named Des Jardine came with William The Conqueror into England The name has been known there from that time The original writing in England seems to have been Gardynar.

THOMAS GARDNER.

Thomas Gardner, the first of the Salem stock, came over in 1624 from Dorsetshire, England, near which the name had flourished for more than three centuries, and settled, under the auspices of the Dorchester Company and Rev John White, with thirteen others, at Gloucester, Cape Ann, upon the grant of Lord Sheffield to Robert Cushman and Edward Winslow, made in January of that year Mr Gardner was overseer of the plantation, John Tyler of the fisheries, Robert Conant soon after being appointed governor. Not realizing the success they anticipated in forming a colony, they removed, in 1626, to Naumkeag, or Salem, which continued the home of Mr Gardner and his descendants down to this present Century He died in 1635

Thomas, his son, an eminent merchant, was born 1592, and died 1674 He held several town offices, and was a member of the general court in 1637 By his wives Margaret Frier and Damaries Shattuck he had 1 Thomas 2 George, 3 Richard, 4 John, 5 Samuel, 6 Joseph, 7 Sarah, wife of Benjamin Balch, 8 Miriam, wife of John Hill, 9 Ruth, wife of John Grafton From these were many descendants Joseph commanded the Salem company in King Philips's war, and commended for his courage by historians, was killed, with eight of his men and six other captains, in an attack on an Indian fort, in the great battle in the Narragansett swamp, December 19, 1675 His wife was daughter of Emanuel and sister of the celebrated Sir George Downing His widow, about 1686, married Governor Bradstreet It is probable that through this connection the noble house erected by the governor, of which an engraving is to be found in Felt's Salem, came into the Gardner family Richard with three of his children removed to Nantucket, where more were born unto him His eldest daughter, Sarah, became the wife of Eleazer Folger, brother of Dr. Franklin's mother

Some of his descendants married with Coffins, Macys, Starbucks, greatly multiplying and continuing down to our own time

Samuel was a merchant, deputy to the general court, and as one of its selectmen, trustee of the Indian deed of the town of Salem, October 11, 1686

George, the second son of the second Thomas, was born before his father came to America, and died in 1679 He engaged in business at Hartford and there accumulated a large estate. His wife was Elizabeth Orne, by whom he had seven children. 1 Hannah, wife of John Buttolph 2 Samuel 3 Mary, wife of Habakkuk Turner 4. George 5 Ruth, wife of John Hawthorne, one of the judges in the trials for witchcraft 6 Ebenezer, who married in 1681, Sarah Bartholomew, and died in 1685, at the age of twenty-eight, bequeathed considerable property by his will, as he had no children of his own, among his brothers, sisters and other kinsfolk, from the mention of whom in that instrument, which information as to the earlier generations of the name has been derived 7 Mehitable.

The second wife of Mr. Gardner was Ruth Turner, a name which is suggestive. His daughter Mary having married one of the same family, this connection of his may have saved her father from being in his old age companionless

Samuel, born in 1648, died in 1724, married 1673, Elizabeth, daughter of John Brown, widow of Joseph Grafton He was a merchant and also cultivated a farm In the Indian war he commanded a company

His children were 1 George, 2 Hannah, born 1676, married John Higginson in 1695, by whom she had four children and died 1718 3 George, born 1679 (The writer desires to call attention to the name George appearing twice as children of the same parents This occurs frequently when a child died without issue another was given the same name) 4 John, born 1681, died before 1724, married Elizabeth, daughter of Dr Daniel Weld He commanded the Salem Company in the battle, August 29, 1708, at Haver Hill, when it was attacked by French and Indians, and slew with his own hands an Indian, some of whose arms and equipments are still in possession of his descendants For several years he represented Salem in the general court, but his constitution not being very strong he engaged in no active business His children were 1. Elizabeth, born 1705, married Jonathan Gardner. a distant relative, who had a title of Commodore, 2. John, of whom hereafter 3 Ebenezer, born 1708, died young 4 Daniel, born 1709, died 1766, married Ann Putnam 5 Hannah, born 1711, wife of Samuel Halton, and mother of Judge Halton, at one time President of Congress 6 Samuel, born 1712, died 1769 Graduate of Harvard, married Esther Orne, by whom he had several children His second wife was Mrs Winslow, daughter of Richard Clarke, one of the consignees of the tea destroyed in Boston Harbor in 1773, and sister of the wife of Copley, the painter He held many of the town offices, represented Salem in the general court, and left an estate of one hundred thousand dollars. His two sons, George and Henry, were gaduates of Harvard, in the classes respectively of 1762 and 1765 The former left the college about five thousand dollars, the marine society for superannuated seamen over seven thousand, and to the poor of Salem nearly fifteen hundred 7. Lydia 8 Bethia, born 1715, died 1773, married Nathaniel Ingersol Their daughter May, who married Habakkuk Bowditch, was the mother of the celebrated mathematician, Dr Bowditch 9 Ruth, married 1st, Bartholomew Putnam, 2d, Jonathan Goodhue

John Gardner, son of John and Elizabeth, whose father was born 1707, died 1784, in a house which stood on the present site of Salem museum He married Elizabeth Putnam, widow of her cousin, William, brother of General Israel Putnam of the revolution, by whom he had: 1 John of whom hereafter 2. Elizabeth, born 1731, died 1754, unmarried, Mrs Gardner had two daughters by Mr Putnam, one wife of Jonathan Orne and the other of Jonathan Gardner By his second wife Elizabeth he had no children, but by his third, May Pearl, born 1733, died 1826, he had Mary, wife of 1st, Abel Hersey, 2d, William Lemon He had no exclusive occupation, and being possessed of a farm and mill between Salem and Marblehead, engaged in a little commerce He commanded a troop of horse, and for some years was sent to the legislature from Salem

John, born 1731, died 1805 His wife was Mary Gale of Marblehead, born 1728, died 1755 His second wife Elizabeth, sister of Col Timothy Pickering of the revolution, and Secretary of State in the Cabinet of Washington and John Adams By her he had three children 1 Elizabeth, born 1759, died 1816, married 1782, Samuel Blanchard, born 1756, died 1813, surgeon in the army of the revolution She was the grandmother of Francis, born 1784, and who married Mary Ann daughter of Francis Cabot, widow of N C Lee, of the first Mrs Robert C Winthrop 2. John, born 1760, died 1792, a successful merchant at Charleston, S C 3 Samuel P

Early in life Mr Gardner commanded a vessel to the West Indies, and during the revolution owned several privateers, all successful but the Black Prince and Hector, in the Penobscot expedition of 1779, by which he was a loser

GEORGE GARDNER (1.)

The name of George Gardner is among the first settlers of Rhode Island, having settled there as early as 1638 He came from England with the first settlers and is the founder of this branch of the Gardner or Gardiner family in America. In writing the history of a family, whose first ancestors in America is found early in the sixteenth and seventeenth centuries, it is often necessary to throw out many traditions cherished for years, as in the case of this family where tradition cannot be substantiated by documentary proofs or evidence

In an old family Bible a record made in 1790, over a century after the name George Gardner is first found in the State records and a hundred years after his death, the statement is made that the ancestor of this family in America was named "Joseph" If for the name Joseph we use that of George the record is probably correct, and George Gardner was born about 1601 as the record states Died in Kingstown, R I, 1679 He married Herodias, widow of John Hicks, between 1641 and 1645 Her maiden name was Long

Seven children were born to them
Benony,
Henry,
George,
Nicholas,
William,
Dorcas,
Rebecca, became (2) wife of John Watson.

He married (2) Lydia Ballou daughter of Robert and Susanna Ballou After his death she married William Hawkings.

Children by (2) wife were
Samuel,
Joseph,
Lydia,
Mary,
Robert,
Jeremiah,
Peregrine

The following is from the State records of Rhode Island

1638 George Gardner was admitted an inhabitant of the Island of Aquidneck

1639 He was freeman

1641-2. He was Senior Sergeant.

1644 He was Ensign

1660 George Gardner with others was witness to a deed given by T Socho, an Indian, to William Vaughn, Robert Stanton, John Fairfield, Hugh Mosieck, James Longbottom, all of Newport, Rhode Island, of land comprising what is now the city of Westerly, R I

1662 He was commissioner from Newport at court held at Warwick, R I, on October 28

1668 He was made overseer of the will of Robert Ballou, his father-in-law

1671. Ben (an abbreviation no doubt for Benony) Gardner, Henry Gardner, George Gardner, Nicholas Gardner were among the list of inhabitants of the Pettaquomscut Plantation

1673 George Gardner was Juryman

HERODIAS (LONG HICKS) GARDNER.

Was born in England.

Before the General Assembly of Newport she declared, "That when her father died in England she was sent to London, and was married unknown to her friends to John Hicks, privately, in the under church of Paul's, called St Faith's church, she being between thirteen and fourteen years old She then came to New England with her husband, and lived at Weymouth two and a half years, thence coming to Rhode Island, and there lived ever since till she came to Pettacomscott

Soon after coming to Rhode Island there happened a difference between her and her husband, John Hicks, and he went away to the Dutch carrying away with him most of her estate which had been sent her by her mother. (Her mother and brother lost their lives and estate in his Majesty's service, she says) After her desertion by John Hicks, she became the wife of George Gardner, and by him had many children.

Testimony as to her marriage to George Gardner was given by Robert Stanton, who declared one night at his house both of them did say before him and his wife that they did take one the other as man and wife

In May, 1658, two years only, after the advent of Mary Fisher and Ann Austin, to whom the distinction is awarded of having been the first missionaries of the society of Quakers who landed in the colonies, Herodias Gardner, who resided at Newport, Rhode Island, left her home and children, of whom she had several, and trudged sixty miles on foot through the wilderness to Weymouth, Massachusetts, to deliver her "testimony," carrying an infant in her arms, and accompanied only by a little maid

The New England Puritans had lost nothing of the intolerance of what they had been, more excusably, the victims in the mother country. They branded their fellow-dissenters with heresy, and greeted them with scourge and prison

On reaching her distination Herodias was arrested and taken before Governor Endicott who harshly addressed her in approbrious language and commanded that she and her attendant should each receive ten lashes on their naked backs This cruel sentence was as barbarously inflicted, the woman meanwhile, holding her child, and only protecting it by her sheltering arms from the lash of the executioner

After the whipping with a threefold knotted whip of cords, she was continued for fourteen days longer in prison

After the savage, inhuman and bloody execution upon her of the cruelty aforesaid she kneeled down and prayed the Lord to forgive them

BENONY GARDNER (2)

George (1).

Benony Gardner, son of George and Herodias (Hicks) Gardner, died 1731. Married Mary ——. She was born 1645, died November 16, 1729, at the home of her son-in-law, Job Sherman, at Portsmouth.

Chidren were

Stephen, born 1667, died Feb 9, 1743, at Bozrah, Conn

Nathaniel, died 1734

William, born, 1671, died 1732

Bridget

Isaac, born Jan 7, 1687-8

Benony Gardner was born possibly about 1647. In 1727 he gave his age in testimony as upwards of ninety

In 1671 he took the oath of allegiance

In 1679 he, with forty-one others of Narragansett, signed a petition to the King, praying that he would 'put an end to these differences about the government thereof," &c

September, 1785 he and wife Mary deeded son Nathaniel land, being the westernmost part of farm where Benony now dwells, and on the same day deeded son Stephen dwelling house, orchard, &c.

In 1713, he and wife Mary deeded land to son Isaac.

DEED FORM BENONY GARDNER TO SON ISAAC GARDNER.

Book 2 Page 108. Noith Kingstown records.

To all persons to whom these presents shall come I Benony Gardnei of Kingstown in the Colony of Rhode Island and Providence Plantation in New England yoeman, Sendeth Greeting Know ye that I Benony Gardner for and in consideration of the full sum of one hundred and fifty six pounds Current passable money of New England to me in hand paid befoie the Sealing & Delivery of these presents by my son Isaac Gardner of South Kingstown which said sum of one hundred and fifty six pounds .. . . . .
. Benony Gardner own and acknowledge ye the Rec. . ..
. and of every part and parcel thereof do acquit . .
. and exhonerate Sd Isaac Gardnei his heir Executors
& Administiators forever by these Presents Have ..
. given granted, bargained Sold Aliened and Confirmed
. . and by these presents do freely and fully absolutely .
. ..give, grant, baigain, sell, Elien Enfeoffe and confiim . .
from Gaidner and my heirs unto the Sd Isaac . . .
Gardner a ceitain parcel oi Tract of Land situated in. ...
. . The Town of Kingstown aforeSd Containing ...
. . ....nenty acres be it more or Less according to the. ..
bounded Southerly upon the Land of John Sweet .
. ...George Gardner, Northerly upon Land of . . .
.. . upon Land of Nicholas Gardner, at or
..Nor Have & To Hold the Sd one hundred .
.. Singular the Buildings. . .
. .. . ry the . .
. . gnes and Every of them from . .. .
freely peacebly and Quietly to take possession .. .
. with all their appurtenances without any Lan .
... eruption or Euation or Disturbance of me the Sd . .
..Benony Gardner assigns or any other person or persons
whatsoever from by oi under me or them. . .
. or any of them also I the . ner do furthermore ..
Covenant and promise to and with the .his heirs
. and Assigns that I the Sd Benony Gardner at . sign- . . . .
ing and Sealing of these presents have full power . .. ..
lawful Authority to bargain Sell and Alien the . .. .
premises ..fiom above Exprest and foi the Conformation .
thereof .Gardner have to these presents Set my hand ..
and Seal this . of May, Anno Dom One Thousand Seven .
. Hundred . in the Twelfth year of her Majesty's .
. Reigh Anna Queen ttain &c Signed Sealed and
. Delivered in the presence ..
. (signed) Peleg Mumford . ...

Daniel Mackoone (signed)

his
BENONY B GARDNER
mark

The above named Benony Gardner of Kingstown the Day and year above Sd. acknowledged the above written Instrument to be his act . .

CHRISTO ALLEN, Justice.

DEED FROM BENONY GARDNER TO SON NATHANIEL.

Book 2. Page 199. North Kingstown records

Explanation for the deeds and records being imperfect, the town records of North Kingstown were destroyed by fire and the pages were burned, only that portion remaining as copied here, the rest having been burned away

., Be it known & Manifest by this Public Instrument of . . .
..... Eighteenth Day of September Annoqrie Dominy. . .
. hundred and five Stile Angliae in the Presents . .
after named, personally appeared, Benony Gar . ....
n in their Majes Colony of Rhode Island & Prov . . .
in New England yeoman, & Mary his wife which. .. ..
. in Consideration of the Love and affection which
bear unto Nathaniel Gardner their Son of King .
. Said and for his better Livelihood and Subsistance . .
. free and vollentry Will and without any Cons . .
ed Bargained Aliened enfoeffed Conveyed and ... ...
... . by these presents Do fully freely Clarly & Abso ... . .
bargaine Alien Enfeoffe Assign Transport and confirm . ..
Nathaniel Gardner His Heirs and Assigns forever . .
. .. or parcel of Land Lying and being in Kingstown . ..
the Weathermost pait being by Estimation
. ...Granter Benony Gardner now Dwells on.. . .
Acres more or less, Butted and Bounded
. a young white oak Marked which .... .
. Stands in A North and South . . . .
. his heirs Executors or Assigns .:
.. ures fields wood Timber wood Land fences .
.... ago feed Rights Privileges Hendrances ....
.. . whatsoever to the Sd Piece or Parce . ..
. . aies appertaining or there with used occup . ..
. ll rights Titles Interest Inheritanse Property. .
, ... whatsoever of whom the said Grantors their Heirs .
. . . of in or unto the above Granted Premises and ... ..
at the Said Granted Nathaniel Gardner his heirs . .. ..
. may from time to time and at all times from . .
.... Occupie Possess and Enjoy the Piece of Land Butt . ... .
...as afore said with all other the Above Granted Pre
or Rights and to their benefits and Behoofs the ....
. without any hindrances Let or Semable of the
. their heirs Executors, Administrators or Assigns .
. .... the Said Benony Gardner & Mary his wife are the . . .
.owners of the above Granted Premises and Stand. .
. Haveing in themselves Good right and Lawful Authority ....
. and Convey the same in manner and form aforsd . ...
.. . to Granters for themselves their Heirs Executors
......ant to and with the said Grantee His heirs or Assigns . .

.. Delivery of these presents according to the true interest . .
. thereof they will defend the above Granted premises
... ner of Persons Claiming Rights, titles or Interest .
.... .either of them in Witness thereof they the Sd
.. . Benony Gardner and Mary his wife hereunto set . .
.. . . their hands and fixed the. ....
year above written and the fourteenth year of the ..
Reign of Her Majesty Anne by the Grace of God over Eng-
.. . . land, Scotland &c. . .. .
... Defender of the faith . . . .
... ed and Delivered . .. . ..
. . .. of us .. ..

(Signed)

his
BENONY **B** GARDNER
mark

her
MARY **M** GARDNER
mark

.... . The above mentioned Gardner personally....... .....
this 1st Day of September 1712 and acknow . ...
Above written Instrument to be his act and .

JOHN ELDRED, Justice

HENRY GARDNER (2).

George (1).

Henry Gardner, son of George and Herodias (Hicks) Gardner, died 1744 He married (1) Joan No children Married (2) Abigail, widow of John Remington and daughter of Edward and Abigail (Davis) Richmond She was born 1656 and died 1744

Their children were

Henry, born Feb 25, 1691; died 1768

Ephriam, born Jan 17, 1693, died 1774.

William, born Oct 27, 1697, died 1732

Martha Elizabeth

Jeffrey Watson in his diary under date April 28, 1744, says "I was at the burial of Uncle Henry Gardner It was adjudged by old people that he was about one hundred years old, as he was a man grown in the Indian War" As the Indian war was in 1675 and "a man grown" might mean twenty-one years of age, but as he took the oath of allegiance in 1671, he must have been at least twenty-one and undoubtedly much older

In 1679 he signed the petition to the King.

In 1683 he was Constable.

In 1685 he was Juryman

His will proved May 5, 1744, was as follows

To wife Abigail, a pacing mare, three best milch cows, six ewes, Negro wench, bed and other household furniture sufficient to furnish a room, and all that said wife dies possessed of she may give to my granddaughters

To sons Henry and Ephriam Gardner, equally a farm in Westerly of 200 acres,

To grandson Henry, son of William deceased, 80 or 90 acres in Westerly when he shall come to age

To granddaughter Hannah Potter, wife of Thomas, negro Patience

To granddaughter Dorcas Gardner, daughter of Ephriam, negro Sarah.

To son Henry half my money, lands, horses, hogs, &c, viz half of all estate not disposed of

To son Ephriam the other half (To Henry a watch and to Ephriam a bible also)

To servant Peter a suit of clothes

To son Ephriam land in Pettaquamscutt

To sons Ephriam and Henry rest of Estate

Inventory, 1016 Pounds, 1s., viz.:

Wearing apparel .... 42 Pounds

Silver money, cane, great bible, books, pewter stillyards, warming pan, 2 woolen wheels, — wheels, 5 cows, heifer, 2 oxen, mare,

negro Betty and child . . . . .120 Pounds

Patience and child...... ....120 Pounds

Charity .. . . 120 Pounds

Sarah . . . .130 Pounds

Boy .. . . 70 Pounds

Will written July 20 1744 Proved October 8, 1744 Widow Abigail and son Henry, Executors.

To son Henry, negro Betty, he paying my four grandchildren 40 Pounds, equally divided

To daughters Martha Sherman and Elizabeth Kenyon all wearing apparel

To granddaughters Dorcas, daughter of Ephriam, Mary, daughter of Henry, Abigail Worden, daughter of William Gardner, deceased, rest of Estate

GEORGE GARDNER (2).

George (1).

George, son of George and Herodias (Hicks) Gardner, was born about 1650 He married Tabitha Tefft, daughter of John and Mary Tefft, Feb 17, 1670, died 1724 She was born 1652, died 1722

He took the oath of allegiance May 19, 1671 His name is on the list of those inhabitants of Narragansett who signed the petition to the King in 1679.

Children were

Joseph

Nicholas, died 1746, married Mary Northup.

Samuel, married Ann Briggs, daughter of Thomas and Martha, 1706

Robert, married Lydia Littlefield, June 14, 1716

John, married Mary Rathbun, of New Shoreham, 1717

George

Hannah, married Josiah Wescott, Jan. 1, 1701, died 1756

Tabitha, born Feb 2 1687, died 1760, married Nathaniel Niles.

Joanna, married Daniel Hill.

DEED FROM GEORGE GARDNER TO SON NICHOLAS.

Book 2. Page 68. North Kingstown records

.. beloved Son Nicholas Gardner of . .
bequeath and freely bestow upon our son. .
. ner his heirs Execrs Adminrs and Assignes And . . .
. iff bequeath and freely bestow upon our aforesaid son ..
. .. parcell of Land Lying Situated and being in Kingstow
. on Eighty Acres more or less is Butted and bounded . .
terly on Land of Thomas Mumford of the .
.ay or Country Rhode, Southerly on Wards Farme Now i .
. .orow Langworthy and Samuel Wescott both of Kingsto
Tract or parcell of Land with all the privileges & Appe .
belonging wee the Said George Gardner and Tabitha Ga . .
Presents given and Granted in name and forme aforeSd
.Nicholas Gardner his heirs and Assignes as is Above Sd .
. . his proper benefir and Behoofe forever To have & to Hold
fore given and Granted premises with the Appurtenances
. belonging unto the aforesai Lands and Each and Every Pa
thereof with all the Uplands and Swamps thereon All these .
and Trees growing, Standing, Lying or being in or upon.....
with all the waterings, water Courses ways & Easer
thereunto or any part of, And further we the Sd George . .
Tabitha Gardner Do by these presents Declare the above
. of Lands to be free and Clear of and from all a.... . . .
of former Gifts, grants, bargaing, Sales Mortgages .... .
or Leases or Incumbrances whatsoever and that
and granted premises are at this present and . .
and Delivery of these presents is unto us the Sd George
& Tabitha Gardner a good and Lawfull Inheritance and na. . .
. Lawfull Authority to Dispose of these premises
. . ... is aforeSd. And do by these presents for . ..
. .Adminstrs and Assignes forever acquit
. . AforeSd Son Nicholas Gardner . .
. Lawfull Claims or Demands of any ....
formation of all the above granted premises ...
..... Tabitha Gardner have hereunto Sett our hands. . .
twenty Nine Day of January In the year of our Lord
. Soveraign Lady Ann over England & Queen ..
. the within written Instrument.... ... .

(signed)

Signed Sealed and Delivered in the presence of us (signed)	his
Nathaniel Niles	GEORGE X GARDNER. mark
Ebenezer Niles	her
James Kinyon	TABITHA X GARDNER mark

The above Signed persons personally appeared this 29th Day of January, 1708-9. and acknowledged the above written Deed of gift to be their volentary act and Deed

THOMAS MUMFORD, Justice.

NICHOLAS GARDNER (2).

George (1).

Nicholas, son of George and Herodias (Hicks) Gardner, was born about 1654, died probably in the year 1712 as the town council of Kingstown in that year granted letters of administration on his estate to his son Nicholas Gardner, Jr In the year 1714, Nicholas Gardner appeared before the town council and asked not to be required to make account until the next council, and informs the said council that as his father had died intestate, he was with information in relation to the estate, and that he believed that his father in his life time intended that his estate should be divided between himself and his two brothers, and, that he proposed that his brother George should have one thousand acres of land, and his brother Exekiel, the farm on the Great Plain. I, therefore, conclude he had three sons His wife was Hannah

Children
Nicholas,
George,
Ezekiel

1671, May 19, Nicholas Gardner took oath of allegiance, the same year he bought land of John Porter.

1673, Nov 2, he bought of John and Herodias Porter, 100 acres of land

1679, July 29, he signed the petition to the King

1701, Mar 26, he and wife Hannah for 48 Pounds, sold John Thomas, of Jamestown, certain lands in Kings Town

1711, Mar 12, he testified as to certain lands calling age fifty seven years or thereabouts.

1712, Administration was granted to son Nicholas.

WILLIAM GARDNER (2).

George (1).

William Gardner, son of George, Sr, and Herodias (Hicks) Gardner, died 1711 Married Elizabeth—Their children were

William,
Ann,
Elizabeth,
Rebecca,
Susanna,
Dorcas,
Tabitha,
Rachael

In 1671, Jan 21st, he bought 200 acres of John Porter, calling himself "Son of George Gardner of Newport" As he must at that time have been twenty one years of age he would have been born about 1650.

In 1679 he signed the petition to the King

In 1688 he was Constable and the same year Juryman

1707, May 23, he deeded son and daughter Joseph and Ann Hull, 204 acres for love, &c.

1706, Jan 8, he deeded land to son John Gould and Elizabeth his wife.

A copy of what remains of the will of William Gardner is herein recorded

WILL OF WILLIAM GARDNER.

Book 1-5, Page 105. North Kingstown records.

.. . .
. .. .during her Natural Life . . .. . .
. . . . . . y son William also one half of my hou... ....
unto my wife one half of my Stock of....... .. ..
one half of my household Goods to be at her disposal . . . .
.. ... ing forty Pounds She shall pay to my Daugh .. .. ..
. .... ecca out of my movable Estate now Given her . ....
. .. . .comes of age or Day of marriage—.. . . ..
.... . unto my Daughter Rebecca my Negro girl............
. . .. and forty pounds in Money to be paid her .. . .
. . ...out of the half of my Estate above Expressed.. ..
... . unto my Daughter Susannah fifty Acres of. . . .. .
.... the Great Neck and twenty pounds in Money to. . . . .
....y my Executor hereafter Named—. .... ..
... ... I give my Daughter Dorcas my Negro . . . . ..
. ..thirty five pounds in Money to be paid by my.. .... ..
... ...give unto my Daughter Tabethy Sixty pounds in.. .... .
. . to be paid her by my Executor———.. .... . .
. . . I give unto my Daughter Rachel half my........... .
d noe in my Son-in-Laws John Goulds possession
... . pounds in money to be paid by my Son John .
. ... . upon paying to Rachel Sixty Pounds to be ....
.. Gould there my son Gould shall have.... . . ...
.... . give unto my Daughter Eliza Wife of John Gould ....
pounds in Money to be paid her by my Executor.... .. .
... ... unto Honar Huling Daughter to Alexander . ...
. ... pounds in money to be paid her by my Executor. ...
my well beloved son William Gardner. . . ..
.. .. ments Wills ....
. . . any ways before this time named . ...
.... attested Ratifying and Confirming this . ...
. .. my last Will and Testament In Witness . ...
.... hereunto Set my hand and Seal this Eigh.... ....
. day of January in the yeare of our Lord God one Thou. ......
.... seven hundred and tenn or Eleven . . .

(signed)
WM GARDNER

Signed Sealed Published Pronounced
and Declared by William Gardner as his
Last Will and Testament signed in the
presence of us the subscribers (viz)

his
Benony **X** Gardner
mark
Elizabeth Huling
Alexander Huling

Mr Benony Gardner, Mrs. Elizabeth Huling, Mr. Alexander Huling appeared the 12th Day of March, Domino and Declared that they saw William Gardner Deceased Sign Seal and Declare this Instrument to be his Last will and Testament ..
he was in his right sense at the signing
and appeared before the Town Council of Kingstown....
Day of March, 1710-11

WILLIAM HALL, Clerk of Council.

WILL OF ELIZABETH GARDNER

Book 3, Page 40. South Kingstown records.

Written February 24, 1736-7. To son William Gardner the sum of Forty Shillings

To William Gardner my Grandson the Sum of Five pounds money as afore sd, to be paid by Executor.

To Grand daughter Tabitha Avery the sum of Forty Shillings

To Grandson John Gardner a Bible with Silver Clasps

To Grandson Thomas Gardner Forty Shillings Money as aforesaid to be paid by my Executor.

To Grand daughter Desire Gardner Little red Trunk

To Susannah King my Granddaughter Five pounds and all the rest of my Estate that remains after paying all the Legacies, Funeral Charges &c. herein mentioned.

To Grand daughter Marberry Potter Eight pounds Money as aforesaid

I give and bequeath unto my Grand children Thomas, Susannah and Mary Potter Fifty Shillings to each and Every one of them to be paid to them by my Executor.

her
(signed) ELIZABETH X GARDNER
mark

Son William Gardner Executor.
(signed)
George Douglas
Mary Watson
John Ball.

DORCAS GARDNER (2).

George (1),

Dorcas, daughter of George and Herodias (Hicks) Gardner, married John Watson He was a tailor In 1687 he was constable 1688 on the Grand Jury. 1690 Conservator of the peace also Deputy

Children:
John born July 22, 1676
Samuel, died Nov. 25. 1799, record of his death says aged 93.
William,
Frances,
Ann,
Herodias.

SAMUEL GARDNER (2).

George (1),

Samuel Gardner, son of George and Herodias (Hicks) Gardner, married Elizabeth He died 1696 She died 1697

One child was born to them

Samuel, born October 28, 1685

JOSEPH GARDNER (2).

George (1),

Joseph Gardner, son of George and Herodias (Hicks) Gardner, married Catherine Holmes, Nov 30, 1693, daughter of John and Frances (Holden) Holmes, born 1669 Died Aug 22, 1726 She was born 1673, died October 28, 1758 Both are buried in Newport Cemetery

Their children were

John, born September 17, 1697. Died 1764
Robert, born August 16, 1699
Francis, born September 7, 1701
Joseph, born April 7, 1703
George, born February 4, 1705
Catharin, born February 1, 1707
Lydia, born March 2, 1709
William, born 1711 Married Mary Carr.
James, born 1713 Married Eliza Sanford
Mary, born 1718

DEED FROM JOSEPH GARDNER TO WILLIAM HAWKINS.

Book 1; Page 217. Providence, R. I., records of Deed

To all persons to whom these presents shall come I Joseph Gardner Now Resident in Newport in ye Colony of Rhode Island & Providence plantation &c Sends Greetings Know ye That I ye Said Joseph Gardner for a Valuable Consideration unto me in hand payed by William Hawkings of Providence in the Colony aforesaid the Receipt whereof I doe hereby acknowledge & therewith doe owne my self to be fully satisfied Contented & Payd have Granted, bargained Aliened & Sold & by these Presents for me my heirs Executors and Administrators doe fully Clearly & Absolutely, Grant, Alien Bargaine, sell & Confirm unto the Said William Hawkings his Heirs and Assigns forever a Certain piece of Land Containing by Estomation twelve acres and it Situated Lieing & being in the Towneship of Newport it being the Land which George Gardner's Deceased, father, to the said Joseph Gardner & Peregrin as by said Will may move at large appeare, To have & to hold the Said land together with all & Singular the Comons, libertys & Privileges advantages ways and Commoditys whatsoever, thereunto belonging as appertaining unto ye Said William Hawkings his heirs & Assigns forever to ye only proper use & behoofe of ye said William Hawkings his heirs and Assigns forever And further ye Said Joseph Gardner for him self his Heirs Executors & Administrators do hereby Covenant & Promise to & with ye said William Hawkings & his Heirs—Said land hereby granted viz, all Priveldges & appertenances thereunto belonging shall hereafter ever be & Remaine in the possession of him, the said William

Hawkings his Heirs or Assignes without the lett hindrances or Molestation of me the said Joseph Gardner or any person Clayming from by or under me And I the said Joseph Gardner the said land above by these presents Granted together with all & singular the premises thereunto blonging Unto him the said William Hawkings his Heirs & Assigns against Me my Heirs & Assigns will warrant & defend by these presents & Memorandum Its agreed by these within Named, in Case the said Joseph Gardner his Heirs or Assignes do they not Molest or hinder the said William Hawkings his heirs or Assignes in a Certain parcel of Land Made over to the said William Hawkings his Heirs & Assignes forever as by a Certain Deed of Sale from the said Joseph Gardner may move at large appeare then this present deed of sale to be voyd & of None Efect or else to Remaine in full force & Virtue, in Wittnes whereof I have hereunto Sett my hand and Seale this Ninth day of January in the yeare of our Lord God 1691 & in th fourth yeare of their Majestyes Reigne William & Mary King & Queen of England &c
Signed Sealed and Delivered in the presence of us
Samuel Whipple,
William Turpin

(signed)
JOSEPH GARDNER

LYDIA GARDNER (2).

George (1),

Lydia Gardner, daughter of George and Lydia (Ballou) Gardner, married Joseph Smith.

The following is from the early records of the town of Providence, R I "Upon the 4th day of April in ye yeare 1689 Joseph Smith (the weaver) & Liddia Gardner, (after lawfull publication) were both joyned together in Marriage by Richard Arnold. both partyes belonging to Providence"

Their children were.
Israel, born at Providence, R I, January 13, 1689-90
Liddia, born July 25, 1692.
Sarah, born at Providence, R I, May 24, 1694
Joseph, born at Providence, R I, December 18, 1695
Robert, born at Providence, R I, May 3, 1697-8
Alice, born at Providence, R. I., January 25, 1699-1700
William, born at Providence, R I, March 15, 1702-3
David, born at Providence, R I, December 10, 1705
Jeremiah, born at Providence, R I, 1707-8

MARY GARDNER (2).

George (1).

Mary Gardner, daughter of George and Lydia (Ballou) Gardner, Married Archibald Walker

The following is from the early records of the town of Providence, Rhode Island:

"Archibald Walker & Mary Gardner Were both joyned together in marriage July ye 18th, 1690"

Charles W., born at Providence, R. I., May 6, 1691

Susanna, born at Providence, R. I., September 28, 1695.

Abigail, born at Providence, R. I., January 15, 1699

Hezekiah, born at Providence, R. I., March 14, 1701-2

Nathan, born at Providence R. I., June 26, 1704.

Ann, born at Providence, R. I., February 14, 1709

Book 1, Page 22. Providence, R. I., records.

Received from my father-in-law Williams Hawkins of Providence the sum of Thirteen pounds in Money-pay And is the full of Twenty pounds Current pay bequeathed to me by the last will of my father George Gardner of Newport on Rhode Island (Deceased) as wittness my hand this 30th day of November, 1683.

(signed)

her
Thomas Ward (signed) MARY GARDNER
John Stanton mark

ROBERT GARDNER (2).

George (1),

Robert Gardner, son of George Gardner and Lydia (Ballou) Gardner was born May 1, 1672, and died May, 1731 Was born probably at Newport Was an ensign in the Rhode Island troops and a member of the legislature He was a naval officer and collector of the port of Newport

He was an active churchman. His name was on the petition to the board of trade, requesting aid in getting a clergyman for Newport.

This was before the Society for Propagating the Gospel was formed in England, before this time all missionary work had been done by the government of England, as the church did not seem to know that she had any thing to do with missions She had few, if any, foreign missionaries after the conversion of Germany. The name of Robert Gardner occurs in the following petition found in Arnold's history of Rhode Island:

"To his Excellency Richard, Earle of Belmont, Capt General and Gov in Chiefe in and over the provinces of Massachusetts Bay, New York and Newhampshire and the territoryes thereon depending in America, and Vice Admiral of the same.

The humble Petition of the People of the Church of England now residing in Rhode Island,—

Sheweth

That your Petitioners and other inhabitants within this Island having agreed and concluded to erect a church for Worship of God according to the discipline of the church of England, and tho' we are disposed and ready to give all the encouragement we possibly can to a Pious and learned Minister to settle and abide amongst us, yet by reason we are not in a capacity to contribute to such an Hon'ble maintenance as may be requisite and expedient Your Petitioners therefore humbly pray that your Lordship will be pleased so farr to favour our undertakings as to intercede with his Majesty for his gracious letters to this Government, on our behalf to protect and encourage us and that some assistance towards the present maintenance of a Minister among us may be granted as your Excellency in your great wisdom shall think most meet, and that your Excellency will also be pleased to write in our behalf and favour to the Lords of Council of Trade and Plantation, or to such Minister of State as your Excellency shall judge convenient in and about the premises

And your Petitioners in duty bound will ever pray,

Gabriel Bernon,
Piere Ayroult,
Thomas Fox,
George Cutler,
Wm. Pease,
Edwin Carter,
Fra. Pope,
Richard Howland,
Wm Bemley,
Isaac Martindale,
Robert Gardner,
Thos. Payne,
Thomas Malleth,
Robert Wrightington,
Anthy. Blount,
Thomas Littlebridge.

This petition was delivered at Newport, 26th Sept 1699

The name of Robert Gardner also occurred in the following letter which is among the earliest documents extant relating to the Rhode Island Church, which is found in the Churchman's Year Book for 1870

The Ministers and Church Wardens of Rhode Island to the Society for the Propagation of the Gospel in F Parts institute A D 1701

Rhode Island, 29th Sept, 1702.

Honored Sirs.

We can not forebear expressing our great joy in being under the patronage of so Honorable a corporation through whose pious endeavours with God's assitance, the Church of England hath so fair a prospect of flourishing in the more remote parts of the world, and amongst the rest of her small branches, ours also in Rhode Island We therefore, Honored Sirs, beg leave to tell you that we look upon ourselves as under your pious care, and accordingly presume to trouble you with small account of our affairs Our church is but young, it not being four years yet completed since we began to assemble ourselves together on that occasion, upon which account the number of such men as can be relied upon to defray the charges of it, is but small at present, altho' there are a good many that constantly attend our worship regularly.

The place wherein we meet is finished outside, all but the steeple which we will get up as soon as we are able, the inside is pew'd well, altho' not beautiful, we have also got an altar, where we have had the communion administered twice to our great joy and satisfaction, chusing rather to partake of that Holy Sacrament without these necessary conveniences that the table in England furnished with (well knowing that they add not to the worthiness of the guests) rather than be without it, not but we are sensible they add much to the decency and order of it The place wherein we live is one of the Chief Nurseries of Quakerism, in all America, but now we have some reason to hope that the Rev. Mr Keith by God's assisting his skill on that disease hath pretty well curbed (if not quite stopped) so dangerous gangrene Their behaviour to us outwardly is almost as civil as is consistent with their religion Although slyly and underhand we are sensible they would pinch us in the bud.

But thanks be to God who hath put it past their power, in that he hath not only raised us up a Queene that is truly a nursery mother but hath blessed us also with the protection of so honorable Corporation, two such encouragements as (by the assistance of God's Grace) are able not only to invigorate our endeavours toward the Promoting of God's true Religion and worship, but flushed us likewise with the hopes of success

Thus Honor'd Sirs, we have laid before you the circumstances of our Church, delivering them unto your hands to do for us what you think best, only begging leave to assure your Honors that whatsoever favors you are pleased to bestow upon us towards the Promoting our Church, shall be accepted with the humblest Gratitude and seconded with the utmost of our abilities, and so we remain Honored Sirs,

Wm Brinley, Warden Your most obedient Servants to command,
Rob't Gardner Warden. JOHN LOCKIER

Robert Gardner is buried in Trinity church yard, near the east end of the Church, the inscription on his tomb reads as follows

"Here lieth intered the body of Robert Gardner, Esq, who was one of the first promoters of the church in this place, he survived all his brethren and had the happiness to see the church completely finished

"He was naval officer and collector of this port for many years, also employed in the affairs of this Colony, and discharged his trust to satisfaction He died ye 1st of May 1731, the day of his birth, aged 69 years"

JEREMIAH GARDNER (2).

George (1).

Jeremiah Gardner, son of George and Lydia (Ballou) Gardner, was born about 1673

He was probably married twice for September 23, 1712, a daughter was born in Newport to Jeremiah and Sarah Gardner His second wife was Grace As the name, Lawton, appears in the list of his grandchildren probably her maiden name was Lawton She died Feb 12, 1776.

Benjamin Gardner was administrator of her estate.

The children by Grace were

Elizabeth, born Nov. 26, 1714 Married John Cottrell

Freelove, born Feb 28, 1716 Married John Albro

Jeremiah, born Jan 28, 1719 Married Tabitha Gardner, daughter of Nicholas (3)

Phebe, born Oct 26, 1722 Married Samuel Browning, Jr., died, June, 1810.

Sarah, born April 6, 1725 Married Simeon Babcock, 1743

Dorcas, born December 28, 1727. Married Dr Benjamin Waite

Abigail, born June 23, 1731 Married Samuel Cottrell

Desire, born Nov. 6, 1734. Married Elisha Clark, April 10, 1763.

Penelope, born Nov 11, 1737 Married William Hiscox, Jr

James, born Nov 11, 1737

Grace Gardner died 1776 and letters of administration were granted to her grandson, Benjamin

Sarah Gardner mentioned as child of first wife died young and daughter by second wife was named same

August 7, 1711, Jeremiah Gardiner of Newport (Weaver) bought 133 acres in Kingstown of Mary Young In April 20, 1714, he bought 180 acres of Isaac Gardner and in 1716, January 9, he bought 70 acres of John Congdon

PEREGRINE GARDNER (2)

George (1).

Peregrine Gardner, son of George and Lydia (Ballou) Gardner We have no record of the date of his birth History states he never married

The following little sketch may be of interest to the reader

Some reminiscences of how, when and where the "young idea was taught to shoot" in olden times, the late Hon William Staples says in his "Annalls of Providence "

"The first schoolmaster in Providence of whom any memorial remains was William Turpin When he came is not known, but he was here the 11th day of June, 1684 On that day he executed an indenture with William Hawkins and Lydia His wife (widow of George Gardner, Sr), in which he covenanted to furnish Peregrine Gardner with board and schooling for one year, for six pounds, forty shillings of which in beef and pork, pork at two pence, and beef at three pence half penny per pound, twenty shillings in corn at two shillings per bushel and the balance in silver money He was to be instructed in reading and writing

'This instrument is in the handwriting of Mr Schoolmaster Turpin and exhibits plenary proof of his ability to teach writing It also proves conclusively that schoolmasters in those days were not very exorbitant in their demands."

NATHANIEL GARDNER (3).

Benony (2), George (1).

Nathaniel Gardner, son of Benony and Mary Gardner, was born about 1674, died 1734 Married Mary ——

Their children were

Benjamin, born February 26, 1705

Mary, born Nov 30, 1707

Penelope, born 1709

Dorcas, born June 10, 1712

Nathaniel, born June 16, 1714

Job, born July 23, 1723

In 1705 his father gave him by deed one hundred acres, being the west half of the farm where Benony then lived

August 25, 1731 Nathaniel Gardner Deeds to George Gardner a piece of land Situated Lying and Being in South Kingstown containing Thirty Acres being part of Sd. Nathaniel Gardner's farm bounded Easterly upon John Dalton, Southerly upon a highway & Westerly on the Sd. Nathaniel Gardner's farm Northerly on Nicholas Gardner's farm Together with all rights privileges &c

(signed)
Dorcas Tibbits,
her
Mary M Stanton
mark
John Pennel

(signed)
NATHANIEL GARDNER.
her
MARY M GARDNER
mark

Will of Nathaniel Gardner.

In the Name of God amen, The Thirty first Day of January, A D 1734, I, Nathaniel Gardner, of South Kingstown in Kings County in the Colony of Rhode Island & providence plantation &c yeoman, being grown Very week In body but of Perfect mind and Memory thanks be given unto God Therefor Calling unto mind the Mortality of my body and Knowing that it is appointed for All men Once to Dye Do make and ordain this my Last Will and Testament That is to Say principally and first of all I give And Recommend my Soule into the hands of god that Gave it and my body I Recommend to the earth to be Burried in Decent Christian Burial at the Discretion of my Executrix and Executor hereafter Mentioned Nothing doubting but at the general Resurrection I shall Receive the Same Again by the Mighty power of God & as touching such worldly Estates wherewith it hath pleased Good to bless me with in this life I give Demise and Dispose of the Same in the following manner and form—

I will and order that all my just Debets be first paid by my Executrix and Executor hereafter named out of my personal Estate in some Convenient time after my Decease

Item--

I give and bequeath unto my Loving wife Mary Gardner the one third part of my homestead whereon I now Live Lying in said Town with one third part of my Orchard And Dwelling house for and During the Time that She shall Remain my widow Excepting that she shall see Cause to Chouse any one Room in Sd House in Liew of the sd Third part of sd House Aforementioned

Item—

I Give and Bequeath unto my sd Wife Two of my Milch cows Such as She Shall se Cause to Chuse out of all my Cows and I all so Give my sd wife one Riding mare That She Usually Rideth upon and one Birdle & side Sadle and farther more I give to my said Wife With Two Feather Beds with the Bed steds and furniture Belonging to Sd two Beds and I all so give to my sd Wife the one half of all the Remaining part of my Household Goods Excepting those particular things that I gave or shall hereafter give to Some of my Children in this my Last will and Testament

I give and Bequeath unto my Loving Son Benjamin Gardner and to his heirs and Assigns forever all That my farm or Tract of Land Situated Lying and being in the New purchase in the town ship of East Greenwich & Containing by Estamation Two hundred and Twenty two Acres and is the third farm in the Second Division in sd purchase Buted and bounded as followeth viz Northerly and Westerly on two highways South on the Land of John McCoun East partly on the Land of Anthony Low and partly on Land of Henry Summers as it is Laid Down per the platt of Sd Purchase made by William Hall Surveyor and farthermore I give and bequeath unto my Sd. son Benjamin Gardner one hundred pounds in Good passable Bills of Credit in Sd Colony to be Levied and paid out of my Estate in Sd South Kingstown by my Executrix and Executor within one year after my Decease

Item—

I give and give and bequeath unto my Loving Son Nathaniel Gard ner and to his heirs and assigns forever all the Westermost half of my homestead farm whereon I now Live Lying in South Kingstown aforesd with all the houseings standing upon sd half of sd Farm

Item—

I Give and Bequeath unto my Loving Son Job Gardner And to his heirs and Assigns forever all the Eastermost half of my Aforesd Homestead farm Lying in Sd South Kingstown whereon I now Live as aforesd And it is to be Understood that my will and Mind is that my aforesd Son Nathaniel Gardner shall have the Use and Improvement of that half of my sd farm which I have hereafore given unto my Said Son Job Gardner until my Son Job shall come to the age of twenty-one And furthermore my will is that my Said Son Nathaniel Gardner shall not Cutt nor suffer to be Cutt any of the wood or Timber that is growing upon Sd Eastermost half of my Sd Home Sted farm while my Son Job Gardner shall come to the age of Twenty one years Nor Carry of Any of the hay that shall hereaftergrow upon sd Eastermost half of Sd farm while he hath the improvement as aforsd

Item—

I give and Bequeath unto my two Sons Nathaniel Gardner and Job Gardner the Cedar and Chestnutt Rails and poles which I now have upon my aforsd Homested farm to be Equally Divided between them when my son Job shall Come to the age of Twenty one years And it is to be farther understood that my will Mind is that if Either of my two sons Nathaniel Gardner or Job Gardner before he or they Shall Come to the Age of Twenty one Years or without Lawfull Issue that then his half of my Aforsd Homested Farm Shall go to the Longest Surveyour of them and to his heirs And Assigns forever

Item—

I give and bequeath unto my sd Son Nathaniel Gardner My Negro man Named Bristo and my Negro Woman named Tene and my Large bible and my Gilded Trunk and my Satchel my woosted Combs and my Razor and whone and all my powdering Tubbs and Likewise all my negroes beding and my Case and Case Bottles and all so I give him my black mare which I Commonly ride upon and Bridle and Sadle

Item—

I give and Bequeath unto My sd son Job Gardner one hundred pounds in passable Bills of Public Credit in the Colony aforsd to be Levied and Paid out of my Estate in sd South Kingstown by my sd Son Nathaniel Gardner when my said Son Job Gardner shall come to the Age of Twenty one years

I give and Bequeath unto my Loving Daughter Mary Kenyon one of my feather beds with the bed stid and furniture that belongs to one of my Sd Beds And I all so Give to my Sd Daughter Mary Twenty pounds in bills of passable Credit in the Colony aforsd. to be Raised

Levied and paid out of my Estate by my Executrix and Executor hereafter named within one year after my Decease

Item—

I give and bequeath unto my Loving Daughter Dorcas Tibbits one of my feather beds with the bed sted and furniture that belongs to one of my said beds and I all so Give unto my Said Daughter Dorcas Tibbits Twenty pounds in Bills of public Credit in the Colony aforsd. to be Raised Levied and paid Out of my Estate by my Executrix and Executor hereafter named within one year after my Decease and All so I give her one Case of Draws

Item—

I give Unto my two Daughters Mary Kenyon and Dorcas Tibbits the one other half of my Household Goods which I have not particularly given away or mentioned in this my Last Will and Testament to be Equally Divided between them And Furthermore My will is and I do Order that my Sd son Nathaniel Gardner shall at his own Cost and Charge find for his mother Sufficient firewood Ready Cutt and Carted to her Door to burn in her Said Room in Sd House All the time that his mother shall Remain my Widow

And further my will is and I Do Order that my son Nathaniel Gardner Shall Allow to his mother the use of negro man Bristow to hoe corn for her every year that she Shall Remain my widow, at any time when She Shall want him most for that Service And it is to be Known and understood that my will and Mind that what I have before given and bequeathed unto my Sd wife in this my Last will and Testament is to be In Liew of her thirds and Dowery

And furthermore my will is and I do Order that my Son Job Gardner shall be kept to school Some Reasonable time at the Cost of my Executrix and Executor till he is of proper age to be putt on apprentice and then to be put on apprentice to Learn Some Good handycraft Trade And I do hereby Constitute and Ordain my Loving wife Mary Gardner my Executrix and My Loving Son Nathaniel Gardner my Executor of thismy Last Will and Testament And I do hereby Utterly Disallow Revoke and Disanul All and Every Other former Testament Wills Legacies and Bequests and Executors by me in any ways before Named Willed and Bequeathed Ratifying and Confirming this and no other to be my Last Will and Testament

IN WITNESS whereof I have hereunto Sett my Hand and Seal the Day and year above written

Signed Sealed Published pronounced
And Declared by the Said Nathaniel
Gardner as his last will and Testament
In the presence of us the subscribers

NATHANIEL GARDNER (seal)

JOB TRIPP
his
ABIEL **X** SHEARMAN
mark
WILLIAM ROBINSON

Job Tripp, Abiel Shearman and William Robinson all appeared before the Town Council of South Kingstown this 10th Day of February 1734 and Did Declare upon Oath that they did See Nathaniel Gardner of Sd. Town Sign Seal and Declare This Will to be his Last Will and

Testament and That they Signed thereto at the Same time in his presence as Wittness And According to the best of their Understanding he was in his perfect mind and Memory

This will being so proved The Town Council Doth approve of ye Same

Inventory taken February 10, 1734 showed 743 pounds

SAMUEL GARDNER (3).

George (2), George (1).

Samuel, son of George and Tabitha (Tefft), Gardiner, married Ann Briggs, daughter of Thomas and Martha Briggs.

Their children were:

Thomas, born May 5, 1707.

Samuel, born Apr 25, 1709

John, born Dec 15, 1717, married Ann Fry, 1740.

Martha, born May 28, 1723, married Thomas Nichols, Aug 13, 1741

Henry, born March 23, 1725, married Elizabeth Rice, Apr, 1746.

JOHN GARDINER (3).

George (2), George (1).

John, son of George and Tabitha (Tefft) Gardiner, died 1752 Married Mary Rathbun, 1717 She was the daughter of Joseph and Mary (Mosher) Rathbun, of New Shoreham She was born March 6, 1697.

Their children were

May, born 1718

Margaret, born May 7, 1720, married Isaac Gardiner, 1736.

Tabitha, married Gideon Gardner.

John, born July 27, 1727, married Amy ——

HANNAH GARDINER (3).

George (2), George (1).

Hannah, daughter of George and Tabitha (Tefft) Gardiner, died 1756 Married Josiah Wescott Jan. 18, 1701 He was born 1675; died Nov 11, 1721 She married (2) Thomas Burlingame

Children were.

Nicholas, born Aug 27, 1702.

Hannah, born Aug 11, 1704

Tabitha, born Dec 7, 1706, married Stetely Wescott, Apr. 15, 1725 He died Oct 8, 1726

Josiah, born March 6, 1709

Nathan, born March 23, 1711

Damaris, born June 12, 1713

Caleb, born Dec 6, 1716

Oliver, born Sept 5, 1720

JOHN GARDINER (3).

Joseph (2), George (1).

John, son of Joseph and Katherin (Holmes) Gardiner, was born Sept. 7, 1697. Jeffry Watson in his diary under date Jan 29, 1764, says:

"This morning the Hon John Gardiner, Deputy Governor, departed this life He is to be buried the second day of February"

1736 he was Deputy, 1743 to 48 he was General Treasurer, and in 1756 he was elected Deputy Governor to succeed Governor Jonathan Nichols who died in office He also died in office

He married Frances Sanford, October 23, 1720. She was the daughter of John and Frances (Clark) Sanford and granddaughter of Jeremiah and Ann Clark. She was born Jan 13, 1702-3

Their children were

Frances, married William Benson Oct 3, 1745

Lydia, married —— Rodman, son of Samuel and Mary (Willett) Rodman

Katharin, married Thomas Rodman July 6, 1750 He was born 1726

Elizabeth, married Capt Peter Wanton

Mary, died May 8, 1788, was (2) wife of Benjamin Wickham.

Sanford, married Ann Newton Dec 4, 1760.

GEORGE GARDNER (3)

Joseph (2), George (1).

George, son of Joseph and Catherine (Holmes) Gardner, was born June 4, 1704 He married Mary Thurston, daughter of William.

Their children were.

Joseph, born July, 1727, died Aug 8, 1727

Daughter, died Oct 17, 1729

William Thurston, born July 7, 1732

Abigail, died June 6, 1764, aged 22 years.

Mary

CATHERIN GARDNER (3).

Joseph (2), George (1).

Catherin, daughter of Joseph and Catherine (Holmes) Gardner, was born February 1, 1707. She married Edward Thurston

Their children were

Susannah, born 1728, died March 14, 1830

Susannah, born 1733 died May 10, 1736

Edward G, born 173— He was a Free Will Baptist preacher near Prov, R. I

John, born 1734, married Mary Brett

Catherin, born 1736, married Watson, March 19, 1761 She had sons John, Edward Thurston

ROBERT GARDNER (3).

Joseph (2), George (1).

Robert, son of Joseph and Kathern (Holmes) Gardner, was born Aug. 1, 1690, married Ann ———

He was admitted freeman of Newport 1722

One child

Freelove, born Oct 24, 1727, married Wiliam Easton.

ELIZABETH GARDNER (3).

Jeremiah (2), George (1).

Elizabeth, daughter of Jeremiah and Grace (——) Gardner, was born November 26, 1714; married John Cottrell about 1732

Their children were

Elizabeth, born April 6, 1733
Hannah, born May 4. 1735, married Elias Burdick, Jan 17, 1754
Dorcas, born May 4, 1737; married Carey Burdick Dec. 27, 1754
Thomas, born Sept. 4, 1739.
Benjamin, born Sept 14 1742
John, born March 12, 1745

FREELOVE GARDNER (3).

Jeremiah (2), George (1).

Freelove, daughter of Jeremiah and Grace (——) Gardner, was born July 28, 1716, married John Aldro.

Their children were

Jeremiah, married Mary Tefft Oct 15, 1758.
Eunice, married James Whit——
Margaret,
A daughter,
Son,
Mary.

PHEBE GARDNER (3).

Jeremiah (2), George (1).

Phebe, daughter of Jeremiah and Grace (——) Gardner, was born October 26, 1722, married Samuel Browning, Jr She died June 15, 1810

Their children were·

Child, born June 3, 1743
Child, born Nov 6, 1745
Child, born Dec 5, 1748
Child, born Dec 19, 1751
William born July 21, 1754, married Sarah Cole Dec 13, 1787.
Gardner, born May 31, 1761, died July 23, 1817.

SARAH GARDNER (3).

Jeremiah (2), George (1).

Sarah, daughter of Jeremiah and Grace (——) Gardner, was born April 6, 1725, married Simeon Babcock, October 3. 1743.

Their children were

Eunice, born Oct 3, 1744
Jeremiah, born March 16, 1746.
Thomas Browning, born July 21, 1748.
Lucy, born June 11, 1750
Dorcas, born Dec. 3, 1753

Jason, born July 9, 1756.
Lydia, born June 20, 1759.
Hannah, born Apr 28, 1762
Lucas, born Apr. 24, 1765.
Jonathan, born April 18, 1768, married Prissella —— of Stonington, Ct Feb. 20, 1795.

NICHOLAS GARDNER, JR (3).

Nicholas (2), George (1).

Nicholas Gardner, Jr., son of Nicholas and Hannah —— Gardner, was born at South Kingstown, R I Died at North Kingstown April 6, 1743 Married Mary A., daughter of Thomas Eldredge, October 13, 1709

Their children were

Nicholas, born Dec. 6, 1710
Ezekiel, born Sept 29, 1712.
Sylvester, born Aug 3, 1714
Hannah, born Sept 2, 1717
Amey, born June 17, 1723
Susannah, born —— 19, 1725
Thomas, born Oct. 1, 1729
Dorcas, born Mar 27, 17—.

He was known as Nicholas of North Kingstown or Nicholas of Exeter Together with William Hall, Nathan Pierce and John Albro he laid out the northwestern boundary of the Pettaquamscutt Purchase About 1737 he moved from the "rock farm' at South Kingstown and passed the remaining six years of his life with his son Sylvester, at Gardner's Four Corners

In 1732 he was a member of the Town Council

June 11, 1734, he was one of the appraisers of the estate of William Eldredge

In 1732 he gave receipt to —— Eldredge, administrator of the estate of his father, Thomas Eldredge, for his share of the property, his wife being daughter of Thomas Eldredge

In 1753 he died and left the following will

IN THE NAME OF GOD AMEN, the twenty sixth day of March Annoque one Thousand Seven hundred and Forty three and in the Sixteenth year of his majestyes Reign George the Second King of Grat Brittain, I Nicholas Gardner of Exeter in the County of Kings in the Colony of Rhode Island &c yeoman Being Sick and weak of body but perfect minde and memory Thanks be Rendered to Almighty God therefor, and calling to mind the Mortality of my Body and Knowing that it is appointed For all men once to Dye do make and ordain this Instrument To be my Last Will and Testament That is to Say Principally and first of all I committ my Soul into the Hands of almighty God that gave it, and my body to the Earth To be buried in Decent Christian Buriall at the Discression of my Executor hereafter Mentioned and as Touching Such Worldly Estate Wherewith it Hath pleased God to Bless me with in this Life I give and Dispose of the same in the following manner and form—

Imprimas—

my will is and I do order That my Executor hereafter mentioned do Emediately after my Decease Rent out all my Land being where I now

Dwell until Such Times as my Son Thomas Shall arrive at the age of twenty one years and the Income or Rents of my Said farm I order my Executor to Satisfy and pay all my just Debts Therewith.

Item—

I order and my will is That my Two Sons (Viz) Nicholas and Ezekiel Gardner do Support there mother Mary Gardner and maintain her equally alike as Long as She Remains my widow Which maintainance Shall be in Liue of her Thirds which She might in any ways Recover by Law

Item—

I give and bequeathe To my Loving Son Nicholas Gardner Five Shillings in passable bills of Public Creditt to be paid by my Exeecutor hereafter Named out of my estate as my money becomes due to me from my Son Ezekial Gardner, to his Heirs and assigns for Ever he haveing already Received his portion

Item—

I Give and bequeathe unto my Son Ezekial Gardner the Sum of five Shillings in passable bills of Public Credit to be paid by my Executor out of my Estate as my money Becomes due to me from my Said Son Ezekiel to his Heirs and assigns for Ever he haveing allready Received his portion—

Item—

I give and Bequeath unto my Son Sylvester Gardner my Negro boy Named Cuff to him his Heirs and assigns for Ever—

Item—

I Give and Bequeath unto my son Thomas Gardner all my Farm whereon I now Dwell Lying and being in the Town of Exeter after he arrives to the age of Twenty one years to him his heirs and assigns for Ever—

Item—

I do order and my will is that my Executor Emediately after my Decease do put out my Said Son Thomas Gardner to Some Good Trade as my Said Executor may think fitt—

Item—

I Give and Bequeath unto my Loving Daughter Hannah Sweet widow to John Sweet Deceased one Hundred pounds in Good Passable Bills of Creditt to be paid and Levied out of my Estate by my Executor hereafter Named at the Expiration or end of Seven years after my Decease—

Item—

I give and Bequeath unto my Loving Daughter Amy Gardner one Hundred pounds in bills of Publick Creditt to be paid out of my Estate by my Executor hereafter Named at the end or expiration of Two years from the Date hereof as also one Negro Gairle Named Pegg and my black mare and Sidesadle and bridle which I bought for her, and also my best Bed and bedsted and all other furniture thereunto Belonging—

Item—

I Give and Bequeath unto my Loveing Daughter Susannah Gardner one Hundred pounds in bills of Publick Creditt To be out of my Estate by my Executor hereafter named at the End or Expiration of Three years from the Date hereof—as also one Negro gairle Named fillis and my will is That my Negro fillises Child Suck until Such Time as Said Child is fitt to weene—

Item—

I Give and Bequeath unto my Son Thomas Gardner my Negro Child Named Cezar to him his heirs and assigns for Ever—

Item—

I Give and Bequeath unto my Loving Daughter Dorcas Gardner one Hundred pounds in Passable bills of Creditt To be paid out of my Estate by my Executor hereafter Named at the End and Expiration of foure years from the date hereof for hir and hir own Disposall, that is to Say to be put to Intrust for hir at That time by my Sons Nicholas and Exekiel Gardner.

I Give and Bequeath unto my Deare and Loveing Wife Mary Gardner that Bed that we Lye on to and for hir owne Disposall as all furniture thereunto belonging—

Item—

I Give and Bequeath unto my two Daughters Susannah and Dorcas Gardner all the Beds and beding that I have not before by this Instrument already Disposed of To be Equally Devided between them as also all the Feathers that I have I Give to my Said Daughters to be Equally Devided between them

Item—

I Give and Bequeath and my will is that all my Iron Puter and brass ware be Equally Devided between my three Daughters Namely, Susannah Amy and Darkas Gardner To them and at There own Disposal—

Item—

I Give and Bequeath and my will is That all my Chanes Axes Betle and Wedges hoas and Streak of the Cart wheals and Plows and plow Irons be Equally Devided Between my two sons Nicholas and Thomas Gardner, and I give to my Son Sylvester Gardner my Grindstone and hone, and I likewise Give to my Son Sylvester Gardner my old Rone mare and if Said mare Shall this yeare have a Colt, Then my Said Son Thomas Gardner Shall have Said Colt when fitt to weene and that the mare be not red till Said Colt is fitt to weene—

Item—

I Give and Bequeath To my Three Daughters Namely Hannah Amy and Susannah Each of them a Silver Spoone—I Give and Bequeath unto my Daughter Darkas Gardner my small red Trunk—

Item—

I Give and Bequeath To my Son Sylvester Gardner all my Swine both great and Small—

Item—

my will and meaning is that my Daughter Hannah Sweet have The Intrust of the Legacy Given hir after the Expiration of five years which will be two years for hir to Receive Intrust—

Item—

I Give and Bequeath and do Order That my two Sons Nicholas and Exekiel Gardner Shall Sell all my Cattle and Sheepe and That they put the money out to Intrust to be Equally Devided amongst all my Daughters Namely Hannah Amy Susannah and Darkas only first of all My Said Sons paying out of Said mony all the Present Debts that I owe—

I Do Constitute and appoint my Trusty friend Job Tripp of North Kingstown in Kings County To be my only and Sole Executor of this my Last will and Testament Rattifying and Confirming this and no other to be my Last Will and Testament In witness Whereof I have hereunto Set my hand and Seal the Day and year first above Written—

his
NICHOLAS O GARDNER (seal)
mark

Signed Sealed Delivered published Pronounced and Declared by the Said Nicholas Gardner to be his Last Will and Testament In presence of us the Subscribers—

Subscribers—
(signed)
Isaac Gardner
his
Palmer X Cleavand
mark
Benoni Hall

Mr Isaac Gardner and Benoni Hall personally appeared before the Town in Counsil of Exeter the 12th Day of aprill A D 1743, and on There Solemn Engagement Declared That They Saw The above Subscriber Nicholas Gardner Deceased Sign Seale publish pronounce and Declare the above Instrument to be his Last Will and Testament and that at the Signing thereof he was of a Sound Disposing mind and memory and that they two and in his presencee Signed Thereunto as witnesses and also Sd Palmer Cleaveland Signed Thereunto as a Witness at the Same time Signed by the order of the Town Counsell of Exeter the 12th Day of aprill 1743.

(signed) BENONI HALL, T Clerke

A True Copy Took from the origanall Examined and Compared by Exekiel Gardner.

This Instrument is Recorded in the 40, 41, 42, 43, and 44 Pages of the book of Records for Wills That Did belong to North Kingstown now being in Exeter No 13 aprill the 14th 1743

By Benony Hall T Clerke

This is Recorded Likewise in the 2, 3, 4, 5, and 6 pages of the book of Records for Wills No 2 August the 17 a d 1744 belonging to Exeter.

By Benony Hall, T Clerke

TABITHA GARDNER (3).

George (2), George (1).

Tabitha, daughter of George and Tabitha (Tefft) Gardner, was born Feb 2, 1687 Died 1760 Married Benjamin Westcott, son of Jeremiah and Eleanor Westcott and brother of Josiah He was born July 4, 1684; died 1765

Their children were

Bethia.

Dorcas, died 1734. Married James Congdon.

Benjamin, married May Carpenter, April 29, 1733
Stutey,
Samuel, born Aug. 28, 1719
Josiah,
Hannah,
Phebe.

GEORGE GARDNER (3).

George (2), George (1).

George, son of George and Tabitha (Tefft) Gardner, died before his father. Married and had a daughter.

Elizabeth, baptised Aug 2, 1725

She is mentioned in her grandfather's will as only child of his son George, deceased

SAMUEL WATSON (3).

Dorcas (2), George (1)

Samuel Watson, son of John and Dorcas (Gardner) Watson, died Nov 25, 1779. The record of his death says aged 93 He married first, Mercy Helme of Rouse and Mary Helme, married second, Hannah Slocum, widow of Samuel Slocum and daughter of Robert Carr.

The following were children.

Benjamin,
Margaret,
Freeborn,
Robert,
Silis,
Nicholas,
Mary, married Edward Slocum, Aug 20, 1774, died 1778
Samuel,
Freeborn,
Hazard.

WILLIAM WATSON (3).

Dorcas (2), George (1).

William Watson, son of John and Dorcas (Gardner) Watson, died about 1740 Married Mary Helme, daughter of Rouse and Mary Helme

One child was born to them:

William

FRANCIS WATSON (3).

Dorcas (2), George (1).

Francis Watson, daughter of John and Dorcas (Gardner) Watson, died 1726 Married Daniel Brown, son of Jeremiah and Mary Brown He died 1726.

Children born as follows

Elizabeth, born March 13, 1705.

Mary, born August 3, 1706
Benjamin, born March 16, 1708
Daniel, born November 15, 1709
Elisha, born January 26, 1711.
Dorcas, May 22, 1713.
John, born February 18, 1714.
Desire, born January 8, 1723

ANN WATSON (3).

Dorcas (2), George (1).

Ann Watson, daughter of John and Dorcas (Gardner) Watson, married Peter Wells, son of Peter Wells He was born 1681, died 1732

Their children were
James, born September 30, 1706.
Ann, born October 20, 1708
Rebecca, born December 30, 1710
Peter, born May 4. 1713.
John, born April 14, 1716
Mary, born 1718
Dorcas, born Sept 17, 1720.
Samuel, born February 2, 1725

HERODIAS WATSON (3).

Dorcas (2), George (1).

Herodias Watson, daughter of John and Dorcas (Gardner) Watson, married John Sheldon, son of John Sheldon, April 11, 1706

John, born February 10, 1707.
Dorcas, born January 4, 1708.
George, born May 25, 1709.
Samuel, born January 15, 1714.
William, born March 27, 1715
Elizabeth, born March 31, 1720
Sarah, born March 26, 1722

BRIDGET GARDNER (3).

Benony (2), George (1).

Bridget, daughter of Benony and Mary (——) Gardner, was born Nov 8, 1687 Married Job Sherman, son of Samson and Isabel (Tripp) Sherman, Dec. 23, 1714 Lived at Portsmouth, R I.

Their children were
Philip, born Dec 12, 1715, married Feb 14, 1744, Alice Sherman
Isabella, born Oct. 31, 1717, married John Watson June 26, 1736
Mary, born Jan 16, 1719-20
Job, born May 20, 1722.
Bridget, born July 11, 1724, married John Sherman, Aug 19, 1747 Died Oct 8, 1753
Sarah, born Oct. 29, 1726.

Alice, born June 25, 1728, married Joshua Earl, of Swansey, May 12, 1748

May, born October 25, 1730

ISAAC GARDNER (3).

Benony (2), George (1).

Isaac Gardner, son of Benony and Mary (——) Gardner, was born January 6, 1687 Married Elizabeth Davis, March 24, 1709 She died May 20, 1759

Their children were.

Mary, born Mar. 30, 1711

Elizabeth, born Mar 24, 1714-5.

Sarah, born May 5, 1716.

Isaac, born May 5, 1718

Benony, born May 31, 1720, married Elizabeth, 1741.

Samuel, born Sept 27, 1722, married Elizabeth Congdon, May 3, 1750.

Penelope, born July 19, 1725, married William Hall, Oct 2, 1741

Silas, born Oct 29, 1727, married Hester Congdon, Dec 20

Gideon, born Jan 8, 1729, married Tabitha Gardner, of John, Sept 29 1750

Bridget, born Aug 21, 1734

WILLIAM GARDNER (3).

Benony (2), George (1).

William Gardner, son of Benony and Mary (——) Gardner, was born 1671 Died December 4, 1732 Married Abigail Remington, daughter of John and Abigail (Richmond) Remington

Their children were

John, born July 8, 1696, died July 6, 1770, aged 74 years

William, born May 21, 1698, died at sea

Abigail, born Sept 24, 1700, died May 22, 1772.

Hannah, born Dec 7, 1704

Lydia, born June 27, 1706.

Sylvester born June 29, 1707-8; died 1786, at Newport, R I

1712, William Gardner was admitted freeman

1708, William Gardner, cordwainer, and Abigail, his wife, sold to John Watson 17 acres of land near Pettaquamscutt Rock

1705, he and wife Abigail, sold to Henry Gardner 250 acres of land that had belonged to wife's father, bounded west by —— ——, south on Thomas Mumford, north on said Henry Gardner and part by William Gardner, Sr, and fresh meadows This is the land in Moorsfield a part of which is still occupied by descendants of Henry Gardner

He united the calling of Lawyer and farmer, which blending of the industrial and intellectual was common in colonial days In the exercise of his profession he had acquired considerable wealth and was the owner of much real estate, which included land on Boston Neck, and extended farther toward the west Among the bequests of his will was a farm of one thouand acres left jointly to three of his grandsons.

He was the father of seven children, six of whom grew into positions of influence Indeed, the Gardner family as a whole, attained a degree of prosperity rare in these olden times One of them rejoiced in the name of "four chimney Amos" And this at a day when one chimney was a cause for great thanksgiving, may be supposed to imply the influence of its possessor

After his death his widow married Col Job Almy, of Newport, Sept. 3, 1740. She died Feb 6, 1763, in her 83rd year, and is buried in the Episcopal churchyard on Tower Hill The records read she was a pleasant tempered woman and a member of the Episcopal church.

Will of William Gardner.

In the name of God Amen the Twelfth day of April Anno Dommie one Thousand Seven hundred thirty two I William Gardner of South Kingstown in Kings County in the Colony of Rhode Island and Providence plantations &c yeoman being in Good Health of body and of Sound and perfect mind and memory Praise be given to almighty God But calling unto mind the mortality of my body and knowing that it is appointed for all men once to dye to make and ordain this my last will and Testament. That is to say Principally and first of all I recommend my Soul to God through the merits death and passion of my Saviour Jesus Christ to have full pardon and forgiveness of all my Sins and to inherit Everlasting life and my body I commit to the Earth to be Decently Buried at the Discretion of my Executor hereafter named and as Touching the Disposition of all such Temporal Estate as it pleases almighty God to bestow upon me I give and dispose thereof as followeth —

I will that my just Debets and funeral Charges be well and truly paid and Discharged by my Executor hereafter named in some Convenient time after my Decease

Item—

I give and bequeath unto my Well Beloved Wife Abigail Gardner one roome in my Dwelling house and two beds and furniture which She Shall See cause to make choyce of with all my plate and so much more of my household Goods as shall be Sufficient to furnish Said Roome with one Negro woman named Moll and one Negro Girl Named Moreah Until my Grandson Josiah Arnold comes To ye Age of Twenty one years. Also one Cow and one Mare of the Value of Thirty pounds, both to be kept on ye Farm during my Wife s Natural Life I also give my said Wife Forty pounds a year to be paid her Quarterly and so much Fire Wood as shall be Sufficient to Maintain one Fire during her Natural Life All which is to be paid kept and performed by my Son John Gardner. But if in case the said Negro Mollie should die before my Wife then my Will is that my sd. Wife shall have ye choyce of one other of my Negro Women and it is to be Understood and it is my Mind and Will that what I have here given my said Wife is in the liew of her thirds —

Item—

I give and Bequeath unto my Well beloved Son John Gardner All that my Homestead Farm in South Kingstown Containing five hundred and Forty Seven Acres to him and his Heirs & Assigns forever.

Item—

I Give and Bequeath unto my Well beloved Son Sylvester Gardner All that my House and Land lying in South Kingstown where my Son John Gardner now dwells Containing in both pieces about Eighty Acres to himself & his Heirs & Assigns forever

Item—

I Give and Bequeath unto my said Son Sylvester Gardner One Negro Boy Named Juda, Two Beds & furniture, One Gelding Horse (that he makes Choice of) with one Bridle and Sadle—I also give & Bequeath unto my said son Sylvester Gardner Fourteen hundred pounds in Bills of Credit to be paid him by my Executor out of my Estate in one year after my Decease

Item—

I give unto my grandson Amos Gardner Three hundred Acres of Land out of my Farm which lies part in North Kingstown and part in Westerly which I purchased of Colb Wanton and others To be taken of ye North side & to extend Southward both ends of a Wedth until it makes up three hundred Acres To him his Heirs and Assigns forever—

Item—

I give and Bequeath my grandson William Gardner Three hundred & fifty Acres of Land in North Kingstown aforesd. to lie in ye same Farm and next to ye three hundred Acres I have given to me Grandson Amos Gardner To him and his Assigns forever Provided & upon Condition that he my said Grandson William Gardner or his Heirs shall give or make Over unto my Son John Gardner his Heirs or Assigns All his or their Right or Claim that Tract of Land in my Homestead Farm called ye Middle Bonnet containing about four Acres Which he may pretend to have or Claim by Virtue of a Deed which I gave his Father But if my sd Grandson or his Heirs shall at any time when required Refuse to Acquit his or their claim to said Land Then I do hereby Declare ye sd Bequest to him to be Null and Void. And I do hereby Give and bequeath the said three hundred and fifty Acres of Land before him to my Son John Gardner his Heirs and Assigns forever—

Item—

I give and Bequeath unto my Grandson James Gardner three hundred and fifty Acres of Land lying in North Kingstown aforesaid being the Southside & remaining part of said Farm I purchased of Wanton &c To him my said Grandson his Heirs and Assigns forever- It is my Mind and Will that my Grandsons Allow each other a Convenient Drift Way to pass through each others Land As Accasion shall require And that my Son John Gardner or his Heirs have ye use and improve ye same until they arrive at ye Age of Twenty one years—

Item—

I give to my two Granddaughters Abigal and Elizabeth Gardner and to each of them One Hundred pounds in Bills of Credit to be paid by my Son John Gardner when they arrive at ye age of Eighteen Years—

Item—

I Give and Bequeath unto my Daughter Abigail Robinson One hundred pounds in Bills of Credit to be laid out in Plate and to be marked with my and my Wifes Names in three years after my decease I also give to her my said Daughter Seven hundred pounds in Bills of Credit three hundred pounds of which shall be paid in three years and four hundred pounds in five years after my decease by my Executor—

Item—

I give and Bequeath unto my Daughter Hannah McSparien One hundred pounds in Bills of Credit to be laid out in plate and to be marked with mine and my wifes Names to be paid in three years After my decease—I also give her my said Daughter Seven hundred pounds in Bills of Credit, Three hundred of which shall be paid her in three years and four hundred in five years after my decease by my executor—

Item—

I give to my Grandson William Hazard fifty pounds in Bills of Credit and ye service of an Indian Named Jeffrey to be paid and delivered to him when he comes of ye age of Twenty One years by my Executor—

Item—

I give to my Grandsons Robert and Caleb Hazard, each Twenty five pounds to be paid by my Executor—

Item—

I give to my Grandson Josiah Arnold a Negro Girl Named Moreah and thirty pounds in Bills of Credit to be paid him by my Executor when he arrives at ye age of twenty one years It is my mind and Will that whereas some part of ye Lands given to my son Sylvester Gardner, being Mortgaged to the Colony that ye same be paid and discharged by my Executor out of my Estate—

Item—

I give and Bequeath unto my well beloved Son John Gardner (whom I appoint my only and Sole Executor of this my last Will and Testament) All the rest and residue of my Estate both Real and personal Be it what kind or Nature soever—And I do hereby disallow Revoke make Null and Void all former Testaments Wills Legacies and Bequests, and Executors by me in any way before Named Willed and Bequeathed Ratifying and confirming this and no other to be my Last Will and Testament in Wittness whereof I have hereunto Set my hand and Seal the day and year first within written—

Signed Sealed Published pronounced (signed)
and Declared by the said William WILLIAM GARDNER (seal)
Gardner as his last Will and Testament
in ye presence of
Francis Willet
his
Nicholas O Gardner
mark
Mary Willet

Letters of Administration were granted to John Gardner March 29, 1733

Inventory of Estate of William Gardner taken by John Watson and Ephriam Gardner Total 4945 pounds 17s 6 p

HENRY GARDNER (3).

Henry (2), George (1).

Henry, son of Henry and Abigail (Remington) Gardner, was born Feb 25, 1691 His home was in Moorsfield in South Kingstown on land inherited from his father. Some of his descendants still own the land which was bought by his father in 1704 from the heirs of John Remington He died in Newport July 16, 1768, and was buried on his own land in Mooresfield He belonged to the Parish of St Paul He married (1) Desire Havens, Aug 4, 1710, (2) Catherine Davis of East Greenwich, Dec 27, 1722

His children by first wife:

Henry, born June 16, 1714.

Christopher

Hannah, baptized Feb 27, 1721, married Thomas Potter Dec 31, 1730

Desire, baptized Feb 27, 1721, died Dec 28, 1723

Children by second wife were

Edward, born Sept 8, 1723, married Elizabeth Tefft, may 23, 1745.

Mary born July 25, 1728, married Jonathan Hazard, Apr 16, 1747.

Abigail, born March 9, 1732, married Thomas Mumford, May 23, 1751.

William, born about 1725.

EPHRIAM GARDINER (3).

Henry (2), George (1)

Ephriam, son of Henry and Abigail (Richmond, Remington) Gardiner, was born January 27, 1693 Died April 11, 1774 Called Ephriam Esq, of North Kingstown Married Penelope Eldred April 28, 1713, daughter of Samuel and Martha Eldred. She died April 19, 1783, in her 89th year

Their children were

Dorcas, born Jan 31, 1714

Penelope born Oct 15, 1716, married Charles Dyer, July 29, 1736

Samuel born Jan 16, 1719, married Amey Easton, July 12, 1749

James, born July 10, 1721, married Waite Coggeshall, Mch 15, 1749

Ephriam, born about 1723, died Sept 10, 1785, married Patience Congdon Mch 21, 1758

Christopher, born June 3, 1726, married May Easton, Sept. 16, 1753 She was a sister to Amey, and daughter of Jonathan and Patience Easton

1778 Ephriam Gardiner, Esq, was admitted freeman from North Kingstown

1747 he was assistant

WILLIAM GARDINER (3).

Henry (2), George (1).

William, son of Henry and Abigail (Richmond, Remington) Gardiner, was born October 27, 1697. Married Margaret Eldred June 12, 1718 She was the daughter of Capt John Eldred Were married by Rouse Helme, Justice

Their children were

John, born Dec 5, 1720

Abigail, born 1721 Married Nov 30, 1738 Jeremiah Worden By Henry Gardiner, Justice.

Henry, born Jan 9, 1726-7 Married Mary Helme, 1750, daughter of Christopher Helme.

Margaret.

Will of William Gardner.

Dated the 19th Day of March 1731 I William Gardner of South Kingstown in Kings County &c yeoman and son of Mr. Henry Gardner of sd town &c being in Good Health of body &c

And as touching the disposition of all such Temporal Estate as it pleases Almighty God to bestow upon me I give and dispose in the same in the following manner and Form—Imprimis—

I give and bequeath unto Margaret my dearly beloved Wife one Mare which is called her mare with her Sadle and bridle and one Negro woman called Betty and one Negro boy called Newport but if my sd Wife should have a Living Child which she is now big with them my will is that the said child shall have the Negro boy called Newport and my son John Gardner shall also pay to the sd Child Two hundred pounds in Currant money of the Colony of Rhode Island If the sd Child Live to the age of twenty one years or at the Day of marriage if that should be sooner I also give to my sd Wife my Now Dwelling house and the one third part of all my Land During the time of her widowhood and afterwards to be and remain as hereinafter Set forth—

Item—

I give and bequeath to my well beloved Sons (viz) John Gardner and Henry Gardner all my Land to be Equally Divided Between them for Quantaty of Acres by a line running East and West a Cross my farme from Samuel Teffts Land to the Wide Highway and my son John to have the East part and my son Henry to have the West part of my sd farme and ye sd Land with ye appurtenances thereunto belonging to Remain to them my sd sons John and Henry and to their Heirs and Assigns forever—

Item—

I give to my well beloved daughter Abigail Gardner one Negro Girl called Jane—

Item—

I give to my well beloved daughter Margaret Gardner one Negro Girl called Florah—And further my Will is that my sd son John shall pay to his sd two sisters Abigail and Margaret Two hundred pounds to each of them when they shall arrive to the age of eighteen years or at the Day of Marriage if that should happen first—

Item—

I also give to my sd. two Daughters Abigail and Margaret Each of them one feather bed and furniture to them—

Item—

I also give to my sd Wife all the Rest and Residue of my movable Estate She paying my Just Debts in Due time and I do hereby Make Constitute and appoint my sd well beloved Wife Margaret Gardner my Executrix and William Robinson of sd South Kingstown in the County of Kings County & Esq My Executor of sd my last will and Testament and I do hereby Utterly Disallow, Revoke, Make Null and Void all other wills Legacies Bequests and Executor by me in any wise heretofore written or bequeathed Ratifying and confirming this and no other to be

my last Will and Testament. In Whttness whereof I have hereunto Set my hand and seal the Day and year first above written
Signed Sealed Published pronounced
and Declared by the Sd William Gardner
as his last Will and Testament.
Henry Gardner Junr. (signed)
Christopher Helme WM GARDNER.
Jeremiah Clark

Estate Apprised by Rouse Helme and Christopher Helme May 8th, 1732

JOHN WATSON (3).

Dorcas Gardner (2), George (1).

John, son of John and Dorcas (Gardiner) Watson was born July 22, 1676, died Nov. 8, 1772 Married (1) Hannah Champlin, daughter of Jeffrey, April 8, 1703. She died Oct 11, 1720 He married (2), Abigail, widow of Samuel Eldred, and daughter of Stephen and Mary (Thomas) Northup, April, 1722 She died Aug 22, 1737. He married (3) Sarah Mowry, Sept 1738, she died March 12, 1764 His children were by his first and second wives

Hannah, born Mar 1, 1703-4, married William Clark, of Latham. He died 1746 She married (2) David Green

Ann, born Mar 27, 1708, died 1771, married Benjamin Allen

John born Mar 13, 1709, died Apr 26, 1791 Married Isabella Sherman, daughter of Job and Bridget (Gardiner) Sherman, June 2, 1736

Jeffrey, born Aug. 3, 1712, died May 10, 1784 Married Bathsheba Smith, daughter of John, Jr, and Mercy (Wescott) Smith, Nov 29, 1732. She was born Apr 7, 1710

Elisha, born Sept 14, 1714, died Sept 11, 1737

Dorcas, born Oct 25, 1716, died 1785 Married Ezekiel Gardiner.

Annie born Oct 18, 1719; married John Lillibridge, 1738

Freelove, born about 1723, married John Champlin, 1743

Mary born about 1725

An obituary notice appeared in the newspaper the week after the death which seems worthy of repeating

"On Wednesday last, Departed this life, and on Saturday was decently interred, John Watson Esqr in the 97th year of his age He was the first child born in Narragansett after the Indian war. He was blest with more than a common share of good sense and was early employed in many important affairs Was several years a member of the General Assembly and sustained other offices of Trust and importance, all of which he executed with integrity and to general satisfaction. He enjoyed an uncommon share of good health, having never been confined to his bed till a few days before his death He retained his memory and Rational facculties to the Last He had eight children, 57 grandchildren, 45 great grandchildren and 3 great, great grandchildren, and a great part of them followed his corpse to the grave He was a Loving husband, a tender father just Majistrate, a good neighbor, a mild master and an Honest man"

In 1708, a few years after his first marriage, he bought of William Gardiner 75 acres "Near Pettaquamscutt Rock" This land was bounded

Easterly on the River, Southerly by Arnold, and Westerly on highway, Northerly by land of Brenton This farm with other lands added to it, has been in the family since that date until about 1890, when J. B. Watson sold it to Mrs Carver It was never sold, but handed down by will or deed of gift till the last date, through the eldest son, whose name for six generations was John John (6), eldest son of John (5), died in infancy and so the farm descended to his second son, Joseph, whose son, Jesse B Watson, sold it to Mrs Carver Five generations of John Watsons are buried on this land John (2) became a large land holder The greater part of his land he gave to his sons by deed of gift before his death

In the diary kept by his son, Jeffrey, is a copy of the publishment of his third marriage It is given here as an illustration of the custom of the times

"Kings County, Sept, A D 1738. These are to publish the Bans of Marriage Between John Watson & Sarah Mowry both of South Kingstown in the County afore Said, and if any person or persons Can Show Just Cause Why these two May not be joined together in Mattrymony, they make their application as the Law Directs, and not to Pull Down nor Deface this publication at their Peril.

Given under my hand and Seal in South Kingstown this 10th Day of September A D 1738.

Per ISAAC SHELDEN, Justice"

PETITION TO THE KING.

Petition from the inhabitants of the Narragansett Country to the King.

To the King's Most Excellent Majesty, the humble Petition and Remonstrance of your subjects, the inhabitants of the Narragansett Country, in the southern part of New England, called by your Majesty's Commission the King's Province

May it please your Majesty: About forty two years since, the father of one of your petitioners, namely Richard Smith deceased, who sold his possessions in Gloucestershire, and came into New England, began the first settlement in Narragansett Country (Then living at Taunton, on the Collony of New Plymouth), and erected a trading house on the same tract of land where now his son Richard Smith inhabits, not only at his cost and charge, but great hazard, not without the consent and approbation of the natives, who then were very numerous and gave him land to sett his house on, living well satisfied in his coming thither, that they might be supplied with such necessaries as often times they wanted, and at their own homes without much travel for the same The said Richard Smith likewise being as well pleased in his new settlement in a double respect, first that hee might bee instrumental under God in the propagating the Gospel among the natives, who knew not God, as they ought to know him, and took great pains therein to his dying day, secondly, that the place might afford him a refuge and shelter in time to come, for the future subsistance of him and his; wherein he was not only deceived in his expectation for losing almost all hee had in the Indian war among the Dutch, where hee likewise made a settlement, chose at last this place of Narragansett for his only abode, no English living nearer to him than Pawtuxel, at his first settling being neare twenty miles from him The place now called Warwick, was not then thought on. Much about that time some gentleman of the Massachusetts Colony removed from their inhabitants and came to the Narragansett Bay and purchased of the natives an Island in said Bay and called it Rhode Island, Mr William Coddington being the chiefest of them and who only purchased the same, and was the first chief sett up among them selves a government by consent for the well ordering of their own affairs, and for the peace and security thereof In process of time, that place called Warwick, was settled by Mr Gorton and Holden and others, whereby Richard Smith, aforesaid, had some neighbors near to him, and afterwards Mr Roger Williams of Province, likewise came to Narragansett and built a house for trade, nearer unto the former house of Richard Smith s who in some short time quitted his settlement, and sold it to the said Richard Smith, who lived there alone for many years, his house being the resting place and rendezvous for all travelers passing that way, which was of great benefit and use to the country, and was at no small cost and charge therein for many years together, to the great relief of all travelers But time, that produces changes, caused him, being wearie of living alone in a desert wilderness, yet having plenty of Indians and wild creatures, to desire neighborhood and invited his neighbors in New England to purchase of the Indians and settle the country with him, which accordingly some well-affected persons of Rhode Island, and some of Massachusetts Collony, Connecticut and New Plymouth joined with the said Richard Smith and his son Richard Smith, your present petitioner, who lived there with his father and made two small purchases of tracts of land by the seaside And much about the same time some of Rhode Island purchased an island in the Bay, called by the natives Quononaqual, and another company of Rhode Island and Boston joined together, but most of Rhode Island purchased another tract of land in the Narragansett Country, to the southward of that above-mentioned, first for the digging of black lead, afterwards for the further settlement, whereby the country came to be inhabited with English to the great cost and charge of the first settlers The country being all this while under no settled government, yet claimed by several Collonies by virtue of grants from some Lord's in England in time of trouble there but no settled government till your Majesty was pleased to grant your gracious Letters Patents to Connecticut and Rhode Island both which including the Narragansett Country, caused great troubles to the inhabitants by making them offenders for not complying with either as they were commanded when in truth they know not whom to submit to, and was the only hindrence of the settlement of that country Some of the purchasers and proprietors thereof choosing to submit unto the government of Connecticut as per article of agreement made between the Agents of each Collony in England, by the Lord Brewerton Cap's Deane, Major Thomson, Doctor Worslev and Cap'n Brookhaven, many appear Yet notwithstand this proved ineffectual to the ends of peace and unity so much desired, to the great grievance and discouragement of the inhabitants that were there minded to improve their settlement, though some of the same purchasers having sold their rights to others, now endeavor to obstruct the rest of their co-purchasers in the enjoyment of theirs, but differences still increasing about the government, your Majesty's commissioners in the yeare 1664 viz Sir Robert Carr, Collonell Cartwright, and Samuel Maverick gave the name of King's Province to the Narragansett Country, and forbid any person of any jurisdiction whatsoever to exercise any authority in the said King's Province, but who should be authorized by them under their hands and seals until your Majesty's pleasure was further knowne. Since which the said Commissioners granted for the orders for settleing part thereof, as to Mr Brown, Cap n Wellett and others Notwithstanding which the government of Rhode Island hath of late forced settlement upon some of our said lands contrary to the said Commissioners orders and your Majesty's letter as lately, at place called East Greenwich In the times of these troubles and contests the Indians proved insolent and very injurious to our petitioners, the inhabitants, not without private abetters as well as was suspected, killed our cattle, destroyed our creatures and plundered some of our horses, soe that wee were hardly able to live among them some of us loosing in some few yearse neare 150 head of cattle

And when complaint was made to our superiors at Rhode Island, wee could have no reliefe, which made some of us apply ourselves to the Massachusetts Collony for redress for these outrages and enormities committed against us, according to an order of your Majesty's granted unto them about the yeare 1663, but still were without remedy, which many of us foresaw would end in a warr with the Indians if not timely and wisely prevented Which afterward came on apace to the ruin and destruction of your petitioners visible estates in that Province So that it became a desolate wildernesse againe, and instead of Christian people, replenished with howling wolves and other wild creatures But it pleased the Lord in his due time to put a period to these warrs, and your petitioners, the former inhabitants, went over from Rhode Island, whither wee retreated with that little wee had left, where it cost us one half of our cattle to keep the rest and carry us over So cold was their charity to their poore neighbors in distress, and then and since imposed taxes on us, when your petitioners had hardly any thing left for the subsistence of themselves and little ones, and settled in the King's Province againe, when very dangerous living in (cellars and holes), under ground, till we got a little beforehand to rebuild, which with our own industry and hard laboure, wee hope in time to effect, if not discouraged and hindered by many that threaten to turn us off May it please your Majesty this being in short, the true state of affairs of the Narragansett Country and the people there inhabiting, from the first settlement to this present time

Your petitioners, the inhabitants thereof, do humbly supplicate your Majesty, as you have been pleased to send your gracious letters to the foure Collonys of New England strictly to will and require them to take care of the inhabitants there at present, so that you would in your princely wisdom and Royal bounty and justice, for the future vouchsafe an eye of favor upon the poore inhabitants your petitioners, the first settlers thereof, in a more peculiar manner, who have been at great cost and charge, and have laid out (most of us) all wee have in this world upon the same, and are not able to subsist, if removed from thence, it being now become in a manner our native country to some of us, and is to many of our children who were there borne and we hope and promise for ourselves and for our children that shall succeed us, that your Majesty in no part of New England shall have no more loyal or faithful subjects than your present petitioners, humbly requesting and desiring that your Majesty would put an end to these differences about the government thereof, which hath been so fatal to the prosperitie of the place, animosities still arising in peoples minds, as they stand affected to this or that government, and may be wronged and injured by either government of these that take place, the transaction of former things being fresh in our memory, and impartiall and equall judicature being the great and earnest desire of your petitioners to live under, being wearied out with the former contests and the troubles wee have met with from both Collonies commanding us, do all of us unanimously and with one consent supplicate your Majesty not to leave us to the government and dispose of those that seek advantage against us The country being large and able to continue many families, may make an entire Province, if your Majesty see cause

And your petitioners shall ever pray, etc, And subscribe your Majesty's humble, loyall and obedient subjects

King's Province, in Narragansett

July 29, 1679

(Signed in our hand)

William Bently,	Henry Gardner,
John Greene,	Richard Smith,
Nicholas Gardner,	Benony Gardner,
John Coale,	Jer. Bull,
George Gardner,	Sam Eldred,
Tho Gold,	Daniel Greene,
Arthur Aylworth,	George Witman,
Sam Wilson,	Hen Reynolds,
Robert Vinin,	James Green,
James Reynolds,	John Eldrid,
James Reynolds, Jun'r	Thomas Sovell,
Daniel Eldrid,	Rob't Spink,
Daniel Swete,	Rob't Spink, Jun'r,
Joseph Delaner,	Sam Alsbery,
John Sheldin,	Alexander Fenix,
William Gardner,	William Ceston,
Henry Tippets,	John Sheldon, Jun'r,
Aron Jackvaier,	William Knowls
Frell Newton,	Thomas Brooks
Rouse Helme,	George Palmer
Joseph Reynolds,	Lodowick Updike,

Indorsed

Petition of the inhabitants of the Narragansett Country Received from Mr Lewyn the 3rd March,1679-80

JOHN GARDNER (4).

William (3), Benony (2), George (1).

John Gardner, the eldest son of William and Abigail (Remington) Gardner, was born July 8 1696, and died July 6, 1770, aged 74 years

He married, first Mary Hill, by whom he had children as follows:

Anstress (Anteis) born March 23, 1721

Hannah, born April 22, 1723, died December 31, 1727

Thomas born March 11, 1725

Amos, born March 27 1729, died September 29, 1827

Mary (Hill) Gardner, died June 11, 1739

John Gardner married, second, Mary Taylor, December 13, 1739 She was a niece of Francis Willet, Esq, of North Kingstown

They were married by Rev Dr McSparren.

Children

Abigail, born September 26, 1740

William, born March 18, 1741-2

Mary, born about 1744, died October 16, 1762, in her 18th year

John, born 1747, died Oct, 1808

Benjamin, born Jan 4, 1750

Sarah, born about 1751, died June 16, 1771, aged 20 years

Lydia, born 1753.

Mary (Taylor) Gardner, died April 24, 1774, in the 60th year of her age

In 1722 he was admitted freeman for South Kingstown.

In 1732 to 36, he was an assistant.

In 1744 he was called Colonel John Gardner and was appointed commissioner for the Colony.

He owned a large estate in Boston Neck, South Kingstown, and also land in Westerly, R I The last he gave to his son Thomas In his will written 1769, probated 1770 he gave to his wife his dwelling house and all the land he bought in Boston Neck of Ephriam and Elezner Smith This tract contained several hundred acres It would seem that at the time of his death he was not living on what he called his homestead, for this farm he left to his son John Gardner, it being the farm where Amos was then living calling it the old homestead farm. This was probably the land bought by William in 1711 of George Witman

He gave to his son John two hundred sheep and ten cows and his clock

To daughter Abigail Updike eleven hundred Spanish Milled dollars, daughter Sarah Gardner thirteen hundred Spanish Milled dollars, and daughter Lydia, fourteen hundred, and grand son James, son of son William, five hundred Spanish Milled dollars His wife in her will 1772, gave grand son James, eight hundred dollars, Daughter Abigail Updike Two Hundred silver dollars, and four silver porridgers, Daughter Lydia Two Hundred dollars, a silver tea pot, milk pot, silver pepper box, eight table spoons, twelve tea spoons, silver sugar tongs

Son John Gardiner two silver porridgers

Son Benjamin two silver porridgers

WILLIAM GARDNER (4).

William (3), Benony (2), George (1).

William Gardner, second son of William and Abigail (Remington) Gardner, was born May 21, 1698, married Elizabeth Gibbs Apr. 16, 1719 He died at sea, supposed to have been killed by pirates.

He had four children as follows:

Abigail, born March 6, 1720.

William, born May 30, 1724
James, born August 5, 1725.
Elizabeth, born June 16, 1728

ABIGAIL GARDNER (4).

William (3), Benony (2), George (1).

Abigail Gardner, third child of William and Abigail (Remington) Gardner, was born September 24, 1700

She married Caleb Hazard, November 19, 1719 By him she had four sons as follows:

William, born April 12. 1721, married Phebe, daughter of Demaris and John Hull, of Jamestown

Robert, born May 1, 1723, he married Elizabeth, daughter of Deputy Governor Robert Hazard

Caleb, born September 22, 1724, died young

Caleb, born September 22, 1726, married Mary ——, died March 4 1784

Mr Hazard died in the year 1726, and his widow, Abigail Hazard, married Deputy Governor, William Robinson, March 2, 1727. He was born 1693 and died 1751

He was the son of Rowland and Mary (Allen) Robinson

The children by second husband were as follows

Christopher, born December 31 1727

William, born August 1 1729, married Elizabeth Wanton, May 17, 1750

Thomas, born January 25, 1731, died 1817 Married Sarah Richardson

Abigail, born 1732, died March 3, 1754.
Sylvester, born 1735, died January 23, 1809
May, born 1736, died 1776
James, born 1738
John, born 1742

HANNAH GARDNER (4).

William (3), Benony (2), George (1).

Third child of William and Abigail (Remington) Gardner, was born December 7, 1704 She married the Rev. James McSparren May 22, 1722. They were married by the Rev James Honyman No children born to them

REV. JAMES McSPARREN, D. D.

A famous clergyman of the olden times, with whom our history has connection, was Rev James McSparren, D D He was among the first emissaries sent to this country by the English "Society for the Propagation of the Gospel in Foreign Parts," and was, in the opinion of many, its ablest missionary He became in 1721, the pastor of St Paul's Church of South Kingstown, Rhode Island, which is now the oldest building of its kind in the United States north of the Potomac river Of

Scotch descent, though born in Ireland, he showed the qualities of his sturdy race in his zealous and untiring work among the Narragansett people, who, to this, day, hold his memory sacred He founded five churches, baptized nearly six hundred people, and, when offered a Bishop's mitre in England, fearing that America would dislike an English ordination, he refused it, saying, 'I would rather live in the hearts of my parishioners than wear all the Bishop's gowns in the world"

The curious title of one of Dr McSparren's books bears evidence of his plainness of speech "America Dissected,' being a full and true account of all the American Colonies, showing the intemperance of the climate, excessive heat and cold and sudden violent changes of weather, terrible and murderous thunder and lightning, bad and unwholesome air destructive to human bodies, badness of money, danger from enemies, but, above all to the souls of the poor people that move thither from the multifarious and pestilent heresies that prevail in these parts

Published as a caution to unsteady people, who may be tempted to leave their native country.

In the great days of Narragansett hospitality and elegance, the congregation of "Old St Pauls' numbered the noblest of the land The Phillipses, the Balfours, the Robinsons, the Hazards, the Potters, the Updikes, and the Gardners were among those that sat in the square, high built pews, and listened to the vigorous tones of the good Doctor. There were at that time no carriages in use, and history has drawn us a pretty picture of the trip to church on Sunday morning, each grave settler, with his wife before him on a pillion, urging his careful-stepping saddle horse over the narrow paths between crowded tree trunks and through rough country fields With them rode Dr McSparren himself, and the fair lady whom he had taken from the Gardner family to be his helpmate in the rural pastorate Of him as well as his wife there remains a portrait, painted by the celebrated Smibert, who came to America with Dean Berkley So that we can picture him round of face, sturdy of figure, invested with all the dignity of curled wig gown, and bands, bending from the clumsy pulpit above the heads of damsels in scarlet cloaks and flaunting plumes, and cavaliers in gold-laced coats and snowy frills, with a background of dusky figures, the slaves for whose welfare Dr McSparren was always zealous

As we have seen the pastor's attention was drawn at an early date to the Gardner family William Gardner, called "William of Narragansett," was the father of Mrs McSparren, and a leading citizen in South Kingston Dr. McSparren was a graduate of the University of Glasgow His health became impaired, and he, with his wife, returned to his native land where he remained some time Small pox became an epidemic while he was on this visit and his good wife contracted the loathsome disease and died June 24, 1755, a few minutes after twelve in the morning and was interred Wednesday evening the 25th

She was buried in Broadway Chapel burying yard in Westminster

The Doctor soon returned to America and his health continued to fail, much more so after the loss of his good wife He grieved this loss and died December 1, 1757 He was buried in the church yard of St Pauls Church (sometimes called Tower Hill Church) in Narragansett, of which church he was pastor thirty seven years.

Doctor McSparren received into his family for classical teaching a few of the more wealthy colonists' sons. Among his pupils were

Thomas Clapp, afterward a famous president of Yale College, and the rector's young brother-in-law, Sylvester Gardner

INTERESTING ST. PAUL'S

A writer in the Westerly Sun says The village of Wickford, in the town of North Kingstown, is a pretty little place, especially pleasant in the summer time, situated as it is on a point of land extending out into the waters of Wickford bay, a branch of Narragansett bay There are several places of interest in and about the village. Perhaps the most interesting is the old Episcopal Church, St. Paul's, which stands down a lane off the main street, a little removed from the quiet bustle of the town Here, in a good-sized lot of land, nearly surrounded by graves wherein sleep some of the forefathers of the hamlet, the old church stands, not in the place where it was built, but as appears upon a plate above the one door of the church now in use, "Built in 1707, removed 1800" It was built some five miles from its present location, at a place called the Old platform, on the side of McSparren hill

As it stands today it is in form of an oblong square, about 34 by 40 feet on the ground and two stories high, a frame building clapboarded and shingled The one door faces the street, having over it beside the inscription above quoted a little ornamental scroll The door is in two leaves On either side on the first floor are two windows with oval tops. The second floor or gallery has five windows in front, the same number of windows on the back, two in each story at the ends, with a round window in one gable furnish light to the place The window panes are many in number, in size 6 by 8 inches.

Entering the door you are in the auditorium Directly in front, across the room, stands the high pulpit, reached by a flight of five high steps on either side The small pulpit a narrow bench against the rear wall, on which two may sit, furnishes an uncomfortable resting place for the occupant of the desk

The room is of the plainest, the massive frame showing every timber and brace Six columns support the galleries, which extend around three sides of the room and are now reached by a flight of stairs at one corner There are thirty pews on the floor, fourteen around the walls being square boxes with a door on the side next to the aisle, while the seats are a board around three sides of the pew. The backs and ends of the pews come up nearly to the shoulders of the persons who sit in them There are sixteen pews in two rows down the middle of the floor These are long and have only one seat in each, a bench running the length of the pew The sides and ends are like the square ones There was no lolling upon soft cushions in the good old days, even if the sermon was two hours or more long

The gallery is plain and the seat on one row furnished the floor of the one above, or else the floor of one row furnished the seat of the one below There once was a tower at one end with a belfry, bell and spire, but that has fallen, or has been taken down The entrance to the gallery was through this when standing

This is the oldest church edifice standing north of Mason and Dixon's line Upon the old site where the church was erected there are still the ancient tombstones erected there in memory of those who lived around the old church, who loved it and that for which it stood,

Amid these towers the memorial cross erected by the churchmen of the diocese in 1869, to Dr McSparren, for many years rector of this the first Episcopal church in Narragansett country

The first work by the Episcopal church in this section was done under the direction of "The Society for the Propagation of the Gospel in Foreign Parts," with headquarters in London The first rector was Rev. Christopher Bridge, followed by Rev William Guy, neither of whom stayed long Rev Mr Honyman of Newport performed the few official acts which were needed for a few years.

In 1721, Rev James McSparren came He labored in this field for about thirty-six years He was succeeded by Rev Mr Fayerweather He was a native of New England but was loyal to his king, and in 1774 resigned his charge and went to Boston, where on Sunday, Sept 18, 1774, he preached "for the king's chaplain before General Gage and his officers and before a very numerous and polite assembly" from the words "Be kindly affectioned one toward another in brotherly love" General Gage's soldiers were then drilling on Boston Common preparatory to war, and the next month hostilities were opened

As the communicants of the church were mostly in or near the village of Wickford, the old church was by vote of the society removed to its present location in 1800

While the parish had a later and more pretentious church edifice near this one, still the old building is kept in repair and services are occasionally held within its walls

A church building was erected in Newport some years before this one, but was taken down and loaded upon a scow and boats, to be taken to Warwick A storm arose while it was on the way and it was destroyed The second building in Newport was burned, so that now this is the oldest church building in the northern part of the United States

The following is the list of the pew holders in 1760, as appears by the record

—— Powel, R Robertson, John Norton, John Cole, Thomas Phillips Samuel Bissel, Charles Dickinson, Henry Gardner, C Phillips, C Dickinson, Samuel Brown, Elisha Cole Thomas Brown, Stephen Cooper, L Updike, Richard Updike Ephriam Gardner, Samuel Albro, Benjamin Mumford, William Gardner, Robert Case, John Gardner, Francis Willet, Benoni Sweet.

FROM ST. PAUL'S CHURCH RECORD

Dec. 25, 1721, Mr William Gardner baptised

Feb 27, 1721, Henry Gardner an adult, baptised

Dec. 23, 1722, Lydia Gardner, a young woman of 16 years baptised

Dec 27, 1722, Henry Gardner, Jr, of Kingstown and Catherine Davis, of East Greenwich, married

1723, Henry Gardner baptised He was born in Narragansett in 1702

Dec 28, 1723, Desire Gardner, child of Henry, Jr. died from scalding, by a kettle of boiling water falling upon her

Apr 5, 1724, Edward Gardner, son of Henry, Jr. baptised

Nov 17, 1724, Josiah Arnold of Jamestown and Lydia Gardner, daughter of William, married.

Aug. 2, 1725, Elizabeth Gardner, daughter of George (an adult) baptised

Aug 2, 1725, Thomas Gardner, son of John, baptised

Oct 18, 1726, Mary was the wife of Long William Gardner

Nov 28, 1726, Abigail Gardiner, aged 69 years, wife of Henry, baptised

Feb. 22, 1727, Lydia, wife of Josiah Arnold and daughter of William and Abigail Gardiner, died

Dec 25, 1733, Jane Gardiner, daughter of John, baptised

Dec 25, 1733, Mary and Abigail, daughters of Henry, Jr, baptised

Dec 25, 1733, at the house of Mr Henry Gardiner, Jr, baptised three children, Hugh Susanna and Ann Essex, children of Mr Essex.

Sept 3, 1740, Job Almy of Newport married to Abigail Gardiner, widow of William, at the house of her son John, Boston Neck

Nov 9, 1749, Thomas Gardiner, son of John of Boston Neck, and Martha Gardiner, daughter of Henry the son of Nicholas, both of South Kingstown

May 23, Thomas Mumford married Abigail Gardner, daughter of Henry of South Kingstown

Oct 10, 1751, Amos Gardiner, son of John and Sarah (Bill) Gardiner of South Kingstown, married

Aug. 24, 1751, eldest son of Thomas and Martha Gardiner was born at Boston Neck

May 8, 1754, Benjah Gardiner, grand child of John Gardiner of Boston Neck and mother-in-law Mary Gardiner

Nov 5, 1767, Henry Richmond Gardner, a child son of Thomas and Catherine, baptised

Jan 7, 1768, Capt Sylvester Gardiner of North Kingstown, married Miss Sarah Beers of Newport at Capt Jos Coggershalls

July 16, 1768, Mr Henry Gardiner son of Henry of Newport, died, buried in his own ground He was one of the parish of St. Paul

May 13, 1770, Samuel Fayerweather Gardiner, child of Thomas and Catherin Gardiner

July 15, 1771, Miss Sarah Gardiner, (daughter of the late John Gardiner of Boston Neck), died

Oct 30, 1787, Nathan (son of Nathan Gardiner, Jr, and Mary Johnson his wife) was baptised

Dec 27, 1787, Susannah, widow of Capt Bardin, and Sarah (wife of Col John Gardiner) daughter of Samuel and Emma Easton

Mar 13, 1788, Robinson and Stephen, sons of Jeremiah and Lucy (Northup) Gardiner baptised

May 4, 1788, William, an adult son of Clarke and Amey (Lillibridge) Gardiner, baptised

May 11, 1788, Lucy an adult daughter of Samuel and E (Easton) Gardiner baptised.

Jan 6, 1790, Walter, an adult son of Samuel and E (Easton) Gardiner, baptised

BENJAMIN GARDNER (4).

Nathaniel (3), Benony (2), George (1).

Benjamin Gardner, son of Nathaniel and Mary (——) Gardner, was born February 26, 1705.

Married Mary Howland, March 22, 1726-7 Married by Christopher Allen, Justice

Their children were.

Abiel, born January 20, 1727-8

Job, born 1730, died March 9, 1806

Benjamin, born 1731, died February 2, 1809

Caleb, born 1732

Nathaniel, born March 17, 1739, died July 18, 1806

Joshua, born 1742, died October 5, 1829

Alse

MARY GARDNER (4),

Nathaniel (3), Benony (2), George (1).

Daughter of Nathaniel and Mary (——) Gardner, was born Nov 30, 1707 She married John, son of John and Elizabeth (Remington) Kenyon, Mar 23, 1726-7, by Christopher Allen, Justice

Their children were

John, born September 29, 1730

Remington, born February 6, 1732

Mary, born February 4 1734

Dorcas, born August 4, 1737.

Hannah, born November 1, 1739

Nathaniel, born January 4, 1741.

Elizabeth, born June 20, 1743

DORCAS GARDNER (4).

Nathaniel (3). Benony (2), George (1).

Dorcas Gardner, daughter of Nathaniel and Mary (——) Gardner was born June 10, 1712. Married March 11, 1730, George Tibbits, of North Kingstown

Their children were

Daughter born January, 1731

Dorcas, born May 18, 173—

George, born August 26, 174—.

Nathaniel

The above records were in condition not clear as to dates

MARY GARDNER (4).

Isaac (3), Benony (2), George (1)

Mary, daughter of Isaac and Elizabeth (Davis) Gardner, was born Mar. 30, 1711. Married March 23, 1732, John Spencer, son of Peleg

Their children were

Benjamin, born Sept 19, 1733

Weight, born March 7, 1735, married Ishmael Spink Dec 5 1752

Elizabeth, born Jan 9, 1737.

May, born March 13, 1745, married Robert Hall, Jan 26, 1764

Isaac, born July 15, 1747

Sarah, born May 24, 1750

ISAAC GARDNER (4).

Isaac (3), Benony (2), George (1).

Isaac, son of Isaac and Elizabeth (Davis) Gardner, was born May 5, 1718 Married (1) Margaret Gardner, daughter of William, Dec 26, 1736. He was born in Exeter and moved from there to East Greenwich. In 17— he was Deputy and was called Lieut Col Isaac Gardner He married (2), Tabitha Avery, at East Greenwich in 1760 She was from Coventry.

Their children were

Peleg, born June 2, 1740

Olive, born June 24, 1742, married Mercy Gorton, of E Greenwich, R I, Sept. 25, 1766

Isaac, born Aug 16, 1744, married Ruth Aylsworth, Oct 11, 1767

Nicholas born May 30, 1748

Waite, born Oct 3, 1751

Mary, born Sept 24, 1754

John, born Nov. 29, 1756

SAMUEL GARDNER (4).

Isaac (3), Benony (2), George (1).

Samuel, son of Isaac and Elizabeth (Davis) Gardner, was born Sept 27, 1722. Married Elizabeth Congdon, May 3, 1750.

Their children were.

Benony, born Mar 30, 1751.

Mary, born Jan 16, 1753

James, born Oct 1, 1754

PENELOPE GARDNER (4).

Isaac (3), Benony (2), George (1).

Penelope, daughter of Isaac and Elizabeth (Davis) Gardner, was born July 19 1725. Married William Hall, Oct 2, 1741.

Their children were.

Penelope,

William,

Gardiner,

Robert,

Benjamin,

Isaac,

Alice, married George Spencer.

Elizabeth, married George Tefft.

Lucy, married Ebenezer Spencer, 1775.

Patience, married James Gardner.

SILAS GARDNER (4)

Isaac (3), Benony (2), George (1).

Silas, son of Isaac and Elizabeth (Davis) Gardner, was born Oct 29, 1727, died 1782. Married 1754, Hester, daughter of John and Patience Northup

Their children were
Lowry, born May 15, 1755, in Warwick, R I
Almy, married John Gardiner, of Exeter, R I
John died 1792
William,
Isaac, married Polly Hefffernon, Apr. 17, 1786
Silas,
Gideon,
Patience.

BRIDGET GARDNER (4).

Isaac (3), Benony (2), George (1).

Bridget daughter of Isaac and Elizabeth (Davis) Gardner, was born Aug 21, 1734 Married Thomas Newcomb, of Poughkeepsie, N Y, June 2, 1754

Their children were·
Elizabeth, born July 14, 1755.
James, born Dec 13, 1756
Frederick born May 4, 1758

LYDIA GARDNER (4).

William (3), Benony (2), George (1)

Lydia Gardner, sixth child of William and Abigail (Remington) Gardner, was born June 27, 1706 She married Josiah Arnold of Jamestown alias Conanicut, married at the home of the bride by Rev Dr James McSparren November 17, 1724

Their children were
Abigail, born June 25, 1725. Died Dec, 1725
Josiah, born 1726
Sylvester Died before four years old

BENONY GARDNER (4).

Isaac (3), Benony (2), George (1).

Benony Gardner, son of Isaac and Elizabeth (Davis) Gardner, was born May 31 1720 Married Elizabeth (——), May 3 1740

Their children were
Othniel, born June 24, 1742, died 1784
Elizabeth, born Dec 21, 1743.
Latham, born Jan 11 1745, died Feb 27, 1747.
Benony, born Aug 18, 1747, died Feb 27, 1749

Ruth, born Jan. 12, 1750, married Job Fowler,, 1770
Benony, born Jan 7, 1752
Lucy born May 15, 1755, died Oct 27, 1756

BRIDGET SHERMAN (4).

Bridget Gardner (3), Benony (2), George (1)

Bridget, daughter of Job and Bridget (Gardner) Sherman, was born July 11, 1724 Died Oct 8, 1753 Married John Sherman, son of John, Aug 19, 1747. He was born March 25, 1725

Their children were
Job, born May 20, 1748, married Lydia Crendall
John, born March 28, 1750
Bridget, born March 20, 1752

SARAH SHERMAN (4).

Bridget Gardner (3), Benony (2), George (1).

Sarah daughter of Job and Bridget (Gardner) Sherman, was born Oct 29 1726 Married (1) Joseph Viall, Dec 11, 1745 (2) Thomas Proctor, Aug 10, 1758 Children of her first husband were

Anstiess, born July 2, 174—
Mary, born Sept 20, 1747

GARDNER BROWNING (4).

Phebe Gardner (3), Jeremiah (2), George (1).

Gardner, son of Samuel, Jr., and Phebe (Gardner), Browning, was born May 31, 1761, died July 23, 1817. Married Izitt Cole, March 27, 1784 She was the daughter of Capt John Cole, and was born March 31, 1763, died June 18, 1843

Their children were
Samuel, born April 12 1785
Mary, born October 24, 1787
Gardner, born March 5, 1791, died young
Gardner, born April 12, 1792
Hannah, born March 28, 1795; died Aug 5, 1848 Married Jeremiah Gardner
William, born Nov 12, 1798, died Sept 19, 1803
Sarah C., born Nov 22, 1800
Izitt Cole, born Aug 13, 1804
Abbie Ann Congdon born Dec 22, 1807, died Aug 2, 18— Married Jeremiah Gardner, March 16, 1826

EZEKIEL GARDNER (4).

Nicholas (3), Nicholas (2), George (1).

Ezekiel, son of Nicholas and Mary (Eldred) Gardner, was born September 29 1712 Died Aug 13, 1780 Married Dorcas Watson (4), John (3), Dorcas Gardner (2), George (1) August 29, 1734

Their children were born as follows:

John, born October 1734-5 died 1706, married Elizabeth Champlin

Hannah born August 25, 1736, married Jeffry Watson, Jr, 1757

Ezekiel, Jr, born August 25, 1738.

Mary born February 20, 1740

Elisha, born June 4, 1742, died June 9, 1777, married Desire Brown, daughter of Beriah

George, born July 2, 1745

David, born February 15, 1747

Nicholas, born May 29, 1749, died July 16, 1812

Peleg, born November 24, 1750

Zebulon, born April 20, 1753

Jeffrey, born 1755

Oliver, born 1757

Will of Ezekiel Gardner

In the name of God Amen this seventeenth day of December in the year of our Lord one Thousand Seven Hundred and Ninety eight, I Ezekiel Gardner of North Kingstown in the County of Washington and State of Rhode Island and providence plantation yeoman being advanced in years, but of a sound disposing mind and memory thanks be given unto God therefor and calling to mind the mortality of my body Knowing that it is appointed unto all men once to die, do make and ordain this Instrument to be my last will and Testament, First of all I give and recommend my Soul into the hands of God that gave it & my body I commit to the earth to be therein decently buried at the Discretion of my executors hereinafter named & as Touching of such worldly state as it hath pleased God to bless me with in this life I give & dispose of the Same in the following manner and Form—

Imprimis

my will is that all my Just debets & Funeral Charges be first well & Truly paid by my Executors—

Item—

I give and bequeath unto my son John Gardner Ten Acres of land of the Northwest corner of the Farm which I purchased of John Whitman with a Dwelling House thereon Standing to be laid off so as to take said House on his Ten Acres, also all that my Farm containing about Seventy-five acres, being the Farm I purchased of my brother Silvester Gardner adjoining the said Ten Acres, all situated in exeter, unto him his heirs & assigns forever also three pair of Sheets to be delivered him by my executors—

Item—

I give and bequeath unto my son Ezekiel Gardner all that my Tract of land which I purchased of John Pinder with a Dwelling House & other buildings thereon standing containing about Seventy acres also that Tract of Land Which I purchased of Jonathan Hassard containing Forty acres all situated in said North Kingstown unto him his heirs and assigns Forever he giving his brother Peleg Gardner a Quit claim of the Twenty acres which I heretofore gave him a deed of on the Whitman farm so called he well and Truly paying and performing what I shall herein order him to pay unto his Sister Mary Gardner Also one

Featherbed beding & Curtains about it being the same bed which I lodge on —

Item

I give and bequeath my son Nicholas Gardner all that my Farm Lying in Exeter containing one hundred & Twenty Two acres which I purchased of Benjamin Northrop with a Dwelling House thereon Standing unto him his heirs and assignes Forever—also Two pairs of Sheets &one Diaper Table Cloth to be delivered him by my executors—

Item

I give and bequeath unto my son Peleg Gardner all the remainder of the Farm which I purchased of John Whitman Situated in Sd Exeter, saving of the Fifteen acres which I gave my son Jeffrey Gardner a Deed of, containing about one hundred and sixty Three acres, unto him his heirs and assigns Forever—also three pair of Sheets to be delivered him by my executor —

Item

I give and bequeath unto my son Zebulon Gardner all that my Tract of Land which I purchased of Benoni Gardner Lying and being in said Exeter containing about one Hundred and Seventyy acres with a Dwelling House and barn thereon Standing whereon he now lives being the Farm which formerly belonged unto James Sweet unto him & his heirs and assigns Forever he having a deed of Fifteen acres thereof, already also Two pair of Sheets and one Diaper Table cloth to be delivered him by executors—I also devise unto my said son Zebulon Gardner & his heirs and assigns Forever Twenty acres of Land Situate in said Exeter being part of the Farm I bought of Benoni Gardner, commonly called the Slocum land to be laid of the east of said Tract —

Item

I give and bequeath unto my Daughter Mary Gardner the sum of Six Hundred good Spanish milled Dollars to be paid unto her by my son Ezekiel Gardner out of the estate which I have herein given him to be paid her the one half Sum in one year after my decease & Three hundred Dollars being the other half in Two years after my decease I also give my said daughter one milch Cow Three good Feather Beds cords beding & Furniture and curtains to each bed—One Set of Curtains more being the Same she calls hers also Two coverlids Twenty pair of Sheets a Cotton Coverlid Two bedspreads & Three blankets to each bed Three Diaper Table cloths, One large Cubbord which stands in th Store bedroom, one low case of Drawers one round Table and Tea Table one Dozen of Cheairs one mettle Teapot and Tea Kittle one Coffee pot which She calls hers together with one half of my Crockry puter and Iron Ware Six Napkins Five Chests one large Trunk my least Great Chair one Ironing Table one Quilt my large looking Glass and Warming pan, one box Iron and heaters & two large Silver Spoons, and all Small things in my house called hers, One Side Saddle & Bridle all to be delivered her by Executors Immediatly after my decease.

Item

I give and bequeath unto my son George Gardner & confirm unto him his heirs and assigns forever The Ten Acres of Land which I heretofore gave him a Deed of which is part of my pinder land Situated in Said Northkingstown—I also give and bequeath unto my said son George Gardner one Silver milled Dollar to be paid him by my executors

Item.

I give and bequeath unto my Granddaughter Honor Gardner, Daughter of my son Elisha Gardner dec d now wife of Gideon Gardner one Silver milled Dollar I order my executors to pay her

Item

I give and bequeath unto my Daughter Hannah Watson the wife of Jeffery Watson the Sum of One Dollar to be paid her by my Executors She having already receiv'd her portion of my Estate.

Item—

I give and bequeath unto my Grandson Alexander Gardner (son of my son Elisha) Ninety Acres of Land Situated in said Exeter of the land purchased of Benoni Gardner, called the Slocum farm, to be next adjoining the Twenty acres which I herein gave my son Zebulun Gardner—to him the said Alexander his heirs & assigns forever, also one Featherbed one pair of Sheets & coverlid to the Same—Said bed was his Fathers—

Item—

I give and bequeath unto my Grandson Jesse Gardner (Son of my son Elisha) Thirty acres of land Situated in Sd Exeter next adjoining the land above given to Alexander, of the said Slocum Farm being the remainder of said Tract, unto him his heirs and assigns forever—

Item—

It is my mind and will and meaning that my above named Grandsons Alexander & Jesse shall make & execute an acquitting unto my son Zebulun Gardner of their respective Rights in the Twenty acres of land which I formerly gave their Father a deed of upon their reciving the land given them as afores'd which land is given them upon that Condition—

Item—

I give and bequeath unto my Granddaughter Dorcas Sherman Daughter of Said Son Elisha Gardner Dec'd one Cow to be delivered her by my executors upon her acquitting of her Right in the Twenty acres of land which I formerly gave her said Father as afores'd —unto my son Zebulun Gardner—

I give and bequeath unto my Granddaughter Elizabeth Gardner daughter of my said son Elisha Dec'd one Cow one Featherbed & beding belonging thereto, one high Case of Draws, one looking Glass, one warming pan & Teakittle, six Chears—and some Iron puter and Crockeryware which was her fathers, also one round Table & Tea Table all to be delivered her by my executors & upon condition that she acquit her right unto her uncle Zebulun Gardner in the Twenty acres of land in exeter which I formerly gave her said Father a Deed on I also give her the Sheets to be delivered her byy Executors—

Item—

I give and bequeath unto my son Oliver Gardner my Silver Tankard & the other half of my Crockery, Iron and puter ware & my Cart & plows & Harrows & all the rest of my Farming Utencils also three beds beding & Furniture Including of one set of Curtains & Six milke Cows one pair of oxen, Thirty Sheep my Desk & Brass Kittle my Negro boy Domine to his own Use & he to maintain S'd Negro when he comes to want—

Item—

I give and bequeath unto my Granddaughter Mary Gardner Daughter of my son Jeffry Gardner Deceas'd the Sum of one Silver milled Dollar to be paid her by my Executors, her said Father having heretofore in his life received of me his part of my estate as I intended for him—

Item—

I give and bequeath unto my Two sons Ezekiel Gardner and Oliver Gardner all the rest and residues of my movable Estate not before by me given away in this my will to be Equally divided between them Share and Share alike they paying all my Just debets Funeral Charges and all Such Legacys as I have herein ordered them to pay and deliver, Lastly I do hereby constitute and appoint my said Two sons Ezkiel Gardner and oliver Gardner Executors to this my will Strictly Requesting of them to see the Same fullfilled according to the True Intent and Meaning thereof hereby making this only to be my last will & Testament In Witness Whereof I have hereunto Set my hand and Seal the day and Date first afore Written—

The word "Dollar" in the Legacy given my son George was interlined before Signing & Sealing

Signed sealed published pronounced & declared
by the Testator Ezekiel Gardner, to be his last well
and Testament in presence of us.

(signed) (signed)
Geo Thomas EZEKIEL GARDNER
Jno Hassard
Martha Hassard

I Ezekiel Gardner of Northkingstown in the County of Washington and State of Rhode Island &c. being aged but yet of sound mind and Memory Whereas on the Seventeenth day of December in the year of our Lord one Thousand Seven Hundred and Ninety Eight I did make publish pronounce and declare in Writing my last will and Testament therein disposing of all my Estate which will I hereby confirm in all its parts Saving of the Alterations herein to me made in which will I did give and bequeath unto my son John Gardner who was then living but Since deceased in the following words "Item I give and Bequeath unto my son John Gardner Ten Acres of Land of the Northwest corner of the Farme which I purchased of John Whitman with a Dwelling House thereon Standing to be laid of so as to take said House on his Ten Acres, also all that my Farm containing about Seventy five Acres being the Farme I purchased of my Brother Silvester Gardner adjoining the said Ten Acres, all Situated in Exeter, unto him his heirs & assigns forever, also three pair of Sheets to be delivered him by my Executors" all which Legacy I hereby declare Void

Item—

I give and devise and Bequeath unto my Grandson Ezekiel Gardner the son of my said Son John Gardner Deceased, Ten Acres of Land of the North West Corner of the Farm which I purchased of John Whitman with a Dwelling House thereon Standing to be laid of so as to take said House he allowing his Mother Elisabeth Gardner to live in & Improve all the New End of said House as Long as she remain my said Sons Widow on his said Ten Acres of Land, also all that my Farm containing about Seventy five Acres, being the Farm I purchased of my Brother Silvester Gardner adjoining the said Ten Acres, all Situated in Exeter, unto him the said Ezekiel Gardner his heirs and assigns Forever, He paying unto his Brothers & Sisters what I shall herein Injoin on him to in this my Codicil I also give him my said Grandson Ezekiel Gardner three pair of Sheets to be delivered him by my Executors—

Item—

I give and bequeath unto my Grand Children herein after Named Children of my Said Son John Gardner deceased, Namely, Dorcas Reynolds wife of Henry Reynolds, Hannah Gardner, Almy Gardner, Mary Gardner, Elisabeth Gardner, John Gardner, and Jeffry Gardner the Sum of one good Silver milled Dollar a piece that is one Dollar to Each of them, to be paid unto them Respectively by said Grandson Ezekiel Gardner the Son of my said Son John Gardner Deceased out of the Estate which I have herein given him within one year after my deceas—

Lastly I make and ordain this my codicil amended to my afore recited will & Testament to be part and parcel of my last will & Testament, In Witness Whereof I have hereunto Set my hand and Seal This Fourteenth day of November in the year of our Lord one Thousand and Eight Hundred

Signed sealed published pronounced and
declared by the Testator Ezekiel Gardner to be part
and parcel of his last will & Testament
in presence of

(signed) (signed)
Geo Thomas EZEKIEL GARDNER
Jno Hassard
Nathan G Hazard

The word Dollar on this
page Interlined before Signing and Sealing—
also the name Elisabeth Gardner in said House or as
put in before Sign & Seal g

The aforesaid will and codicil was presented unto the Court of Probate in Northkingstown & read before the s'd Court on the 22d day of April A D 1805, and personally appeared before the said Court George Thomas, and John Hassard and Martha Hassard the Subscribing Witnesses to the said will and all on their Solemn Engagements declared that they saw the Testator Ezekiel Gardner esq'r late of said Town deceased Sign seal publish pronounce and declare the same to be his last will & Testament and at the Time of Signing and Sealing thereof he the Testator appeared to them to be of a Sound disposing mind and memory, & that they three in the presence of the Testator, and each other Subscribed their Names to the Same as Witnesses, and on the Same day before said Court personally appeared the said George Thomas, John Haszard & Nathan G Hassard the Subscribing Wittnesses to this Codicil (anexed to Said Will and all on their Solemn Engagements declared that they Saw the Testator Ezekiel Gardner Esq'r deceased Sign Seal Publish pronounce and declare the said Codicil to be part & parcel of his Last Will and Testament, and at the Time of Signing and Sealing of the Same he the Testator appeared to them to be of a Sound disposing mind & memory and they three in presence of the Said Testator and Each other Subscribed their Names to the Same as Wittnesses. This Will and Codicil being thus proved is approved on & allowed by the said Court of probate above said to be good and Vallid Will

Wits. GEO THOMAS, Probate Clk

This will and Codicil is recorded on the 277 278 279 280 281. & 282d pages of the probate books recording of Wills &c in North kingstown this 23d day of April A D 1805

(signed)) WS GEO THOMAS, Tn Clerk

LYDIA GARDNER (4).

Nicholas (3), George (2), George (1).

Lydia, daughter of Nicholas and Mary (Northup) Gardner, married May 7, 1730, John Spencer, son of Michael and Elizabeth Spencer He was born Jan 5, 1700.

Their children were

Nicholas, born June 27, 1731

Isabel, born Aug. 10, 1733, married George Weaver, son of Jonathan Sept 28, 1749

Silas, born Nov 18, 1735, married Dorcas Gardner, daughter of Caleb, 1758

Michael, born Jan. 6, 1744-5

George, born Feb 28, 1752

TABITHA GARDNER (4)

Nicholas (3), George (2), George (1).

Tabitha, daughter of Nicholas and Mary (Northup) Gardner, married Jeremiah Gardner, son of Jeremiah and Grace Gardner He was born 1719

Their children were

Lydia, born June 15, 1741, married John Northup

Phebe, born May 27, 1745, died July 27, 1771 Was (2) wife of John Northup

Benjamin, born Nov 9, 1746, married Tabitha Browning, May 22, 1766 She was born Sept 4, 1748, died July 13, 1821

Mary,

Amos,

Jeremiah.

MARY GARDNER (4).

Nicholas (3), George (2), George (1).

Mary, daughter of Nicholas and Mary (Northup) Gardner, married Peleg Tripp June 28, 1728

Their children were

Peleg,

Caleb,

Mary,

Lydia,

Tabitha

NATHAN GARDNER (4).

Nicholas (3), George (2), George (1).

Nathan, son of Nicholas and Mary (Northup) Gardner, was born 1721, died April 13, 1792 Married Katherin, daughter of Nathaniel and Mary (Hannah) Niles She was born March 25, 1725, died June 16, 1772 He married (2) Thankful ——

Their children were

Mary, born Mar 5, 1743, died before her father, probably unmarried

Nathan, born May 15, 1747, died Mar, 1802, married Mary Johnson, Feb 2, 1782

Sarah, born Dec. 28, 1751, died Nov 11, 1778; married John Hazard

MARY GARDNER (4).

Robert (3), George (2), George (1).

Mary, daughter of Robert and Lydia (Littlefield) Gardner, married William Hall, Aug 25, 1754 He was son of Benony and Elizabeth (Gardner) Hall

Their children were

Benony, born June 20, 1755

Waite, born Feb 4, 1757, died July 2, 1758

Isaac, born April 6, 1761.

ANNA GARDNER (4).

Robert (3). George (2), George (1).

Anna, daughter of Robert and Lydia (Littlefield) Gardner, was born about 1722 She married Robert Reynolds, July, 1742

Their children of whom we have record were

Joseph, married Elizabeth Gardner, April 12, 1765

William Hall, married Lydia Reynolds, Dec. 20, 1771.

HENRY GARDNER (4).

Nicholas (3), George (2), George (1).

Henry, son of Nicholas and Mary (Northup) Gardner, was born according to his tombstone inscription, in 1704, died 1791 Married Abigail Eldred, June 30, 1726 She was born 1708 Died March 6, 1773.

Their children were

Hannah, born 1727 Married William Champlin.

Martha, born 1731. Died Feb 21, 1793 Married Nov. 9, 1749, Thomas Gardiner, of Boston Neck, son of John and Mary.

Mary, married Col Joseph Stanton, of Charleston, R I, his second wife

Abigail, born 1740 Died July 24, 1758 Married Nicholas Spencer

1739 he was admitted freeman 1741 Deputy for New Shoreham 1743 was in South Kingstown 1750-56, he was Deputy from South Kingstown.

CALEB GARDNER (4).

Nicholas (3), George (2), George (1).

Caleb son of Nicholas and Mary (Northup) Gardner, died Nov 22, 1796 Married Isabella Sherman, daughter of Abiel and Dorcas (Gardner) Sherman, Feb 20, 1734.

Their children were:

Sarah, born Apr 29, 1736, married —— Bos.

Dorcas, born Mar 16, 1739, married Silas Spencer

Nicholas, born Dec 8, 1744, died 1784, married Sarah ——

Tabitha, born Apr 8, 1748

Experience, born Nov 1, 1751 Married Pardon Mowney, son of John and Amy (Gibbs) Mowney.

Mary, born ——, married (1) Joseph Perkins (2) Elisha Potter Mentioned in her father's will as daughter, Mary Potter

SUSANNAH GARDNER (4).

Nicholas (3), Nicholas (2), George (1).

Susannah, daughter of Nicholas and Mary (Eldred) Gardner, was born —— 19, 1725, died August, 1783 She married Capt Robert Northup about 1745. He was son of David and Susannah (Congdon) Northup He died September 5, 1783

Their children were

David, born May 9, 1746, married Anstess Crandall, March 9, 1789

Dorcas, born Nov 30, 1748

Nicholas, born Oct 26, 1751

Hannah, born Aug 12, 1755

Benjamin, born Dec 18, 1757

William, born June 4, 1760

DANIEL HILL (4).

Joannah Gardner (3), George (2), George (1).

Daniel, son of Daniel and Joannah (Gardner) Hill, was born Nov 17, 1721, married Elnathan Greene Oct 29, 1747 She was the widow of Thomas Greene and daughter of John Rice

Their children were

Tabitha, born Dec 12, 1750

Elnathan, born Apr 12, 1753

Daniel, born March 27, 1755

Sarah, born July 6, 1760

SUSANNAH HILL (4).

Joannah Gardner (3), George (2), George (1)

Susannah daughter of Daniel and Joannah (Gardner) Hill, was born August 6 1724, married Ayers Ellis, March 28, 1755

Their children were.

Jeremiah, born Dec. 11, 1755, married Amy Austin, —— 29, 1802
Augustus, born Apr 9, 1758, married Desire Slocum, daughter of Charles, of Portsmouth, Oct 3, 1779
Elizabeth, born June 26, 1760
Joannah, born Sept 22, 1763

TABITHA HILL (4).

Joannah Gardner (3), George (2), George (1).

Tabitha, daughter of Daniel and Joannah (Gardner) Hill, was born in Kingstown, Dec 3, 1711, died January 8, 1749 She married Ephriam Howard of Mass, March 31, 1742 He died Aug 9, 1759

Their children were
Ephriam born Feb 28, 1743, married Elizabeth Meyers Apr 12, 1764
Caleb born Dec 4, 1745
Daniel, born June 12, 1748.

MARY HILL (4).

Joannah Gardner (3), George (2) George (1).

Mary, daughter of Daniel and Joannah (Gardner) Hill, was born Feb 21, 1718, married, March 31, 1748, John Case

Their children were
Nathaniel, born Oct 31, 1748
Tabitha, born June 25, 1751

MARTHA GARDNER (4).

Samuel (3), George (2), George (1).

Martha, daughter of Samuel and Ann (Briggs) Gardner, was born May 28, 1723, in East Grenwich. She married Thomas Nichols, Aug. 13, 1741.

Their children were
Rebecca, born Jan 10, 1742, died young
Rachel, married Job Whitford, Oct 27, 1777
Rebecca, born Jan 10, 1744, married William Sweet, Jr, March 0 1769
Anne born July 2, 1755

THOMAS GARDNER (4)

Samuel (3), George (2), George (1)

Thomas, son of Samuel and Ann (Briggs) Gardner was born May 5, 1707, died 1774 Married (1) Aliah Downing, Feb 17, 1731. She was a daughter of Mrs Mary Browning. Married (2) Katherine ——

Their children were
Mary, born Nov 23 1744
Richard born Feb 3, 1745
Thomas born Mch 23, 1746
Samuel, born May 13 1750, died in Newport.
Tabitha, born May 24, 1752.

Will of Thomas Gardner.

In the Name of God Amen this Thirteenth day of October in the year of our Lord one Thousand Seven Hundred and Seventy Four, I Thomas Gardner of South Kingstown in the County of Washington and State of Rhode Island and providence plantation yeoman being advanced in years but of Sound disposing mind and memory thanks be given unto God therfor and calling to mind the mortality of my body Knowing that it is appointed unto all men once to die, do make and ordain this Instrument to be my last will and Testament, First of all I give and recommend my Soul into the hands of God that gave it & my body I commit to the earth to be therein decently buried at the Discretion of my executor hereinafter named & as Touching of such worldly estates as it hath pleased God to bless me with in this life I give and dispose of the same in the following manner and Form

Imprimis—

my will is that all my Just debets & Funeral Charges be first well &truly paid by my Executor—

Item—

I give and Bequeath unto my wife Katherin all the household stuff & goods which she brought me, Her choice of Negro Women Freelove or Kate The Use & Improvement of the West part of My Dwelling House & a privilege in the Kitchen for & During ye Time she shall remain my widow also one Cow to be kept by my Executor for and During her widowhood in lieu of her Right and Dower of Third.

Item—

Son Thomas Gardner should he be still alive my Silver Tankard & all ye money at present due to me by Note bond & Book all of which to remain in hands of my executor & should he not return I give & bequeath all ye above to my executor.

Item—

Son Henry Richard Gardner my Negro Boy Prince one Feather Bed Bedsted and furniture when he shall arrive to ye age of twenty one years, one half of ye mortgage I have upon my Estate of Jeffry Watson Esq to be paid by my Executor when he comes of age & one large Silver Spoon also instruction in reading writing and arithmetic to be paid for by Executor

Item—

I give and bequeath unto my son Samuel Gardner Negro girl Lydia one feather Bed Bedsted when he shall arrive at ye age of twenty one years & one half of ye mortgage I have upon ye Estate of Jeffry Watson Esq to be paid by my Executor when he comes of age and one large silver spoon also instructions in Reading Writing & Arithmetic all to be paid by my Executor Also I give and bequeath unto my Sons Henry Richard & Samuel Gardner my New Coat, Breeches and three Silver Teaspoons to be equally divided between them, Also I give and bequeath unto my grandsons Joseph Hull & Thomas Hull one Large Silver Spoon each.

Item—

I give and Devise unto my son Richard Gardner my mansion House Barn Cribb out Houses together with all my Lands adjoining being in South Kingstown aforesaid to him his Heirs & Assigns forever Also my negro man James & one of my negro women also all my Stock of

Cattle Horses Sheep & Hogs together with my farming utensils & all my other Estate both Real and Personal not hereinbefore Disposed of he paying ye Several Legacies hereinbefore given away & I do hereby Constitute ordain & appoint my son Richard Gardner sole Executor of this my last will & Testament

Revoking Disannulling & Discharging all other & former wills & testaments by me heretofore made or said to be made I ratify & Confirm this & no other to be my last will & Testament ye day and year first above written.

Signed sealed published & pronounced &
declared by the Testator Thomas Gardner to
be his last Will & Testament in the
presence of us.

W Hammond THOMAS GARDNER (seal)
John Gardner.
Joseph Torrey.

William Potter, Clerk of Council.

Recorded ye sixteenth of December 1774.

SAMUEL GARDNER (4).

Samuel (3), George (2), George (1).

Samuel, son of Samuel and Ann (Briggs) Gardner, was born April 25, 1709 Married Mary ——, 1735.

In 1734 he was admitted freeman from East Greenwich, he was then called Samuel Gardner, Jr In 1744 he was called Samuel Gardner of Exeter

We have but one record of issue

Ann, born May 2, 1736 Married Jonathan Olin, Feb 24, 1757

JOHN GARDNER (4).

Samuel (3), George (2), George (1).

John, son of Samuel and Ann (Briggs) Gardner, was born in Greenwich, R. I, Dec 15, 1717. Married

Children were

Samuel, born Aug 29, 1742 Died, Dec 18, 1762 Married Catherine Greene

Mary, born Feb. 12, 1745

Abigail, born Feb 1, 1747

Ruth, born Mch. 20, 1750

William, born Feb 9 1756 Married Hester Nichols, Feb 27, 1780

MARY GARDNER (4).

John (3), George (2), George (1).

Mary, daughter of John and Mary (Rathbun) Gardner, married Josiah Mumford, Nov 29, 1739 He was the son of Peleg and Mary (Bull) Mumford.

Their children were
Waite, born June 27 1742, died Oct 7, 1743
William Gardner, born Nov 26, 1744. married Elizabeth about 1769
Josiah, born May 30, 1747. married Deborah Lillibridge, born Dec 30, 1749.
Mary, born June 17, 1751, died Feb 26, 1752
Sarah, born May 1, 1753
Hannah, born Jan. 18, 1755

JOHN GARDNER (4).

John (3). George (2), George (1).

John son of John and Mary (Rathbun) Gardner, was born July 27, 1727 Married Ann —— about 1746
Their children were
Abel, born Sept 2, 1747 Married Dorathy Waite, born May 2, 1750. Died 1814 Married —— Gardner In her will she mentions daughters, Sarah B Gardner and Dorcas Gardner, who was to have a legacy from her aunt Dorcas Gardner. Also brother John Gardner, of Exeter
Zelpha, born Jan 14, 1752, died 1752
John, born Apr 7, 1753; married Mary, daughter of Samuel and Ann Gardner, Apr 7, 1775
Henry, born Apr 5, 1755
Samuel Green, born May 13, 1757
Mary Gardner, born Apr 7 1759
Ann, born July 1, 1761
Margaret, born Aug 27, 1767

NICHOLAS GARDNER (4)

Nicholas (3), Nicholas (2), George (1).

Nicholas, son of Nicholas and Mary (Eldred) Gardner, was born in Kingstown, Dec 6, 1710. married (1) 1729, Martha Havens, daughter of William Havens of North Kingstown She died Sept 25, 1746 Nicholas Gardner died in 1801. He was a large land holder and owner of many slaves
Children
Mary, born Sept 22, 1732, married Oliver Reynolds Feb 28, 1759
William, born Sept 19, 1734, married Martha Reynolds, Mar. 2, 1760.
Margaret, born June 13, 1736
Nicholas born Mar 2, 1738, died June 6, 1815
Martha, born Aug 31, 1739, married Stephen Arnold Mar 3, 1760.
Ann, born May 28, 1741, married Samuel Morey
Elizabeth, born Sept 22, 1743; married Daniel Champlin
Huling, born Aug 18, 1745, married Elizabeth Northup daughter of Immanuel
Nicholas Gardner, married (2) Dorcas, who died Mar 23, 1775 Children as follows
James, born Oct 26, 1750, died Feb 4, 1795
Sylvester, born Aug. 30, 1752, married Hannah Reynolds

Francis, born April 4, 1755, married Watey West
Dorcas, born Mar 12, 1760, died 1811
1746 and 1754 he was Deputy
1759 he was added to the war committee
1767 he was Lieutenant Colonel

ABIGAIL GARDNER (4).

Henry (3), Henry (2), George (1)

Abigail, daughter of Henry and Catherin (Davis) Gardner, was born March 9, 1732 Married Thomas Mumford, May 23, 1751
Their children were
Henry, born May 28, 1753 Died Oct 21, 1753
Thomas, born June 26, 1755

SAMUEL GARDNER (4).

Ephriam (3), Henry (2), George (1).

Samuel, son of Ephriam and Penelope (Eldred) Gardner, was born Jan 16, 1719 died 1802. Married Amy Easton, —— 12, 1749 She was the daughter of Jonathan and Patience Easton, died 1810
Their children were
Walter Clarke,
Sarah, married John Gardner, Dec 13, 1772
Susannah, born 1751, died June 16, 1808
Samuel Eldred, born 1765, died Sept 9, 1830
Elizabeth,
John,
Emily,
Ephriam,
Lucy,
Thomas Rodman

1778 Samuel Gardner's estate was mortgaged to Thomas Brown for one hundred and sixty-seven Spanish Milled dollars The same year, May, 1778, the General Assembly voted that the sheriff for the County of Kings inquire into the present valuation of the estates of Samuel Gardner and William Robinson in South Kingstown The report of the Sheriff Beriah Brown, was to the effect that the estate of William Robinson was mortgaged to his brother Sylvester Robinson for four thousand and — Spanish Milled Dollars, payable 1773 He said Sylvester who is possessed of the premises said that William owed him also a sum of money not included in the mortgage

Also the estate of Samuel Gardner was mortgaged as above Elijah Babcock, the present occupant was to pay Samuel Gardner 150 dollars and five hundred weight of post

In February 1779, the Assembly ordered that the sheriff take possession of the estate of Samuel Gardner in South Kingstown immediately Said Gardner being then with the enemy in Newport

In 1777 his daughter Susannah, was allowed to go to Newport with a flag of truce to see her father.

WILLIAM GARDNER (4).

William (3), William (2), George (1).

William, son of William and Mary Gardner, died Feb 6, 1781. Married Freelove Joslin

Their children were

Clarke, born Aug 3, 1737 married Ann Lillibridge, Nov 1, 1759 She died Aug 17, 1785

Thomas, born Mar 7, 1738, married Abigail Parker, June 21, 1764

Stephen, born June 7, 1740, married Dorcas Watson.

May, born Feb 13, 1744

Patience,

Desire, born Nov 26, 1749

Gideon, born Nov 15, 1751, died Feb , 1757

HENRY GARDNER (4).

Henry (3), Henry (2), George (1).

Henry, son of Henry and Desire (Havens) Gardner, was born June 16, 1714 Married Ann Champlain, daughter of Christopher and Elizabeth (Dennison) Champlain, June 27, 1736 She was the great granddaughter of John Howland, one of the passengers on the Mayflower She was born March 29, 1714, died 1798

Their children were

Christopher, born Feb 7, 1737, married Mercy Wheeler, daughter of Thomas and Desire Wheeler Jan 23, 1760

George, born Jan 3, 1739, died June 20, 1756

Jonathan, born Oct 14, 1741 married Mary Mowry, July 22, 1764.

Henry, born June 10, 1748 married Ruth ——

James, born Sept 30, 1749, married Abigail Telft, June 27, 1771

Desire, born Mar 31, 1751

MARY GARDNER (4)

Henry (3), Henry (2), George (1)

Mary, daughter of Henry and Catherin (Davis) Gardner, was born July 25, 1728, married Jonathan Hazard April 16, 1747 He was the son of Robert and Sarah (Borden) Hazard.

Their children were

Catharin, born Mar 9, 1748, died young

Henry born Apr. 6., 1749, married (1) Martha Clarke, (2) Rebecca Crouse, widow of Caleb Eldredge

Catharine, born Aug 30, 1751

Robert, born June 24 1753

Sarah, born July 23, 1755

Mary, born 1757

Edah, born 1759.

JAMES GARDNER (4).

Ephriam (3), Henry (2), George (1).

James, son of Ephriam and Penelope (Eldred) Gardner, was born July 10, 1721

Married Waite Coggeshall, daughter of Joseph

Their children were

David, born Dec 19, 1751, died Feb 10, 1755
May, born Nov. 3, 1752
Waite, born Sept 2, 1754, died Dec 9, 1813
Ann, born Mch 29, 1759
James, born Sept 4, 1762
Susannah, born Dec 6, 1763
Abigail, born Sept. 7, 1766
Samuel, born Jan 22, 1769, died 1801
Wanton, born June 1, 1771

THE KINGSTOWN REDS

Among the body of troops formed for the safety and defense of the colonies in Rhode Island was the independent company called the "Kingstown Reds." It seemed to have been a very active organization, and is frequently referred to in the events which occurred within the State Only one roll of this company has been found among the public records and that refers to the company in May 1776 It is believed to be the only list extant and for that reason has been printed

KINGSTOWN REDS MAY, 1776.

John Gardner, Captain
Thomas Potter, First Lieutenant
Rouse T Helme, Second Lieutenant
Rowland Brown, Ensign.

Privates.

John Weight,
James Cottrell,
Richard Gardner,
Jeremiah Sheffil,
Jone Rose,
James Pearce,
John Petrill,
Allen James,
James Rose,
James Helme, Jr,
George Tefft,
Nathan Gardner,
Benjamin Perry,
Walter Watson,
William Rodman,
Frederick Gardner,
James Purkins,
William Aplin,
James Champlain,
William Dyer, Jr.,
Nathan Cotrelle,
Jeremiah Brown,
Henry Reynolds,
Christopher Brown,
George Wilson
Caleb Waistcoat
Robert Helme,
John Weeden,
Lory Gardner,
John Tory,
David Douglas,
James Tefft,
William Clarke,
Solomon Tefft,
James Potter,
Nicholas Easton Gardner,
Allin Gardner,
Ephriam Gardner,
John Clark, Jr

Copied from the Revolutionary Rolls, State archives.

CALEB GARDNER, OF NEWPORT, R. I. (4),

William (3), Joseph (2), George (1).

Sea-Captain, born in Newport, Rhode Island, in 1739, died there December 24, 1806 Living near the harbor and owning a boat, he was in boyhood familiar with the waters and islands of Narragansett Bay, and as a young man became a sea captain, sailing his own ship to China, to the East Indies and made other long voyages Before the beginning of the Revolution he had retired from the sea and engaged in mercantile pursuits in his native town. The war found him a strong Whig He raised a Company, was assigned with it to Richmond's regiment, of which he became Lieutenant Colonel, and was later a member of the counsel of war and of the Rhode Island state government He was residing in Newport in 1778, when the French squadron Count d Estaing was blockaded by the greatly superior British fleet under Admiral Howe A sudden and dense fog prevented an immediate attack of the English, but they occupied both entrances to the harbor, and waited for daylight Captain Gardner had noted from his house top through his spy-glass the position of the hostile fleets, and, as soon as it was dark, rowed himself to the ship of the French Admiral, offered to pilot him to a safe position, and with his own hand steered the Admiral's ship through a channel which he had known from boyhood, the other vessels, with all lights extinguished, following singly in his wake

Having piloted the French beyond the enemy and to clear water, he returned to the island, reached his own house before daylight, and was among the groups along the water front who marveled when the fog lifted, at the disappearance of the French fleet Count d'Estaing's report of the affair to Louis XVI was confidential, since its disclosure would have exposed his guide to the dangerous displeasure of the English government, and to the Tory element in Rhode Island, but the King, through his Embassador in the United States, the Chevalier de la Luzerne, sent to the amateur pilot a sum of money with which the latter bought an estate near Newport, and built upon it a house, portions of which still remain in the cottage known to the visitor of today as "Bateman's"

Throughout the war Captain Gardner was a trusty adviser of the French officers in Rhode Island and of General Washington, who was his friend and correspondent After peace was declared he was made French Consul at Newport, where he resided till his death, being president of a bank, warden of Trinity church, and a head of the volunteer fire department of the town

His great grandson, Dorsey, born in Philadelphia, August 1st, 1842, is a grandson of Dr John Syng Dorsey He removed to Trenton, N J, in 1854 and entered Yale in 1860, but was not graduated In 1864-5 he published the "Daily Monitor," a journal established at Trenton in support of the Lincoln administration in the conduct of the war and with the special purpose of creating public sentiment through New Jersey against the extension of the exclusive privilege of transportation between New York and Philadelphia which was then possessed by the Camden and Amboy railroad company In 1866-8 he was one of the editors and proprietors of the "Round Table," a weekly literary and critical journal published in New York After spending several months in Europe he held editorial positions on the "Commercial Adviser" and the "Christian Union" of New York until he removed to Florida in 1869 Returning thence to Philadelphia in 1872, he became one of the secretaries of the United States Centennial commission and was charged with the publication of all the official documents relating to the International exhibition of 1876, including its catalogue and eleven volumes of final reports Subsequently he assisted in the state department at Washington, D C, in the preparation of the official report on the Paris International Exhibition of 1881 by the United States Commission—General C McCormick He has published "Quatre Bras, Ligny, and Waterloo a narrative of the campaign in Belgium, 1815" (Boston and London 1882) and "A condensed etymological dictionary of the English language, 'A rearrangement on an etymological basis, of the "American Dictionary of the English Language" of Dr Noah Webster, Springfield, Mass, and New York 1884, London 1886.

SYLVESTER GARDNER (4)

Nicholas (3), Nicholas (2), George (1).

Sylvester, son of Nicholas and Mary (Eldridge) Gardner, was born Aug 3, 1714 He married Lydia Dawley, 1736

Children

Palmer, born Sept 19, 1737, died 1798
John.
Daniel, born 1746
Tabitha, died between 1768 and 1772
Joseph, born 1747 died Dec 15 1816
Benjamin, born 1748, died Aug 12, 1825
Lydia

He had deed from his father Nicholas on March 30, 1737 of 70 acres 'of that land which was purchased of Peter Reynolds, bounded on north by highway east by John Wightman, south by College lands, west by land which I have given my son Ezekiel" This land lies in the southeast angle of Gardiner's Four Corners in Exeter Sylvester settled there and built his house, he afterwards sold this land to his brother Ezekiel

On the first Wednesday of May, 1757, Sylvester was admitted as freeman of West Greenwich

On March 17, 1761, he purchased a farm of 70 acres from Abraham Matteson at West Greenwich This deed was witnessed by Jeremiah Gardner and Amos Stafford This land as nearly as can be ascertained was about two miles south of West Greenwich near the Connecticut line and about six miles south of the station Greene on the New York and New England railroad

This farm Sylvester and Lydia his wife conveyed April 13 1766 to their son Palmer This deed of gift was witnessed by John and Tabitha Gardner before George Dyer, justice of the peace

Lydia Dawley, wife of Sylvester (4) was reared one mile north of Gardner's Four Corners For twenty years she and her husband lived at the Four Corners before removing to West Greenwich The exact location of the house in which they passed these earlier years of their married life is distinguished today by the heap of rock that was once the chimney, now all but overgrown by the sward

Across the street once lay the earthly remains of Nicholas (3) and Mary (Eldridge) Gardner, within recent years, however, this sacred dust has been removed to the Allenton Grove Cemetery and there reinterred with new markers

A silhouette of Sylvester (4) has fortunately been preserved by his descendants, so that his profile appears at the second volume of this work

ANN GARDNER (5).

Nicholas (4), Nicholas (3), Nicholas (2), Geeorge (1).

Ann, daughter of Nicholas, Esq, of Exeter and Martha (Havens) Gardner, was born in Exeter, R I, May 28, 1741 Married Samuel Morey Feb 28, 1762

Children were

Martha, born July 5, 1762.

Dorcas born Jan 13, 1765

Hazard, born Apr 18, 1766

Sarah, born Apr 18, 1766

Elizabeth born Feb 14, 1768

Gardner, born in W Greenwich Feb 4, 1770

George, born in W Greenwich March 28, 1772, died in Exeter, 1772

Enoch, born in W Greenwich March 28, 1772, died in Exeter, Mar, 1772

Ann, born in W. Greenwich Aug 21, 1773

ELIZABETH GARDNER (5).

Nicholas (4), Nicholas (3), Nicholas (2), Geeorge (1).

Elizabeth Gardner, daughter of Nicholas and Martha (Havens) Gardner, was born September 22, 1743 Married Benjamin Champlin February 8 1763 They were married by Elder Samuel Albro

The following children are all that are recorded

Nicholas, born January 18, 1764

Daniel, born October 3, 1769

HULING GARDNER (5).

Nicholas (4), Nicholas (3), Nicholas (2), George (1).

Huling, son of Nicholas and Martha (Havens) Gardner, was born August 18 1745, died Sept 26, 1825

He married Elizabeth Northop daughter of Immanual Northop, of North Kingston, February 1 1767 She died Feb 20 1836, in her 94th year Both are buried in Allenton Grove Cemetery, Allenton, R I

Children:

Sarah, born October 7, 1768

Gould, born October 17, 1772 Died Nov 23, 1843

Wanton, born December 5, 1775

Mary, born March 22, 1778.

EZEKIEL GARDNER, JR (5).

Ezekiel (4), Nicholas (3), Nicholas (2), George (1).

Ezekiel, Jr., son of Ezekiel and Dorcas (Watson) Gardner, was born August 25, 1738 Married Susannah Congdon, daughter of William and Ann (Clifford) Congdon, 1764 He was called "Judge Ezekiel Gardner"

Their children were

David, born August 6, 1764 married Lydia Sanford

Mary born March 3, 1766, died Nov 23, 1831, married Vincent Gardner

Ezekiel, born Jan 19, 1768, married Ruth Tillinghast

Hannah, born March 6, 1770, married Jonathan Arnold.

Dorcas, born Feb 3, 1772, married Nicholas Northop.

Susannah, born April 28, 1774, married Giles Pierce His (2) wife

Ann, born March 15, 1776; unmarried

Elisha, born Jan. 28, 1778, married Sarah Hazard

William, born Oct 10, 1780, died June 2, 1848, unmarried

Palmer, born Apr 29 1783 married Elizabeth Browning

Oliver, born May 20 1785, married Mary Browning

Jesse, born Mar 7, 1789, married Elizabeth B Northup.

Amey, born Mar 7, 1789, married Elisha Pierce

Jeffrey, born Oct 21, 1791, married Mary Himes

Will of Ezekiel Gardner, Jr.

In the Name of God Amen this Tenth day of May in the year of our Lord one Thousand eight Hundred and eight I Ezekiel Gardner of North Kingstown in the County of Washington and State of Rhode Island and providence plantations Esq'r being some advanced in age but of a Sound disposing mind and memory thanks be given unto God therefor, and calling unto mind the Mortality of my body Knowing that it is appointed unto all men once to die, do make and ordain this Instrument in Writing to be my last will and Testament that is to Say Principally and First of all I give and recommend my Soul into the hands of God who gave it and my body I commit to the Earth to be therein decently Buried at the discretion of my Executor hereinafter Named, as Touching of Such worldly Estate wherewith it hath pleased God to Bless me within this life I give and dispose of thee farm in the following manner and form—

Imprimis—

my will is and I hereby order that all my just debts and funeral Charges be first well and Truly paid out of my Estate by my Executrix and Executor hereinafter Named—

Item—

I hereby order that my Executrix and Executor to this my will do Lease out all my land with the Buildings thereon Standing Situated in said North Kingstown (saving the new End of my now Dwelling House on my homestead Farm) also to Let out all my Stock (Saving of one Milche Cow) with my homestead Farm and other Lands on Boston Neck for the purpose of Supporting of my True and Loving wife Susanna Gardner, and my Four daughters unmarried Namly Dorcas Gardner Susanna Gardner, Ann Gardner and Almy Gardner until my Just debts are paid by the rents and profits thereof, and thereby order that my said executors Lease the same out to the best advantages and appropriate the rents and profits thereof accordingly for paying my Just debts and Supporting of the above named persons said Terme—

Item—

I give and bequeath unto my True and Loving wife Susanna Gardner after my Just debts are paid the rents and profits and Improvement of my homestead Farm with the buildings thereon Standing Situated in North Kingstown aforesaid for so long Time as She remains my widow She supporting of my daughter Ann Gardner Said Terme the which gift and bequeath I give my said wife in Liue of her Right of Dower and power of thirds in my whole Real estate also four milche Cows and Ten Sheep My Old Gray mare Side Saddle and bridle and my Turkeys and Geese I also give my said wife Two feather beds bedsteads beding Furniture and Curtains to the same belonging Ten green windsor Chairs one Large Mahogany leaf Table one Chistee Leaf Table one pair of Iron dogs Stand in my new Great Roome Two Chests one Standing in the Old Great Roome & the other Standing in Nancy's bedorom my Looking Glass in the old Great Roome, Two Cases of Drawers one standing in the New Chamber & the other in the old Chamber all my Crockery and tea Ware in my new Closet, all my puterware one half of my Kitchen Ironware, my Tea Tray Server and Glass ware Standing in my New Great Roome all also in Liue of her Rights of Dower as aforesaid and the use of the new End of my House for her and four daughters, to Live in until my debts are paid a aforesaid—

Item—

I give and bequeath unto my Son David Gardner the sum of one dollar to be paid him by my executors in one year after my decease I also give him my Said son David Gardner all that he owes me or any ways Indebted unto me for—

Item—

I give and bequeath unto my Daughter Mary Gardner the wife of Vincent Gardner within one year after my Just debts are paid the sum of Two Hundred and fifty dollars to be paid her by my son Elisha Gardner out of the Estate which I shall herein give him—

Item—

I give and bequeath unto my Daughter Hannah Arnold the wife of Jonathan Arnold within one year after my Just debts are paid the sum of Two Hundred and fifty dollars one hundred and fifty dollars of which to be paid her by my son Ezekiel Gardner out of the Estate which I shall herein give him and the other one Hundred dollars to be paid her by my son William Gardner out of the Estate herein given him—

Item—

I give and bequeath unto my son Ezekiel Gardner after my Just debts are paid my Lot of Land called the old pinder Lot containing about Eighty acres be it the Same more or less with the buildings thereon Standing also my Lot of Land called the Jacob pinder Lott containing about Twenty Six acres be it the same more or less Situated in North Kingstown aforesaid to him and his heirs and assigns forever he paying his sister Hannah Arnold the one hundred and fifty dollars which I order him to pay also I give him my Said son Ezekiel Gardner one Feather beding & bedstead and furniture with Curtains to the bed & being the same bed which my father gave me & to be delivered him by my Executors

Item—

I give and bequeath unto my son Elisha Gardner after my Just debts are paid the Farm whereon he now lives with the buildings thereon Standing in Said North Kingstown being the Farm which I purchased of Christopher Greene of Warwick containing about one hundred & Thirty acres be it the Same more or less to him his heirs and assigns Forever he paying my Daughter Mary Gardner the Two Hundred and fifty dollars which I have herein ordered him to pay her—

Item—

I give and bequeath unto my son William Gardner after my Just debts are paid The Farm which I bought of John Hagadorn called the Major Gardner Farme with the buildings thereon Standing Situated in North Kingstown aforesaid containing about one hundred and forty acres be it the Same more or less to him his heirs and assigns forever he paying of my Daughter Hannah Arnold the one hundred dollars which I ordered him to pay her—

Item—

I give and devise unto my Son Oliver Gardner after my Just debts are paid My Forty acre Lott of Land which my father bought of Jonathan Hazzard of the Allen Farme containing of Forty acres be it the same more or less Situated in Said North Kingstown to him his heirs and assigns Forever.—

Item—

I give and devise unto my three daughters Namely Dorcas Gardner Susanna Gardner and Almy Gardner after my Just debts are paid all that my Tract of Land Situated in North Kingstown aforesaid with the buildings thereon Standing containing about Forty Seven acres be it the Same more or less being the Tract of Land which I purchased of William Northop to be equally divided between them share and share alike to them and their heirs and assigns Forever also Two Fether beds bedsteads beding with calico Curtains Each, Two of Said beds and Said Dorcas and Susanna Calls theirs with Curtains, and the said Almy to have likewise Two beds bedsteads and beding with Checked Curtains, all to be delivered them by my Executors —

Item—

I give and devise unto my Grandson David Gardner the son of son David Gardner after my Just debts are paid my Lot of Land which I purchased of David Green containing about fifteen acres with a Dwelling House thereon Standing Situated in said North Kingstown be it the Same more or less to him his heirs and assigns forever if he lives to arrive to Lawful age Leaving Lawful Issue of his own body, but if in case he should die before he arrives to Lawful age or should die leaving of no Issue in that Case I give the same House and Lot of Land unto my three sons Namely Palmer Gardner Jesse Gardner and Jeffrey Gardner to be equally divided between them Share and Share alike to them and to their heirs and assigns forever —

Item—

I give and bequeath unto my Two Grand Daughters Susanna Gardner and Mary Gardner daughters of my son David Gardner all of the

Household goods which their father sold me and gave me a bill of sale of to be equally divided between them and delivered them by my Excutors —

Item—

I give and bequeath unto my Sister Mary Gardner one milke Cow and all my wearing apparel to be delivered by my Executors at the Time of my decease

Item—

I give and bequeath unto my Son William Gardner one fether bed and beding being the same he now lodges on to be delivered him by my Executors—

Item—

I give and bequeath unto my wife Susanna Gardner one brass Kittle and Great Chear, one Carpet, one third part of the provision which I shall have on hand at the Time of my decease all in Line of her thirds as aforesaid—

I order my Executors to this my will to sell and dispose of my Cheese on hand at the Time of my decease and appropriate the proceeds thereof towards the paying of my Just debts & Charges—

and my mind and will and meaning, that whereas Pardon Tillinghast of West Greenwich holds a mortgage or mortgages on the House and land herein given my said son William Gardner which mortgages tis my meaning I consider to be debts which I owe and order the Same to be paid out of the rents and profits of my Said Real Estate so that he my Sons land given him is not to be incumbered with said mortgages —

Item—

I give and bequeath unto my Three sons Namely Palmer Gardner Jesse Gardner and Jeffrey Gardner after my Just debts are paid, after the decease or marriage again of my said wife which shall happen I give devise and bequeath my homestead Farme with the buildings thereon where I now dwell called the Rome farme unto them and their heirs and assigns Forever to be equally divided between them Share and Share alike I also give my three last named sons all the rest and residue of my Estate of any Name or Nature soever not herein other ways disposed of—they Supporting of my Daughter Ann Gardner with Sufficient Victuals, washing Lodging Clothing in Sickness and in health during the Terme of her Natural life Lastly I hereby Nominate and appoint my True and Loving wife Susanna Gardner Executrix, and my Brother Oliver Gardner Executor to this my last will and Testament to see the same well and Truly executed according to the True Intent and meaning hereof hereby making Void all former wills and bequeaths by Me heretofore makeing of this only to be my last will and Testament—In Witness whereof, I have hereunto Set my hand and Seal The day and date first above Written (signed)

EZEKIEL GARDNER

Signed sealed published pronounced
and declared by the Testator Ezekiel Gardner
Esquire to be his last will and Testament
in the presence of us the Subscribers

N B the 7th line from the bottom of the first page being the words "of the New End of my House for her and her four daughters to live in until my debts are paid as aforesaid" was Interlined or put in before Signing and Sealing

(signed)
Martha Thomas
William Browning
Sarah Browning
George Thomas

I, Ezekiel Gardner of North Kingstown aforesaid do hereby make and establish the following Codicil to this my last will and testament vis

I give and bequeath unto my beloved wife aforesaid Ten Cows and Ten Sheep in addition to those already given her I do hereby revoke and make null and void the devise in my will giving my Grandson David Gardner his heirs &c the lot and Land purchased of David Green containing fifteen acres I give and Devise to my Son David Gardner the lot of land with the dwelling house thereon standing which I purchased of David Green containing fifteen acres to him his heirs and assigns forever—

I do hereby revoke and make null and void that clause or Clauses in my will which orders my real estate and Stock to be leased out for the payment of my debts and Maintenance of my Wife and Daughters—

And I do hereby order and direct that all my Just debts and funeral expenses be paid in the following manner

My Son Ezekiel Gardner shall pay Six hundred Dollars out of the Estate by me given him And my Son Elisha Gardner shall pay Nine hundred Dollars out of the estate by me given to him And my remaining debts and Expenses shall be paid equally by my Sons Palmer, Jesse, and Jeffrey Gardner out of the estate by me given them

I do hereby revoke and make null and void that part of my will which gives to my three daughters Dorcas, Susanna, and Almy Gardner their heirs &c the tract of land which I bought of William Northup

I give and devise to my daughter Susanna Gardner to her heirs and assigns forever the tract of land which I bought of William Northup containing forty seven acres more or less on condition that she shall maintain or take care of my daughter Nancy after the decease of her mother during the term of said Nancys Natural life out of the profits of said land.

I do hereby revoke and make null and void that devise in my will which gives to my son Oliver Gardner his heirs &c my lot of land called the forty acre lot bought by my father of Jonathan Hassard

I give and devise to my sons Palmer, Jesse, and Jeffrey Gardner my lot of land called the forty acre lot bought by my father of Jonathan Hassard to them their heirs and assigns forever to be equally divided between them I Give and bequeath to my son Oliver Gardner fifty Dollars to be paid by my sons Palmer Jesse and Jeffrey Gardner. I Give and bequeath to my daughter Dorcas Northup two hundred Dollars to be paid her by my son William Gardner out of my Estate to me given him I also give her my said daughter Dorcas fifty Dollars to be paid her by my sons Palmer, Jesse, and Jeffrey Gardner out of the estate by me given them I give and bequeath to my Daughter Almy Pierce three hundred Dollars to be paid her by my sons, Palmer, Jesse and Jeffrey Gardner

I also give to my said daughter Almy Pierce four milch cows two feather beds and bedding and one brown horse

In testimony of the foregoing Codicil I have hereunto set my hand and seal this fourth day of July in the year of our lord Eighteen hundred and fourteen at North Kingstown aforesaid

(signed) EZEKIEL GARDNER

Signed Sealed pronounced and declared
by Ezekiel Gardner esq'r, as and for a Codicol
to his last will and Testament in presence of us
(signed)
Peleg Gardner
Hannah Gardner
Willet Carpenter

At a Court of Probate held in North Kingstown on the 18th day of August A D 1814 The annexed last Will and Testament and Codicil of Ezekiel Gardner Esquire, late of said North Kingstown deceased, was presented and read in Court, and Martha Thomas, William Browning, and Sarah Browning three of the Subscribing Witnesses to the same, appeared in Court, and on Solemn Oath did Severally declare that they saw the Testator Ezekiel Gardner esq'r (in his lifetime) Sign and Seal and heard him pronounce and declare the same to be his last Will and Testament, and that they subscribed their names thereto, in the presence of the Testator, and of each other, and in the presence of George Thomas esquire, and that he appeared to them to be of a sound-disposing mind and memory at the same time—Also the Codicil annex to said Will was read in Court and Hannah Gardner and Willet Carpenter two of the Subscribing Witnesses to the same appeared in Court, and on solemn Oath did Severally declare that they saw the Testator Ezekiel Gardner esq r Sign and seal and heard him pronounce and declare the same as and for a Codicil to his last Will and Testament and that they Subscribed their names as Witnesses thereto in the presence of the Testator, and of each other and of Peleg Gardner, one other of the Subscribing Witnesses and that he appeared to them to be of a sound disposing mind and Memory at the same time The said Will and Codicil being thus proved the same was approved by said Court to be of a good and Valid Will, with the Codicil thereto annexed

(signed) JNO REYNOLDS, T CL'K

Recorded on the 28, 29 30, 31, 32, 33, 34, 35, 36, 37, 38, and 39th Book No 21, for probate records in North Kingstown August 22d 1814

(signed) JNO REYNOLDS, T CLK

Inclosed is the Last Will & Testament
of Ezekiel Gardner Esqr made
and Sealed up May 10th, 1808
Susan N Gardner, Exec'x
Oliver Gardner Execu'r
Martha Thomas
William Browning

Sarah Browning
Geo. Thomas
Witnesses
Fees $2 65

Witnesses to a Codicil to this will July 4th, 1814
Peleg Gardner
Hannah Gardner
Willet Carpenter

NICHOLAS GARDNER, ESQ. (5).

Nicholas (4), Nicholas (3), Nicholas (2), George (1).

Nicholas Gardner, Esq , son of Nicholas, Jr., of Exeter and Martha (Havens) Gardner, was born March 2, 1738. Died June 6, 1815 Married first Honour Brown daughter of Beriah Brown of North Kingstown who was forty years sheriff She was born May 10, 1740, died August 19, 1760 No issue.

Married second Deborah Vincent, of Exeter, October 19, 1762 She was born 1740, died May 23, 1813 They are buried at Allenton Grove cemetery, Allenton, R I

Honour, born January 3, 1763, died May 20, 1817. Single
Vincent, born December 9, 1764, died July 17, 1851
Elizabeth, born April 10, 1767, died June 10, 1776.
Nicholas, born August 11, 1769
Beriah, born November 16, 1771-2, died February 2, 1853
Willet, born February 13, 1774 married Abigail Gardner, of Daniel.
Elizabeth, born October 6, 1776
Benjamin C , born April 27, 1779 died 1859

Nicholas Gardner, Esq , married third Ruth Tillinghast No children

THE LAST MEETING 'NEATH THE SHADE OF THE ANCIENT OAK AT THE OLD HOMESTEAD.

In the staid old town of Exeter but a short distance west of what was once known as Gardner s Corners yet stands the firm old dwelling erected by the fifth Nicholas Gardner, and retained as his pleasant home until the day of his death

Nicholas was the father of five sons and two daughters, all of whom passed their youthful days in the home circle on their native plains, and all except the sixth Nicholas and Honor lived to reach a good old age The mother's name was Deborah Vincent and with pure veneration that name has been passed down through the family of every one of her sons

Most surely it must have been a pleasant, quiet home in those days of long ago Not far away from the back door of the mansion was and is still standing an ancient oak, whose wide-spreading branches, as yet unmolested, withstood the storms of more than one century, and whose summer shade is still a pleasant resort for the youth of the present generation It was here beneath the shades of this venerable oak that the sons and daughters of Nicholas spent many hours of recreation in the happy days of their childhood.

More than three score years has passed away and the brothers were scattered abroad, all except Benjamin, the youngest, who still retained the homestead of his father All were farmers by occupation, Vincent and Beriah in their native State, Willett and Nicholas married and settled amid the pleasant hills of Berkshire then called a far western country Betsey was the good wife and companion of Deacon Clark Sisson and was settled on the homestead of the Sissons not far from Pine Hill

All except Nicholas and Betsey had quite numerous families, of whom few are left

Years passed on and one bright summer afternoon in the year of 1843 there was a gathering 'neath the cooling shade of the old ancient oak Vincent, Beriah, Willett, Benjamin and Betsey had once more assembled there, even as it were in the days of their second childhood, for three of that number were then over eighty years of age and good old Pero their childhood companion and once a slave to their grandfather, was close to ninety Again to-day, although so many years have passed away and all of that number have long since passed to that land unseen by mortal eyes, I cannot neither would I, cease to remember the emotions of my own heart as I witnessed the meeting and parting of that aged band as they for the last time sat around that tree, the fairest spot of their childhood

The same shadows from those wide-spreading branches were cast around and the same little murmuring brook that led from the neighboring bog seemed to repeat the same sweet refrain as in the days when their father and mother watched so tenderly over their youthful footsteps, the bubbling spring at the foot of the hill still gave forth its pure waters, while the moss-covered stones in the old well seemed to welcome them back to sip from the brim of the iron-bound bucket once more But alas! the many changes that those intervening years had wrought were made visible as they gazed around their native home Well might their aged hearts yearn for the friends that once were so dear and the music of voices that was hushed long ago Father and mother had long since been laid side by side and were peacefully sleeping in that quiet little enclosure beside the road 'neath the shade of the bending locust Their youthful friends had all grown old, while but here and there, like scattering trees on the hillside, there was scarcely one left to view with them the scenes so dear to every feeling and appreciative heart

This was the last meeting where they all assembled at the old homestead and as before stated long since they too all have been laid to rest

Vincent and Benjamin were buried near their father and mother in the family ground at the homestead Beriah in Elm Grove Cemetery near to those of his companions and children, Betsy rests by the side of her companion near the home where they dwelt so peacefully and happy Nicholas with his wife was buried in his home lot near the banks of the Mohawk in the land of the Oneidas, and Willett rests near his ever-loving companion in the fair land of the Cayugas near his western home 'mid the pleasant hills and dales that encircle the beautiful Owasco and Moravia

One more century is nearing its close and we too are growing old Our locks are whitening as the snows of many winters and the elastic step which is failing us, tell that we too must soon be gathered with our kindred and fathers beyond the misty river We would not murmur, neither should we complain for "His mercies endureth forever," and the good spirit even with the voice of nature tells us that it should be so

I still love to roam over the plains and hills of dear old Exeter It was the home and abiding place of our ancestors in the good old pilgrim days of "long, long ago' It often brings back to my memory the little group that gathered around the father's knee in that far western home, while with eager ears they would listen to stories he would tell of his native home in Exeter, away down near the Narragansett shore, often repeating the names and the doings of many of the industrious and happy people of that day and date The Gardners, Sweets Dawleys, Reynolds, Arnolds, Browns, Halls, Greens and the Hendricks with many others whose descendants now inhabit and most honorably represent the old town where their ancestors once resided Most vividly we remember the story of the killing of the great bear in the swamp and the exhibiting of his body at the old meeting house on the hill, with many of the incidents that transpired 'neath the shade of the now decaying chestnut tree that is still standing there We also remember about being carried over the Queen's River, which we children then thought to be a mighty stream, on the good and faithful Pero's shoulders These were stories of ye olden days and even now in fancy's dream we sometimes love to muse and hear them repeated o'er and o'er again

H G O GARDNER

DORCAS GARDINER (5).

Caleb (4), Nicholas (3), George (2), George (1)

Dorcas, daughter of Nicholas and Isabella (Sherman) Gardiner, was born March 16, 1739; died —— Married Silas Spencer 1758. He was born Nov 18, 1735; died ——.

Their children were

Gardiner

There were other children but we have no record of them

NICHOLAS GARDINER (5).

Caleb (4), Nicholas (3), George (2), George (1).

Nicholas, son of Caleb and Isabella (Sherman) Gardiner, was born December 8, 1744, died 1784. He married Sarah ——

Their children were

Caleb died 1806 Married Mary ——; she died 1809

Elisha,

Warren

EXPERIENCE GARDINER (5)

Caleb (4), Nicholas (3), George (2), George (1).

Experience, daughter of Caleb and Isabella (Sherman) Gardiner was born Nov 1, 1751, married Pardon Mowrey, son of John and Amey (Gibbs) Mowrey He was born December 27, 1748, and died at East Greenwich, R I, August 6, 1831 Their children were·

Mary, died March 7, 1809 Married (1) Joseph Perkins, (2) Judge Elisha R Potter, Nov 7, 1790

Peter,

Pardon

NATHAN GARDINER (5).

Nathan (4), Nicholas (3), George (2), George (1).

Nathan, son of Nathan and Katherin (Niles) Gardiner, was born May 15, 1747; died March 11, 1802 Married Mary Johnson, February 2, 1782 She died July 13, 1807

Their children were

Mallone,

Niles,

Nathan,

Katherin.

Items from grave stones on the Niles Gardner farm, Moorsfield, R. I.

William Gardiner, died March 11, 1802, aged 54 years.

Nathan Gardiner, Esq, died June 16, 1772, aged 47 years

Nathan Gardiner, Esq, died ——, 1792, aged 71 years

Mary, wife of Nathan Gardiner, died July 13, 1807, aged 43 years

Niles Gardiner, died July 7, 1845, aged 51 years

SARAH GARDINER (5).

Nathan (4), Nicholas (3), George (2), George (1).

Sarah, daughter of Nathan and Katherin (Niles) Gardner, was born December 28, 1751, died November 11, 1778 Married John Hazard, son of Benjamin He was born 1746, died 1813

Their children were

John, born 1775, died 1806 Married Francis Gardner

Nathan Gardiner, married Frances (Gardner) Hazard, widow of his brother John

WILLIAM GARDINER MUMFORD (5).

Mary Gardiner (4) John (3), George (2), George (7).

William G, a son of Josiah and Mary (Gardiner) Mumford was born November 26, 1744, married Elizabeth ——, about 1769.

Their children were

Paul, born Jan 8, 1770

Dorcas, born Apr 8, 1772

Annie, born May 20, 1774

Silas, born Mar 4, 1776

Oliver, born Jan 12, 1778

Augustus, born Jan 29, 1780

Elizabeth, born Feb 4, 1782

Darius, born May 8, 1786, married Susan Oatley, daughter of Joseph and Mary (Hazard) Oatley

ABEL GARDINER (5).

John (4), John (3), George (2), George (1)

Abel, son of John and Annie (——) Gardiner, was born Sept 2, 1747, married Dorothy, daughter of George and Ruth Sweet She was born Nov 12, 1742

Their children were

Sweet, born June 1, 1773

George, born Aug 19, 1775, married Abigail Dean, Feb 20, 1800.

Mary, born Aug 14, 1777.

Amy, born Aug 16, 1780, married James Tillinghast, Feb 5, 1801

WAITE GARDINER (5).

John (4), John (3), George (2), George (1)

Waite, daughter of John and Annie (——) Gardner, was born May 2, 1750, died 1814 Married (——) Gardiner

In her will she mentions her brother John Gardiner of Exeter, and two daughters·

Sarah B,

Dorcas W

HANNAH GARDINER (5).

Henry (4), Nicholas (3), George (2), George (1).

Hannah, daughter of Henry and Abigail (Eldred) Gardiner, married William Champlin, son of William and Sarah Champlin. He was born October 6, 1724

Their children were

William, born Nov 6, 1745

Hannah, born Dec 9, 1747

Martha, born Jan 27, 1750.

Mary, born Aug 16, 1751, married Edward Bliven, Jan. 6, 1774.

Henry, born Jan 18, 1756.

Samuel, born Sept 18, 1758, married Freelove Boss, Jan 12, 1780

Olive, born Mar 17, 1761, married Thankful Gavitt, Jan 25, 1779

The first child born in New Shoreham, the second in South Kingstown and the rest in Westerly, R I

MARY GARDINER (5).

Henry (4), Nicholas (3), George (2), George (1)

Mary, daughter of Henry and Abigail (Eldred) Gardiner, became the second wife of Col Joseph Stanton in 1752 He was an officer in the French and Indian war and participated in the engagement at the capture of Louisburg

Their children were

Gardiner, died single

Malborough, died single.

Henry married Cynthia Lewis

Abigail Gardiner, married Rev William Gardiner Children, Mary, Abigail, Malborough

SARAH GARDINER (5).

Caleb (4), Nicholas (3), George (2), George (1).

Sarah, daughter of Caleb and Isabella (Sherman) Gardiner, was born April 29, 1736, married Peter Boss

Children were

Peter,

Tabitha,

Sarah

BENJAMIN GARDNER (5).

John (4), William (3), Benony (2), George (1).

Benjamin Gardner, son of John and Mary (Taylor) Gardner, was born January 4, 1750 Married Elizabeth Wicks (Weeks) daughter of Thomas Wicks (Weeks) of Warwick, January 13, 1774. Married by the Rev John Graves

They resided at Middletown Rhode Island

Children were

Thomas, born at Boston Neck, North Kingston, January 20, 1775, died August 11, 1775

Wicks (Weeks), born at Tower Hill, South Kingston, Sept 12, 1777

Benjamin, born at Boston Neck, August 3, 1779, died 1780

Elizabeth, born at North Kingston, August 3, 1781, died at Middletown May 29, 1786

Albert, born April 25, 1786

Edwin, born December 9 1787, died Jan 23 1805 Drowned at sea

James Sayer, born March 18 1789

Benjamin, December 31, 1790

Elizabeth Gardner, wife of Benjamin Gardner, died May 8, 1796, in her forty-second year Benjamin Gardner then married Ann Coggeshall December 1, 1799 She died January 5, 1800 No children. He married (3) Mary Howland, March 5, 1801 One son

Benjamin Howland, born Jan 23, 1805

LYDIA GARDNER (5).

John (4), William (3), Benony (2), George (1).

Lydia Gardner, daughter of John and Mary (Taylor) Gardner, was born 1753 Married Robert Champlin

To them was born one daughter

Mary who married Colonel McRea of the United States army and lived at Newport Robert Champlin died and the widow married John Faxon

Had children, but we have no record of them

SARAH GARDNER (5).

John (4), William (3), Benony (2), George (1).

Sarah Gardner, daughter of John and Mary (Taylor) Gardner, was born about 1751. Died June 16, 1772 Unmarried

Her will dated 1772 reads:

"I, Sarah Gardiner, Gentlewoman &c"

Mentions mother Mary Gardiner to her one thousand Spanish Milled dollars Brothers John and Benjamin sister Abigail Updike, sister Lydia Gardner, to each —— Spanish Milled dollars

WILLIAM GARDNER (5).

John (4), William (3), Benony (2), George (1).

Son of John and Mary (Taylor) Gardner, married Eunice Belden of Hartford, Conencticut, October 21, 1764

There was born to them one child, James, born about 1765-6 Died 1810.

No children

William Gardner was a merchant at Hartford, Connecticut, and died there June 17, 1766, from wounds caused by the blowing up of the school house

ABIGAIL GARDNER (5).

John (4), William (3), Benony (2), George (1)

Abigail Gardner, daughter of John and Mary (Taylor) Gardner, was born September 26, 1740 Married Lodowick Updike January, 1759 He was born July 12, 1725 He was a lawyer Died June 6 1804

Children born to them were

Daniel, born 1761, died 1842, married Adolissa Arnold of Exeter

James, born 1763, died 1855, unmarried Lived at Wickford, R I

Anstis, born 1765, died 1864, married William Lee of Providenee, R I

Mary, born 1767, died 1842; married Nathaniel Mundy, Wickford, R I

Abigail, born 1769, died 1862, married Joseph Reynolds, Wickford, R I

Sarah, born 1771, died 1850, married David Hagan, Wickford, R I.

Lodowick, born 1774, died 1833 married Rhoda Baker

Alfred, born 1779, died 1869, married Dorcas Reynolds, Wickford, R I

Gilbert, born 1781, died 1819, married Hannah Dennis

Wilkins, born 1784, died 1867, married Abigail Watson, Kingstown, R I

Lodowick Updike, Sr, the only son of Daniel Updike, the Colony Attorney, was born July 12, 1725 He was educated under private tutor, in conformity with the practice of that age The pupils lived in the family and were the companions of the instructors, and such were selected by the parents as were the most skilful in imparting literature and science, and best calculated to mould the character and polish the manners of youth His last instructor was the Rev. John Checkley, rector of the church in Providence, an Oxford scholar and learned divine. Mr Updike in after life, was accustomed to relate amusing anecdotes of this distinguished man Mr Updike studied for the bar but never practiced

He inherited the large estate of his father in North Kingston, and resided on it, as an intelligent and gentleman farmer until his death

His son, Wilkins, was the Author of "Updike's history of Narragansett Church"

JOHN GARDNER (5).

John (4), William (3), Benony (2), George (1).

Col John Gardner, son of John Gardner, Sr, and Mary (Taylor) Gardner, was born 1747, died Oct 18 1808 Married Sarah Gardner, daughter of Captain Samuel Gardner, December 13, 1772 She died June 16, 1816 Born 1744

Their children were

Sarah married Thomas Jenkins of Hudson, N. Y

Robert, married Miss Day, of Catskill, N Y He was some years U S Consul to Sweden He was lost at sea No issue

John, died without issue

William, died without issue

Emma, married Philo Day of Catskill, N. Y

Harriet, married Russell Day of Catskill, N Y

Sylvester

Col Gardner was an accomplished gentleman of the old school, and of popular manners He early rose into public favor, and was an active Whig in the revolution He was elected representative to the General Assembly from South Kingston, his native town, for the years 1786-7, by the Paper Money party

In 1788-9 he was elected by the popular vote of the state a delegate to the Confederated Congress but did not take his seat in that body Colonel Gardner inherited the patrimonial estate of his ancestors, the farm next south of the South Ferry containing five hundred acres, reputed the most fertile tract in Narragansett He died October 18, 1808 aged sixty-two His wife survived him some years They left seven children.

Both are buried in the old cemetery on McSparren Hill, Exeter.

ANSTRESS (ANTIS) GARDNER (5).

John (4), William (3), Benony (2), George (1).

Anstress Gardner, oldest child of John and Mary (Hill) Gardner, was born March 23, 1721 She married Rowland Robinson December 31, 1741 (She was a niece of Governor William Robinson's second wife) The following children were born

Hannah, born May 10, 1750, married Peter Simons She died 1773

Mary, born August 15, 1751, died 1777, unmarried

William, born September 13, 1758, married Ann Scott, a widow of Newport, Rhode Island He died 1804

Anstress (Gardner) Robinson, died at South Kingstown, December 23, 1773

THOMAS GARDNER (5).

John (4), William (3), Benony (2), George (1).

Thomas Gardner, third child of John and Mary (Hill) Gardner, was born March 11, 1725 He was married to Martha, daughter of Henry who was the son of Nicholas Gardner, November 9, 1749, by the Rev. James McSparren

Their children were

Frederick, born August 24 1751
Benaiah, born March 8, 1754
Abigail, born April 29, 1756
Thomas, born August 27, 1758

AMOS GARDNER (5).

John (4), William (3), Benony (2), George (1).

Amos Gardner, youngest child of John and Mary (Hill) Gardner, was born March 27, 1729, died Apr. 3, 1793 He was married to Sarah Bill October 10, 1751, by Rev James McSparren. She died Apr 13, 1777

Their children were

William,
James,
Amos, born 1756 married Abby Knowels
John married Eunice Hazard She was born Feb 4, 1764, died 1832
Mary, married Harvy Sherman

WILLIAM HAZARD (5)

Abigail Gardner (4), William (3), Benony (2), George (1).

William, son of Caleb and Abigail (Gardner) Hazard, was born April 12, 1721, married Phebe, daughter of John and Demaris Hull of Jamestown, September 12, 1744

Their children were

Lydia, married John Field, June 8, 1763
Josiah, born Dec. 20, 1748, married Mary Carr, May 31, 1772
Abigail, married Sylvanus Wyatt, Oct. 5, 1796
William, born March 21, 1753.
John, born Jan 20, 1755
Benedict, born Jan 26, 1758
Mary, born March 24, 1762

ROBERT HAZARD (5).

Abigail Gardner (4), William (3), Benony (2), George (1).

Robert, son of Caleb and Abigail (Gardner) Hazard, was born May 1, 1723, died 1771 He was a physician He married his cousin Elizabeth Hazard, April 3, 1752 She was the daughter of Deputy Gov. Robert Hazard

Their children were

Abigail, born Aug 29, 1753, married Jared Starr of New London, Conn, Sept 11, 1780

Esther, born July 26, 1755; died March 25, 1831. Married (1) Silas Niles, (2) Jared Starr of New London, Conn.

Elizabeth, born Nov 28, 1757

Sylvester, born July 27, 1760, died Feb 14, 1812 Married Elizabeth, daughter of Richard and Sarah Greene She died March 16, 1816, aged 52

Nancy, born Apr 20, 1764 Unmarried.

Charles, born July 14, 1766, married Ann Bowers of Newport, Feb, 1795.

Francis, born 1769, died 1814. Married Rebecca Truman

CHRISTOPHER ROBINSON (5).

Abigail Gardner (4), William (3), Benony (2), George (1).

Christopher, son of William and Abigail (Gardner) Robinson, was born December 31, 1727, died 1807 Married Susannah Champlin, daughter of Christopher and Hannah (Hill) Champlin, 1754 She was born January 11, 1735-6, died Nov 28, 1783

Their children were

Abigail, born Jan 20 1755, died 1803 Married Stephen Potter. He died 1793

Christopher, born Nov 26 1756, died Apr 27 1807. Married Elizabeth Anthony Dec 30 1790 She died 1849

George, born June 14, 1760, died 1780 He was taken prisoner in the privateer Revenge, in 1778 He was carried to New York and placed on board the prison ship Jersey, at Long Island, N Y, where he died with the ship fever at that place

Elizabeth, born Aug 5, 1763, died 1822 Married Mumford Hazard of Newport Feb 18, 1796 No issue

William, born ——, died 1803 Married Francis Wanton She died 1816

Jesse born ——, died 1808. Married Hannah T Sands She died 1848

Robert married Sarah Congdon, daughter of Samuel, March 15 1795 She died 1802 He married (2) Ann DeBlois, 1807 She died 1850 He died 1831

Hannah, born 1769, married John Perry Nov, 1783 She died Aug 29, 1849 He died 1834, aged 69

Matthew, born 1772, died 1821 Married (1) Mary L Potter, 1797 She died 1801, aged 24. He married (2) Mary ——, 1802 She died 1836, aged 54.

WILLIAM ROBINSON (5).

Abigail Gardner (4), William (3), Benony (2), George (1).

William, son of William and Abigail (Gardner) Robinson, was born Aug. 1, 1724 Removed to Newport 1761, where he died May 30 1793 He married Elizabeth, daughter of Philip and Hannah (Rodman) Wanton, May 17, 1750

Their children were:

Hannah, born Feb 21, 1751, married Dept Gov George Brown, 1768 He was born 1746, died 1836

Abigail, born Aug 24, 1753, married John Thurston, April 23, 1772 He was son of Peleg.

Philip, born Oct 6, 1755, died in Newport May 30, 1808 Married (1) Elizabeth, daughter of Peleg and Mary Thurston, Oct 7, 1779. She died in child-birth with twins June 22, 1782 He married (2) Martha, daughter of John and Martha Slocum, Oct 2, 1783 He married (3) Elizabeth Clark, Dec. 4, 1788.

He married (2) Elizabeth, daughter of Thomas and Mary Richmond, March 12, 1761 She died in New York July 4, 1794, of small-pox, aged 53

THOMAS ROBINSON (5).

Abigail Gardner (4), William (3), Benony (2), George (1).

Thomas, son of William and Abigail (Gardner) Robinson, was born 1731 died at Newport, R I, Nov 10 1817, aged 86 He married, March 21, 1754, Sarah daughter of Thomas and Mary Richardson She was born March 31, 1733, died Aug 1, 1817

Their children were

William, born Dec 30, 1754, died Feb 2, 1838 Married Sarah Franklin, of New York City She died 1811, aged 52.

Thomas, born Apr 18, 1756, died Sept 2, 1756

Mary, born Oct 27 1757, died Nov 31, 1829 Married John Warson, of Philadelphia He died 1828.

Abigail, born Jan 21, 1760; died very aged Unmarried

Thomas Richardson born Dec. 4, 1761, married Jemima Fish, Dec 5, 1787

Rowland, born May 8, 1763, died Sept 7, 1791, on a voyage home from England

Joseph Jacob, born June 5, 1765 died Feb 19, 1844, at Middletown

Amy, born Apr 15, 1768, married Robert L Brown of New York.

ABIGAIL ROBINSON (5).

Abigail Gardner (4), William (3), Benony (2), George (1).

Abigail, daughter of William and Abigail (Gardner) Robinson, was born 1732, died 1754 Married John Wanton, Aug. 10, 1752. One child

William Robinson, born Feb. 11, 1754; died aged a few months.

SYLVESTER ROBINSON (5).

Abigail Gardner (4), William (3), Benony (2), George (1).

Sylvester, son of William and Abigail (Gardner) Robinson, was born 1734, married Alice Perry, Dec 18, 1755

Their children were

James, born Oct 3, 1756, married Mary Altmore of Philadelphia, 1796

William, born Dec 20, 1760.

Mary, born Dec 15, 1763, died March 26, 1837

Abigail, died May 6, 1818 Married Thomas H. Hazard He died Dec 10, 1825

Twin sons. No further record of them

MARY ROBINSON (5).

Abigail Gardner (4), William (3), Benony (2), George (1).

Mary, daughter of William and Abigail (Gardner) Robinson, was born October 8, 1736 died March 12, 1814 Married John Dockery of Newport. Feb 17, 1757

Their children were

Abigail, born Oct, 1759, died Dec 18, 1759

John B, born 1760, married Mary Congdon, daughter of William and Freelove (Taylor) Congdon, Sept 6, 1779

Hannah born 1762, died single

William Robinson, born Aug, 1764, died May 19. 1785

Mary, born June, 1768. died Jan 27, 1820 Married David Williams, of Newport

Susannah, born 1769, died Sept. 2, 1769

JAMES ROBINSON (5).

Abigail Gardner (4), William (3), Benony (2), George (1).

James, son of William and Abigail (Gardner) Robinson, was born 1738, married Anna Rodman, daughter of Samuel and Mary (Willett) Rodman, Sept 4, 1762

Their children were:

Abigail born 1768 died 1805 Married John Robinson, son of John and Sarah (Peckham) Robinson, 1794.

Ruth, born 1769; died 1839

Mary, born 1771, died 1826 Married John Bowers

Ann, born 1772, died 1790

James, born 1774, died 1781

JOHN ROBINSON (5).

Abigail Gardner (4), William (3), Benony (2), George (1).

John, son of William and Abigail (Gardner) Robinson, was born Jan. 13, 1742-3, died June 23, 1805. He married Sarah, daughter of Benjamin and Mary (Hazard) Peckham, Jan 13, 1761 She was born 1744, died 1775 He married (2) Hannah, daughter of Matthew and Abigail (Gardner) Stewart

Children were

Benjamin, born Aug 5, 1763, died Nov. 29, 1823 Married Elizabeth, daughter of Deputy Governor George Brown, 1791 She was born 1770; died Aug 25, 1855

Sarah, born Dec 10, 1764, married Samuel Taber, of Waterfield, Conn, Feb 14 1782 He was born Oct 26, 1750; died Sept 6, 1798.

William, born Apr 25, 1766, married Phebe Dennison of Stonington, Conn, March, 1802

John, born Dec 16, 1767, died 1831 in New Brunswick, N J Married Abigail, daughter of James and Ann (Rodman) Robinson, (2) Ruth Gardner.

Sylvester, born July 12, 1769, died 1807 Married Eliza, daughter of John and Marcia (Pele) Rodman, of Westchester County, N Y

Thomas, born May 5, 1771, died 1786

James No record of birth He was child of second marriage

JOHN KENYON (5).

Mary Gardner (4), Nathaniel (3), Benony (2), George (1).

John, son of John and Mary (Gardner) Kenyon, was born Sept 29, 1730 Married Freelove Reynolds, June 8, 1754

Their children were

Gardner, born Sept 24, 1755

Mary, born Nov 18, 1757, married Stephen Watson, March 2, 1780

John, born July 3, 1760

Zebulon, born Aug 25 1764

Freelove, born July 30, 1766.

Freeman, born July 28, 1769

Remington, born July 20, 1771

Lewis, born July 20, 1774

Amos, born July 18 1781

Job, born June 24, 1783, married Betsey Benjamin, Feb. 14, 1807

Reynolds, born Aug 21, 1786; married Penelope Dyre, March 8, 1810

Lydia, born March 18, 1789.

Joseph Greene, born May 19, 1792

OLIVER GARDNER (5).

Isaac (4), Isaac (3), Benony (2), George (1).

Oliver, son of Isaac and Margaret (Gardner) Gardner, was born in Exeter, R I, June 24, 1742 Married Mercy Gorton, daughter of William and Mercy (Matteson) Gorton, Sept 25, 1766 She was born June 3, 1744. He was called Capt. Oliver Gardner.

Their children were.

Sarah, born Sept 5, 1767, married Benjamin Gardner, son of Caleb of East Greenwich, Oct 10, 1791.

Hannah, born June 21, 1769

Mercy, born May 27, 1771, married Wanton Rice, Oct 2, 1791

Mary, born Aug. 16, 1773, died Sept 28, 1773

Oliver, born Feb 21, 1775

Margaret, born Dec 23, 1777 married Gideon Bailey of Norwich, Oct 7, 1796

Isaac, born Dec. 8, 1779

Elizabeth, born March 9, 1781, married Nathan Bowen of Warwick, R I, June 10, 1798

Nicholas, born May 19, 1783

William, born June 4, 1787

John, born June 26, 1789

These children were all born and married in Warwick, R I.

ELISHA WATSON (5).

Isabella Sherman (4), Bridget Gardner (3), Benony (2), George (1).

Elisha son of John and Isabella (Sherman) Watson, was born August 5, 1748 married (1), Miriam Babcock (2), Susannah, daughter of Judge Freeman Perry.

Their children were

Mary, born Apr 6, 1775, married John Watson, Jr

Elisha, born Oct. 1, 1776, married Ann Cole

Joseph Dennison, born Aug 30, 1778, died Nov. 17, 1854

Asa, born May 24, 1780

George, born March 24, 1782

William, born Dec 26, 1783, married Mary Cole

Children by (2) wife were

Freeman, born May 16, 1787, married Phebe Watson, daughter of Job and Phebe (Weeden) Watson

Susannah, born March 13, 1789, married George Watson

Elizabeth, born Jan. 24, 1790; married Benjamin Brown

Miriam, born Oct 30, 1793, married Stephen Browning

ISABELLA WATSON (5).

Isabella Sherman (4), Bridget Gardner (3), Benony (2), George (1).

Isabella, daughter of John and Isabella (Sherman) Watson, was born May 7, 1753, married —— Gardner

Their children were

Isabella,
Ezekiel,
Dorcas.

JOHN GARDNER (5).

West Greenwich.

Sylvester (4), Nicholas (3), Nicholas (2), George (1).

Born at West Greenwich, February 19, 1772

John Gardner, a tailor by trade, childless and bereft of his wife, his sister, Tabitha Reynolds, and his parents, executed the following

Being weak and poorly in body and not expecting to live in this world but a very short time, first of all I recommend my soul into the hands of God &c.,

Item—

To my honored mother-in-law, Elizabeth Gardner, three dollars

Item—

To my sister Tabitha's daughter Lydia Reynolds twelve shillings when she shall arrive at the age of eighteen years

Item—

To my beloved brother Palmer Gardner's four children, viz—Abigail, Dorcas, Lydia and Sylvester six shillings apiece to be paid out of my estate by my executor to Palmer Gardner for their use soon after my decease

Item—

All of the rest of my estate be it of what nature soever to be equally divided between my four brothers and sister namely Palmer, Daniel, Joseph, Benjamin and Lydia Gardner.

Lastly, I nominate &c my beloved brother to be my sole executor

Witnesses his
Henry Tanner Signed JOHN X GARDNER
Nathan Dawley mark
Benjamin Tillinghast

West Greenwich, Feb 19, 1772

TABITHA GARDNER (5).

Sylvester (4), Nicholas (3), Nicholas (2), George (1).

Tabitha, daughter of Sylvester and Lydia (Dawley) Gardner, was married June 19 1768, to Samuel, son of Samuel Reynolds at West Greenwich, Benjamin Tillinghast, Justice, officiating Her brother John, in his will executed Feb 19, 1772, leaves a bequest to her daughter, Lydia

Reynolds (6), and omitting in the same Tabitha's name from the number of his surviving brothers and sisters leads us to believe that she died prior to 1772 No clew has been found to the subsequent history or offspring of her daughter Lydia (6)

LYDIA GARDNER (5).

Sylvester (4), Nicholas (3), Nicholas (2), George (1).

Lydia, daughter of Sylvester and Lydia (Dawley) Gardner, is mentioned only in the will of her brother John where she appears as the youngest member of the family Neither she nor her parents figure at Hancock and it is probable that devoting herself to their care through their declining years she terminated her career in West Greenwich and was there laid to rest beside them

WALTER WATSON (5).

Isabella Sherman (4), Bridget Gardner (3), Benony (2), George (1).

Walter, son of John and Isabella (Sherman) Watson, was born May 7, 1753, died May 1, 1801 Married Abigail, daughter of Thomas Hazard She was born Dec 25, 1751, died Feb. 2, 1837

Children were

Walter, died young

Isabella, born 1785, died Jan 9, 1858 Was (2) wife of John J Watson

Abby, born June 22, 1792, died March 31, 1843 She married Wilkins Updike, son of Lodowick and Abigail (Gardner) Updike

ISAAC GARDNER (5).

Isaac (4), Isaac (3), Benony (2), George (1).

Isaac, son of Isaac and Margaret (Gardner) Gardner, was born August 16, 1744, married Ruth Aylsworth, Oct 11, 1767

One child of whom we have record

Isaac, married Alice Wicks of Warwick, R I

ELIZABETH GARDNER (5).

Benony (4), Isaac (3), Benony (2) George (1).

Elizabeth, daughter of Benony and Elizabeth (——) Gardner, was born 1743, married Benjamin Champlin, son of Jeffry and Mary Champlin, February 8, 1763

Their children were

Nicholas, born Jan 18 1764

Daniel, born Oct 3, 1769, married Penelope Allen, Dec. 22, 1788.

JOHN WATSON (5).

Isabella Sherman (4), Bridget Gardner (3), Benony (2), George (1)

John, son of John and Isabella (Sherman) Watson, was born May 23, 1737, married Desire, daughter of Thomas and Mercy (Williams) Wheeler October 17, 1764 She was of Stonington, Conn

Children were

John, born June 24, 1768, married Mary, daughter of Elisha and Marion (Babcock) Watson, Dec 18, 1794

Thomas,

Wheeler, married (1) Mary Champlin, daughter of Stephen. Married (2) Sarah Peckham, daughter of George H. and Sarah (Taylor) Peckham

Rufus,

George, born Dec 16, 1783

Desire, married Peleg Peckham, son of Benjamin and Mary (Hazard) Peckham

Hannah,

Mercy,

Bridget

JOB WATSON (5)

Isabella Sherman (4), Bridget Gardner (3), Benony (2), George (1).

Job, son of John and Isabella (Sherman) Watson, was born Aug 7, 1744 Married Sarah Hazard, daughter of Robert and Sarah (Borden) Hazard, Feb 12, 1766

Their children were

Isabell, born Sept 22, 1766

Job, born Oct 25, 1767, married Phebe Weeden, Jan 18, 1787

Robert, born Feb 28, 1769; died Dec 30, 1790 Married Catherine Weeden

Walter, born June 10, 1770; married Mary Carr

Borden, born Nov. 1, 1772, married Isabella Babcock.

John, born Nov 1, 1774, married Sarah Brown, daughter of Deputy Governor George and Hannah (Robinson) Brown, Jan. 24, 1799 He married (2) Isabella Watson, Aug 4 1805.

HANNAH ROBINSON (6).

Hannah Robinson was the daughter of Roland Robinson and Anstress or (Antis) (Gardner) Robinson She was styled "the unfortunate Hannah Robinson," she was the celebrated beauty of her day, and if unbroken tradition is sufficient authority, the appellation was justly bestowed

The late Doctor William Bowen of Providence frequently conversed about her and observed, "that Miss Robinson was the most perfect model of beauty that he everknew, and that he frequently visited at her father's home Her figure was graceful and dignified, her complexion fair and beautiful, and her manners urbane and captivating. That the usual mode of riding at that period was on horseback; of this exercise she was exceedingly fond, and rode with such ease and elegance, that he was passionately fond of her and proposed to her a matrimonial union She replied, that his wishes to promote her happiness were highly flattering, that as a friend she should ever entertain for him the highest respect, and in that character should be ever extremely gratified to see him but that she was bound to disclose to him, however reluctant she felt to give him pain, that she was engaged' He further observed, 'that though disappointed in the hope he had so ardently cherished, the refusal was imparted with such suavity and tenderness, united with personal respect, that though disappointed he felt consoled"

The late Hon Elisha R Potter, Judge Waite and others who knew her fully confirmed Doctor Bowen's testimony in respect to her personal beauty and accomplishments Mr Peter Simons, a young gentleman of Newport became early attached to Miss Robinson They had been school mates and the attachment was reciprocal Her father without any apparent reason, was hostile to the connection, and his efforts were unwearied to prevent their union Mr Robinson in temperament was constitutionally irritable, rash and unyielding His antipathies, when once fixed, no reason or argument could remove Mr Simons had, early in life, become attached to Miss Robinson, it had been reciprocated, their dispositions were congenial, time had cemented their affections, she had plighted her faith, and no promises or threats could induce her to violate the vows she had made, she could become a martyr she could suffer but she could not betray her own heart or the faith another had reposed in her. And as might have been expected, the violent and unreasonable measures adopted by her father, instead of subduing only increased the fervor of their attachment Her conduct was constantly subjected to the strictest scrutiny If she walked her movements were watched, if she rode, a servant was ordered to be in constant attendance, if a visit was contemplated, he immediately suspected it was only a pretense for an arranged interview, and even after departure, if the most trifling circumstances gave color to the suspicion, he would immediately pursue and compel her to return In one instance she left home to visit her aunt at London, Connecticut, her father soon afterwards discovered from his window a vessel leaving Newport and taking a course for the same place Although the vessel and the persons on board were wholly unknown to him, his jealousies were immediately aroused Conjecturing it was Mr Simons intending to fulfill an arrangement previously made, he hastened to London, arriving a few hours only after his daughter and insisted her instant return No persuasion or argument could induce him to change his determination, and she was compelled to return with him

Her uncle, the late Col. John Gardner, commiserated the condition of his unfortunate niece He knew her determination was not to be changed, or her resolution to be overcome by parental exaction, however severe, and aware that the wrong she had suffered, and the perplexities she had undergone, had already sensibly affected her health, and would soon destroy her constitution, with a generosity and disinterestedness that belonged to his character contrived interviews between Mr Simons and Miss Robinson unknown to her father The window where she sat, and the shrubbery behind which his person was concealed at these evening interviews, were still shown by the family residing there in 1847

These were perilous meetings, for such was the determined antipathy of the father that detection would probably have resulted in the instant death of Mr Simons, but, as is usual in such cases, their precautions were in proportion to the eminence of their danger

All efforts to obtain the consent of her father, aided by the influence of her mother, having proved unavailing, and seeing no prospect of his ever becoming reconciled to their union, she abandoned all further efforts to reconcile him to her wishes and consented to make arrangements for an elopement Having obtained her father's consent to visit her aunt Updike, near Wickford, she left home, accompanied by the servant who usually accompanied her On arriving at the gate that led to her aunt's house Mr Simons was in waiting with a carriage, as had been previously arranged, and disregarding the espostulations of the servant —who feared for his own safety should he return without her—she entered the carriage and that evening they were married in Providence

The intelligence of the elopement, when communicated to Mr Robinson by the servant, roused all the fury of his ire He offered a reward for their apprehension, but no discovery could be made Every friend and relative became accessory to their concealment Even the name of the clergyman who performed the nuptial ceremony could never be ascertained

But the anticipated happiness of the beautiful ill-fated young lady was destined to be short-lived The severity with which she had been treated, the unkind and harassing perplexities she had endured, had so materially affected her health, and preyed upon her constitution, that, in a few short months she exhibited evident symptoms of a speedy decline At the urgent solicitations of her mother, Mr Robinson finally permitted the daughter once more to return, but it was too late, the ceaseless vigils of a mother's love could not restore her, and in a few short weeks this beautiful and unfortunate woman—the victim of a father's relentless obstinancy—expired in the arms of her husband

Many visit the cemetery where the remains and the victim of parental severity repose—a spot consecrated by the ashes of one whose life was a hallowed sacrifice of devotion and fidelity to the selected object of her earliest affections.

WICKES GARDNER (6).

Benjamin (5), John (4), William (3), Benony (2), George (1).

Wickes Gardner, son of Benjamin and Elizabeth (Wickes) Gardner, was born September 12, 1777, at Tower Hill, South Kingstown, died August 17, 1840 Married Waitey Rhodes, December 19, 1802

Their children were:

Betsey Wicks, born Feb 27, 1804
Thomas, born July 25, 1805
Malachi Rhodes, born Dec. 21, 1807
Mary, born Feb 1, 1810
Edward, born Feb 14, 1812
Benjamin, born July 1, 1821, died Nov. 2, 1901

JOHN ROBINSON (6).

John (5), Abigail Gardner (4), William (3), Benony (2), George (1).

John, son of John and Sarah (Peckham) Robinson, was born Dec. 16, 1767, died 1831 He married (1) Abigail, daughter of James and Ann (Rodman) Robinson Married (2), Ruth, daughter of Judge Gardner The first two children were by first wife, the rest by second

James,
Marian,
Emily,
Elizabeth,
Albert,
Edwin,
Cornelia.

JOHN HAZARD (6).

Sarah Gardner (5), Nathan (4), Nicholas (3), George (2), George (1).

John, son of John and Sarah (Gardner) Hazard, was born 1775, died 1806 He married Frances, daughter of Capt Daniel and Sarah (Hazard) Gardner, April, 1800

Children were

Martha born about 1801, married Ormus Stillman

Frances, born about 1803, married Elnathan Brown, 1827, he died 1830, and she married (2) Ormus Stillman

NATHAN GARDNER HAZARD (6).

Sarah Gardner (5), Nathan (4), Nicholas (3), George (2), George (1).

Nathan, son of John and Sarah (Gardner) Hazard, married Frances (Gardner) Hazard, widow of his brother John.

Children were

William Robinson, born Jan 11, 1810, died Sept 26, 1873 Married Sarah Potter

Sarah, born July, 1811 · unmarried

Catherin, born June 2, 1818 married Peleg Noyes

John born Apr 30, 1821, unmarried

FREDERICK GARDNER (6).

Thomas (5), John (4), William (3), Benony (2), George (1).

Frederick, son of Thomas and Martha (Gardner) Gardner, was born Aug 24, 1751, married Lucy Northup, daughter of Stephen

Their children were

Robinson, baptized March 13, 1788, died 1806

Stephen,

Abigail, baptized Jan 7, 1790 Was first wife of Silas Gardner

Simeon Stuart, died 1807.

AMOS GARDNER (6).

Amos (5), John (4), William (3), Benony (2), George (1)

Amos, son of Amos and Sarah (Bill) Gardner, was born 1756, died Sept 29, 1827 He married Abigail Knowles, daughter of Robert. She was born 1743, died June 29, 1840. He lived in the 'four chimney house' about three quarters of a mile west of the South Ferry in South Kingstown, R I He was employed for many years to carry the mails from Newport to New London, Conn.

Children were:

Thomas Bill, born Nov 21, 1778, died Mar 4, 1860 He married Sarah A Sheffield Married (2) Ruth Knowles daughter of Daniel

Robert, died in South America, he was poisoned by an enemy

Lodowick Lewis, born 1784, died Sept 23, 1787

John Collins, born 1786, died May, 1790.

Daughter, married Cranston Gardner

Jeanette married George Arnold.

Josiah, born Jan 18, 1796; died Oct 25, 1864 Married Mercy (——) (2) Abby Potter

Charlotte, born 1797, died Dec 13, 1859 She became (2) wife of Geo Arnold.

Charles, born 1799, died 1802

Abby, married William Arnold.

Mary, married John R. Gardner of Prince Edward Island.

James Alfred, born 1801, died Aug 9, 1879 Married Maria Fish of Newport, daughter of Job and Mary She died Jan 11, 1892, in her 89th year One son of whom we have record was Amos, who died May 10. 1902, aged 75 Interred in Allenton Grove cemetery, R I

JOHN GARDNER (6).

Amos (5), John (4), William (3), Benony (2), George (1).

John, son of Amos and Sarah (Bill) Gardner, was born in South Kingstown, 1758, died in Prince Edward Island Jan 5, 1842 He married Eunice Hazard, daughter of Thomas and Eunice (Rhodes) Hazard She was born Feb 14, 1764, in Rhode Island and died March 9, 1832, in P E Island Children were

William Hazard, born in R I, Apr 25, 1786, died in P E Island He married Ann Clarke Feb 7, 1811

Sarah born at P. E Island Dec 4, 1789

Ann Matilda, born May 29, 1791; married James Reynolds

Thomas, born May 8, 1796

Bowdoin, born May 8, 1796.

John Rhodes, born Apr. 24, 1798, married Mary Gardner, daughter of Amos, about 1821. Married (2) Mary Harper.

George Scott, born Sept. 9, 1800, died young.

Sarah Sophia, born Mar 17, 1804, died Sept 27, 1827

Maria Waitstill, born Apr 7 1806 married James Harper

Eunice Susannah, born May 13, 1809, married Joseph ——.

MARY GARDNER (6).

Amos (5), John (4), William (3), Benony (2), George (1).

Mary, daughter of Amos and Sarah (Bill) Gardner, was born 1763, married Harry (or Harvy) Sherman about 1789

Children were.

Sarah Ann, born 1790, married Milton Cady, Aug 20, 1815, died 1851.

Lucy, born 1792, died July 25, 1863, became (2) wife of Daniel Daily, of Providence

Elizabeth, married Peter Forbes

Mary, married Ralph Post.

HANAH ROBINSON (6).

William (5), Abigail Gardner (4), William (3), Benony (2), George (1).

Hannah, daughter of William and Elizabeth (Wanton) Robinson, was born Feb 21, 1751, died 1823 She married George Brown, Apr 24, 1768 He was for many years a member of the General Assembly "In 1795 he was appointed by the Legislature second Justice on the bench of the Supreme Court of the State, and held the office until 1799, when he was elected by the people Lieutenant Governor of the State over Lieut. Governor Samuel J Potter after a severe and close canvass Governor Brown was a courteous and amicable gentleman, and exemplary communicant of the Episcopal church and a liberal contributor to its support He sustained an unreproachable character through life and died Jan 20, 1836, in the 91st year of his age and was buried in the church-yard at Tower Hill" His remains were afterwards removed to Westerley and placed in River Bend Cemetery Governor Brown had a large estate in Boston Neck and on Tower Hill, that he inherited from his father and uncle, Thomas Browne He with his brother, Rowland, built a large house on Tower Hill, and for some few years kept an Inn, but on the death of his uncle Thomas, from whom he inherited a fine estate in Boston Neck he moved to that place. Gov Brown kept up a fine establishment and entertained right royally, keeping a great number of slaves for house and farm labor When Robert Gardner, Consul to Sweden, came from his mission abroad he opened his home and gave a grand entertainment to his friends and neighbors. Miss Nancy Brown, one of Gov Brown's beautiful daughters, when she was over eighty years of age could still remember and loved to talk about this splendid affair, of which she was evidently the presiding genius, being taken in to supper by Mr Gardner and placed at the head of his table His elegant dress with its fine lace ruffles at wrist and knee and white satin vest sprigged with pink rose buds fondly lingered in her memory Gov Brown did not approve of the attentions shown to his daughter by "Consul Gardner" as he was called, and to his disapproval and contempt of the would-be lover when he called at the house the morning after the entertainment to enquire after the health of Miss Nancy, the Governor, instead of ordering some of his fine wines or Holland cordials to be brought in, left the room and returned with a pewter tankard filled with cider, and pewter tumblers, instead of the silver tankard and fine cut glass that were always used for his family and friends. Miss Nancy in telling the story, would add, "Can one imagine my mortification to see that elegant gentleman treated in such a contemptuous way, or wonder that he never came to see me again." Miss Nancy died at an advanced age unmarried

Children of George and Hannah (Robinson) Brown

Elizabeth, born 1769, married Benj , son of John and Sarah (Peckham) Robinson, 1791 , died Aug 25, 1855.

Mary, born 1771 , married Hezekiah Babcock

William born 1775, married Nancy Dockray Mar. 29, 1798.

Sarah, born 1778, died young

Abigail, born 1778; died unmarried

Nancy, born 1783, died unmarried.

Hannah, born 1786

John Brown, married Mary Robinson, daughter of Christopher

George, married Mary Brown, his first cousin.

BERIAH GARDNER (6).

Nicholas (5), Nicholas (4), Nicholas (3), Nicholas (2), George (1).

Beriah, son of Nicholas Esq., and Deborah (Vincent) Gardner was born November 16, 1771 , died February 12, 1853 He married first Phebe Gardner who died April 3, 1808, aged 36 years He married second Elizabeth Hammond, daughter of Joseph, son of Judge William and Chloe (Wilbur) Hammond, October 25, 1808 She died September 1, 1863, in her 76th year. He with his two wives are buried in Allenton Grove cemetery, Allenton, Rhode Island.

The children by his first wife were

Beriah, born March 28, 1794, died April 28, 1794

Elizabeth, born June 27, 1795 , married Aldridge Bissell, Genesee, N. Y

Nicholas Vincent, born December 13, 1797, died April 10, 1857

Mary H , born March 9, 1800, married Beriah Reynolds . died Sept 1858

Beriah, born March 27, 1802, married Francis Hefferman , died Sept. 19 1876.

Ezekiel M , born February 6, 1804, married Susan Reynolds , died Sept 14, 1876

Phebe, born February 25, 1806 Died at Cedar Springs, Kent Co . Mich , Jan 20, 1892, married Allen Spooner

Deborah V , born January, 1808, married Alexander Nichols of New York, died Sept 30, 1865

Children by his second wife were·

Joseph H , born February 22, 1811 , died Nov 23, 1893, in Joshua township, Fulton Co , Ill.

James A , born January 23, 1813, died December 24 1852

Harriet Cottrell, born March 11, 1815; died Nov 7, 1896 married Capt Stephen Boyer Reynolds

Lucy A , born July 21, 1817; married Thomas R. Rathbun , died Oct 19, 1878

Benjamin C, born September 11, 1821, died October 22, 1863.
Aldridge B, born May 25, 1823 married Agnes Jackson of New York
William N, born December 15, 1828, died August 30 1875

VINCENT GARDNER (6).

Nicholas (5), Nicholas (4), Nicholas (3), Nicholas (2), George (1).

Vincent, son of Nicholas and Deborah (Vincent) Gardner, was born December 9, 1764, died July 17, 1851 Married Mary, daughter of Ezekiel and Susannah (Congdon) Gardner, May, 1764. She was born March 3, 1766, died November 23, 1831

Their children were
Deborah, married Malborough Gardner
Susan, born 1793, died April 11, 1815
David V, born October 27, 1794, died May 8, 1843 Married Hannah Waite
Honour born September 19, 1796, died February 20, 1877
William, born June 11, 1797, married Rebecca Wood
Mary, born January 5, 1799, married Howland Brown
Amey, born October 1, 1801, married Samuel Brown
Elizabeth, born September 7, 1803
Vincent born September 7, 1804, died April 22 1872.
Martha, born November 11 1807, married William Northop
Dorcas born August 31, 1809, married Jeremiah S Gardner
Nancy, born October 12, 1811, married Elisha Brown

BENJAMIN C. GARDNER (6).

Nicholas (5), Nicholas (4). Nicholas (3), Nicholas (2), George (1).

Benjamin C Gardner, son of Nicholas, Esq, and Deborah (Vincent) Gardner, was born April 27, 1779, died Aug 28, 1859, married Mehitable Spencer daughter of Ann Spencer of North Kingstown, R. I, Aug. 21, 1803 by William Northup Eld

She was born 1781 Died July 20, 1845 Both are buried in Allenton Grove cemetery, Allenton, Washington County, R I.

Their children were
Sarah, born September 1, 1803, died October 12, 1881
Nicholas, born April 14, 1805, died August 12, 1853
Ann born September 21, 1806, died March 3, 1888
Willet, born June 27, 1808, died October 19, 1830
Deborah, born September 23, 1810, died April 15, 1899
Clark S, born June 27, 1812, died November 1, 1883
Alfred, born July 26, 1814
Perry G, born June 24, 1816, died July 20, 1866
Benjamin, born July 5, 1818 died August 15, 1876
Joseph W, born August 22, 1820, died September 2, 1824
All were born at Exeter, Washington County, Rhode Island.

HANNAH GARDNER (6).

Ezekiel, Jr. (5), Ezekiel (4), Nicholas (3), Nicholas (2), George (1).

Hannah, daughter of Ezekiel, Jr, and Susannah (Congdon) Gardner, was born March 6, 1770, married Jonathan N Arnold.

Children were:
George, married —— Nichols
Mary, born 1810, died Feb 10, 1897, never married
Elizabeth, married William Weeden
Susan married —— Spink
Joseph, married Ruth Fry.

DORCAS GARDNER (6).

Ezekiel Jr. (5), Ezekiel (4), Nicholas (3), Nicholas (2), George (1).

Dorcas, daughter of Ezekiel and Susannah (Congdon) Gardner, was born Feb 3, 1772, married as (2) wife of Nicholas Carr Northup, March 6, 1811.

Children were:
Nicholas C, born April 18 1812.
John C, born May 13, 1815, died Apr 20, 1857

ELISHA GARDNER (6).

Ezekiel, Jr. (5), Ezekiel (4), Nicholas (3), Nicholas (2), George (1)

Elisha, son of Ezekiel and Susannah (Congdon) Gardner was born January, 1778, married Sarah Hazard He died 1834.

Children were
Palmer, born 1803; married Lydia Sheffield Gardner daughter of Oliver, Esq
Sarah, born ——, married John Brown.
Jesse,
Susan,
Amey,
Ezekiel,
Abby,
John,
Jeffrey,
Elisha,
Mary,
William

PALMER GARDNER (6).

Ezekiel, Jr. (5), Ezekiel (4), Nicholas (3), Nicholas (2), George (1)

Palmer, son of Ezekiel, Jr, and Susannah (Congdon) Gardner, was born April 29, 1783, married Elizabeth Browning

Children were
Dorcas, married Whiting Searle.

Elizabeth, married Willet Gardner

Mary, married Isaac H Jecoy

Ruth, married Jonathan Arnold, had a daughter who married Albert F Ellsworth

JESSE GARDNER (6).

Ezekiel, Jr. (5), Ezekiel (4), Nicholas (3), Nicholas (2), George (1).

Jesse, son of Ezekiel, Jr, and Susannah (Congdon) Gardner, was born March 7, 1789 He married Elizabeth Bliss Northup, daughter of Nicholas Carr Northup and wife Ann She was born June 11, 1789

Children

Ezra N, born Jan 24, 1818, married Maria Cole, May 18, 1840

John,

Nicholas, married —— Cole, daughter of William

Albert,

Immanuel,

Elizabeth

MARY GARDNER (6)

Ezekiel, Jr (5), Ezekiel (4), Nicholas (3), Nicholas (2), George (1)

Mary, daughter of Ezekiel, Jr, and Susannah (Congdon) Gardner, was born March 3, 1766 married Vincent Gardner, son of Nicholas and Deborah (Vincent) Gardner. She died Nov 23, 1831

Children were

Deborah, married Malbro Gardner

Susan,

Honor, born Sept 19, 1796, married (1) Stukley Brown, (2) Capt Christopher L Phillips and had children Christopher, Susan Elizabeth Mary Nichols, Honor Angelia Margaret B

William born June 11, 1797, married Rebecca Wood

David, born Oct 27, 1798, married Hannah Waite, had children Charles and Vincent

Mary, born January 5, 1799, married Howland Brown

Amy born October 1, 1801, married Samuel Brown

Elizabeth, born September 7, 1803

Vincent, born Sept 7, 1805 died 1872.

Martha, born November, 1807, died Oct 19, 1895 Married William Northup

Dorcas, born Aug 1, 1809, died March 11, 1885

Nancy A, born Oct 12 1811, died May 9, 1887 Married Elisha Brown One child Amey Ann

ROBERT GARDNER (6).

Zebulon (5), Ezekiel (4), Nicholas (3), Nicholas (2), George (1)

Robert, son of Zebulon and Katherin (Wilcox) Gardner, was born in Exeter, R I, died in West Greenwich, R I, 1845 He married Mercy Tillinghast, daughter of John and granddaughter of Pardon Tillinghast

Their children were:
John T., born 1802, died Apr 12, 1878
Hannah, married John S Sweet.
Olive,
Mercy, married Stephen A Gardner
Zebulon, born 1810; married Eliza B Lawton
Robert, born 1814, died Feb 22, 1866
Dorcas,
Fanny, born 1818, died Apr 28, 1840
Mary A, born 1821, died March 18, 1837.
Catharine, born 1823, died July 10, 1837
Ann W

Robert was a thrifty farmer occupying after his father the homestead property, where, with his good wife, he passed in rural peace the noontime and evening of his life until its close

His sturdy good sense and his position for some years as magistrate in the local Court, are both preserved in the title "Judge Gardner," by which he has been known and is till remembered, he was also a member of the legislature

His children were all born at Exeter and in the same house John the eldest, at the death of the father became in a sense, the head of the family, and prior to his death was one of the most prosperous farmers in the town

BENJAMIN GARDNER (6).

Zebulon (5), Ezekiel (4), Nicholas (3), Nicholas (2), George (1).

Benjamin, son of Zebulon and Katherine (Wilcox) Gardner, was born about 1780 He married Susan Northup

Children were
Zebulon, born about 1800, married Elizabeth Rathbun
Harrington,
James,
Benjamin,
Samuel,
Sarah,
Mercy,
Mary,
Rathbun.

GOULD GARDNER (6).

Huling (5), Nicholas (4), Nicholas (3), Nicholas (2), George (1).

Gould, son of Huling and Elizabeth Northup was born 1771, died 1843. He married Sarah Tanner, daughter of Samuel and Sarah Tanner She was born 1777, died Jan 12, 1826

Their children were
William H, married Patience Hendricks, Dec 7, 1817
Joseph Wanton, born 1799, died 1881, married Mary Hendricks
Cornelia, born 1802, died Apr 2, 1869
Susan, born 1807, died Apr. 23, 1861

Ray,
Mary, born Apr 27, 1812, died June 12, 1885
Sarah

MARY ANN GARDNER (6).

Peleg (5), Ezekiel (4), Nicholas (3), Nicholas (2), George (1).

Mary Ann, daughter of Peleg and Hannah Gardner, was born Nov 15, 1800, she married Timothy Clarke Collins, Oct 2, 1823 She died Oct 19, 1863 He was born Jan. 4, 1799, died May 5, 1867

Their children were
Mary Ann, born Dec 24, 1825, died Feb 19 1847
Abel Clark, born Aug 17, 1828
Peleg G, born Aug 17 1828
Hannah C, born Oct 15, 1831
John, born Apr 23, 1836, died Feb 29, 1847.

EZEKIEL WATSON GARDNER (6).

Peleg (5), Ezekiel (4), Nicholas (3), Nicholas (2), George (1)

Ezekiel W, son of Peleg and —— Gardner, was born Oct 7, 1776, died at Potter, N Y. Apr. 19, 1866 He married Mary, daughter of Silas and Esther (Hazard) Niles, March 2, 1806 She was born Jan 13, 1779, died Dec 15, 1868

Their children were.
Peleg, born Nov 27, 1808, died Jan 15, 1880
John born Aug 19, 1810, died Nov 6 1876
Elizabeth, born Dec 16, 1812, died July 27, 1851. Married John Underwood, Oct, 1839 Two children Isabella W, Henry C
Ezekiel W born Oct 30, 1814, died Oct 10, 1875
Mary E, born June 29, 1823, died March 23, 1896 Married John Underwood Jan 3, 1853 One child John A

DAVID GARDNER (6).

Ezekiel, Jr. (5), Ezekiel (4), Nicholas (3), Nicholas (2), George (1).

David, son of Ezekiel Jr, and Susannah (Congdon) Gardner, was born August 6 1764 Married Lydia Sanford, daughter of Joseph and Mary (Clark) Sanford

Their children were
Susan, born 1801.
David, born 1802.
Mary, born 1807
Lydia, born June 29, 1809
Joseph C, born 1811, died August 10, 1876
Ann, born 1813
Abbey E, born 1815

EZEKIEL GARDNER (6).

Ezekiel, Jr. (5), Ezekiel (4), Nicholas (3), Nicholas (2), George (1).

Ezekiel, son of Ezekiel, Jr, and Susannah (Congdon) Gardner, was born Jan 19, 1768, married Ruth Tillinghast

Children were

Ruth, born 1796, died Apr 24, 1882, unmarried

Ezekiel, born 1798, died Aug 11, 1817

Hannah, born 1800, married as (2) wife of Hazard Burlingame

Pardon Tillinghast, born Oct 13, 1804, died Jan 25, 1888

Oliver, born 1808, died Feb. 26, 1893

George, born Sept 20, 1810, died May 31, 1858.

AMEY GARDNER (6).

Ezekiel, Jr. (5), Ezekiel (4), Nicholas (3), Nicholas (2), George (1).

Amey, daughter of Ezekiel, Jr, and Susannah (Congdon) Gardner, was born March 7, 1769, died Sept 7, 1821 She married Elisha Pierce

Children were

Joseph born Aug 23, 1815, died Nov 20, 1836

Susan G, born Dec 23, 1816, married Benjamin Smith

Ezekiel C, Elisha, twins, born March 25, 1818

Amey, born Dec 24, 1820, married Benjamin Champlin, Sept 28, 1837

JEFFREY GARDNER (6).

Ezekiel, Jr. (5), Ezekiel (4), Nicholas (3), Nicholas (2), George (1).

Jeffrey, son of Ezekiel Jr, and Susannah (Congdon) Gardner, was born Oct 21, 1792, married Mary Himes

Children were:

William,

Ezekiel, married, Sept 12, 1847, Susan Elizabeth Phillips, daughter of Christopher L Phillips She was born July 1, 1825 One child Charles M P, born Aug 2, 1851

ROBERT GARDNER (6).

Christopher (5), Henry (4), Henry (3), Henry (2), George (1).

Robert, son of Christopher and Mercy (Wheeler) Gardner, was born May 25, 1795 He married Lucinda Grant Elliott, April 7, 1825 He married (2) Sarah Barber

Children were

Oscar, born Jan 25, 1826, married Lydia A Sherman, 1848. She died 1888 He married (2) Hannah J Northup, 1889.

Edgar T, born Dec 15, 1827, married —— Brownell,

Rufus, born Oct 30, 1829

Daniel, born April 1, 1832, died Aug, 1833

Children by (2) wife were:
Darwin,
Charles,
Mary

MARY GARDNER (6)

Christopher (5), Henry (4), Henry (3), Henry (2), George (1).

Mary daughter of Christopher and Mercy (Wheeler) Gardner, was born January 19, 1781, died March 25, 1864 She married Clark Rodman, son of Robert and Margaret (Carpenter) Rodman, 1800 He was born Feb 16, 1781, died April 12 1859

Their children were

Christopher, born July 18, 1801, married Nancy Taber of Newport

Margaret Clarke, born May 13, 1803, married Elisha Kenyon

Daniel, born Aug. 3, 1805, died Aug 5, 1881 He married Elisa Brown

Clarke, born Sept 3, 1808 died Mar 25, 1864 Married Fanny Crandall, (2) Sarah Straight

Elizabeth, born July 11, 1810, died Feb 8, 1867 Married William Hammond

Mary Ann, born Mar 16, 1813; died young

Robert, born Sept. 1, 1815, died young

Robert, born Oct. 9, 1818, married —— Taylor

Phoebe, born Feb 13, 1822, married W. E Pierce

Thomas C, born Apr 25, 1826, died Oct 8, 1869. Married Caroline Sherman.

GEORGE B. GARDNER (6).

Nicholas E. (5), Christopher (4), Ephriam (3), Henry (2). George (1).

George B, son of Nicholas Easton Gardner, was born 1787, died Aug 5, 1859 He married Lucy Ann ——. She was born 1798, died Nov 17 1841

Children were

Eunice B, died young

Penelope, died 1834 aged 7 years

Sarah Penelope, died 1835, aged 1 year

BENJAMIN GARDNER (7).

Wickes (6), Benjamin (5), John (4), William (3), Benony (2), George (1).

Benjamin Gardner, son of Wickes and Waitey (Rhodes) Gardner, was born July 1, 1821, at Warwick, R. I., died November 2, 1901, at Providence, R I Married Caroline Greene of Warwick, R I, September 26, 1844 She died January 4, 1869, at Providence, R I

Seven children were born to them:

Walter Scott, born June 10, 1846, died Sept 29, 1852.

Richard Wickes, born Aug 10, 1848, died June 22, 1859.
Harriet Rhodes, born June 24, 1854, lives at Westboro, Mass
Elizabeth Wickes, born Jan 23, 1857, teacher at Warren, R I
Caroline, born Feb 26, 1860, died Mch 24, 1861
Charles Carroll, born Jan. 23, 1863
Albert Greene, born Apr 11, 1865
Benjamin Gardner was a graduate of Brown University

ANNIE GARDNER (7).

Benjamin C. (6), Nicholas (5), Nicholas (4), Nicholas (3), Nicholas (2), George (1).

Annie, daughter of Benjamin Champlin and Mehitable (Spencer) Gardner, was born September 21, 1806, died March 3, 1888, married James Davis Date of marriage not known.

One child was born to them·

Lucy Emeline, born Jan. 28, 1837

EZRA N. GARDNER (7).

Jesse (6), Ezekiel, Jr. (5), Ezekiel (4), Nicholas (3), Nicholas (2), George (1).

Ezra son of Jesse and Elizabeth B (Northup) Gardner, married Maria Cole, May 18, 1840 She was born July 31, 1820, a daughter of Edward and Margaret (Pierce) Cole

Children were.

Maria C, born Mar. 5, 1842
Emma, born Aug. 1, 1844; died Oct 2, 1844
Sarah P, born Sept. 2, 1846, married Cyrus Brown, died Aug 26, 1872 Two children Cyrus P, Joseph Theodore, born July 27, 1852
Albert,
Immanuel,
Elizabeth

PARDON TILLINGHAST GARDNER (7).

Ezekiel (6), Ezekiel, Jr. (5), Ezekiel (4), Nicholas (3), Nicholas (2), George (1).

Pardon T son of Ezekiel and Ruth (Tillinghast) Gardner, was born Oct 13, 1804, died Jan 25, 1888 He married Harriet G. Burlingame

Children were

Hannah N, married William A Spaulding
Ruth Ann, married Daniel Congdon
Daniel T, born 1840.
Alice F.

OLIVER GARDNER (7).

Ezekiel (6), Ezekiel, Jr. (5), Ezekiel (4), Nicholas (3), Nicholas (2), George (1).

Oliver, son of Ezekiel and Ruth (Tillinghast) Gardner, was born 1808, died 1893 He married Harriet Sherman

Children were

Ezekiel, married Nancy B Brown.
Ruth, married Elisha D Browning
Oliver, married Susan Gardner
Harriet, married Almond C Huling
Samuel,
Rhoda,
Alfred

GEORGE GARDNER (7).

Ezekiel (6), Ezekiel, Jr. (5), Ezekiel (4), Nicholas (3), Nicholas (2), George (1).

George, son of Ezekiel and Ruth (Tillinghast) Gardner, was born Sept 20, 1810, died May 31, 1858 He married Mary Ann Burlingame

Children were

Frances Ann, born Apr. 1, 1835, died Mar 20, 1895, married William W. Congdon

George Henry, born July 14, 1837

NICHOLAS GARDNER (7).

Benjamin C. (6), Nicholas (5), Nicholas (4), Nicholas (3), Nicholas (2), George (1).

Nicholas Gardner, son of Benjamin C and Mehitable (Spencer) Gardner, was born April 14, 1805, died August 12, 1853 Married Abigail Arnold of Exeter, Rhode Island

The following children were born to them

Mary Angeline, born April 5, 1829, died January 5, 1899
Benjamin Arnold,
Frances Ann, died in her seventeenth year
Willet, born April 12, 1833, died Aug 4, 1904
Nicholas Spencer,
Abigail Mehitable,
Susan Elizabeth, born February 3, 1840
Cornelia Maria died in infancy
Charles Wilson, born December 4, 1844
Frances Manton, died in infancy

SARAH GARDNER (7).

Benjamin C. (6), Nicholas (5), Nicholas (4), Nicholas (3), Nicholas (2), George (1).

Sarah Gardner, daughter of Benjamin Champlin and Mehitable (Spencer) Gardner, was born September 1, 1803, died October 12, 1881. Married Gideon Bailey, son of Caleb and Elizabeth (Barber) Bailey, January 1, 1829 He was born July 29, 1802, died April 28, 1880

Children were

Willet Anthony, born Feb 1, 1835; died March 19, 1850

Mary Ellen, born July 12, 1837, living

BENJAMIN GARDNER (7).

Benjamin C. (6), Nicholas (5), Nicholas (4), Nicholas (3), Nicholas (2), George (1).

Benjamin Gardner, son of Benjamin C. and Mehitable (Spencer) Gardner, was born July 5, 1818, died August 15, 1876. Married Mary Reynolds, daughter of John and Catharine (Tripp) Reynolds, February 12, 1839 She died September 24, 1861.

Children were

Thomas T, born October 14, 1839, died April 25, 1846.

Joseph O, born October 13, 1842

Philander F., born February 16, 1846; died April 15, 1885

Alonzo J, born December 27, 1848, living at Allenton, R. I

Benjamin T, born August 27, 1851, died April 2, 1874.

VINCENT GARDNER, JR. (7).

Vincent (6), Nicholas (5), Nicholas (4), Nicholas (3), Nicholas (2), George (1).

Mary (6), Ezekiel (5), Ezekiel (4), Nicholas (3), Nicholas (2), George (1)

Vincent, son of Vincent and Mary (Gardner) Gardner, was born Sept 7, 1804, died April 22, 1872, married Mary Reynolds, daughter of Jonathan, Jan. 29, 1829 She was born in Wickford, R I, Aug 16, 1807. Married by Rev Lemuel Burge.

Children:

Mary Eleanor, born February 22, 1830, living at Chattanooga, Tenn

Jonathan Vincent, born May 23, 1832, living at Wickford, R I

Susan Elizabeth, born October 17, 1834, died November 3, 1842

Susan Elizabeth, born November 1, 1845, died February 9, 1873

Leander, born September 3, 1848, died May 6, 1835; single.

DORCAS GARDNER (7).

Vincent (6), Nicholas (5), Nicholas (4), Nicholas (3), Nicholas (2), George (1).

Mary (6), Ezekiel (5), Ezekiel (4), Nicholas (3), Nicholas (2), George (1).

Dorcas Gardner, daughter of Vincent and Mary (Gardner) Gardner, was born August 1, 1809, died March 11, 1885 Married Jeremiah S Gardner

Children were·

Thomas Vincent, born January 3, 1834, died October 3, 1881

Jeremiah S., born May 13, 1838

Edward C, born May 7, 1840, died young

Phebe E, born June 18, 1841

Edward C, born January 3, 1846

AMEY GARDNER (7).

Vincent (6), Nicholas (5), Nicholas (4), Nicholas (3), Nicholas (2), George (1).

Mary (6), Ezekiel, Jr. (5), Ezekiel (4), Nicholas (3), Nicholas (2), George (1)

Amey Gardner, daughter of Vincent and Mary (Gardner) Gardner, was born October 1, 1801 Married Samuel Brown

Children were

Jeremiah,

Mary G. born April 21, 1830; died Nov 10, 1856, married John G. Pierce Children were Izitt G, born February 12, 1855, died March 31, 1880 Thomas J, born June 20, 1858.

Eleanor L, born 1832, died 1885

ELIZABETH GARDNER (7).

Vincent (6), Nicholas (5), Nicholas (4), Nicholas (3), Nicholas (2), George (1).

Mary (6), Ezekiel, Jr. (5), Ezekiel (4), Nicholas (3), Nicholas (2), George (1)

Elizabeth Gardner, daughter of Vincent and Mary (Gardner) Gardner, was born September 7, 1803 Married (1) Benjamin Gardner They had one child

Mary E Married (2) Henry S Sherman April 19, 1849 They had children as follows John B, Mary E William H Sarah, Jesse, Deborah married Pardon —— Married (2) John Caswell and died July 29, 1889.

NICHOLAS VINCENT GARDNER (7).

Beriah (6), Nicholas (5), Nicholas (4), Nicholas (3), Nicholas (2), George (1).

Nicholas V, son of Beriah and Phebe (Gardner) Gardner, was born Dec 18, 1797, died April 10, 1857, married Hannah S Baker She was born Sept 8, 1806, died Jan 21, 1879

Children.

Nicholas Jonathan (called "Captain Joe"), born Oct 15, 1837, living at Wickford, Rhode Island He married Phebe Cozzens Nov 27, 1866 She died May 15, 1905 No children

Phebe Elizabeth, born July 15, 1829, living at Wickford, R I, married William H Lewis Children. Hattie, born 1854, died 1906, Elizabeth, born 1857 Living at Wickford

JOSEPH WANTON GARDINER (7).

Gould (6), Huling (5), Nicholas (4), Nicholas (3), Nicholas (2), George (1).

Joseph Wanton, son of Gould and Sarah (Tanner) Gardiner of Exeter, was born Sept 26, 1799, died Oct 6, 1881 He married Mary W Hendricks, daughter of James of North Kingstown, Feb 19, 1829 She was born Apr 14, 1811, died Feb 6, 1897 Both are buried in Allenton Grove Cemetery, Allenton, R I

Children were

Harrison, born May 18, 1830, died Oct 7, 1857 His wife, Hannah B., died Nov 9, 1900

Greene, born Nov 24, 1831

Mary Fields, born Sept 10, 1834

Joseph Warren, born Mar, 1836 Living at Brewster, Nebraska

Owen G, born Jan 8, 1845

Massena T, born Nov 9, 1846.

Ansel B, born Jan 29, 1849.

Calvin, born Apr 24, 1851.

CHARLES CARROLL GARDINER (8).

Benjamin (7), Wickes (6), Benjamin (5). John (4), William (3), Benony (2), George (1)

Charles Carroll Gardiner son of Benjamin and Caroline (Green) Gardiner, was born January 23, 1863, at Providence, R I Married (1) Annie Louisa Cooke, daughter of Edwin S and Louisa W Cooke of Smithfield R I, October 17, 1889 She died May 21, 1893 No children

Mr Gardner married (2) Ethelind Richards, November 8, 1900 She was the daughter of Rev C A L and Mary White (Wiltbank) Richards, who reside at Providence R I

One child has been born to them

Charles Carroll, Jr, born June 28, 1905

ALBERT GREEN GARDINER (8).

Benjamin (7), Wickes (6), Benjamin (5), John (4), William (3), Benony (2), George (1).

Albert Green Gardner, son of Benjamin and Caroline (Green) Gardiner, married Annie Marion Dow, of Cambridge, Mass, June 19, 1900

Their children are

Elizabeth Trott, born Apr 23, 1901.

Caroline Greene, born Sept 21, 1904

Z. HERBERT GARDNER (8).

Zebulon (7), Robert (6), Zebulon (5) Ezekiel (4), Nicholas (3), Nicholas (2), George (1).

When the family of Zebulon and Eliza (Lawton) Gardner, at Fall River was broken up by the death of the mother, the youngest son, Z Herbert then but two years old, found a home with his father's brother John T, and from then lived at the Gardner homestead in Exeter, a part of which he inherited from his uncle at his death in 1878

From his uncle's home he had such meager chances for an education as the small rural school might give until old enough to attend the seminary at East Greenwich, after which he was in Bryant & Stratton's school at Providence, and later in 1868, he graduated at Schofield's Commercial College in that city

Mr Gardner has always been a republican Beside filling several minor offices, he was three years commissioner of the town asylum, and in 1879, 1880-81 he represented Exeter in the lower house of the state legislature After an interval of one year, he was promoted by his fellow townsmen to a seat in the State Senate, and re-elected in 1884 For three of those five terms, he was chosen without opposition

In 1879 he married Martha A Crandall, of Phoenix, R I

Children were

John T, born Aug., 1882

Z Herbert, Jr, born Feb, 1884

Thomas C, born Feb, 1887

LUCY EMELINE DAVIS (8).

Annie Gardner (7), Benjamin C. (6), Nicholas (5), Nicholas (4), Nicholas (3), Nicholas (2), George (1).

Lucy Emeline Davis, daughter of James and Annie (Gardner) Davis was born January 28, 1837 Married John Tillinghast Greene, son of Pardon and Deborah (Sisson) Greene, March 20, 1862

Their children were

Frank Wilson born Jan 23, 1863, married Ella Jencks Bartlett, daughter of Smith Jencks and Marietta (Dow) Bartlett, May 5, 1899.

Fred Davis, born July 19, 1864, died Apr 27, 1883

Nellie Abbott, born Sept 18, 1865.

Annie Bell, born Oct 25, 1869

NICHOLAS SPENCER GARDNER (8)

Nicholas (7), Benjamin C. (6), Nicholas (5), Nicholas (4), Nicholas (3), Nicholas (2), George (1).

Nicholas S, son of Nicholas and Abigail (Arnold) Gardner, was born at Exeter, R I, May 21, 1835, married Susan F Holmes in St Louis, Mo, Nov 13, 1867 He died in St Louis, Mo, March 11, 1891

Two sons

Charles Holmes, born Sept 13, 1868, in Warsaw, Mo, married Mary Belle McClurrey in St. Louis, Mo, Dec 17, 1895 He died June 1, 1900, in St. Louis No children

Herbert Spencer, born in Warsaw, Mo, Dec 22, 1872 married Maria Platt Read in St Louis, Mo, Apr 8, 1896 One son Edward Read, born Sept 11, 1897

WILLETT GARDNER (8).

Nicholas (7), Benjamin C (6), Nicholas (5), Nicholas (4), Nicholas (3), Nicholas (2), George (1).

Willett Gardner, son of Nicholas and Abigail (Arnold) Gardner, was born April 12, 1833, at Exeter, Rhode Island Died August 4, 1904, at Riverside, California, where his family now reside Married Lucia Avery of Providence, Rhode Island, September 9, 1868

They have two sons as follows

Frank Avery, born in Providence, R I, Nov 22, 1870

Willett Arnold, born in Roscoe, Mo, June 9, 1872

AMEY ANN BROWN (8).

Nancy G Gardner (7), Mary (6), Ezekiel, Jr. (5), Ezekiel (4), Nicholas (3), Nicholas (2), George (1).

Amey Ann, daughter of Elisha and Nancy G (Gardner) Brown, was born July 15, 1836, died 1887, married Thomas C Pierce

Their children were

John F, born Aug 17, 1852.

Christopher P, born Sept 28, 1854

Thomas W, born Nov 21, 1859

Amey Ann, born March 6, 1869

GEORGE HENRY GARDNER (8).

George (7), Ezekiel (6), Ezekiel, Jr (5), Ezekiel (4), Nicholas (3), Nicholas (2), George (2).

George Henry, son of George and Mary Ann (Burlingame) Gardner, was born July 14, 1837 He married (1) Nancy Greene, (2) Rachel F George

Children by first wife

George E, born Mar 4, 1862,

Abby P, born Mar 24, 1863
Children by second wife
Francis Murry, born 1872
Ada Josephine, born 1875
Harriet Langworthy, born 1880
Mary Esther, born Apr 15, 1881, died Mar 10, 1887.
Ruth Emeline, born June 28, 1889.

ALONZO J GARDNER (8).

Benjamin (7), Benjamin C. (6), Nicholas (5), Nicholas (4) Nicholas (3), Nicholas (2), George (1).

Alonzo J Gardner, son of Benjamin and Mary (Reynolds) Gardner, was born December 27, 1848, in Exeter, Rhode Island Married Mary E Wilcox, daughter of George W. and Clarissa (Johnson) Wilcox, September 17, 1871

Their children were
Mary B, born June 17, 1872, died May 8, 1902.

Arthur Lynwood, born April 27, 1879, married Bessie Waterman Luce April 16, 1907, daughter of Clarence J., and Mary Anna (Duffy) Luce

Infant son, born March 23, 1881, died April 19, 1881
Ethel B., born April 26, 1885
All were born in North Kingstown, R I

MARY ELLEN BAILEY (8).

Sarah Gardner (7), Benjamin C (6), Nicholas (5), Nicholas (4), Nicholas (3), Nicholas (2), George (1).

Mary Ellen, daughter of Gideon and Sarah (Gardner) Bailey, was born July 12, 1837, married Martin Andrews, son of Holden and Elizabeth (Bailey) Andrews, January 1, 1870 He was born May 31, 1834, died March 4, 1899

Children
Annie Holden, born May 17, 1871.
Clarke Willett, born July 18, 1872
Louisa Bailey, born Nov 17, 1874, unmarried

CHARLES F. GARDNER (8).

Zebulon (7), Robert (6), Zebulon (5), Ezekiel (4), Nicholas (3), Nicholas (2), George (1).

After being educated in the East at Phillips' Academy in Andover, Mass, and at Yale College, he located in California became the head of a family and an Attorney at Law in Sacramento city He was appointed receiver of public moneys there, by President Arthur, and held the position six years.

ROBERT GARDNER (8)

Zebulon (7), Robert (6), Zebulon (5), Ezekiel (4), Nicholas (3), Nicholas (2), George (1).

Robert son of Zebulon and Eliza (Lawton) Gardner, was born 1842 At the age of 17 years, he emigrated to California, and became a prominent business man there He was in the flour, grain and lumber business for 10 years He was a delegate from California in the National Republican Convention which met in Baltimore, June, 1864, to nominate Lincoln for the second time President of the United States

He was appointed by President Grant in March, 1869, register of the Humboldt land office for Humboldt district, Cal

He was nominated for State Surveyor General by the republican state convention in Sacramento in June, 1871, on the ticket with Newton Booth for Governor, and was elected for four years, renominated for State Surveyor General in June, 1875, on the ticket with Timothy G. Phelps, for Governor The ticket was defeated, caused by a split in the Republican party He lived in 1889 in Oakland, Cal

JOSEPH WARREN GARDINER (8).

Joseph Wanton (7), Gould (6), Huling (5), Nicholas (4), Nicholas (3), Nicholas (2), George (1).

J Warren son of Joseph Wanton and Mary W (Hendricks) Gardner, was born March, 1836, in North Kingstown, R. I. Living in Brewster, Neb

Children were
Claude, born 1867
Grace, born 1869
Blanche, born 1871
Joseph Ray, born 1873
Earl born 1876.
Walter Scott, born 1877
Marie, born 1881.

OWEN GARDNER (8).

Joseph W. (7), Gould (6), Huling (5), Nicholas (4), Nicholas (3), Nicholas (2), George (1)

Owen Gardner, son of Capt Joseph W and —— Gardner, married Susan A, daughter of William Tisdale, 1866

Children were
Eleanor G
Clarence E
Owen G, Jr.
Linwood A

Mr Gardner was business manager of the R I Telephone three years, and engaged in the wholesale confectionery business several years on the road

HARRINGTON GARDNER (8).

Zebulon (7), Benjamin (6), Zebulon (5), Ezekiel (4), Nicholas (3). Nicholas (2), George (1).

Harrington, son of Zebulon and Elizabeth (Rathbun) Gardner, married —— Gardner, daughter of Randall Gardner

We have record of only an adopted son

Herbert.

MARY ELEANOR GARDNER (8).

Vincent, Jr. (7), Vincent (6), Nicholas (5), Nicholas (4), Nicholas (3), Nicholas (2), George (1).

Mary Eleanor, daughter of Vincent Jr and Mary M (Reynolds) Gardner, was born Feb 22, 1830 Living at Chattanooga, Tenn She married Rev Charles H Payne

Children

Charles Vincent, born Sept 20, 1858, at Taunton, Mass Living

Frank Leonard born Oct 7, 1860, at East Bridgewater, Mass, died Apr 29, 1863, at Prov, R. I

DR. CHARLES H. PAYNE.

In his youth Charles Henry Payne had to encounter such obstacles as were common to New England boys in humble circumstances, and some that were peculiar to his own situation, but he displayed the tenacity and energy which in later years were synonyms for as well as causes of, successful achievement in various but closely related fields He studied in the public schools, prepared for college in the East Greenwich Seminary, and was graduated from Wesleyan University Having the ministry in view he went to the Concord Biblical Institute, and was admitted on trial in the Providence Conference in the spring of 1857, and stationed at Sandwich He had been a local deacon for some time, and in his third year in Conference was sent to East Bridgewater Rapidly rising in popular esteem, he was transferred at the end of that year to First Church, Fall River From Fall River, at the end of his two years, he went to Broadway, Providence, R I, and there at the close of his second year was stationed for a third year, though, his health having failed, he had a colleague

He then thought it improbable that he would be able to preach again and made arrangements to go into business. At that time Dr Cyrus D Foss, who had been for two years pastor of South Fifth Street Church in the Eastern District of Brooklyn was transferred to the New York Conference, to the disappointment of the people who desired him to return for a third year Dr James Porter, one of the Book Agents, then attended South Fifth Street Church and having known Dr Payne from his youth and holding a high opinion of his abilities, suggested him as a suitable person for pastor, saying, "As sure as he comes every pew will be rented, and he will build you a new church" Dr Payne was transferred, entering the New York East Conference in the spring of

1866 Dr Porter therein prophesied truly Not a "crowd compeller" in the ordinary sense of the word, those whom he attracted were by his pastoral persuasiveness induced to take permanent sittings The fragile man, who appeared as though dyspepsia was to be followed by consumption, gave to that church an organic unity which it had never had, and produced a universal spirit of co-operation, the result of which was the erection of the imposing St John's Church, long the admiration of all Methodist visitors, and still one of the best structures in the denomination As its pastor in 1868 he met William Morley Pushon, the English orator, immediately after his landing in New York en route to the General Conference and took him to the church where he preached in the evening of the dedication the first of his brilliant series of discourses on this continent

Dr Payne remained but one term in the New York East Conference, being sought for in Philadelphia to make necessary and erect the Arch Street Church in that city Having done this work,—in many respects more arduous than that which he had performed in Brooklyn,—he was sent to Spring Garden Street Church, and at the close of his term there was transferred to St Paul's Church, Cincinnati In 1876 he was elected President of the Ohio Wesleyan University, and there remained until 1888, when he became Corresponding Secretary of the Board of Education

The mind of Dr Payne was unusually clear, it was also precise, familiar with distinctions and definitions, an obscure sentence never fell from his lips His acquaintance with literature was extensive, and style and its cultivation occupied much of his thought His spirit was critical of words, things, thoughts and their embodiment in men and institutions It is probable that he never uttered a word of slang All his public communications were on a high plane, and his private conversation, if published, would not have subjected him to harsh criticism. He saw defects and noted them, applying the same principles to himself and others Always, till with some mitigation in the last few years, he was a dyspeptic His temperament was intensely nervous This gave him the great advantage of being always animated whenever he spoke in public The reaction of an audience upon him was a nerve stimulant, but it subjected him to the dangerous temptation of permitting an undue draft upon his vital resources The art of self-care he had mastered as respects food and regimen, and could practice self-denial heroically in everything but work

His temperament carried with it its usual accompaniment of sensitiveness He was easily worried, might be irritated, but was never seen in a passion.

His voice, a somewhat sharp baritone, almost thin, but with great carrying power, was singularly penetrating It admitted of use upon at least two full octaves, and at times his low notes gave great force and happily modified the acuteness of some of his tones He abounded in gesticulation The application of his powers to the platform abounded in surprises to the auditor who heard him for the first time: for one would expect, from his appearance, mildness and perhaps feebleness of manner, and scholarly hesitation for the right word Instead, he would hear a man who might have spoken on the platform with Garrison and

Phillips in the days of their most portentious fulminations, without weakening the effect

As a sermonizer he blended system with much power of elaboration, and could deliver distinctions as though they were descriptions A discourse on "Divine Providence," which he delivered in the Park Street Church when it was still the representative orthodox church of Boston and was without a pastor, made such an impression that the committee on pulpit supply began negotiations with him to accept its pastorate Long afterward we requested him to preach that sermon in a pulpit of which we had control, and could easily understand the impression which it had made

As a pastor his success was achieved without obsequiousness, indiscriminate flattery, or officiousness hence it greatly reinforced his sermons What he did as an author was sufficient to show what he might have done had he given more attention to that form of literary work. His writings were based chiefly upon his addresses, and were in every way creditable to him.

Money-raising was with him reduced to an art A clear presentation of the cause, a tenacity in appeal, and a transparent plan, all fused with an earnestness born of strong desire to succeed, together with preliminary preparation, gave him unusual success The churches that he built are his monuments

As a college president he was among the best, subject to the disadvantage of his temperament, which could be fretted by details He was true to his principles, and the Ohio Wesleyan University derived substantial and permanent benefits from his administration

As Corresponding Secretary he identified himself with his cause His mind was continually at work, and whether in preparing the program for Children's Day, conceiving a scheme for the establishment of a University Senate, conferring with the burdened authorities of struggling schools, or aiming at a general elevation of the average curriculum, he was alike ready to concentrate his whole faculties and to avail himself of the suggestions and labor of others If he could find no hymns expressive of the idea which he wished to set forth, he would compose them or have them composed

Dr Payne sympathized with reformatory movements Sometimes, having gone to the uttermost verge of radicalism he would hesitate, step back, and survey the scene Again, a spirit of conservatism would take possession of him as he saw the waves of controversy rising higher and higher, but his general course was in the direction of modifications in Church and State in the interest of human progress The "Western Christian Advocate" in an excellent article speaking of him as five times a delegate from the Cincinnati to the General Conference, says that "except in committees, where he was always valuable and influential, he was not at his best in the General Conference He lacked the readiness for rough-and-tumble debate His steel was too finely tempered to clash with the rude broadswords wielded there"

Concurring in the general estimate, in the spirit only of brotherly appreciation we suggest that the primary difficulty was not in the temper of the steel but in the general movement of his mind when under a sense of limitation and responsibility The platform and the pulpit left him to make selections from the abundance of his thoughts at his own will This, whether the Damascus blade or the rude broadsword be swung, is impossible in the General Conference To change the figure, one must select almost by an instinct smooth or rough stones, as he needs them, and while in the very act of hurling them

Dr Payne possessed one gift which any Gospel minister, unless menacled by a liturgy, might covet,—the power of public prayer We have long classed him with a few men who, from our human point of view, seemed to utter words in public prayer in the Sabbath congregation, alike acceptable to devout hearers on earth and presumptively in view of His great mercy, to the "eternal power whose high abode becomes the grandeur of a God"

J M BUCKLEY, D D

JONATHAN VINCENT GARDNER (8)

Vincent, Jr. (7), Vincent (6), Nicholas (5), Nicholas (4), Nicholas (3), Nicholas (2), George (1).

Jonathan Vincent, son of Vincent, Jr, and Mary M (Reynolds) Gardner, was born May 23, 1832 Married Charlotte E Hall, February 24, 1859

Their children were born as follows

Henry Vincent, born February 15, 1860, at Wickford, R I. Living

Arthur Gerald, born May 26, 1868, at Wickford, R I Living

SUSAN ELIZABETH GARDNER (8).

Vincent, Jr. (7), Vincent (6), Nicholas (5), Nicholas (4), Nicholas (3), Nicholas (2), George (1).

Susan Elizabeth, daughter of Vincent, Jr, and Mary M. (Reynolds) Gardner, was born November 1, 1845, died Jan 9, 1873 Married Thomas D Nichols July 10, 1870

Children born to them were

George Vincent,

Mary Charlott

AMEY ANN BROWN (8).

Nancy G. Gardner (7), Mary (6), Eekiel, Jr (5). Eezkiel (4), Nicholas (3), Nicholas (2), George (1)

Amey Ann daughter of Elisha and Nancy G (Gardner) Brown, was born July, 1836, died 1887, married Thomas C Pierce

Their children were

John F, born Aug 17, 1852.

Christopher P, born Sept 28, 1854

Thomas W, born Nov. 21, 1859.

Amey Ann, born March 6, 1869

JOSEPH GARDNER REYNOLDS (8).

Harriet C. Gardner (7), Beriah (6), Nicholas (5), Nicholas (4), Nicholas (3), Nicholas (2), George (1)

Joseph G., son of Capt Stephen B and Harriet Cottrell (Gardner) Reynolds, was born July 12, 1853 Married Rebecca G Tillinghast, January 1, 1879 living at Wickford, R I

Their children were

Marion T born Jan 24, 1880, living

Stephen B, born May 16, 1882, living, married Gracie Clark, June 20, 1906

Joseph G., Jr, born April 9, 1886

Bessie T, born April 17 1890 died Feb 16 1906

Howard E, born April, 1896, died June 11, 1896

FRANK WILSON GREEN (9).

Lucy E Davis (8), Annie Gardner (7), Benjamin C (6), Nicholas (5), Nicholas (4), Nicholas (3), Nicholas (2), George (1).

Frank Wilson Green, son of John T and Lucy E (Davis) Green, was born January 23, 1863 Married Ella Jencks Bartlett, daughter of Smith Jencks and Mariette (Dow) Bartlett, May 5, 1899

No children.

FRANK AVERY GARDNER (9).

Willett (8), Nicholas (7), Benjamin C (6), Nicholas (5), Nicholas (4), Nicholas (3), Nicholas (2), George (1)

Frank Avery Gardner, son of Willett and Lucia (Avery) Gardner, was born Nov 22 1870 Married Alice Azelina McCormick of Riverside, Cal, November 24, 1887

One son has been born to them

Myron Milice, born November 22, 1900

ANNIE HOLDEN ANDREWS (9)

Mary E Bailey (8), Sarah Gardner (7), Benjamin C (6), Nicholas (5), Nicholas (4), Nicholas (3), Nicholas (2), George (1).

Annie Holden Andrews, daughter of Martin and Mary Ellen (Bailey) Andrews, was born May 17, 1872. Married Richard Bowen, son of Amos M and Eliza R (Henry) Bowen, September 18, 1905 He was born April 8, 1872.

No children

CLARKE WILLET ANDREWS (9)

Mary E. Bailey (8), Sarah Gardner (7), Benjamin C (6), Nicholas (5), Nicholas (4), Nicholas (3), Nicholas (2), George (1)

Clarke Willet Andrews, son of Martin and Mary Ellen (Bailey) Andrews, was born July 18, 1872 Married Annie Frances Bliven, daughter of Charles Courtland and Lucetta (Briggs) Bliven, October 17, 1900 She was born March 1, 1878

One child has been born to them

Justin Meredith, born August 28, 1902

MARY B GARDNER (9)

Alonza J. (8), Benjamin (7), Benjamin C. (6), Nicholas (5), Nicholas (4), Nicholas (3), Nicholas (2), George (1),

Mary B. Gardner, daughter of Alonza J and Mary (Wilcox) Gardner was born June 17, 1872, died May 8, 1902 Married Isaac E Lewis, son of John P and Mercy A (Willis) Lewis, April 28, 1896 He died October 29 1897

One child was born to them

Marjorie Ethel, born August 6, 1897, died June 22, 1898

HENRY VINCENT GARDNER (9)

Jonathan V. (8), Vincent (7), Vincent (6), Nicholas (5), Nicholas (4), Nicholas (3), Nicholas (2), George (1).

Henry Vincent, son of Jonathan V and Charlotte E (Hall) Gardner, born February 15, 1860, at Wickford, R I Is now living at Providence, R I Married Elizabeth A Clark June 1, 1883 No children.

ARTHUR GERALD GARDNER (9).

Jonathan V (8), Vincent (7), Vincent (6). Nicholas (5), Nicholas (4) Nicholas (3), Nicholas (2), George (1).

Arthur Gerald, son of Jonathan V and Charlotte E (Hall) Gardner, was born May 26, 1868, at Wickford, R I Now living at Providence, R I. Married Sarah J Cosgrove, November 1 1893

The following children have been born to them:

Charlotte Beatrice, born July 3, 1895 Living.

Dorothy Elizabeth, born Dec. 7 1898 Living.

CHARLES C. GARDNER.

Charles C Gardner son of Oliver A and Annie E (Williams) Gardner, married Mary E Good, daughter of Cyrus Good, November 1 1883

Their children were
Clarence O, born October 6, 1884
Eugene C, born February 7, 1886
Harry R, born August 25, 1887
Lola E, born March 12, 1889
Charles O, died in infancy
Bertha A, born October 14, 1893
Cyrus A, born June 3, 1903
All were born in Iowa.

CONNECTICUT.

STEPHEN GARDINER (3)

Benony (2), George (1).

Stephen Gardiner, son of Benony and Mary Gardiner, was born about 1667, at Kingstown, Rhode Island Died February 9 1743, in Bozrah, Conn , and buried in the Gardiner cemetery on a large farm near Gardiner's Lake, now owned by Alvah Frances Gardiner.

Married Amy Sherman, daughter of Benjamin and Hannah (Mowery) Sherman, of Kingstown, about 1700. She was born October 25, 1681

Their children were·

Amy, born June 13, 1701

Lydia born October 10, 1702

Stephen, born February 24, 1704

Benjamin, born April 18, 1706.

Peregrene, born January 24, 1707, married Susannah, daughter of John and Mary (Hazard) Robinson, Mar 30, 1737

Daniel, born December 14, 1709, died July 31, 1755

Sarah, born October 25, 1711, married Jonathan Smith, August 24, 1732.

Hannah, born May 2, 1713

Mehettable, born May 22, 1715

Abigail, born July 9, 1717, married Richard Smith, of Groton, Conn , April 21, 1744

David, born June 28, 1720. died 1798

Jonathan, born April 18, 1724

1705. his father deeded land to son Stephen with house thereon in Kingstown

1731 Stephen deeded the same land to his uncle, John Watson, for 2,300 pounds, signed as Stephen Gardiner of South Kingstown (The town was divided into North and South Kingstown in 1722) This homestead farm was possibly on or near Tower Hill

1736 A number of deeds of this date are recorded in Norwich, Conn , relating to the purchase of land in Colchester by Stephen Gardner, of South Kingstown In Colchester other deeds are found dated 1733 Signed by Stephen Gardner of Norwich From this time till 1742 he appears in the records as buying land in Colchester and Bozrah and Montville around Gardiner's lake

Coggeshall history of Montville says "Stephen Gardiner married, 1700, Amy Sherman, daughter of Benjamin and Hannah (Mowry) Sherman, of Kingstown, Rhode Island Settled in New London County, Connecticut He bought the Great Pond afterwards called Gardiner's Lake. The following inscription on his tombstone at Gardiner's Lake was deciphered a few years ago by Mr James Arnold of Providence, Rhode Island

"Here lyes ye body of Stephen
Gardiner, who died February ye
9, 1743 and in ye 76 year of his age"

BENJAMIN GARDNER (4).

Stephen (3), Benony (2), George (1).

Benjamin Gardner, son of Stephen, Sr, and Amy (Sherman) Gardiner, was born April 18, 1706, died 1776, married Content ——. His will is recorded in Vol 6, Page 26, Probate Records, Norwich, Conn Written February 13, 1762 Probated May 7, 1776 The children were as follows

Ezekial,
Simeon,
Margaret, married —— Congdon
Benjamin,
Sherman,
Desire, married Avery
Content.

DAVID GARDNER (4).

Stephen (3), Benony (2), George (1).

David Gardner, son of Stephen and Amy (Sherman) Gardiner, was born 1720, died 1798, married Jemima Gustin October 1, 1744

Children
Amy,
Sarah,
Anstress,
David, born April 20, 1753, died January 20, 1823
Isaac

JONATHAN GARDNER (4)

Stephen (3), Benony (2), George (1).

Jonathan, son of Stephen and Amy (Sherman) Gardiner, was born April 18, 1724, in South Kingstown, R I, died August 22, 1792, at Bozrah, Conn He married (1) Mary Houghton She died Feb 29, 1760 He married (2) Alice or Abiah Fitch, of Montville, twin daughter of Daniel and Sarah (Sherwood) Fitch She died Feb, 1812

Children by first wife were
Jonathan, born Dec 2, 1758 died May 6, 1847
By second wife were
Lemuel, born July 10, 1762, died March 11, 1850 Married Jemima Lathrop, Oct 28, 1789
Sarah, married Russell Leffinghall

DANIEL GARDNER, SR. (4),

Stephen (3), Benony (2), George (1)

Daniel Gardner, son of Stephen and Amy (Sherman) Gardner, was born Dec 14, 1709, in Narragansett, R I, died 1758 in Bozrah, Conn Married Bathsheba Smith, of New London, Conn She was born 1705

Children

Bathsheba, born October 20, 1736
Daniel, born October 9, 1738, died May 12, 1806.
Presieve, born January 29, 1741
William, born March 10, 1743
Stephen, born April 25, 1745
Anne, born September 7, 1748
James, born November 19, 1750
Sylvester, born April 19, 1753.
Elizabeth, born July 2, 1755

Will recorded in Vol 2, Page 372, book of Probate Records at Norwich, Connecticut Probated March 28, 1758 Distribution made April 7, 1758

DAVID GARDNER, JR. (5)

David (4), Stephen (3), Benony (2), George (1).

David Gardner, Jr, son of David, Sr, and Jemima (Gustin) Gardner, was born April 20 1753 Died January 20, 1823

Married Dennis Holmes about 1772 She died November 14, 1801, aged 49 years Married, second, Mary Lathrop, third, Olive Metcalf, who survived him He was a farmer and lived near Gardiner's Lake, Connecticut.

His children were born as follows

Amasa, born November 1, 1776
David, born August 2, 1778
Azel, born August 5, 1780
Lucinda, born November 12 1782.
John born February 1, 1786
Anstress, born June 24, 1787
Erastus, born July 16, 1789
Artemas, born January 15, 1792
Salmon, born December 5, 1804

JONATHAN GARDNER, JR (5)

Jonathan (4), Stephen (3), Benony (2), George (1).

Jonathan Gardner, Jr, son of Jonathan and Mary (Houghton) Gardner, was born December 2, 1758

Married Jerusha Hyde Stark, only daughter of Silas and Jerusha (Hyde) Stark, January 22, 1783

The children born of them were as follows

Jerusha, born November 21, 1783
Mary, born January 10, 1786
Roderick, born July 20, 1788. Died January 1, 1848

LYDIA GARDNER (5).

Stephen (4), Stephen (3), Benony (2), George (1).

Lydia, daughter of Stephen Gardner, was born March 20, 1727 Died Oct 22, 1804 Married John Jenkins, of Gardiner's Lake, New London County, Connecticut

Their children were:

John, born November 27, 1751, died March 19, 1827
Stephen, born February 22, 1753 died September 20, 1808
Benjamin, born July 18, 1754, died March, 1787
Amy, born January 12, 1757, died March 24, 1834
Thomas, born January 19, 1761, died April 22, 1812
William, born October 30, 1764, died November 1, 1846
Wilkes, born July 28, 1767, died April 1, 1838.

DANIEL GARDNER, JR (5)

Daniel (4), Stephen (3), Benony (2), George (1).

Daniel Gardner, Jr, son of Daniel, Sr, and Bathsheba (Smith) Gardner, was born October 9 1738, died May 12, 1806; married Elizabeth Clark, of New London Conn, July 6, 1763 She was born 1733, died July 12, 1806 They resided at Gardiner's Lake, Conn.

Their children were

Daniel, born May 10, 1764-5, died Aug., 1789
Clarke born March 2, 1766
Ebenezer, born April 17, 1768
Jabez, born September 2, 1770
Elizabeth, born August 24, 1772
Sylvester, born March 26, 1775
Charles, born March 2, 1778
Nicholas, born March 27, 1779, died June 21, 1814
A daughter, born March 27, 1779

His will, recorded in Vol 10, Page 563, New London, Conn, Records, mentions his children and grandchildren

Wife Elizabeth Gardner
Three sons (viz) Clarke, Sylvester, Nicholas
Grandson Giles Gardner, eldest son of my son Daniel Gardner deceased
Grandson Daniel Gardner, son of my son Daniel Gardner, deceased
Grandson George Gardner eldest son of my son Jabez, deceased
Jemima Gardner, daughter of my son Jabez deceased
Elsa, daughter of said Jabez, deceased
Jabez, son of said Jabez, deceased
My daughter Elizabeth Gardner
Son Sylvester Gardner, Executor

his
(signed) DANIEL X GARDNER
mark

Inventory taken June 6, 1806

LEMUEL GARDNER (5)

Jonathan (4), Stephen (3), Benony (2), George (1).

Lemuel, son of Jonathan and Aliah (Fitch) Gardner was born July 10, 1763, at Bozrah, Conn., died July 10, 1839. He married Jemima, daughter of Capt. Jedediah Lathrop, Oct 28 1789. She was born Dec 31, 1767, died Mar 11, 1850. They lived successively in Bozrah, Norwich and Montville.

Children.

Lorinda, born in Bozrah, Jan 15, 1790, and married, in 1810, Levi Whaley, of Montville. Children: Levi Gardner, Charles Lathrop, David Chauncey, Theodore Dwight, Mary Anne, Jane, Maria, Sarah Ann.

Almira, born May 27, 1792.

Sidney, born in Bozrah, Apr. 17, 1795, and married June 23, 1823, Maria, daughter of Thomas Fanning, of Norwich. Children were: Sidney Alfred, Sarah Ann, Frederick Lester and Charles Henry.

Amelia, born in Bozrah, June 6, 1799, married in November, 1840, Rev. Christopher Leffingwell, a Baptist minister of "Leffingwell Town."

Sarah, born in Norwich, May 28, 1806, died Oct 15, 1821. Single.

John F., born in Norwich, Nov 5, 1808, and married Feb 25, 1829, Martha Crary of Preston. Children: Henry, Albert, Mary, Helen.

ABIGAIL GARDNER (5).

William (4), William (3), Benony (2), George (1).

Abigail, daughter of William and Elizabeth (Gibbs) Gardner, was born March 2, 1719, died January 30, 1784.

Married Matthew Stewart, October 19, 1735. He was born October 16, 1701, and emigrated to this countryy from Ireland and settled at New London, Connecticut. He died June 28, 1778.

Their children were:

Abigail, born Jan 29, 1738, died Mar 18, 1752.

Daniel, born Aug 22, 1739, died Sept 22, 1740.

Matthew, born Nov 5, 1741, died Sept 6 1758.

William, born Mar 6, 1745, died July 11, 1787, married Jane Winthrop, of New London, Conn., a descendant of Gov. Winthrop. She died 1798, left one child, Ann.

Hannah, born Dec 12, 1746, died Feb 14, 1814.

Anna, born Oct 19, 1748, died Oct 11, 1769. Unmarried.

Daniel, born Aug 21, 1751, died Mar 24, 1752.

Mary, born Feb 14, 1753, died Nov 29, 1841, married Joshua Starr of New London, Conn.

Walter, born June 17, 1755, died at sea 1777. Unmarried.

Abigail, born Oct 12, 1757, died Aug 27, 1762.

Frances, born Oct 21 1761, died March 8 1854, married Major John Handy, oldest son of Captain Charles Handy. She was his third wife.

Major Handy was a merchant in Newport. He entered the revolutionary army and was promoted to the rank of Major. He died in Newport in 1838, aged 72 years. He read the Declaration of Independence to the military and people from the Court House steps in Newport in 1776, as ordered by the Legislature, and at the semi-century celebration in 1836 Major Handy read it again to the military and people from the same place

JOHN GARDNER

John, son of —— ——, married Phebe Lathrop Dec 13, 1780 She was born July 1, 1762

Children, all born in Bozrah, were

John, born May 7, 1783, and married Violate, daughter of William and Sybil (Lathrop) Crocker

Rebecca, born May 31, 1785.

James, born June 27, 1788

Jemima, born July 22, 1791

Jedidiah Lathrop, born Sept 4, 1793

Phebe, born July 9, 1801

Uriah, born Nov 18, 1805.

RODERICK GARDNER (6)

Jonathan, Jr. (5), Jonathan (4), Stephen (3), Benony (2), George (1).

Roderick Gardner son of Jonathan, Jr, and Jerusha Hyde (Stark) Gardner, was born July 20 1788, in Bozrah, Conn Died January 1 1849, and is buried near Gardner's Lake at North End He married Amy Miner, of Lynne, Conn, May 23, 1813

Their children were born as follows:

Dyer Hyde, born February 11, 1814, died 1884 at Charleston, S C.

Ulysses Selden, born December 16, 1815, died 1884, married Lucy Abel, of Colchester

Adolphus Morgan, born August 10, 1817, died 1881

Andrew Jackson, born February 20, 1819 died 1896

Russell Smith, born December 16, 1820, died 1886, married Fannie Abel, of Norwich

Lucius Leander, born August 31, 1822-3, died 1892.

Mary Miranda, born October 10, 1824, died 1898.

Austin, born July 2, 1826

Anson, born May 19, 1829, died 1896

Albert Avery, born August 20, 1831, died 1878.

Emma Elizabeth, born August 24, 1833

Elisha Miner, born July 13, 1836

JERUSHA GARDNER (6).

Jonathan (5), Jonathan (4), Stephen (3), Benony (2), George (1).

Jerusha daughter of Jonathan and Jerusha H (Stark) Gardner, was born November 21, 1783, died ——, married Col Avery Morgan, of Groton Conn, October, 1802 He was born May 20, 1781, and was the son of William and Lydia (Smith) Morgan

Their children were born as follows, the first two in Groton, the other five in Colchester.

Lyman Gardner, born Dec 31 1803, married Elizabeth Washington Newton, Sept 30, 1828.

Lydia Smith, born Oct 7, 1806, married Eliphalet Adams Bulkley, Jan., 1830. He was born June, 1804

Jedidiah Starr, born Sept 1, 1809, married Caroline Adams, April 23, 1827-9

William Avery, born Sept 2, 1812, died Jan 8, ——; married Diana Ingham, April 8, 1835 She died Dec 2, 1850

Mary Gardner, born Sept 24, 1815, married Frederick Green, May, 1838

Nathan Denison, born Oct 22, 1818, married Mary B Churchill, of Portland, Feb 14, 1842 She died June, 1852

Henry Packer, born July, 1821, married Eunice Hicks, of Brooklyn, April, 1850

MARY GARDNER (6).

Jonathan (5), Jonathan (4), Stephen (3), Benony (2), George (1).

Mary, daughter of Jonathan and Jerusha H (Stark) Gardner, was born Jan 10, 1786, in Bozrah, Conn, married Dr Charles Bingham, May 27, 1810 He was born 1784, died 1842

Their children were born as follows

Harriet, born Mar 6, 1811, married Edward Miles August 27, 1844

Lucius, born June 21, 1813, died April, 1814

Lucius C, born February 4, 1815, at Mount Morris

Jerusha M, born January 14, 1819.

NICHOLAS GARDNER (6).

Daniel (5), Daniel (4), Stephen (3), Benony (2), George (1).

Nicholas, son of Daniel and Elizabeth (Clark) Gardner, was born March 27, 1778, died June 21, 1814 He married Sarah Wright, June 21, 1804 She was born June 19, 1779, at Port Hadden, Conn, died March 15, 1873

Their children were

Rebecca Dixon, born March 16, 1805

Elizabeth Clark, born Apr 19, 1807, died 1863, married Jonathan Olmstead, 1837

Eunice Wright, born June 9, 1809, married Harvey Gillett, March 26, 1839

Nicholas G, born Sept. 16, 1811

Robert Dixon, married Phebe Gardner Wilkes, Sept 5, 1839

FREDERICK GARDNER (6)

Thomas (5), John (4), William (3), Benony (2), George (1).

Frederick, son of Thomas and Martha (Gardner) Gardner, was born Aug 24, 1751, married Lucy Northup, daughter of Stephen

Their children were

Robinson, baptized March 13, 1788, died 1806
Stephen,
Abigail, baptized Jan 7, 1790 Was first wife of Silas Gardner.
Simeon Stuart, died 1807

AZEL GARDNER (6)

David (5), David (4), Stephen (3), Benony (2), George (1).

Azel Gardner, son of David and Dennis (Holmes) Gardner, was born August 5, 1780, died in Bozrah, Conn, Nov 14, 1868. Married Amy Rogers, daughter of Jehial and Amy (Vibber) Rogers, of Montville She died Jan 21 1866

Children
Ann, born Mar 15, married Thomas Leach
Cyrus, born June 25, 1815, married Lucy Swan
Darius, born Mar 31, 1818, married Lucinda Butts
Francis, born Dec 8, 1819, married Elizabeth Avery
Amy, born May 14 1823, married Elisha M. Rogers

CLARKE GARDNER (6)

Daniel (5), Daniel (4), Stephen (3), Benony (2), George (1).

Clarke, son of Daniel and Elizabeth (Clark) Gardner, was born Nov 24, 1766, married Elizabeth Harding, daughter of Capt Stephen Harding

Their children were
Ebenezer, born Sept, 1790
Mary R,
Charles,
Albert

CYRUS GARDNER (7)

Azel (6), David (5), David (4), Stephen (3), Benony (2), George (1).

Cyrus Gardner, son of Azel and Amy (Rogers) Gardner, was born June 25, 1815, died August 25, 1895, aged 80 years and two months Married Lucy Swan in 1840

Their children were born as follows

Orrin, born 1842, married Eveline Glover and lives at Gardiner's Lake, Conn

Norton, born 1844, died 1867

Charles, born March, 1847, married Nellie Lattimer and lives at Gardiner's Lake

Alvah Francis, born Oct 14, 1851 married Fannie Ross and lives at Yantic, Conn. They have one son, Frank Norton Gardner born Oct 12, 1880

Alvah F Gardner was born on the old homestead and lived there for many years, but has retired and is living at Yantic, Conn

Cyrus Gardner was a farmer and lived on what is known as the Gardner homestead which has been owned by the family for more than

200 years He was very active in both religious and political matters He represented his native town in the legislature in 1864, and held many important town offices and positions of trust. He was a trustee of the Gardiner's Lake Methodist Episcopal Church for many years, which office he held at the time of his death

LYDIA SMITH MORGAN (7)

Jerusha Gardner (6), Jonathan (5), Jonathan (4), Stephen (3), Benony (2), George (1)

Lydia Smith Morgan, daughter of Avery and Jerusha (Gardner) Morgan, was born Oct 7, 1806, at Bozrah, Conn Married Eliphalet Adams Bulkeley, son of John Charles and Sally (Taintor) Bulkeley, of Colchester, Conn Jan, 1830

The children were born as follows:
Mary, born Oct 21, 1833
Charles Edwin, born Dec 16, 1835
Morgan Gardner, born Dec 26, 1837.
Mary Jerusha, born Sept 27, 1843
Eliphalet Adams, born Dec 17, 1848
William Henry, born Mar 2, 1849

EBENEZER GARDNER (7)

Clarke (6), Daniel (5), Daniel (4), Sephen (3), Benony (2), George (1).

Ebenezer, son of Clark and Elizabeth (Harding) Gardner, was born Sept, 1790 married Matilda Denison Welch. She was born January, 1793, died 1881 at Hartford, Conn

Their children were
Edward E,
Henry Vibber born March 24, 1817
Joanna Foote,
Lester Cotton.

REV AUSTIN GARDNER (7)

Roderick (6), Jonathan, Jr (5), Jonathan (4), Stephen (3) Benony (2), George (1).

Austin Gardner, son of Roderick and Amy (Miner) Gardner, was born July 2, 1826. Married Emily Jane Baker daughter of Marshall and Betsey (Noble) Baker, of Benson, Vermont, in Hamilton, North Carolina, June 28, 1854

Children were born to them as follows
Dwight Baker, born June 16, 1855
Genevieve Theresa, born February 5, 1857.
Samuel Austin, born June 28, 1858
Harry David John, born April 19, 1860, died November 26, 1888
Frederick Robertson, born July 16, 1866, died Nov. 13, 1868

"My first schooling, aside from the common school, was at Bacon Academy Colchester Conn, in 1844 I did not begin a collegiate education until 1849, at East Greenwich Rhode Island I am an alumnus of that institution, matriculating at Wesleyan University in 1852, the class of 56 Was married at Hamilton, North Carolina, to Emily J Baker, of Benson, Vermont, June 28, 1854 Was principal of the Normal Academy of Manchester, Conn, 1856-8, and in the fall of 1858 entered the theological institute of East Windsor Hill and graduated in 1860

"My first parish was West Grandville, Mass, where I was ordained October 1860 In 1867 was called to found the Union church at Ludlow Mills, six miles east of Springfield In 1869 I was called to Canton Center, Conn, and January 1, 1873, to West Suffield, Conn I was then called to Buckingham, Conn, in 1876 and was installed pastor till 1889, when I was called to Warren, Conn, where I remained eight years In 1897 was called to Ashford, Conn, and retired to Willington in 1901, and am serving the church there at the present time

"It will be forty-six years the thirtieth of this month (October, 1906) since my ordination I am a life member of the A B C F M, the A M A, Seaman Friend Society, the Bible Society and am life director of the Congregational Missionary Society and the American Tract Society

"My life has been a busy one I have had remarkable health and strength up to four score years surely I have been under the care of an indulgent Providence, of whom I can only say from the depths of my heart, "Blessed be His holy name forever and forever"

The above remarkable letter came to the writer from this aged man of God When we began correspondence and till we received his parental line we concluded we were corresponding with a man of middle life

We have received from this aged father much family record that he has supplied from memory and to understand he is past the four score years with the blessing of memory is remarkable Many of the families we had secured the data from record and compared with what he gave us from memory and found him correct We look forward to the national reunion when we trust he will be spared to meet with us and enjoy the fellowship of this large family that will gather at Newport and Narragansett

MORGAN GARDNER BULKELEY (8)

Lydia Smith Morgan (7), Jerusha Gardner (6), Jonathan (5), Jonathan (4), Stephen (3), Benony (2), George (1).

Morgan Gardner Bulkeley, son of Eliphalet A and Lydia S (Morgan) Bulkeley, was born Dec 26, 1837, at East Haddam, Middlesex County, Conn Married Francis Briggs Houghton, daughter of James Frank and Caroline L Houghton, who resides at San Francisco, Cal

To them was born the following children

Morgan Gardner, Jr born Dec 25, 1885

Eleanor Houghton, born April 7 1893

Houghton, born August 9, 1896

Morgan Gardner Bulkeley, Sr., was educated in the district school of his native town and in the district and high school of Hartford, Conn, to which city his father removed in October, 1846 Commenced a business life in Brooklyn, New York, 1851 In 1872 returned to Connecticut and located in Hartford Has been identified with the business of the municipality and as a member of the Court of Common Council and as Mayor of the city from 1880 to 1888 Was chosen governor of the state of Conenctiut in 1889 and held the office until 1893 In January, 1905, was chosen United States Senator for the six-year term commencing March 4, 1905 Senator Bulkeley is connected with the following historical and Patriotic Societies Society of the Loyal Legion, Grand Army of the Republic, Department Commander of Conencticut, President of the Sons of the Revolution, Sons of the American Revolution, President of the Society of the war of 1812

HENRY VIBBER GARDNER (8).

Ebenezer (7), Clarke (6), Daniel (5), Daniel (4), Stephen (3), Benony (2), George (1)

Son of Ebenezer and Matilda D (Welch) Gardner, was born March 24, 1817, married Mary Foote, of Elizabeth, New Jersey, April 19, 1846

Their children were·

Marietta,

Harriette Foote,

Mary Watson

SAMUEL AUSTIN GARDNER (8).

Austin (7), Roderick (6), Jonathan, Jr (5), Jonathan (4), Stephen (3), Benony (2), George (1)

Samuel Austin Gardner, son of Austin and Emily Jane (Baker) Gardner, was born June 28, 1858 Married Mary E Fisk

The following children were born to them

Harold Irving,

Amy L ,

Linda B

Harold Irving Gardner graduated at Yale in 1904, and is a Senior in Hartford Theological Seminary

HARRY DAVID JOHN GARDNER (8)

Austin (7), Roderick (6), Jonathan, Jr. (5), Jonathan (4), Stephen (3), Benony (2), George (1).

Harry David John Gardner, son of Austin and Emily Jane (Baker) Gardner, was born April 19, 1860 Died November 26 1888. Graduated at Williston Seminary in 1880 Amherst College in 1884, Hartford Theological Seminary 1887. Was called to be a missionary with the Zulu mission as the strategic point He was to have married Miss Mary J Hills and to go to South Africa early in 1889, but was seized with appendicitis and died, after an illness of only three days at the age of twenty-eight, and is buried in Buckingham Connecticut, where his father was pastor about fourteen years He was a fine singer, organist and preacher and beloved by all who knew him

Rev William Gardner, Rio, Wis, says of him

"Of Harry Gardner's college life it seems scarcely necessary to say anything to his classmates Chosen captain of our class, nine at our first class meeting, he was prominent in athletics all through his course, playing in nearly every position on the college nine with an enthusiasm and success which made him a general favorite, while his manly, straightforward disposition won the sincere respect of all who knew him

His name, which combined the names of his father's seminary class-mates, commemorated the fact that he was seminary class boy He prepared for college at Williston Seminary and in the fall of 1884 entered Hartford Theological Seminary where he grew rapidly in power of thought and expression 'I wish some one had waked me up four years ago,' he said in a letter written at the close of his first year there

In college he was very diffident when speaking in public, but he became a ready and forcible speaker whose words carried weight because of the whole souled earnestness and honesty of the man behind them

He was engaged to Miss Mary J Hills and expected to be married in December, and to sail with her in January to his chosen field of work —a place where no one else wanted to go—Natal, Africa

While making the final preparations for marriage and departure, he was attacked by perityphlitis, which developed into peritonitis, and caused his death on the fourth day of his illness, at the home of his parents, Rev Austin and Emily J Gardner"

CHARLES HENRY GARDNER (9).

Henry Vibber (8), Ebenezer (7), Clarke (6), Daniel (5), Daniel (4), Stephen (3), Benony (2), George (1)

Charles Henry Gardner was born January 23, 1849 Died August 8, 1896 Married, first, Annie Parker, of Pittsburg, Pa She died in 1881 Second Margaret Morrison Jackson, daughter of William Bennet and Elizabeth (Blake) Jackson, of Utica, N Y, April 26, 1887

Children by first wife were

Irvine Parker, born January 2, 1875, at Fayetteville, N Y

William Thaw, born April 23, 1877, at Fayetteville, N Y

Charles Henry, born Dec 20, 1879, at Utica, N Y

Children by second wife were

Arthur born Feb 21, 1888

Anson Blake, born Aug 19, 1890

Edward Summers, born Oct, 1894

Charles Henry Gardner was born at Long Hill, Conn Was a member of the class of 1870 at Trinity College, Hartford, Conn B D Neshota, Wis Trinity Church Clayville, was his first parish

After his first marriage he resided in Fayetteville, where he was in charge of Trinity church.

His first wife died in Utica, N Y, where Mr Gardner was rector of Trinity Parish for nine years In the Fall of 1886 he accepted the charge of Trinity Cathedral, Omaha, Neb, and was Dean there until his death

His three younger sons were born in Omaha, Neb, and all his sons are living, the three older being in business in the west, Irvine and Charles at White Earth, Minn, William T at Ashland, Wis The younger sons reside with their mother in Washington, D. C.

ELLA GARDNER (9).

Henry Vibber (8), Ebenezer (7), Clarke (6), Daniel (5), Daniel (4), Stephen (3), Benony (2), George (1)

Married Dr Charles Hart of Bethel, Conn
They have several children

MARIETTA GARDNER (9).

Henry Vibber (8), Ebenezer (7), Clarke (6), Daniel (5), Daniel (4), Stephen (3), Benony (2), George (1)

Unmarried Resides at Brockport, N Y

FREDERICK GARDNER (9).

Henry Vibber (8), Ebenezer (7), Clarke (6), Daniel (5), Daniel (4), Stephen (3), Benony (2), George (1)

Married Nellie —— He is not living. He resided at East Aurora, N Y

They had several children

MARY GARDNER (9)

Henry Vibber (8), Ebenezer (7), Clarke (6), Daniel (5), Daniel (4), Stephen (3), Benony (2), George (1)

Married Thomas Dobson of Brockport, N Y
They have two sons and one daughter

GEORGE E GARDNER (9).

Henry Vibber (8), Ebenezer (7), Clarke (6), Daniel (5), Daniel (4), Stephen (3), Benony (2), George (1)

Married Jessie Lewis of Lowville, N Y He was a student at Fayetteville, N Y, at Hobart College, Geneva, N Y., and at Berkley Divinity School, Middletown, Conn, and a clergyman of the Protestant Episcopal church at Utica, N Y, and at St Joseph, Mo, where he died about 1892

He left no children

Henry Vibber Gardner (8), father of the foregoing was a clergyman at Elizabeth, N J

His wife was Miss Mary Foote of Elizabeth. N. J

BENJAMIN BILLINGS GARDNER.

Benjamin B, son of William Benjamin and Mary Ball (Billing) Gardner, was born May 25 1865, at New London, Conn He married Mary Rogers, daughter of James Strickland Rogers, of New London.

Child

Charles Benjamin Gardner, born Sept 8, 1890, in New London, Conn

RUFUS GARDNER

Rufus Gardner was born in Newport, R I, 1747 and died in 1809, in New London, Conn He was Captain of a sloop which plied between New York and New London for years, carrying freight and passengers, from the close of the Revolutionary war until his death He was an old sailor during the Revoution He was a mason, the emblem of that fraternity appearing on his grave stone in Cedar Grove cemetery He married Lydia Harris, who was born in New London, and came of an old family

Children

Christopher, died young

Rufus, died young

Mercy, married a Mr Williams of New York

Lydia, married Robert Buttles of New York.

Henry

Lucy, married James McKibben, a New York broker

Douglas W

Harriet, married a Mr Burke of New York

Champlin, married a Miss Packer

HENRY GARDNER

Henry Gardner son of Rufus and Lydia (Harris) Gardner, was born February 21 1798, on Ocean Ave, New London Died August 20, 1863, at Waterford, Conn He kept store and tavern in Waterford at the corner of Old Lyme Road and the road to Jordan village He was post master for more than thirty years from Jackson's administration to the time of Lincoln, being first appointed by President Jackson as a staunch Jacksonian Democrat He was a radical politician, and a leader in the local ranks of the people He was an intelligent man, well qualified and had a great memory He compromised on the slave question because he was opposed to the Rebellion

He was a man of determined disposition and could be stern at times, though he was of a genial temperament He was a very honorable man, scrupulous to a degree in financial matters, and set a fine example to his family and associates He was a good christian, a devout member of the Baptist church and always had evening prayers in his home He married (1) in 1824 Mary Miner, daughter of Stephen Miner of Waterford, who was a Revolutionary pensioner She died in the fall of 1839

Children

Mary Miner, married John Powers of Black Point, East Lyme, and died there

Henry, Jr, married Matilda Clark of East Lyme and lived and died in that place He was a fisherman by occupation

Lucy Wheeler married Lyman Clark, a fisherman of Niantic and is living in Middletown with her daughter

Christopher was a sailor and died at Snug Harbor

Andrew Jackson, was a carpenter, died 1864, married Mary E Manwaring of East Lyme

Thomas W, living in New London, Conn Married widow of Andrew Jackson, his brother

On March 1, 1840, Henry Gardner married (2) Wealthy Ann Powers, who died February 22, 1893, aged sixty-nine years She was a daughter of Joshua and Wealthy Ann (Morgan) Powers and a descendant of Richard Rose Morgan who settled in what is known as the Gilead district of the town of Waterford, and was granddaughter of Samuel Powers who came from Waterford, Iowa, and married Zilah Rogers, daughter of James Rogers who was among the first settlers of that place Samuel Powers settled at Black Point, being one of the first settlers of New London To Henry and Wealthy Ann (Powers) Gardner was born the following children.

Washington R

James Morgan, born Oct 5, 1845, is a physician and public speaker, is engaged in teaching English in European Countries He is an accomplished linquist, speaking English, Italian, Spanish, French and German, and accompanies parties as Doctor and interpreter He married Flora Rogers, daughter of George F Rogers of Fulton Market, N Y One child: Violet, who married Robert Kissick of Westerly, R I He died 1904, leaving one son Robert Gardner Kissick Mrs Kissick married (2) Dr Thomas Edward Robinson of Westerly, R I

Wealthy Ann, born Jan, 1848 married William Davis of Noank and is living at West Mystic, Conn No children

Lydia Elizabeth, born 1850, married George W. Hewitt, of Waterford.

Harriet Burke, born 1852, married Fitch S. Comstock, died same year of marriage

Ella, born 1855, became the (2) wife of Fitch S Comstock Children, Carrie Comstock, married Dr George Culver, of Jersey City, where they live Ira Comstock lives with his parents

Carrie, died young

WASHINGTON R. GARDNER

Washington R, son of Henry and Wealthy Ann (Powers) Gardner was born in Waterford in a house which stood at the forks of the Lyme Turnpike and the Jordan Road He received his early schooling in Waterford, and later attended Bartlet Grammar school in New London, taught by Professor Jennings, leaving same at the age of seventeen years he took up the carpenter trade under John L Beckwith, of East Lyme, remaining with him about one year Living in New London, he was with Bishop Bros, manufacturers of sash blinds, etc, for three years was subsequently in New Haven and had charge of the window frame department of Hatch and Norton for six years In the fall of 1869 he located on the farm known as the Chapel homestead, the birthplace of his wife, comprising 60 acres, and has there carried on general farming together with plying his trade as contractor and builder, in which he has met with substantial success

Mr Gardner has been a factor in the administration of public affairs for a number of years He has served for several years on the Board of relief in his town, and has been chairman of the Board of Assessors for the past eight years

In 1883 he was representative in the General Assembly of the State from Waterford and served as a member on Humane Institutions and again represented his town in 1884 when he served as a member of the Finance Committee, and is now the Democratic candidate for State Senator in the twentieth Senatorial District His political connection is with the Democratic party

Fraternally he is a member of Union Lodge No 31, F & A M, of New London, Pequot Lodge, I O O F, of New London In religious connection he is a member of the First Baptist Church of Waterford with which his wife also united

Mr Gardner was married Nov 26, 1863, to Mary Adelaide Chappell, daughter of Rev Gurdon T Chappell Three children

Harry Chappell, born Nov 5 1869, died aged 18 years with typhoid

James Isham, born Aug 22, 1875, in Waterford, attended the Nathan Hale Grammar school of New London, The Hopkins Grammar school of New Haven, and the Hill House High school of New Haven, which latter place he graduated in 1898

He is book-keeper for C D Boss & Son, New London Conn He married Earnestine Miller Goddard of New London, Conn, formerly teacher in the Robert Bartlett School

Strong Griswold born June 28 1879, at Waterford Attended the Nathan Hale Grammar School at New London, The Hill House High school in New Haven and the Bulkeley High School at New London, graduating from the latter in 1899 He is a commercial agent and traveling salesman for Austin Nichols & Co, New York City He married Edith Rosamond Kenyon of Waterford, Conn

MAINE.

DR. SYLVESTER GARDINER (4)

William (3), Benony (2), George (1).

Sylvester Gardiner seventh, and youngest child of William and Abigail (Remington) Gardner, was born June 29, 1708 He married Ann Gibbons of Boston, September 20-December 11, 1732

Their children were born as follows

William, born June 13, 1736, died without issue.

John, born December 4, 1737.

James, born September 9, 1739.

Ann, born April 21, 1741

Hannah, born July 18, 1743

Rebecca,

Abigail.

Dr Gardiner married, second, Love Epps of Salem, Mass She died and he married, third, Catherin Goldthwait, who survived him and married a Mr Powell He had no children by his last two wives.

Sylvester Gardiner, son of William Gardiner, known as "William of Narragansett," was born on the farm next south of the Ferry estate

His health was feeble and his constitution slender. His father was apprehensive that his system was not sufficiently robust to constitute him an efficient farmer Upon the expression of these apprehensions, his son-in-law, Doctor McSparren, suggested the propriety of educating this son for some professional pursuit and that the expenses of obtaining such an education should be deducted from the portion of the estate intended for him He promised that if his father-in-law would permit him to have the direction of the education of the son upon these terms, he would make him more of a man than all of the rest of the family

The father replied "take him" Doctor McSparren then placed him in Boston to complete his primary education, and subsequently directed his attention to the study of medicine He was then sent to England and France, where he empoyed the best advantages for eight years

Once upon the Continent the mind of the student imbued with the firm principles of his brother-in-law, received a shock in the licentiousness of the Parisian customs His sojourn in France was during the minority of Louis XV, when the agitator of the South Sea Bubble and the shameless profligacy of the nobles were sowing the seeds of the terrible revolution. The striking piety and good sense of the youth carried him in safety through all the dangers to which he was exposed, and he returned to America with a degree of professional knowledge unexampled at that period

He not only practiced successfully but promoted the knowledge of the healing art, by reading lectures, illustrated by anatomical preparations He was among the most distinguished of his profession in the day in which he lived.

By his professional success and by the means of a large establishment for the importation and sale of drugs he accumulated an immense estate and purchased large tracts of land in Maine

As long ago as 1640, the land, including what is now the city of Gardiner, Maine, and extending "from the Cobbosseecontee River to the Western Ocean, fifteen miles on either side of the Kennebec," had been granted by Governor William Bradford to "the freeman of the Colony of New Plymouth."

This Company made various attempts to settle the Country, which proved failures for several reasons, among which were the severity of the climate, the number of hostile Indians, and the company's monopoly of trade and fishing, at a time when monopolies were particularly distasteful to England where they were giving way to freer systems

For nearly a century the land in that vicinity only occasionally leased, and then under restrictions, was held mainly as a hunting and fishing ground In accordance with the progress of the Nation, an increase of settlers was deemed desirable, and in 1749, a corporation was formed under the name of the 'Plymouth Company,' consisting of nine proprietors who immediately set about the improvement of the "Kennebec Purchase" The company, for the most part was made up of staunch adherents to the English Crown, who at once chose Dr Gardiner perpetual moderator of their meetings, and committed to him, trust calling for the most judicial management. Still there was no great influx of settlers, and in 1754 Dr Gardiner determined to take more energetic measures He obtained a grant of land embracing Gardiner and Pittston, though its limits were not included in these towns. He had selected the situation with a practical eye, because of the facility for mills afforded by the waters of the Cobbossee Already a large sloop which he had built, was running from Boston to the Kennebec, and before long, he had cleared a farm of four hundred acres in Gardinerstown as Gardiner was then called, and had erected upon it a suitable dwelling-house, in which lived his son William, charged with the care of the estate

Even then it was not easy to procure settlers, especially so as the tide of immigrants from England had been checked with her war with France But Dr Gardiner spared no efforts in this direction and gradually increased the size of the little colony at great expense and trouble to himself

In other localities he encouraged the foreign element, Dresden, for instance, being colonized by Germans and Irish, but it seemed to have fallen to the lot of Gardinerstown to attract for the most part, an English speaking population Of all his vast estate in Maine, which was even then valued at $150,000, and which included much of Dresden, Pittston, Chelsea, Augusta, Hallowell, Norridgewock and Winslow Dr Gardiner showed an especial preference for the growing town that bore his name, and though the money he spent to aid the settlers was often a total loss to him, he was unwearied in his efforts for their comfort and encouragement So energetic was he that before 1772 he had built in Gardinerstown two saw-mills, a grist mill, a fulling mill, a potash manufactory, a wharf, and many houses and stores

When we consider the difficulty to travel in the early days, those achievements seem little less than wonderful If the great water-way of the Kennebec was closed, since there was no carriage roads, then the owner's visits to his estate must have led him through narrow woodland paths or over the frozen surface of the river, often heavy with drifting snow, and beset with dangers from wild beasts and savage Indians. It was in the eighteenth century that Madam Sarah Knight, the school teacher of Benjamin Franklin, had journeyed along the more perilous route from Boston to New York, and this feat, hitherto unequaled by woman, had given her lasting fame. So wonderful indeed did her trip appear, that upon her return the worthy dame wrote an account of her hardships and thrilling adventures, and farther chronicled her deliverance with a diamond upon her school room window.—

"Through many toils and many frights
I have returned, poor Sarah Knights
Over great rocks and many stones
God has preserved from fractured bones."

As late as 1750 'Chairs" were among the favorite conveyances in towns and cities, though the women still rode much upon horseback, and here and there appeared the clumsy calash, or the heavy square-typed chaise.

In 1755 we find recorded a great event in the history of Maine.—"Judge Paine passed through Wilk in a chaise, and all the village thronged to Kimball's tavern to see it."

In the Revolution Dr. Gardiner adhered to the royal cause and when the enemy evacuated Boston he went to Nova Scotia and finally went to England, and his great estate was confiscated and sold, embracing nearly one hundred thousand acres in Maine.

In a letter to Mr., afterward Governor, Bowdoin, dated Poole, Eng., April 10, 1783, he says: "There is now an entire change in our ministry which you will hear of before this reaches you and with them most likely a change of political measures. God grant us all grace to put an end to this devouring war, so contrary to our most holy religion, and unite us all once more in that bond of peace and brotherly union so necessary to the happiness of both countries, which God grant may soon take place, and give us all an opportunity once more to greet one another as friends."

Upon the conclusion of peace he returned to this country and resided at Newport in his native state, where he took a house and resumed the practice of physics and surgery, which he followed until his death, which took place after a short illness August 8, 1786, in the eightieth year of his age.

The colors of the shipping in the harbor were displayed half mast and every other mark of respect shown by the inhabitants on the mournful occasion.

Dr. Gardiner was a munificent patron of the church and contributed ten acres of land for a glebe (parsonage) at Gardiner in Maine, and twenty-eight pounds sterling for the minister, forever, which has been the partial means of sustaining a respectable church in that state.

JOHN GARDNER (5)

Sylvester (4), William (3), Benony (2), George (1)

John son of Dr Sylvester and Ann (Gibbons) Gardner, was born 1731, died 1793 Married Margaret Harries, of Haverfordwest, Wales.

Children

John Sylvester John, born 1765, died 1830

Anne,

William.

John Gardner was sent to England to complete his education; studied law at the Inner Temple, and was admitted to practice in the Courts of Westminster Hall He was an intimate associate at this time with Churchill, the poet, and John Wilks, the reformer He practiced a short time in the Welsh circuit and married a Miss Margaret Harries, of a respectable family of South Wales, but being impatient to get a lucrative practice, he procured the appointment of Attorney General of the Island of St Christopher in the West Indies, where he removed with his family about the year 1765 He practiced law with great success at St Christopher and the Island of Jamaica until the termination of the American Revolution by the peace of 1783 when he removed to his native town

He removed in 1786 to an estate left by his father at Powalborough, in the district of Maine, where he practiced law and whence he was sent as representative to the Massachusetts legislature from the year 1789 till his death, which happened by the loss of a packet in which he took passage for Boston for the purpose of attending the General Court in 1793-4

He was a thorough republican and violent whig in politics, and in religion was a Unitarian, in consequence of which he took a leading part in the alteration of the liturgy of Kings Chapel, Boston, and other changes by which that church became a Unitarian Congregational Society

From a dislike of his principles, both in politics and religion, his father by his will settled the greater portion of his estate upon his sister s son, Robert Hallowell, who afterward took the name of Robert Hallowell Gardner

The forfeited property in Maine of Dr Sylvester Gardner was chiefly recovered by his heirs, in consequence of some informality in the legal process of the Attorney General.

ANN GARDNER (5)

Dr Sylvester (4), William (3), Benony (2), George (1)

Ann, daughter of Sylvester and Ann (Gibbons) Gardner, was born April 21, 1741, died 1807 Married early in life Arthur Brown, son of the powerful Irish Earl of Altamont The Episcopal Church erected at Gardinerstown, Maine, was named St Ann, for this daughter

She was a famous beauty and was painted by Copley in the guise of the huntress Diana

Children

John Brown, died 1814 Married, 1784, Rosa Mary, daughter of Admiral Sir Richard Hughes Children Arthur of Newton, Roscommon, Ireland, born 1786, died 1870

George Townsend.

HANNAH GARDNER (5).

Dr Sylvester (4), William (3), Benony (2), George (1)

Hannah Gardner, daughter of Sylvester and Ann (Gibbons) Gardner, was born July 18, 1743-4; died 1796 Married Robert Hallowell, of Boston, 1771 He was born 1739, died 1818

Children were:

Hannah, born 1773, died 1796

Nancy, born 1774, died 1775

Anna, born 1776, died 1800

Rebecca, born 1777, died 1779

Robert, born 1782, died 1864 His name was changed to Robert Hallowell Gardner after he reached his estate

Robert Hallowell was Collector of Customs in the port of Boston at the time of his marriage to Hannah Gardner He was of a fine English family, and as evidenced by his epitaph in the graveyard of Christ Church, "a man of firm integrity, distinguished courtesy, and strong affection" He was the father of Maine's beloved "Squire Gardner"

ABIGAIL GARDNER (5).

Dr Sylvester (4), William (3), Benony (2), George (1)

Abigail Gardner, daughter of Sylvester and Ann (Gibbons) Gardner, married Oliver Whipple, of Cumberland, Rhode Island, afterwards of Portsmouth, R I

Their children were

Sylvester Gardner, unmarried

Hannah B married Hon Frederic Allen, a noted poet and geologist Children Charles, Edward, Hannah, Eleanor Ann, married Martin Gay, M D, of Boston, Margaret, married —— Elton; Augustus, unmarried

Abigail (Gardner) Whipple was a woman of most exalted character She gave proof of her deep piety in a solemn written covenant still preserved, in which she dedicated herself unchangeably to God This covenant she renewed in writing from time to time, and, for this purpose, was raised by her attendants to a sitting posture upon her deathbed, where she traced the few falterinf lines of a completed vow

REBECCA GARDNER (5)

Dr Sylvester (4), William (3), Benony (2), George (1)

Rebecca, daughter of Dr Sylvester and Ann (Gibbons) Gardner, married, 1763, Philip Dumaresq of Boston who traced his lineage from nobles of the Isle of Jersey He was born 1738.

Their children were
James, born 1771, died 1826 Drowned in the Kennebec river
Philip, born 1772, died 1806 No children
Francis, M D., of Jamaica, W I Had descendants
Sylvester, died young.
Anne, married (1) John Ferguson of Ayrshire, Scotland (2) Charles Gow
Rebecca,
Susannah,
Francis,
Hannah,
Abigail

REV. JOHN SYLVESTER JOHN GARDNER (6).

John (5), Dr. Sylvester (4), William (3), Benony (2), George (1).

John Sylvester John, son of John and Margaret (Harries) Gardner, married 1794, Mary Howard of Augusta She died at Newport, R I., Sept. 16 aged 74

Children.
William Howard, born 1797, died 1882
Mary Louisa,
Elizabeth, unmarried

John Sylvester John Gardner was rector of Trinity Church, Boston, from 1805 till his death, which occurred July 29, 1830

He was an eloquent Divine and was highly esteemed by society for his talents and virtue He wrote the English language with great purity and elegance and was not without a happy talent for poetry

The following from Channing's 'Early Recollections of Newport

'The peculiar salubrity of the climate of Newport attracted a large number of clergymen from various quarters during the summer months The fact that many intelligent Southerners made it their home, drew attention to its charms, and even then were quite noticeable the handsome carriages and gay horses which they kept

Among the ministers I frequently listened to was Dr Gardner and others The arrival of the gentleman from time to time caused a great stir in the town, and the churches, for the time being, were thronged by those who seldom attended church, except to hear "some new thing"

Dr Gardner, of Trinity Church, Boston, was wonderfully presentable—of good figure and expressive countenance He had one peculiar habit—that of carrying an umbrella, however fair the weather

His mode of reading was admirable A gift to which no other clergyman during his day could lay claim"

ANN GARDNER (6).

John (5), Dr. Sylvester (4), William (3), Benony (2), George (1).

Ann Gardner, daughter of John and Margaret (Harries) Gardner, married James N Lithgow

Children.

Alfred, unmarried
Llewellyn, unmarried
Louisa, married Mr Williams

WILLIAM GARDNER (6)

John (5), Dr. Sylvester (4), William (3), Benony (2), George (1).

William Gardner, son of John and Margaret (Harries) Gardner, married Sarah, daughter of Richard Allen of Boston

Children

Margaret Harries, married Thomas Nelson of Castine One child, Margaret Patterson. Married Rev Thomas Fales.

George married Caroline Tallman of Bath One child William, unmarried.

Mary Anne, born 1812 Married Isaac Elder of Portland. One child, Mary Anne Osgood

JAMES DUMARESQ (6)

Rebecca Gardner (5), Dr Sylvester (4), William (3), Benony (2), George (1).

James, son of Philip and Rebecca (Gardner) Dumarseq, married, 1797, Sarah Farwell, daughter of Ebenezer Farwell, of Vassalboro, Maine

Children were

Philip, of Swan Island, born 1804, died 1863; married, 1836, Margaretta, daughter of Francis DeBlois of Boston

Jane Francis Rebecca

Louisa, married John Rice. No children

ROBERT HALLOWELL GARDNER (6)

Hannah Gardner (5), Dr. Sylvester (4), William (3), Benony (2), George (1).

Robert H, son of Robert and Hannah (Gardner) Hallowell, was born 1782, died 1864 After reaching his estate he took the name of Gardner Married Emma Jane Tudor of Boston, Mass 1805 She was born 1785, died 1865

Children were

Emma Jane born 1806, died 1845 Unmarried

Anne Hallowell, born 1807, died 1876

Robert Hallowell born 1809, died 1886, married Sarah Fenwick Jones She was born 1814, died 1869 No children

Delia Tudor, born 1812, died 1836, married George Jones No children

Lucy Vaughn, born 1814, died 1847 Unmarried

John William Tudor, born 1817, died 1879

Henrietta, born 1820, died 1880, married, 1846, Richard Sullivan

Frederic, born 1822, died 1889

Eleanor Harriet.

WILLIAM HOWARD GARDNER (7).

John Sylvester John (6), John (5), Dr Sylvester (4), William (3), Benony (2), George (1).

William Howard, son of John Sylvester John and Mary (Howard) Gardner, married, 1823, Caroline Perkins, she died 1867. She was the daughter of Handasyde Perkins of Boston

Children

William Prescott, born 1824, died 1860

Edward, born 1825 died 1859 Married Sophia Mifflin, Philadelphia Children William Howard, Eugenia, Edward Gardner, Elizabeth, Maud

Mary Cary, born 1827, died 1863 Married 1856, William Nye Jarvis of Boston.

John Sylvester, born 1830; died 1856 Unmarried

Caroline Louisa, born 1832, died 1888 Unmarried

Charles Perkins, born 1836 Married 1864, Emma Fields Glidden Child Mary Caroline, born 1867 Married 1887 William Robinson Cabot One child, Mary Geraldine, born 1892

MARY LOUISA GARDNER (7)

John Sylvester John (6), John (5), Dr Sylvester (4), William (3), Benony (2), George (1)

Mary Louisa Gardner, daughter of John Sylvester John and Mary (Howard) Gardner, married John Cushing of Boston.

Children

John Gardner, married Susan Dexter Children. John and Alice

Thomas Forbes, married Child· Edith

Robert Maynard, married. Children Grafton Dulany, Mary Louisa, Howard Gardner, Olivia

William,

Mary Louisa, married Edward Boit Children Edward D died young John, died young Florence, Jane Hubbard, Mary Louisa, Julia Overing

FREDERICK GARDNER (7).

Robert H. (6), Hannah (5) Dr Sylvester (4), William (3), Benony (2), George (1)

Frederick, son of Robert H and Emma J (Tudor) Gardner, married Caroline Vaughn, daughter of William of Hallowell, Me

Children were

Emma Jane, married, 1872, Rev Henry Ferguson of Stamford, Conn Children were Samuel, Eleanor Margaret, Henry Gardner, Charles Vaughn

William Tudor, born 1850, died 1863.

Frederic, married 1886, Sallie Merrick, of Germantown, Penn Children Frederic Merrick, William Henry, Francis Vaughn

Henrietta,

Alfred, born 1862, died 1879

ANNE HALLOWELL GARDNER (7).

Robert H (6), Hannah (5), Dr. Sylvester (4), William (3), Benony (2), George (1)

Anne H, daughter of Robert H and Emma J (Tudor) Gardner, married, 1832, Francis Richards He was born 1805, died 1858

Children were

Francis Gardner, born 1833, died 1884, married Anne Ashburner, daughter of Samuel of London Children· Francis Ashburner, Anne Hallowell

George, born 1837, died 1837

George Henry.

Sarah, born 1840, died 1855

John Tudor, married Cora Howard Children Amy, Madelene, Dorothy, Ruth

Robert Hallowell, married Ellen Swallow

Henry married Laura Elizabeth Howe, daughter of Dr Samuel G Howe Children Alice Maud, Rosalind, Henry Howe Julia Ward, Muad, born 1881, died 1882, John, Laura Elizabeth

JOHN WILLIAM TUDOR GARDNER (7).

Robert H. (6), Hannah (5), Dr Sylvester (4), William (3) Benony (2), George (1).

John W T, son of Robert H and Emma J (Tudor) Gardner, married, 1854, Anne Elizabeth (Hays) West, daughter of John Hays of Carlisle, Penn

Children were

Robert Hallowell

Eleanor

Anna Hays, born 1859, died 1860

Francis Richards, born 1860, died 1880

John Hays, John Tudor, twins

JANE FRANCIS REBECCA DUMARESQ (7)

James (6), Rebecca Gardner (5), Dr. Sylvester (4), William (3), Benony (2), George (1).

Jane F R daughter of James and Sarah (Farwell) Dumaresq, married Thomas Handasyde Perkins of Boston

Children were

Thomas Handasyde, married Elizabeth Jones Chadwick Children. Jesse Grant, Mary

Augustus Thorndike, died 1891, married Susan Hammond Timmins Children Henry Dumaresq, Elizabeth Greene, Winifred Scott Singleton

Phillip Duramesq

Francis Codman, born 1830 died 1842

Louisa Dumaresq, married William Morris Hunt Children Morris, Elleanor, Enid Dumaresq, Mabel, Paul

PHILLIP DUMARESQ (7)

James (6), Rebecca Gardner (5), Dr Sylvester (4), William (3), Benony (2), George (1).

Phillip Dumaresq, son of James and Sarah (Farwell) Dumaresq, married Margaret, daughter of Francis DeBlois, of Boston Their children were

Phillip Kearney married Sophia Hurlbert Children Philip, Sophia, Lillian, Margaretta, Coletta

James Saumerez,

Herbert,

Francis,

Margaretta,

Frances Perkins, born 1840, died 1855

Florence Saumerez married, 1864, George Wheatland Children Philip Dumaresq, married Alice Ellerton Pratt, Florence Dumaresq, married Jacob Crowninshield

Rogers,

Peabody,

George

FREDERIC GARDINER (7).

Robert H (6), Hannah (5), Dr. Sylvester (4), William (3), Benony (2), George (1)

Frederic Gardner youngest son of Robert Hallowell and Emma Jane (Tudor) Gardiner was born at Oaklands, Gardiner, Maine, September 1822 Died July, 1889 Married Caroline Vaughan daughter of Oliver Vaughan of Hallowell, Maine, 1846 She was born July, 1825 Died January, 1906

Children were

Emma Jane, born October, 1847

William Tudor, born April, 1858, died 1863

Frederic born April, 1858

Henrietta born Feb , 1860

Alfred, born April 1862

EMMA JANE GARDINER (8)

Frederic (7), Robert H. (6), Hannah (5), Dr Sylvester (4), William (3), Benony (2) George (1).

Emma Jane Gardiner, daughter of Frederic and Caroline (Vaughan) Gardiner, was born October, 1847 Married to Rev Henry Ferguson M A LL D

Born April, 1847 Priest in the Episcopal Church Professor in Trinity College and lately Rector in St Paul's school, Concord, N H

He was son of John Ferguson

Children

Samuel, born Nov, 1874 B S M A Electrical Engineer Present address General Electrical Works, Schenectady, N Y

Eleanor Margaret, born June, 1876 Sculptor Graduate of the Students' Art League of New York

Henry, born June 1882 M A (Harvard), Geological Engineer. Present address, Cleveland Cliff Iron Works, Ishpeming, Mich

Charles Vaughan, born August, 1885 Student at Trinity College

FREDERIC GARDINER (8)

Frederic (7), Robert H. (6), Hannah (5), Dr Sylvester (4), William (3), Benony (2), George (1).

Frederic Gardiner, son of Frederic and Caroline (Vaughan) Gardner, was born April, 1858 Married Sally Merrick, September, 1885 She was born September, 1859 Daughter of William Henry Merrick Mr Gardiner ordained Presbyter in the Episcopal Church, Head Master of Yates

Children are

Frederic Merrick, born June, 1887

William Henry, born May, 1889

Frances Vaughan, born September, 1892

ROBERT HALLOWELL GARDINER (8).

John W T (7), Robert H (6), Dr Sylvester (4), William (3), Benony (2), George (1)

Robert H, son of John W T. and Ann E (Hays, West) Gardiner, married Alice, daughter of Edward Bangs, of Boston

Children were

Robert Hallowell,

Alice,

Sylvester, born 1889, died 1889

Anna Lowell,

William Tudor

Robert H Gardiner is one of the very modest members of this family In our correspondence with him early in the work we were not aware it was he to whom we were writing until apprised of the fact by another member of the family

We will reproduce a part of Mr Gardiner s address at the Philadelphia Convention on accepting the office of President of the Brotherhood of Saint Andrew, as well as the press notices of his parentage and life

"You have done me, through your counsel, a very great honor in electing me your President, and I thank you for it most warmly, and I assure you that with all my strength of heart and mind and soul I will try to show you that I appreciate it and to be a leader worthy of our great Brotherhood army For who could ask a nobler opportunity than to be the chosen leader of ten thousand men and boys, consecrated by daily converse with God our Father source of our life of body, mind and soul, to the splendid effort to bring men nearer to Christ through His Church?

For my part I would rather be President of this Brotherhood than have any other office in the gift of man For with all our weakness, all our errors, all our failures, we are seeking to lay the only foundation on which peace and righteousness, justice and morality ever have stood, or ever can stand, permanently No honor can be done to a man greater than to give him an opportunity for a useful service to the world, and the highest office is but the greatest opportunity for such service.

The most earnest efforts of a statesman and the philanthropist will come to naught unless the Nation and the individual rest firmly on the Rock of Ages—the only general and enduring foundation for national or individual peace, prosperity and righteousness You and I have chosen for the underlying and controlling motives of our lives the noble effort to bring all men to a personal allegiance to the King of Kings, that so, by the obedience of all men everywhere to His laws, His Kingdom may be established here and now upon this earth, and his world made what He means it to be"

TWO SKETCHES OF MR GARDINER.

1. By Rt. Rev Robert Codman, D. D., Bishop of Maine.

Since Mr Robert H. Gardiner has been elected President of the Brotherhood of St. Andrew several interesting biographical sketches have appeared in the Church papers, giving the facts of his life and ancestry We find him descended from a whole line of New England men, "furious and clamorous for the Church" We learn that he has been brought up in the atmosphere of Boston and Harvard University We see that he is constantly filling positions of trust and responsibility in the Church, and of late years, though a practicing lawyer in Boston, he has taken up his legal residence in Gardiner, Maine, that he might identify himself with and carry on the great Church interests there which were the life's work of his uncle, grandfather and great grandfather As they were, so is he now, Warden of Christ Church, Gardiner, member of the Standing Committee of Maine and delegate to both Diocesan and General Conventions Though a prominent trustee with immense business interests in Boston, he is an active member of the Board of Missions in Maine, Chairman of the College Committee of the Brotherhood Treasurer of the Christian Social Union and interested in every organized effort for Christian progress

These facts show the character of the man Filled with an all-absorbing desire to be useful to other men and make this world better because he has lived in it, he has fully persuaded himself that the power, the real lasting power for good, lies in Jesus Christ and in the work of His Church Through this faith he has learned to know and to love Christ with that personal devotion which enables a man to sacrifice all he can in the Master's service Hence his qualification and enthusiasm as a Brotherhood man With a gentle humility because he knows he is working, not in his own, but in his Master's strength, he has a wonderful persistency in pursuing his ends Thus firm, cheerful and always with a pleasant smile he wins his point in the end in spite of all obstacles He can take advice and weigh it He can say his prayers and wait, but at all times his sense of duty is his guide In his judgment he has all the advantage of a trained legal mind, never disturbed by temper or selfishness He has mixed with men as a fellowman, and with a genuine social interest in men If he errs in his judgment of men it is out of his sympathy for them and his hope for their better side Hence his qualification for the office of President of the Brotherhood But Mr Gardiner makes no "hobby" of the Brotherhood He believes that the Brotherhood vow is the Churchman's vow That the Brotherhood prayer is the Churchman's prayer, and that the Brotherhood work is best training in a Churchman's duty The Brotherhood is the training school for the sons of the Church to teach them how to be faithful and valiant soldiers of Christ

Mr Gardiner is a loyal Churchman—loyal to the Book of Common Prayer Yet he is not one of those who would harness his own or the devotion of others in the forms, beautiful as they are, in that one book With him the Prayer Book is the best form of fellowship with God, and he believes in using the Communion Service frequently and with special intention With his social instincts he recognizes the force of the Master s words, "If two of you shall agree on earth,' and he believes in the usefulness of Corporate Communions to promote the spiritual life in the Chapters, in order that in the power, of that life its members may be drawn closer to the Master and feel the greater enthusiasm for the Master's work He does not believe in work without prayer. There, after all, lies the great power in Mr Gardiner's life He has his faults and weaknesses as all men have He knows what struggle is because he has struggled But he is a prayerful man in private, in his family and in the Church May God help him teach all who meet him the lesson of lessons how to pray and how to pray better!

II. By Edmund Billings, Boston, Second Vice-President Brotherhood of St Andrew in the United States.

Mr Gardiner's first ancestors came from England to Rhode Island in 1635 The family settled in Boston Neck, Narragansett, where they were prominent citizens and Churchmen The Rev James McSparren, a Missionary of the Society for the Propagation of the Gospel, married Hannah, a daughter of William Gardiner, and it was through his influence that his brother-in-law, Sylvester Gardiner, was sent to Europe to receive there a thorough education as a physician On his return Sylvester established himself in Boston, where he gained a large practice He marritd a daughter of Dr John Gibbons, of Boston, who is mentioned in a letter to the Bishop of London, in 1731, as "furious and clamorous for the Church" Dr Gibbons graduated at Harvard in 1715, and was Warden of King's Chapel in 1725 and 1726, as Dr Gardiner was in 1738 and 1739, and for the most of the time from 1756 to 1775 They both served, often together, on many important Church Committees, not only for the management of King's Chapel, but for the founding of Christ and Trinity Churches Dr. Gardiner published a book of family prayers His daughter married Robert Hallowell, the last English Comptroller of the Customs of Boston

Dr Gardiner had large holdings of land in Maine, where he had been zealous to establish the Church, having built and partially endowed Churches at Pownalborough, now Dresden, and Gardiner. By his will he entailed his large estate at Gardiner, Maine excluding his eldest son who had been active in transferring King's Chapel from the Church to Unitarianism On that estate he charged an annuity to be paid to the Rector of the Church at Gardiner, providing that the Rector should be appointed by that one of his descendants who, at the time of the vacancy, ocupied the estate Dr Gardiner died in 1786 and was buried under Trinity Churh, Newport On the death within a year of his son, William, his grandson, Robert Hallowell, succeeded to the estate, and on coming of age, took the name of Robert Hallowell Gardiner He built the present Church at Gardiner and devoted his life tothe service of the Church, serving on the Standing Committee of Maine, as Treasurer of the Diocessan Board of Missions, and for many years representing the Diocese in the General Convention To one or more General Conventions, he and his son, the Rev Frederic Gardiner, afterwards a Professor at Gambier and at the Berkeley Divinity School, were elected Deputies from Maine and his eldest son and namesake from Georgia

On his death he was succeeded as Treasurer of the Diocesan Board of Missions and as Deputy to the General Convention by his eldest son His second son, John William Tudor Gardiner, was an officer in the regular army of the United States in which he remained till his death, though he was with difficulty persuaded not to enter the ministry in middle life, and while he was stationed at Fort Tejon, California, his eldest son, Robert Hallowell Gardiner, the subject of this sketch, was born there This present R H Gardiner was baptized by Bishop Kip at Fort Tejon, confirmed in Montreal by the Metropolitan of Canada, and after graduating at Harvard in 1876, and teaching in De Veaux College, New York, and the famous Roxbury Latin School, established himself in the practice of law in Boston He was one of the founders and Treasurer and Warden of the Church of the Redeemer, Chestnut Hill, and served in Massachusetts as Treasurer of the Episcopal City Mission of Boston and the Diocesan Board of Missions and as a member of the Standing Committee

He had succeeded on his uncle's death in 1886 to the family estate at Gardiner and in 1900 established his legal residence there He has served the Church in Maine as Warden of Christ Church, Gardiner, and as a member of the Standing Committee and the Diocesan Board of Missions and Vice-President of the Church Club, and was a Deputy to the General Convention of 1904 While a citizen of Massachusetts, he was active in the Republican party, being one of the founders of the Republican Club of Massachusetts He was Treasurer of the Christian Social Union and is Vice-President of the National Consumers' Laegue He is one of the charter members (about 1894) of the Chapter at the Church of the Redeemer, Chestnut Hill, Mass, and later of that at Christ Church, Gardiner, and has been for some years President of the Boston Local Council For the last two years he has been Chairman of the College Committee of the Brotherhood of St. Andrew.

SAMUEL FERGUSON (9).

Emma Jane Gardiner (8), Frederic (7), Robert H (6), Hannah (5), Dr Sylvester (4), William (3), Benony (2), George (1).

Samuel Ferguson, son of Rev Henry and Emma Jane (Gardiner) Ferguson, was born November, 1874 Married Marguerite Price, November, 1903

One child has been born to them as follows

Samuel Ferguson Born 1904

MASSACHUSETTS AND NEW YORK.

STEPHENTOWN

This town was named in honor of Stephen Van Rensselaer formed from Renssalaerswyck, on March 29, 1784 Petersburg was taken off in 1791 and parts of Berlin and Nassau in 1806 It forms the southeast corner of the County, and is bounded on the north by the town of Berlin, in the same County, on the south by the town of New Lebanon, in Columbia County, on the east by the State of Massachusetts and on the west by the town of Nassau, in Rensselaer County, it contains 33,-538 acres of land

The town was first settled about the year 1765, by pioneers from the States of Connecticut and Rhode Island, who entered the town at the southeast corner, and located as the early settlers were wont to do, upon the rocky hills of that location (An explanation as to the term town used herein will clear the mind of the reader The term is the same used at present for a subdivision of a County at present known as a township)

Some doubt exists in the town in regard to the actual "first settler" of the town By some the honor is claimed by Asa and William Douglas, who settled in the town in the season (year) of 1765-66; while others insist that the first settlement was made by Elnathan Sweet, Nathaniel Rose, Joseph Rogers, Benjamin Gardner or others.

It is thought probable that several of the first settlers of the town came in about the same time The tombstone of both Asa and William Douglas and Joshua Gardner simply declare them to be "one of the first settlers of the town" While the following Douglas history is a diversion of the Gardner record we introduce it here as it confirms a belief that the Douglas and Gardner families were closely allied, socially and in marriage, for a few generations, coming as they did to America at the same time, settling in the same place in Massachusetts, and from there to Connecticut, Rhode Island and New York

Asa Douglas was a descendant of William Douglas, who was born July 26, 1610, came from Scotland and landed at Boston in 1640 From thence he went to New London, Connecticut, and died July 26, 1662 Asa came from Pittsfield, Massachusetts, in the year 1766, in search of some good land which he was to receive in compensation for certain services which he had performed in behalf of the government

Finding no satisfactory land there, and meeting an Indian chief who informed him that there was good land in "Jericho Hollow," a name that was given to the "hollow" west of the Berkshire hills, he repaired there and took up 1,000 acres which then laid within the territory of Massachusetts Here he established himself with his family, which subsequently consisted of his wife, Rebecca, seven sons and five daughters.

One-half of the land is now within the State of New York, and is divided into six farms, Mrs Emeline A Hubbard, a descendant of Asa Douglas, Leonard Doty, Charles Shumway, Ambrose Sweet, Kirk Gardner, the widow and heirs of Silas Gardner, the last two of whom reside in Massachusetts. Other early settlers in the town, some of whom were among the first, were men by the name of Moon, Rowland Hall, Dr. Nicholas Harris, and the Gardner brothers, Joshua, Caleb, Nathaniel, Benjamin and others, no more names given Joshua Gardner in 1774 cut his way through the woods from the old "East Road" that passed from Lebanon Springs, up over the mountains to the place where he located

The records are clear as to the coming to Stephentown of some Gardners who were brothers of Benjamin first mentioned and from these families numerous branches have gone forth.

In the research we have found the following names and official relations sustained to the government

Assistant Justice of the Court.

George Gardner appointed by the Governor of New York, 1771.

Powell Gardner appointed by the Governor of New York, 1802

Powell Gardner succeeded himself for four terms and then at the close of a term of another appointee was reappointed and held the office till March, 1815, when William Gardner was appointed

State Officers.

Stow Gardner was elected and entered upon the duties of the office of Attorney General December 8, 1853

Representatives in the Assembly.

George Gardner, in 1811

Field and Staff.

William L. Gardner, Adjutant.

Nathan B Gardner, Lieutenant

William Lamport Gardner, Ensign (Grenadiers).

Daniel Gardner was a prominent attorney, Rensselaer County, New York

Railroad Lines.

The Troy and Stockbridge road, incorporated by act of legislature in 1836 Capital stock 6000 shares, $50 00 each Commissioners named in bill were Daniel Gardner and others, including Russel Sage.

Early Manufactures

We record the following as evidence of the aggressiveness and leadership characteristic of the family

At Troy, N Y., 1838, Jefferson Gardner purchased an interest in a collar and cuff factory In 1851, Nathaniel Wheeler of Wheeler, Wilson and Co, came to Troy, bringing with him one of the recently invented sewing machines Alluding to the results of his visit Wheeler remarked. "I particularly brought the attention of the manufacturers of cuffs and collars, to the machine, most of whom shook their heads doubting the practicability of stitching collars by machinery Among my visitors was Jeff Gardner who seemed to be less skeptical, investigated the subject and concluded to give the machine a trial. Early in the spring of 1852 he put them in practical operation in the shops" Others followed after he had demonstrated the possibility of using the machines

GARDNER FAMILY REUNION.

Saturday, September 15th, 1906, witnessed, at the home of Rufus Sweet of Stephentown, N Y, a reunion of one of the oldest families in America The founder of this family was one George Gardner, who, in 1638 forsook old England for New England, settling in Rhode Island, and it was his descendants who, nearly three centuries later, celebrated their first family reunion in the land of their adoption

It is but comparatively few years since the ancestors of the living members of this family cleared the very ground whereon the present gathering met On this occasion one could but reflect that the distance from the ox team to the automobile is not so very great after all, and from the steam shuttle to the hand loom and the spinning-wheel one is made to feel he can almost touch hands There were a number present at the Stephentown reunion who, in the earlier days, had spun by hand and woven by hand, and whose ancestors, but one or two generations removed, had struck into the wilderness, and come "west" with the pioneers.

As a family, the Gardners have played a creditable part in the development of the new country, and the useful position it now occupies is testified to by the very considerable number of prominent and able members it includes

The early history of this family in America is much the same as that of the other settlers who helped give birth to the young nation First, there is the abode among the coastwise towns, and then the hardier ones, with ax and rifle, push westward There is the blazed trail, the little clearing, the log cabin, and the wilderness begins to flourish under the arm of the settler Gradually the frame house rises where the cabin stood, and broad fields stretch away where the meagre crop once grew between the stumps of the clearing Hardy beginnings, these, which, as in the case of all pioneers, fostered a hardy race Emerging from its forest pathway, populating the farms, and entering the cities, this family has increased and prospered, till today its living members number about 5,000,—a surprisingly vigorous growth for its small beginning But perhaps this early growth was not unusual; for in the settlement days large families were more the fashion than now The brood of ten was by no means the exception,— and, as a member of the family expressed it, "Ten times ten are a hundred"

During the past two years a Mr Charles M Gardner, of Buffalo, N Y., has undertaken the task of collecting the complete history and genealogy of the Gardner family, and the final sheets of this work are nearly ready for the printer The history begins with the early English ancestors, and brings the record down wherever possible, to the present day

To accommodate the widely scattered members of the family, the reunion of the eastern and the western branches was held separately, the gathering of the western branch taking place in Ohio about three weeks before the one which occurred in Stephentown The attendance at the reunion held in Ohio, numbered between 200 and 300 and at Stephentown about 30

Following the example of its western relative, the eastern branch organized as a family association, for the purpose of establishing a wider acquaintance among the members of the Gardner family and like the former voted to make its reunion an annual event It is expected that the attendance next year will be very large, when a fine program, including addresses, will be arranged

The officers of the eastern association, chosen for the ensuing year, are as follows President and treasurer, Rev Daniel Shepardson, Hancock, Mass , vice president, Fred Gardner, Stephentown, N. Y , secretary, Miss Mary Shumway, Hancock, Mass

C M FORD

JOB GARDNER (4).

Nathaniel (3), Benony (2), George (1)

Job, youngest child of Nathaniel and Mary (——) Gardner, was born July 23, 1723, married Ann Fry, of East Greenwich, in 1748 He was mate of the "Ranger", also owned land in East Greenwich, for July 17, 1755, Job Gardner and wife Ann deeded land to Joseph Billington (2) married —— Greene He removed to Stephentown, N Y., about 1787

Children

Mary, born 1749
Nathaniel, born 1751
Thomas, born 1753
Amy, born 1755
Ann, born 1757
George, born 1759
Samuel, born 1761.
Augustus, born 1763
Hannah, born 1765
William, born 1767
Benjamin, born 1769

JOSHUA GARDNER (5)

Benjamin (4), Nathaniel (3), Benony (2), George (1)

Joshua Gardner, son of Benjamin and Elizabeth (Howland) Gardner, was born 1742, in Kingstown, Rhode Island, he married, first, Mercy Tanner, daughter of Palmer Tanner, at Kingstown, R I, February 22, 1763. They were married by Elisha Clark, Justice

Joshua Gardner removed from Rhode Island to Stephentown, New York, in 1764-5 He took up a tract of land which he increased until he owned about four hundred acres

The following inscriptions were taken from the grave stones in the old cemetery on the hill back of what is now the Baptist cemetery of Stephentown, New York, and on land originally owned by him

"In memory of Mercy Gardner, wife of Joshua Gardner, who died December ye 11th, 1804, in the 63rd year of her age"

"In memory of Elcy Gardner, wife of Joshua Gardner, who departed this life March ye 4th, 1816, in the 60th year of her age"

"The grave of Joshua Gardner, who died October ye 5th, 1829, aged 87"

'He emigrated to this town from Connecticut in 1764 and was one of the first settlers of the soil where he now lies buried—married to three wives and had twelve children, all of whom died before him"

The above is all the information we have been able to obtain relative to him or his family

CAPT. CALEB B. GARDNER (5).

Benjamin (4), Nathaniel (3), Benony (2), George (1)

Caleb B, son of Benjamin and Mary (Howland) Gardner married Amy Aylesworth, Mar 18, 1761 In the West Greenwich records her name is written "Almy" She was born Dec 28, 1739, died Dec 24, 1811 Caleb B was born Apr 27, 1741, died Aug 3, 1806

Children of whom we have record

Russell, born July 20, 1762, married —— Clark

Amy, born Aug 3, 1764, married William Hall.

Mary, died at Hancock, Mass, Mar 15, 1797, in the 31st year of her age, and is buried on the homestead now (1907) owned by Kirk E Gardner She married Arvin Wood Two children of whom we have record Betsy, born Apr 13, 1794, died Aug 15, 1876, married Adam Clark Wanton G, died May 21, 1798, aged 1 year 2 months 14 days

Caleb, born Mar 17, 1769, married —— Reynolds He died in Rio Janeiro

Silas, born July 15, 1771

John, born Aug 19, 1778, died Jan 10, 1863

Olive, died at Hancock, Mass, Aug 20, 1826, in the 53d year of her age, married Hezekiah Noyes

Job, born Aug 19, 1776, died in Sherburn, N Y

Adam, born June 14, 1781, married —— Corliss

Platt, born July 10, 1786, died July 27, 1806 Buried at Hancock

Captain Caleb B Gardner came from Rhode Island. On the thirteenth of April, 1767, bought of Asa Douglas of Connecticut one hundred acres for £75

Soon he had 1,000 bushels of wheat in one year from said farm delivered at Schodac landing on the Hudson, in sleighs, and with the proceeds paid for the farm

In a few years he was the owner of five hundred acres including the Douglas homestead which was the adjoining farm, and which is in the Gardner family at this writing, 1907 Kirk E Gardner, great-grandson of Caleb B Gardner, owns and lives on the old farm Caleb B built his house and barn large and strong and both are now in use

The house was built in 1795, as a stone tablet in the cellar walls bearing date and names of Caleb B and his wife, Amy Aylsworth, certifies

The barn which was built ten or fifteen years previous was, according to tradition, used by the Baptists for the holding of their first services in Hancock

The house was the first hotel in Hancock, and an old clock, the first in town, built in the wall on one side of the bar room, is still there with its metallic face In the house also may be seen the signs of "Caleb B Gardner's Inn 1790," and J. Gardner's Inn' J. Gardner, his son, kept the house as a hotel till about 1840

The following is the deed of transfer of one hundred acres of land to Caleb Gardner at Hancock, Massachusetts

To all People to whom these Presents shall come

Greeting, know ye, that I, Asa Douglas of Canaan in the County of Litchfield and Colony of Connecticut, Yeoman do for and in Consideration of the Sum of Seventy-five pounds lawful money, of the province of the Massachusetts Bay, to me in hand before the Ensealing hereof, well and truly paid by Caleb Gardner of Dutchess County and province of New York—Yeoman—The Receipt whereof I do hereby acknowledge, and myself therewith fully satisfied and contented, and thereof, and of every Part and Parcel thereof do exonerate, acquit and discharge him—said Caleb Gardner his Heirs, Executors and administrators, forever by these Presents Have given, granted, bargained, sold, aliened, conveyed and confirmed, and by these Presents, do freely, fully and absolutely give, grant, bargain, sell, aliene, convey and confirm unto him the said Caleb Gardner, his heirs and Assigns forever, one certain farm of land lying and being in the County of Berkshire and the Province of the Massachusetts Bay, being part of that Grant of Land of Deans and others Being at the westermost end of lot number four and lot number five running easterly at the Lot Line Runs the width of both Lots, till it contains one hundred akers Bounds as follows, Easterly, Southerly, and Westerly on Land of said Douglas and Northerly on land of Timothy Hollenbeck—Being part of said Grant—To Have and to Hold the said granted and bargained premises, with all the appurtenances, Privileges and commodities to the same belonging, or in any way appertaining to him the said Caleb Gardner his Heirs and Assigns forever To his and their only proper use Benefit and Behoof forever And I the said Asa Douglas do for myself, my Heirs, Executors and Administrators, do Covenant, Promise and Grant to and with the said Caleb Gardner his Heirs and Assigns, that before Ensealing hereof I am the true, sole and lawful owner of the above bargained Premises, and am lawfully seized and possessed of the same in my own proper Right as a good perfect and absolute Estate of Inheritance in Fee Simple; and have in myself good Right full Power and lawful Authority, to grant, bargain, sell convey and confirm said bargained Premises in manner as foresaid, and that the said Caleb Gardner his Heirs and Assigns, shall and may from time to time, and at all times forever hereafter, by force and virtue of these Presents, lawfully, peacebly and quietly have, hold, use, occupy, possess and enjoy the said demised and bargained Premises, with the appurtenances, free and clear, and freely and clearly acquitted, exonerated and discharged of from all, and all manner of former or other Gifts, Grants, Bargains, Sales, Leases, Mortgages, Wills, Entails, Jointures, Dowries, Judgments, Executors or Incumbrances of what Name or Nature soever, that might in any measure or Degree obstruct or make void this Present Deed Furthermore I the said Asa Douglass for myself Heirs, Executors and Administrators do Covenant and Engage the above demised Premises to him the said Caleb Gardner his Heirs and Assigns against the lawful claims or demands of any Person or Persons whatsoever, forever hereafter to Warrant, Secure and Defend by these Presents, in witness whereunto I have set my Hand and Seal this thirteenth Day of April in the Seventh year of his Majesties Reign George the third of Great Brittain &c, Ano dominum 1767 Signed Sealed and Delivered in the presence of

David Vaughn,
George Hollelston.
Asa Douglas,
Berkshire

ALSE GARDNER (5),

Benjamin (4), Nathaniel (3), Benony (2), George (1)

Alse Gardner, daughter of Benjamin and Mary (Howland) Gardner, was born about 1747, married Justus Brockway He was born about 1747 He died 1827, aged about 80 They are both buried on the old Simeon Gardner family burying ground, on what is now known as the Lapp farm.

The graves have no markers She was a sister of the early settlers, Benjamin, Caleb, Joshua, Job and Nathaniel Gardner

Her children were

Justus. Children but we have no record of them
Jesse,
Benjamin, no record
Samuel,
George, born April 24, 1791, died January 27, 1846
Simeon, went to Ohio. No further record
Lucy,
Alse,
Elizabeth, no record
Thankful, no record

BENJAMIN GARDNER (5)

Benjamin (4), Nathaniel (3), Benony (2), George (1)

Benjamin Gardner, son of Benjamin and Mary (Howland) Gardner, was born about 1731, at Exeter, R I, died Feb 2, 1809, at Stephentown, N. Y married Elizabeth Olin She was born in Rhode Island, 1737, died at Stephentown N Y, March 4, 1813 Both are buried on the old homestead farm at Stephentown, now owned by Rufus Sweet

Their children, born in Exeter, R I, were

Simeon, born Oct 22, 1754
Alice, born May 6, 1756
Mary, born Jan 31, 1757
Benjamin, born Sept 13, 1759, removed to Ohio
Elizabeth, born Sept 12, 1761
Howland, born Sept 1, 1763
Nathaniel, born Oct. 11, 1765
- Caleb, born Feb 14, 1768
Olin, born at Stephentown, N. Y, is buried beside his parents

Lease

This indenture made the sixteenth day of January in the yeare of our Lord 1787 Between Stephen Van Rensselaer Esq Lord and Proprietor of the Manor of Rensselaer Wick in the County of Albany of the 1st part and Benjamin Gardner of the County of Albany of the 2nd part

Witnesseth, That for in consideration of the sum of five Shillings Lawful Money of the State of New York to him the said Stephen Van Rensslear now paid and more especially for and in further consideration of the Rent Covenants Conditions Provisions and Agreements hereinafter refered contained and expressed he the said Stephen Van Rensselaer Hath Granted Bargained And Sold Aliened Released & confirmed & by these Presents Doth Grant Bargain and Sell Alien Release And Confirm unto the said Benjamin Gardner in his actual Possession now Being by virtue of a Lease thereof by Indenture to him made bearing Date and Day before the Date hereof and by Force of the Laws transfering of titles into Possession & to his Heirs & Assigns forever—All that certain Tract of Land or farm Situated, lying & being in the said Manor on the East side of Hudson s River butted bounded & described as follows to wit

Saving & always excepted to the said Stephen Van Rensselaer his Heirs and Assigns out of the present Grant & Release all Mines & Minerals that are now or may be found on the premises hereby granted & released & also all the Creeks Kills Streams & Runs of Water & so much ground within the Same Premises as he the said Stephen Van Rensselaer his heirs & assigns think requisite and appropriate at any Time hereafter for the erection of Mills Dams & any Works & Buildings whatsoever for the convenient working of the said Mines or for the Use of the said Mills & the said Benjamin Gardner for himself his Heirs Executors Administrators & Assigns doth hereby covenant & agree to & with the said Stephen Van Rensselaer his Heirs & assigns that the said Benjamin Gardner his Heirs and assigns Executors & Administrators shall and will forever hereafter well and faithfully pay & deliver the Rent and Quality & Quantities of Wheat or Species so by the above condition secure at the Time and Times therein mentioned to the said Stephen Van Rensselaer his Heirs & Assigns he the said Benjamin Gardner his heirs & assigns will faithfully discharge & pay all Taxes charges or Assessments ordinary or extraordinary taxes charges or assessments or to be taxed charged or assessed upon the said hereby released Premises.

In testimony whereof the Parties to the Presents have hereunto interchangeably set their Hands and Seals the Day and year first above written

Sealed and delivered in the
presence of
I A. Magely,
Benj F Egberts

Benjamin Gardner

Lease

Benjamin Gardner 129 acres and
108 Rods 10¾ Bushels of wheat yearly

NATHANIEL GARDNER (5).

Joshua (4), Robert (3), George (2), George (1)

Nathaniel Gardner, son of Joshua and Sarah (Spink) Gardner, was born in Kingstown, R I, April 10, 1744, died July 14, 1801 Married Martha Brown, also of Kingstown, Aug 1, 1762 She was born 1743, died Aug 11, 1841, in Hancock.

Their children were

Joshua, born Mar 11, 1764, married Lydia Gardner, daughter of Palmer

Robert, born Feb 3, 1766, in Exeter R I

Elizabeth born July 6, 1770, died in Hancock, Mass, Aug 18, 1856

Martha born in Exeter, R I; married Griffin Reynolds, Sept 22, 1793, removed to west

Waity, born in Exeter, R I, married George Dyer, Apr 7, 1796.

Eunice, born Nov 19, 1773, died May 6, 1851.

Mary, born Aug 12 1784, in Hancock, Mass, married O Cortell.

Hannah, born 1789, in Hancock, Mass, died 1803

Nathaniel Gardner emigrated to Hancock, Mass (then Jericho valley), settling on the land now owned and occupied by William A Gardner, and which has been owned and occupied by his descendants since that time Martha made the journey from Rhode Island on horseback, carrying her baby in her arms, their road being indicated by marked trees They lived and died and are both buried on the farm where he settled.

Martha lived a widow for forty years and died at the age of 99 years It is said sometime during the Revolutionary war Nathaniel decided to enlist as a soldier but, his brother Ishmael, unmarried, said: "Nathaniel, yau stay at home and care for your wife and little ones I will go as I have no one dependent upon me One of us ought to go so I will be the one" He went,but did not return, having been killed at the battle of Bennington.

Nathaniel was Captain of the First Company of Militia of the town at the time the Regiment of King and Kent Counties, R I., were ordered to be divided into two Regiments His name does not appear among those given as appointed officers of the reorganized companies At about this time he removed to Hancock, Mass He was Captain of the military company of the town and was in service in the Revolutionary war. The only official record of this is among the Revolutionary State Papers at Boston, that he marched from Hancock to and in defense of other towns This was probably during the time of the battle of Bennington Hancock muster rolls were not preserved All of the militia was called out All had voluntarily served in anticipation of call As early as 1764 every man in the militia had been called to serve

JOB GARDNER (5)

Benjamin (4), Nathaniel (3), Benony (2), George (1)

Job Gardner, son of Benjamin and Mary (Howland) Gardner, was born in North Kingstown Rhode Island, about 1730, died at Stephentown, New York, March 9, 1806 Married Hannah Briton; she died at Stephentown, New York December 26, 1781, aged 48

Children were:
Lobdel,
William,
Benjamin,
Wheelock

NATHANIEL GARDNER (5).

Job (4), Nathaniel (3), Benony (2), George (1).

Nathaniel, son of Job and Ann (Fry) Gardner, was born in Rhode Island in 1751, died Feb. 1813 of influenza in Stephentown, N Y His wife died Nov 11, 1837 He with his wife Marcy (Spencer) Gardner moved from East Greenwich, Rhode Island, in 1787, to Stephentown, Rensselaer Co, New York, where he purchased a farm

Their family consisted of ten children:
Dorcas—Mrs Russell Cowles.
Job,
Nathan,
Charlotte—Mrs. Samuel Herrick, of Owasco, N Y
Ann,
Eliza,
John, born Feb 22, 1791
Charles, born May 13, 1793
Richard, 1795
Ruth, 1797—Mrs Daniel Rhodes

PALMER GARDNER (5).

Sylvester (4), Nicholas (3), Nicholas (2), George (1).

Palmer Gardner, son of Sylvester and Lydia (Dawley) Gardner, was born in Exeter, R I, September 19, 1737, was married in West Greenwich to Hannah, daughter of Joseph and Mary Nichols, in 1763 Her line of descent was as follows Hannah (4), Joseph (3), John (or Benjamin (2), Thomas (1). Thomas Nichols was admitted as a freeman at

Newport in 1664 and located in East Greenwich in 1677. She was born December 8, 1731

Their children were

Abigail, born Mar 2, 1764, in W Greenwich, R I, died 1825.
Dorcas, born 1766, died 1811
Lydia, born 1768, died 1838, married Joshua Gardner (6) See line.
Sylvester, born Aug 11, 1770, died July 30, 1830
Mary, born June 17, 1772, died Sept 6, 1853
Joseph Nichols, born Nov 14, 1773, died Nov 22, 1845
Palmer, born Mar 14, 1775, died July 19, 1817
Amy, born 1777
Hannah, born April 1, 1781, died Oct 9, 1825
Daniel

June 1, 1761, was issued the following —

Commission

By the Honorable Stephen Hopkins, Esq, Governor and Captain General of the English Colony of Rhode Island and Providence Plantations in New England in America

To Palmer Gardner, Gentleman, Greeting You, Palmer Gardner, being by the General Assembly of the Colony elected and chosen to the place and office of Captain of the 3d company or trained band of the Town of West Greenwich in the County of Kent in the Colony aforesaid are hereby in the name of his most sacred Majesty George III by the grace of God King of Great Brittain &c, authorize and impowered and commissioned to have, take and exercise the office of Captain of the Company aforesaid and to command, guide and conduct the same or any part thereof

And in case of any invasion or assault of any enemy to infest or disturb this, his Majesty's plantation you are to alarm and gather together the number under your command or such part thereof as you shall deem sufficient and with them to the utmost of your skill and ability you are to resist, expel, kill and destroy the same in order to preserve the interest of his Majesty and his good subjects in these parts

You are also to follow such further instructions and directions as shall from time to time be given forth either by the General Assembly, the Governor or General Counsel or other of your superior officers

And for your so doing this shall be a sufficient warrant

Given under my hand and the seal of the County aforesaid, the 13th day of June in the 1st year of his said Majesty's reign 1761

(Signed) STEPHEN HOPKINS

By his Honor's command.
(Signed) HENRY WARD, Secy

On March 1, 1769, Palmer Gardner sold his farm in West Greenwich to Josiah Matteson, and removed to Hancock Mass, where he bought 199 acres upon the east side of the turnpike between Hancock and South Williamstown and about two miles from the former The present owner of the property is Milton Pease, of Stephentown, N Y, whose great grandfather, Griffin Eldredge, bought it from the heirs of Palmer Gardner

This valley northward from Hancock is extremely picturesque, high wooded hills on either side. Along this street lived the Townsends, Hands, Wilsons, Douglases, Cogswells and Eldredges, most of them Rhode Island people, acquaintances there of the Dyers and Gardners Of the latter there were descendants of Benony (2), George (2), and Nicholas (2), and here in the fifth and sixth generation these intermarried in several instances

A Pioneer.

Often have I enjoyed trying to picture to myself the sort of man Captain Palmer Gardner, of Hancock Mass, must have been To the very meager traditions that have come down to me I have joined in imagination some recurring characteristics among his descendants. That he was held in high esteem by his fellow pioneers among those glorious hills and smiling valleys on the confines of the great Commonwealth of Massachusetts does not need to be repeated 'There were giants in those days and he was one of them A man whom physical stature alone marked him as of regal mien, it might be said of him as of Israel's first king, that 'when he stood among the people he was higher than any of the people from his shoulders and upward' When he and his consort were met driving through the country, they were the chief matter of interest in the landscape for they occupied so much of it

The relation of physical to mental and moral bigness is interesting It is not difficult to trace it among those descendants of Capt Palmer Gardner who inherited his massive frame, and even among some who did not Then his first the gentleness the sweetness, the simplicity that is so often found among people who rightly belong to the favored children of God, and so surely among them who approximate true greatness. Then there is the breadth of sympathy strong indeed which is the only effective basis of the most useful lives lived among men Again, there is the bouyant, happy disposition which ever reflects God's warm sunshine into the hearts and lives of those about I do not know that many of the family possessed exceptional intellectual gifts, but they had strong, practical common sense

Reference may be expected to the deeply religious nature and moral earnestness of this people Few sons and daughters of Massachusetts were not such These people enjoyed their religion It was full of radiance of the better kind Two of them went as heralds of the Cross to the Empire of the Rising Sun and beyond One, through an exceptionally long life retained among her friends the reputation of the Angel her husband had called her before their marriage

Another was known as the Saint of the Community in which she lived Who would not rejoice to claim friendship with such?

Pioneers were they! Pioneers they still are Pioneers of Gardners of joy and happiness Happy is the nation which can claim such resourceful folk among its foundation stones! Blessed are they who are conscious of such rich blood coursing in their veins

REV FLOYD APPLETON, D D

CAPT. DANIEL GARDNER (5)

Sylvester (4), Nicholas (3), Nicholas (2), George (1).

Capt Daniel Gardner, son of Sylvester and Lydia (Dawley) Gardner, was born in Greenwich, R I, 1746, died November 28, 1807, and is buried on the farm at Hancock, Mass, formerly owned by him He married Abigail Hall of West Greenwich, March 21, 1771 She was born in 1746, died November 21, 1775, and is buried at Hancock, Mass

Two children

Christopher, born 1773, died 1777

John, born 1775, died 1776

Daniel Gardner married for his second wife Alice ——, she was born June 13, 1746, died Feb 25, 1791

Children

Abigail, born in Hancock, Mass, Nov 16, 1777, died Dec 16, 1852, in Moravia, N Y.

Lydia, born Feb 1, 1779, died Sept 7, 1841, married John, son of Caleb B and Amy Gardner

Daniel Gardner married, third, Christina Hall, cousin of Abigail and Alice She was born April 3, 1772, died Dec 27, 1842.

Children

Elcy, born Dec 29, 1796; died Jan 24, 1882

Sally, born Nov 25, 1799, died June 23, 1871.

March 7 1768, in consideration of 15 pounds, Peleg Dawley conveyed to Daniel Gardner 25 acres contiguous to the lands of Henry Tanner and Sylvester Gardner

In 1770 Daniel Gardner emigrated to Hancock, Mass (then called Jericho) where he purchased 370 acres of land and in 1793 he erected a large two-story house, which a few years ago was destroyed by fire, but the chimney is still standing His widow lived there until her death and his daughter, Sally, passed her entire life there, with the exception of one year Her son, Dwight, lived and died on the old homestead, after which the farm was sold and passed out of the family It is now owned by Miss Fannie Carpenter of Lebanon Springs The marble tablet bearing the date of erection is in the possession of Dr. Gardner Smith

JOSEPH AND BENJAMIN GARDNER (5).

Sylvester (4), Nicholas (3), Nicholas (2), George (1).

Joseph and Benjamin followed their brother Palmer to Hancock, Mass, and their remains were laid to rest in the Dawley burial ground just north of the spot where may be seen today the ruins of their brother Daniel's spacious residence which was erected in 1793

Tradition states that Joseph was a hunchback Neither he nor Benjamin married They wore the Quaker garb If we may divine from their epitaphs the feelings of these bachelor brothers who were so near of an age and never separated till Joseph died, we can readily appreciate their wistful memories of Rhode Island where they laid to rest their parents and maiden sister Lydia, before turning their steps to Massachusetts, and the sense of isolation Benjamin experienced after the death of his brothers and the migration of their children to New York state and Canada

The grave stone of Joseph at Hancock, Mass, contains the following inscription

Joseph Gardner died December 15, 1816
aged 69 years

"Far from my native land I've come
To lay my body here
O may my soul to God return
To dwell within his cear."

The following is from Benjamin's grave stone

Benjamin Gardner died August 12, 1825,
aged 77 years

"Why should I longer live to mourn
The loss of one in age and all
My equal true? Since strength is gone
I'd go where virtue cannot fall"

NATHANIEL GARDNER (5).

Benjamin (4), Nathaniel (3), Benony (2), George (1)

Nathaniel Gardner was born March 17, 1739, married Eunice Sunderlin, May 18, 1760, died July 18, 1806 She was born Dec 28, 1738, died Jan. 11, 1781 He was son of Benjamin and Mary (Howland) Gardner

Children were

Lois, born Dec 28, 1760; married —— Hammond, died Jan 23, 1850

Isaac, born Mar 14, 1762

Mary, born Jan. 30 1764, married a Brownell, died July 29, 1831

Stephen, born Feb 27, 1767 died July 4, 1826

Isabel, born Jan. 20, 1769

Zephaniah, born Oct 20, 1770

Zebulon, born Dec 28, 1773, died July 8, 1775.

Joshua, born Nov 2, 1774

Dorcas, born Aug 18, 1776

Benjamin, born July 22, 1778

GEORGE GARDNER (5)

Ezekiel (4), Nicholas (3), Nicholas (2), George (1).

George, son of Ezekiel and Dorcas (Watson) Gardner, was born July 2, 1745, married Mary Reynolds She became a disciple of the Friends and remained one of their firmest adherents, personally and doctrinely, through life Leaving her husband behind, she came with her children with the early settlers of the Friends' colony to the New Jerusalem She settled first near the Friends residence, on land which later belonged to Charles J Townsend She was a valued member of the Friends Society, and often interchanged visits with the Friends, and subsequently with Rachel Malin She died in 1845, nearly 95 years old.

Children were

Dorcas, born 1779

Abner, born 1781

George, born 1783

Other children of which we have no record

Albon Crocker, 1799

DEED TO MARY GARDNER

The following transfer of property is recorded page 379, Book A, Ontario County, transferred to Wayne County, New York·

To all people to whom these presents—

Know ye that I John Reynolds of East Greenwich in the County of Kent in the state of Rhode Island &c, yeoman, for and in consideration of the love, good will and affection that I have and do bear to my sister Mary Gardner now residing in Jerusalem in the County of Ontario and state of New York &c, and to assist her in her needy circumstances, do give, grant, bargain convey and confirm and by these presents do absolutely give, grant, bargain, convey and confirm unto the said Mary Gardner, and to her heirs and assigns separate distinct and exclusive of her husband George Gardner of the County of Washington and state of Rhode Island A certain tract or parcel of land situated lying and being in the county of Ontario, containing ten acres, in lot No two, in the Gore (so called) said lot was surveyed by Jabez French August ye 1st 1793 which appears by his draught of the same, and the hereby conveyed premises is bounded as followeth, Beginning on the north line of said lot No two where the brook running from near Elnathan Bartford's house crosses the same, thence nearly south about thirty rods to a crooked winding white oak tree marked S C thence east parallel with the north line of said lot, No two, so far that a line running north to said north line will cut off said ten acres of land, thence north to said north line—thence west along said west line to place of beginning, and is part of the land which James Parker William Potter and Thomas Hathaway have a patent from the people of the state of New York, for, Together with all and singular the rights hereditaments and appurtenances to the same belonging, or in any wise appertaining, Excepting and reserving to the people of the state all the gold and silver To have and to hold the above described and granted premises unto her the said Mary Gardner and to her heirs and assigns forever, as a good indefeasable estate of inheritance forever, hereby giving and granting to the said Mary Gardner the full and sole power of occupying and selling and disposing of the above described premises as fully and completely as if she was legally discharged from her said husband,

In witness whereof I have hereunto set my hand and seal this twenty sixth day of August in the year of our Lord One Thousand Seven Hundred and ninety six

Executed in the presence of
Oliver Parker,
James Parker.

John Reynolds, S.

Ontario County,

Be it remembered that on the eighteenth day of June One Thousand Eight Hundred came before me, Arnold Potter one of the Judges of said County, James Parker to me personally known, and made oath that he saw John Reynolds with whom he was acquainted execute the above instrument as his valuntary act for the use and purposes therein mentioned & that he with Oliver Parker signed the same as witnesses in the presence of each other I have examined it and finding therein no erasures or interlineations do allow it recorded

Arnold Parker

I certify the foregoing to be a true copy of the original recorded examined and compared this 13 day of May, 1801, 9 o'clock A M

OTHNIEL GARDNER (5)

Benony (4), Isaac (3), Benony (2), George (1).

Othniel, son of Benony and Elizabeth (——) Gardner, was born 1742 in Rhode Island, died 1783 He married Lydia Reynolds, a famous beauty; after his death, she married a Babcock Othniel Gardner with wife Lydia, removed from Block Island, R I, to Stephentown, N Y., about 1769 In 1775 he signed a compact to organize a new colonial government of New York State He was an officer in the Revolutionary army He died at Petersburg, N Y, leaving a family of six children, and was buried in the Reynolds cemetery at Petersburg His two oldest sons were born in Exeter, R I He was sheriff of the county during the Revolution

George, born 1766, died 1840, married Louisa Dawley
Jesse, born 1768, removed to the west
Elizabeth, born 1770, married a Mr West.
Lucy, born 1772, married Francis Moone
Charlotte born 1774
Asa, born 1776, died at Troy, N Y, 1820

JOHN GARDNER (6).

Caleb (5), Benjamin (4). Nathaniel (3), Benony (2), George (1).

John, son of Caleb and Amy (Aylsworth) Gardner, was born August 19, 1778, at Hancock, Massachusetts, died January 10, 1863, married Lydia, daughter of Daniel and Abigail (Hall) Gardner, March 22, 1798 She was born February 1, 1779, died September 7 1841

Children were
John H, born January 2, 1799, died August 25, 1821
Minerva B., born November 14, 1800

Silas H., born January 17, 1803, died September 6, 1857
Daniel H., born November 7, 1807, died September 8, 1875.
Lydia L., born April 30, 1810

LUCY BROCKWAY (6).

Alse (5), Benjamin (4), Nathaniel (3), Benony (2), George (1).

Lucy Brockway, daughter of Justus and Alse (Gardner) Brockway, married, first, Mr Curtis, second, Stephen Maine

One child was born to them

Orlando G Maine

SAMUEL BROCKWAY (6).

Alse (5), Benjamin (4), Nathaniel (3), Benony (2), George (1)

Samuel Brockway, son of Justus and Alse (Gardner) Brockway, married

His children were

Susan, who married Orelias Webster No further record
Samuel,
Alonzo,
Henry.

GEORGE BROCKWAY (6).

Alse (5), Benjamin (4), Nathaniel (3), Benony (2), George (1)

George Brockway, son of Justus and Alse (Gardner) Brockway, was born April 24 1781 Died January 27, 1846 Married, first, Susanna Shaw, July 11, 1811 Second, Susanna Babcock December 31, 1818.

Their children were.

Hiram Franklin, born January 30, 1812. Died September 14, 1832
Alse, born January 10, 1814.
George W., born June 21, 1816
Susanna, born January 30, 1820 Died August 16, 1822.
John S., born April 15, 1821
Polly, born February 12, 1823
Sally Ann (Sarah), born April 8, 1825
Justus, born June 8, 1827
Silas, February 18, 1829.
David, August 31, 1830.
Susan Mariah, born September 13, 1834.
Orlando, born April 19, 1836.

ALSE GARDNER BROCKWAY (6)

Alse (5), Benjamin (4), Nathaniel (3), Benony (2), George (1)

Alse Gardner, daughter of Justus and Alse (Gardner) Brockway, married, first, George Worden, second Orelias Webster.

Children by her first husband all died young. Children by second husband were.

Nelson,
Gilbert,
George,
Constant,
Chloe,
Martha,
Charles,
Frank

SIMEON GARDNER (6).

Benjamin (5), Benjamin (4), Nathaniel (3), Benony (2), George (1).

Simeon, son of Benjamin and Elizabeth (Olin) Gardner, was born in Rhode Island, Oct 22 1754, died at Stephentown, N Y, Sept 18, 1817 He had three wives, the first was Louise—who died June 28, 1793, in the 42d year of her age and is buried in the upper cemetery on the Rufus Sweet farm His second wife was Dorcas, who died June 28, 1813, in the 63rd year of her age, and is buried beside his parents by the house on the Rufus Sweet farm His third wife was Abigail, who died Apr 11, 1867 in her 89th year We have record of only one child who was born of the last wife

Simeon, Jr, died May 9 1831, aged 15 years

CALEB GARDNER (6).

Benjamin (5), Benjamin (4), Nathaniel (3), Benony (2), George (1).

Caleb Gardner, son of Benjamin and Elizabeth (Olin) Gardner, was born Feb 14, 1768, died May 19, 1842, married Eunice Northup, August 20, 1789 She was born 1766, died Nov 12, 1840 Both are buried in the Baptist cemetery at Stephentown, New York.

Children were

Caleb, Jr, born Oct 30, 1789, died January 9, 1861
Olive, born Mar 23, 1792
Ira, born Jan 23, 1794, died March 11, 1869
George, born May 22, 1796, died Sept, 1865
Nicholas, born May 4, 1798, died November 16, 1872
Francis, born May 4, 1798, died November, 1877
Sylvester, born Mar 10, 1801, died March 10, 1888
Israel, born Aug 10, 1803 died November 28, 1845

Caleb Gardner became a large land owner, owning and occupying about four hundred acres north of Stephentown, N Y He built and lived in the house which still stands at this present writing No deaths have ever occurred in this house although it has always been occupied He was a member of the Baptist church of Stephentown, N Y, and is buried in the Baptist cemetery

ELIZABETH GARDNER (6).

Nathaniel (5), Joshua (4), Robert (3), George (2), George (1)

Elizabeth, daughter of Nathaniel and Martha (Brown) Gardner, was born July 6, 1770, in Exeter, R I, died August 18, 1856, in Hancock, Mass Married Griffin Eldridge, of Hancock, April 30, 1788, son of Thomas E, who came from Rhode Island Eight children were born to them, and their many descendants are now residing in Williamstown and Hancock, Mass Deacon Lyman Eldridge was a grandson of theirs We were unable to get the names of the children

MARTHA (PATTY) GARDNER (6)

Nathaniel (5), Joshua (4), Robert (3), George (2), George (1).

Martha or Patty, daughter of Nathaniel and Martha (Brown) Gardner, was born in Exeter, R I Married Griffin Reynolds, Sept. 22, 1793

Children:
Gardner,
James,
Clark R; married Almira Persons

EUNICE GARDNER (6).

Nathaniel (5), Joshua (4), Robert (3), George (2), George (1)

Eunice Gardner, daughter of Nathaniel and Martha (Brown) Gardner, was born November 19, 1773 Died May 6, 1851 Married Daniel Smith, son of William Smith of Hancock He was born December 9, 1769 Died November 28, 1838 Their children were born as follows

Infant, born Aug 9, 1790, died Aug 9, 1790
Hannah, born July 4, 1791, died Mar 25, 1870
Rebecca, born May 28, 1793, died Feb 7, 1872
Augustus, born June 21, 1795, died June 4, 1852
Gardner, born May 16, 1797, died June 18, 1849
William, born June 17, 1799, died Mar 10, 1884
Hiram, born June 17, 1801, died Apr 24, 1823
Amanda Malvina, born Apr 1, 1803; died Mar 27, 1845
Waty, born July 17, 1805, died Apr 18, 1894
Sally Mariah, born Oct 21, 1807, died Sept 15, 1869.
Eliza Cranston, born Dec 20, 1809, died Aug 11, 1841
Lydia Caroline, born Jan 15, 1812 died Feb 17, 1833
Ethima Laruna, born Apr 21, 1814, died May 21, 1814

MARY GARDNER (6).

Nathaniel (5), Joshua (4), Robert (3), George (2), George (1)

Mary Gardner, daughter of Nathaniel and Martha (Brown) Gardner, was born Aug 12, 1784, in Hancock Mass Married Oliver Cottrell, Mar. 16, 1800 They reared a large family One son Joshua established a fur store in Albany, N Y, which was continued after his death as Cottrell and Leonard Mary died in Albany at the residence of her son Joshua

ROBERT GARDNER (6)

Nathaniel (5), Joshua (4), Robert (3), George (2), George (1).

Robert Gardner, son of Nathaniel and Martha (Brown) Gardner, was born February 3, 1766, died April 9, 1846, at Hancock, Mass Married Amy Arnold, March 14, 1786 She was born November 18, 1765; died April 26 1838

Children were

Perry Green, born May 28, 1787, died Aug 20, 1856, married Esther Ely, Jan 10, 1810.

Honor, born Sept 10, 1789, died Jan 27, 1875, became (2) wife of Norman Southworth, of Coldwater, Mich Judge Charles Legg of that place was a grandson There are also other descendants of her in Coldwater.

Sarah, born Aug 13, 1791; died Feb 1, 1817, married Norman Southworth

Nathaniel, born Oct 23, 1793

James, born May 18, 1797, died May 7, 1830; married Laura Hazard His descendants are living in Detroit, Mich, and southern Wisconsin

Martha, born March 30, 1800, died Jan. 14, 1814

Nicholas, born Feb 6, 1802, died Mar 7, 1875, married Dorcas Hadsell He had two sons, James and William, both died unmarried

CAPT JOSHUA GARDNER (6).

Nathaniel (5), Joshua (4), Robert (3), George (2), George (1)

Joshua, son of Nathaniel and Martha (Brown) Gardner, was born March 11, 1764, died Feb 2, 1830, married Lydia, daughter of Palmer and Hannah (Nichols) Gardner She was born 1768, died Nov 16, 1838 Lived on the old farm home in the town of White Creek, Washington Co, N Y Both are buried in the old cemetery at Waite Corners

Their children were

Ann (Nancy), born Oct 10, 1791, married Eliphalet Dyer

Ishmael, born Feb 9, 1789, married Cynthia Dyer

Daniel, lived to be over 70, died of spinal disease; unmarried

Joshua E, born Dec 17, 1805, married Julia Russell, sister of George

Delia born June 16, 1799, married (1) Rev John Alley, (2) Christopher Snyder

Susan, born May 6, 1802, married George Russell

Eunice Minerva, born Feb 10, 1811, married Reuben Ely Gorton

Lydia, born Aug 20, 1796, died Aug 20, 1798

Lydia Louise, born Jan 5, 1808, married Sylvester Millman

Robert H, born Aug 10, 1818, died Feb. 22, 1819.

Edward D, born Oct 22, 1822, died Mar 9, 1823

Julia, born May 18, 1832, died July 28, 1833

Joshua Gardner, born March 11, 1764 in Exeter Rhode Island, came with his parents to Hancock, Berkshire County, Mass., in about 1774-5 After his marriage he settled in Arguile, Wash Co, N Y On March 17 1791, he moved to the town of White Creek, also Wash Co, purchasing a farm of David Sprague Here in 1813 he built a brick house, one of the first of the kind in the county. Here he lived in Baronial style Was captain of the military company of the town and annually for many years dined his company and others of the regiment, giving them ox-roasts The Douglass family were near friends and made them frequent visits with Stephen A (later the Hon and nominee for U. S Presidency) who was then a babe

ABIGAIL GARDNER (6)

Palmer (5), Sylvester (4), Nicholas (3), Nicholas (2). George (1).

Abigail Gardner, daughter of Palmer and Hannah (Nichols) Gardner, was born March 2, 1764, in West Greenwich, R. I, died 1825, married Samuel Dyer, son of George and Ann (Nichols) Dyer He was born April 1, 1761, died —— His parents removed from West Greenwich to Hancock, Mass, where their farm was near that of Palmer and the cousins grew up together

Their children were

Nichols, no issue

Mary, married Mr Mascraft (or Masters)

Sarah,

Milton,

Hannah, married Daniel Lum of Geneva, N Y

Horace,

Nancy married Dr O P Laird, of Oneida Castle, N. Y Two children Orville, and Kate who married Harvey Woodford, of Canastota, N Y They lived at Deerfield, N Y, near Utica

DORCAS GARDNER (6).

Palmer (5), Sylvester (4), Nicholas (3), Nicholas (2), George (1).

Dorcas Gardner, daughter of Palmer and Hannah (Nichols) Gardner, was born at West Greenwich, R I, 1766, died in Floyd township, Oneida Co, N Y, about 1813, married Nathan Townsend about 1784, at Hancock, Mass He was born in 1764 at Cornwall Bridge, Conn

Children

Nathan, born Jan, 1785, died Dec. 3, 1799

Gardner, born Aug 26, 1786

William born 1788 died Sept. 29, 1868

Hannah,

Halsey,

Palmer,

Rhoda, born about 1797

Ingham.

Nathaniel, born June 24, 1804, died 1864

Betsey

Nathan Townsend was fourth in line from Martin Townsend of Watertown, Mass, whose lineage is traced by Martin I Townsend, of Troy, N Y, to Hinton in the Hedges and Paynham, Norfolkshire, Eng., where William the Conqueror bestowed lands upon one of his generals, named De Haville, from whom sprang the Townsends of England, Ireland and America

Jonathan, son of Martin, of Watertown, Mass, settled in Hebron, Conn, in 1713 Martin, second son of Jonathan, born 1728, married Rhoda Ingham of Hebron, April 29, 1753 In 1765 in company with his brother Amasa, Martin removed by way of Cornwall Bridge upon the Housatonic River and Stockbridge Mass, to Hancock Asa Douglas, great-grandfather of Hon Stephen A. Douglas, they found located near Stephentown

The journey from Conecticut was made by Martin with the aid of one horse on which Mrs Townsend rode with her infant son Nathan, and on which their household stuff was also loaded, while the father and the two elder children, Hannah and Martin, made their toilsome way on foot, along the bridle trail.

Till a log house could be erected shelter was found beneath a roof of boughs supported by crotched stakes in front of a huge basswood log

Six hundred acres of excellent land were here purchased and eventually brought under cultivation Martin, before his death in 1800, saw his children married and established in circumstances of comfort and independence

In 1800 Nathan Townsend and wife Dorcas, removed to the Town of Floyd twelve miles north of Utica, N Y, and there spent the remainder of their lives

In this locality Mr Townsend took up 1,000 acres of the richest and most beautiful land in the state and upon this farm raised a numerous and stalwart family, placing them in most comfortable circumstances

Rhoda (Ingham) Townsend removed from Hancock, Mass, to Floyd, N Y, and passed the later years of her widowhood with her son, dying in 1823 at the advanced age of 92

Nathan Townsend was a man influential and highly esteemed in the community, and was a member of the State Legislature in 1812-13. He attained the age of 90 years and his sons, William, Palmer, Ingham and Gardner all exceeded four score years

SYLVESTER GARDNER (6).

Palmer (5), Sylvester (4), Nicholas (3), Nicholas (2), George (1).

Sylvester Gardner son of Palmer and Hannah (Nichols) Gardner, was born at Hancock, Mass, August 11, 1770, died July 30, 1830, at Eagle Village N Y He married Sarah Cogswell (7), Solomon (6), Nathan (5), Joseph (4), Samuel (3), John (2) John (1), of Hancock, Mass, April 26, 1798 She was born Feb 26, 1775, at Hancock, died July 12, 1853

Their children were

Palmer born Feb 23, 1803, died Jan 19, 1888.

Hannah, born Sept. 15, 1806.

Dorcas, born Jan 20, 1809, died Aug 4, 1832
Sylvester Cogswell, born Mar 24, 1811, died Sept 7, 1869.
William Nichols, born July 22, 1813, died Aug 24, 1839
Sarah Ann, born Feb. 6, 1815; died Jan 3, 1894

In 1810 Mr. Gardner removed with his family to Manlius, Onondaga Co, N Y, and resided upon a farm at Eagle Village, two miles east, until his death His wife survived him twenty-three years He was Assemblyman at Albany in 1822 He was a man of tremendous energy and of a genial spirit which made him a general favorite throughout the countryside He and his wife were members of Christ Church (Episcopal) in Manlius, one of the first churches built in Onondaga County.

A word as to how Mr Gardner came to settle in Manlius, N. Y His wife had a sister Chloe, who married Major Joseph Strong and died in Fabius, N. Y, in 1799 Major Strong s second wife, Lucy Elderkin, of Manlius, wished him to be a merchant Accordingly he opened up a store in Manlius and one at Onondaga Valley To stock these he borrowed $1,000 from his brother-in-law Sylvester Unable to pay this, he turned over to Mr Gardner his farm and residence at Eagle Village, two miles east of Manlius and removed to Ohio The house was new and handsome, it commanded a superb view westward across the valley to Pompey and northward to the limits of the county at Oneida Lake A double row of Lombardy poplars marked the spot for miles around The farm consisted of 150 acres of choice land, only 20 of which were under cultivation While clearing the rest of it Sylvester also conducted a general store at Eagle Village in partnership with Thomas Cranston, a man of Rhode Island origin He kept open house for his kinfolk from the east in their migration westward

MARY GARDNER (6).

Palmer (5), Sylvester (4), Nicholas (3), Nicholas (2), George (1).

Mary, daughter of Palmer and Hannah (Nichols) Gardner, was born at Hancock, Mass, June 17 1772 died Sept 6, 1853 She married John Wilson, of Hancock Their farm was next south of her father's. John died in Hancock Mary died in Smyrna, N Y at the home of her son Samuel

Children

Samuel W, born Jan 15, 1792

Sally C, born July 10 1795. married Nathaniel Gardner (7) of the George (2) line Feb 11, 1820 See record of Nathaniel

Lydia, born at Hancock, Mass, Apr 20, 1803, married Heman Hand of Hancock

JOSEPH NICHOLS GARDNER (6)

Palmer (5), Sylvester (4), Nicholas (3), Nicholas (2), George (1).

Joseph N, son of Palmer and Hannah (Nichols) Gardner was born at Hancock, Mass, November 14, 1773, died at Stanbridge, Quebec,

November 22, 1845 He married Deborah daughter of James Reynolds, Sr, about 1800 She died in April, 1846

Children were

Two sons who died in Hancock

Morency, born Aug 12, 1805, at Hancock Hill, Stanbridge, P Q

Lester, born Feb 7, 1808

James Palmer, born Apr 25, 1812

Susan, born Jan 10, 1814; died 1901, unmarried

Emily, born Sept 7, 1817

Orcelia, born Sept 6, 1821

Calista, born Sept 2 1824

A daughter who died in infancy.

James Reynolds, Sr, father of Mrs Gardner, settled at St Armand, Quebec, south of Stanbridge, a little prior to 1812 The wife of James Reynolds, Jr., Deborah's brother, was Hannah Gardner, who was, perhaps, a daughter of Hannah Reynolds and Sylvester (5), Nicholas (4), Nicholas (3), Nicholas (2), George (1) James Reynolds, Jr, and Hannah settled at Stanbridge at the time Joseph Nichols Gardner and Deborah did, viz 1812 Patience Reynolds, a sister of Deborah and James Jr, married Tamplin Smith, of Hancock, son of William Walker and Polly (Tamplin) Smith, and brother of Daniel and Willard, who married Eunice Gardner (6), Nathaniel (5), Joshua (4), Robert (3), George (2), George (1), and Amy Gardner (6), Palmer (5), Sylvester (4), Nicholas (3), Nicholas (2), George (1), respectively After her marriage Eunice declined to return with Daniel to Canada, so Daniel and Willard exchanged farms and Amy rode the 200 miles to Canada on horseback One of the points where this little colony from Massachusetts settled they named Hancock Hill

Joseph Nichols Gardner and his wife Deborah are buried in a family burying ground within sight of their farm home at Stanbridge Their graves are marked by grey marble slabs, which are (1906) in a good state of preservation

Though he had lived in Stanbridge for a few years prior to 1808 it was in 1812 that Joseph Nichols Gardner settled there permanently His sympathies were with the British government Theologically his ideas differed from those of his Baptist kindred at Hancock, and he became a devout Universalist Death found him, Bible in hand, discussing theology from the standpoint of his persuasion After his removal to Canada, communication between him and his relatives at Hancock and in New York State would seem to have been infrequent and as a result in the next generation the families knew practically nothing of each other

They were brought again into touch as the result of conversation in which Rev William Gardner, Rio, Wis, chanced to engage a fellow passenger in southern Vermont the summer of 1904 The man was Judson Sornberger, of Manchester, Vt, who stated that he was born in Stanbridge near Hancock Hill that his grandfather, William Smith, removed thither from Hancock, Mass, and that his boyhood recollections of the locality included the name 'Palmer Garner,' as the surname was pronounced there in Canada

Investigation proved that William Smith was a brother of Tamplin, Daniel, Willard and Nathaniel, and that the union of the names Palmer and Gardner was not a mere coincidence and that "Old Nick," as he is to this day affectionately styled throughout the locality, was no myth, but a very substantial and influential citizen of the Dominion, and the progenitor of a large group of grandchildren and great-grandchildren who were totally in the dark as to whether their grandsire had any brothers and sisters and what were his antecedents back of Hancock, Mass They were already querying dubiously among themselves as to their problematical cousins in the States, and eager to learn the truth concerning them The discovery has therefore been a mutual delight

Helen Gardner Stanton has very kindly acted as sponsor and historian of her house and receiving Miss Sarah Gardner, sister of Rev William Gardner, Rio, Wis, as a guest last May (1906) introduced her to the numerous cousins throughout the neighborhood

The utility of a family history is illustrated by the following circumstance: In Sherbrooke resided, as was found two second cousins, granddaughters of Abigail (6), and Joseph Nichols (6) When an attempt was made to bring them together it developed that for ten years they had been well acquainted and co-workers in the Congregational Church, all unaware of the kinship which existed between them, but, sad to say, Lily Dyer Morey had passed away shortly before and to her acquaintance with Eva Gardner Hubbard was denied the additional charm of cousinship

PALMER GARDNER (6).

Palmer (5), Sylvester (4), Nicholas (3), Nicholas (2), George (1).

Palmer, son of Palmer and Hannah (Nichols) Gardner, was born in Hancock, Mass, March 14, 1775; died in Hancock, July 9, 1817 He married Rhoda Greene, March 14, 1801 She was born Oct 18, 1781, died January 1, 1852 Palmer was a shoemaker and tanner His tannery was upon the Kinderhook Creek at the foot of Potter mountain at the north end of the village of Hancock He was a man of large physique, weighing 300 pounds He was buried beside his parents in the small triangular field just across the street from the old home Neither his nor his parents' graves are marked today

Children were

Hannah, born in Rhode Island Nov 24, 1803, died in Syracuse, N Y, May 30, 1890

Sarah, born in Hancock, Dec 25, 1805, died 1876

Sylvester, born in Hancock, Feb 9, 1808; was of a roving disposition, strayed from home, engaged in rafting and was never heard from since

Emeline, born Aug 24, 1810, died Sept 7, 1845

Patience Calsina, born in Hancock, Mass, Aug 31, 1813, died Dec 4, 1906, at Sioux City, Iowa Buried at Fayetteville, N Y

Marietta, born Apr 4, 1816, died Apr 10, 1837 She was adopted by her cousin Rhoda McViccar, and is interred in the McViccar lot in the village cemetery at Fayetteville, N Y

AMY GARDNER (6)

Palmer (5), Sylvester (4), Nicholas (3), Nicholas (2), George (1).

Amy, daughter of Palmer and Hannah (Nichols) Gardner, was born in Hancock, Mass, Feb, 1777, died Jan 23, 1870, at the home of her son Ezekiel, in Elkhorn, Wis She married Willard Smith, son of William and Polly (Tamplin) Smith of Hancock, Mass, in 1794 He died 1850 and both are buried at Lafayette, Walworth County, Wis They lived for a while in Hancock, upon the corner just north of her father's, they then exchanged farms with his brother Daniel, since Eunice Gardner, after her marriage to Daniel, refused to go to Canada with him Amy made the journey of 200 miles to Canada on horseback Later they resided in Mannsville, Jefferson County, N Y.

Children were

Sylvester Gardner, born June 16, 1796, died June 24, 1879
Mary Ann (Polly), born Sept 7, 1798, died Mar, 1853.
Palmer, died in Canada at the age of two years of smallpox
Hannah Gardner, born Nov 17, 1804-5, in Canada, died 1897-8
William Walker, born Jan, 1807, died 1870
Ezekiel Brown, born Feb 17, 1809, died Mar 10, 1884
Annie Maria, born Jan 23, 1811, died Dec 17, 1892.
Daniel P born Feb 4, 1813, died in Hancock Mass, aged 11 years
Harriet Newell, born Jan 27, 1815, died Sept 22 1900, at Macon, Mich
Charlotte E, born Apr 26, 1817, died 1893

JOHN GARDNER (6)

Nathaniel (5), Job (4), Nathaniel (3), Benony (2), George (1).

John, son of Nathaniel and Marcy (Spencer) Gardner, was born Feb 22 1791, at Stephentown, Rensselaer Co, New York Married Feb, 1824, to Elizabeth Smith, daughter of John and Mary (Harris) Smith of Lebanon, New York

Nine children were born to them

John Smith, born June 12, 1825
Job, born March 27 1827
Amanda Malvina, born July 24, 1829
Frances Helen, born April 28, 1831
Lucy M, born April 19, 1834
Desevignia Starks, Nov 14, 1837
William D Stead, Oct 13, 1839.
Nathaniel, July 21, 1844
Mary Elizabeth, Aug 17, 1847

Mr Gardner remained at the home of his birth until Nov, 1856, when he removed to West Point, Wis, where he followed the occupation of a farmer until his death, Aug 28, 1879

He enlisted as a soldier in the war of 1812 and served until the close of the war Mrs Gardner died Nov 23, 1879

CHARLES GARDNER (6)

Nathaniel (5), Job (4), Nathaniel (3), Benony (2), George (1).

Charles, son of Nathaniel and Marcy (Spencer) Gardner, was born May 13, 1793, at Stephentown, New York, died Apr 9, 1892, married Lucy Ammerman April 10, 1823 She died Feb 25, 1890

Five children were born to them

Russell,

Amanda,

Jennie,

Byron, deceased

Alfred, deceased

Mr Gardner remained at home until the death of his father in 1813 and then apprenticed himself to a wool carder and cloth dresser In March, 1815, with his trade as his capital, a few dollars in money, his wardrobe tied in a handkerchief, he started for Ohio alone on foot in search of a new home He wandered through the southern and central part of Ohio and as far north as Southern Michigan until June, 1816 On his return home he reached Norwalk, Ohio Here he thought he had reached the desired goal, and in a short time was on his way back to Stephentown In December of the same year he, with his brother Richard, started for their new home, locating on the Huron river, near the center of Peru township in Huron County. Mr Gardner died April 9, 1892 Mrs Gardner died Feb 25, 1890.

GEORGE GARDNER (6)

Othniel (5), Benony (4), Isaac (3), Benony (2), George (1).

George Gardner, son of Othniel and Lydia (Reynolds) Gardner, was born in 1766, in Rhode Island Died 1840, at Troy, N Y Married Louisa Dawley

Children were

Emma, married John Patterson, of Troy, N Y, and was mother of Elias J Patterson, a lawyer of Broadway, New York City

Olivia, married Elias Patterson, of Troy, N Y, and was mother of Commodore Thomas Patterson of the United States Navy

Daniel, Born Aug. 21, 1799, died Jan 12, 1863

Mary, married Dr C S Goodrich, of Troy, N Y

Jane, died single

Louisa, married John A Hall, of Troy, N Y

He was at one time Judge of the County Court The first newspaper published in Troy, N Y, was "The Recorder" a small four-column page folio The only two extant copies known are No 208 of Vol IV preserved in the library of the Troy Young Men's Association issued on Tuesday, Aug 18, 1795, "printed by George Gardner, near the court house," and No 192, Vol III, printed at Lansingburgh, on Tuesday, April 28, 1796, by Gardner and Hill

DORCAS GARDNER (6)

George (5), Ezekiel (4), Nicholas (3) Nicholas (2), George (1).

Dorcas, daughter of George and Mary (Reynolds) Gardner, was born 1779, married Eleazer Ingraham, Jr. They lived some years in the Friend's Settlement and subsequently removed to Pultney, where both died in advanced age

Children were
John,
Abigail,
Mary,
George,
Rhoda,
Rachel,
Nancy

ABNER GARDNER (6)

George (5), Ezekiel (4), Nicholas (3), Nicholas (2), George (1).

Abner, son of George and Mary (Reynolds) Gardner, was born 1781, married Mary, daughter of Rowland Champlin, 1814. She was born in Vermont in 1795 They lived and died on lot 22 He died 1860, she in 1858

Children were
Mary S, died 1839 aged 24 years Single
George W,
Rowland J,
Abner

GEORGE GARDNER (6).

George (5), Ezekiel (4), Nicholas (3), Nicholas (2), George (1)

George son of George and Mary (Reynolds) Gardner, was born 1783, died 1866, married Lydia A daughter of Peleg Gifford She died 1854, aged 59 years

Children were

Mary, married John Bartholomew of Milo, N Y, died leaving three children Cecelia, Lewis, Sarah

Ruth, married Perry Bills and moved to Ohio

Abner, married Miss Warner of Cohocton, where they settled Four children

Phebe, married Peter French of Naples and died leaving five children

George married (1) Agnes Welker of Barrington, (2) Miss Deming of Barrington Two children were born of each marriage Almeda Byron, Ulysses G, and one other

Lydia, single, resided with her brother George

BENJAMIN GARDNER (6).

Nathaniel (5), Benjamin (4), Nathaniel (3), Benony (2), George (1).

Benjamin, son of Nathaniel and Eunice (Sunderlin) Gardner, was born July 22, 1778, died Aug 1, 1854; married Polly Allen, Sept, 7, 1805. She was born Dec 31, 1805, died April 14, 1864

Children were

Maria, born June 2, 1806, died July 18, 1882

Amanda, born Nov 12, 1807, died Aug 14, 1891

Ann, born July 17, 1809, died ——

Dewitt, born Mar. 28, 1819, died Nov 15, 1897

HANNAH GARDNER (6).

Palmer (5), Sylvester (4), Nicholas (3), Nicholas (2), George (1)

Hannah, daughter of Palmer and Hannah (Nichols) Gardner, was born April 1, 1781, died Oct 9, 1825, is buried at Eagle Village, Manlius, N Y She was married, Dec 25, 1805, to Robert Henry, son of Isaac He was born April 20, 1779, died at Medina, Ohio, Sept 29, 1862 Was a wagon maker by trade Farmer in Ohio They lived in Cambridge, N Y, and later at Eagle Village After the death of his wife, Hannah, Robert Henry married (2) Almira (Clark) Scouten and removed to Ohio in 1833

Children by Hannah were

Sylvester G, born Dec 15, 1806, died Sept 17, 1887

Isaac R, born April 22, 1810, married Mary Ranson and died Aug 11, 1862, at Olmstead Cuyahoga Co, Ohio

Myron H, born Aug 16, 1812, died January 12, 1874.

James Harvey, born July 23 1815, died April, 1884

Milton Dyer, born Dec 23, 1817, married Mary Ann Boyd, died March 17 1904-5, at Independence, Kan

Hannah Maria, born April 10, 1820, married Marcus Prentiss Ashley, living at Hawarden, Iowa, with her son James Alton She is the survivor of her generation

DANIEL GARDNER (6)

Palmer (5), Sylvester (4), Nicholas (3), Nicholas (2), George (1).

Daniel, son of Palmer and Hannah (Nichols) Gardner, was born 1783, died 1853 He married Lenche (or Diana) Van Buren, of Dutch Stock, a relative of President Van Buren They lived at Berlin, N Y where Daniel kept a store It is said that Daniel had a very sweet, musical voice and was often paid five dollars for a single performance of singing

Children were

Jane Anne,

Polly Anne.

James Van der Poel, born in Hancock, Mass, 1808, died in Utica, N Y, 1882 He married (1) Miss Webber, (2) Miss Williams, (3) Sophia Wells Williams, 1846 The following is from the Utica Herald.

"James V P Gardner, one of the oldest and best known residents of the city and one of the pioneers in the stage line business, died of paralysis Saturday, aged 74 years His funeral services were held at the Reformed Church yesterday afternoon and was largely attended Mr. Gardner came to this city in 1825 since which time he has resided here He went directly into the office of Jason Parker as book-keeper, and afterwards became associated in business with F S Faxton Silas D Childs and John Butterfield in conducting a line of stages from Albany to Buffalo His associates of those days have all passed away and he was probably the last representative of the stage route pioneers of Utica's early days When the railroad was built from the east to the west, he still conducted stage routes running north and south He was associated with John Butterfield in running a line of stages from Utica as far as Ogdensburg and later he was interested with S Brownell in running a line of stages from Utica to Norwich About the year 1855 he went to California by the overland route, settling up with the agents and making contracts for the Overland company After his return he was for some time engaged in business with the Overland company in New York From the time when he first came to Utica in 1825 up to the year 1866 was engaged in the stage business A year before the Utica, Chenango and Susquehanna Valley railroad was built he sold his stage route running to Norwich. He came to Utica a poor boy and by his industry and enterprise accumulated considerable wealth

Since retiring from the stage business, however, he lost much of his property by unfortunate investment He lived at the corner of Genesee and Cottage Streets till 1874 when the house was sold

Mr Gardner was a self-made man of high character and public spirited He was always kind to those in trouble and very generous He was a member of the Reformed Church since he came to Utica and gave to it liberally of his means He was thrice married His first wife was a daughter of Edward Webber of Vernon His second wife was a daughter of Thomas Williams of Vernon His third wife, who survived him, is a daughter of the late William Williams who at one time conducted a printing establishment on the site of the Herald office He leaves an adopted son, Dr Dwight Gardner Mr Gardner will be missed most by the older residents of the City"

Sophia Wells (Williams) Gardner, third and last wife of James V P Gardner was one of sixteen children Her father Col William Williams was a printer in Utica He was of Puritan stock and his father Thomas Williams participated in the Boston Tea Party and was one of the Roxbury Minute men Her brother S Wells Williams was a famous missionary diplomatist and scholar in China and acted as interpreter for Matthew Galbraith Perry at Yeddo in 1854 Another brother Henry Dwight Williams was commissioner of imperial customs in China while still another, Rev W Fredric Williams, was a pioneer missionary in Turkey

Henry Dwight Williams, son of Frederic, was adopted by Mr. Gardner He was educated at Hamilton College and the college of Physicians and Surgeons in New York, but his promising career as practitioner in Utica was cut short by death in 1883 His brother, Talcott Williams, is editor of the Philadelphia Press and prominent in literary circles.

ABIGAIL GARDNER (6).

Daniel (5), Sylvester (4), Nicholas (3), Nicholas (2), George (1).

Abigail, daughter of Daniel and Alice (Hall) Gardner, was born at Hancock, Mass, Nov 16, 1777, died 1852 She married Francis Willet, son of Nicholas and Deborah (Vincent) Gardner, Dec 15, 1797, at Hancock He was born at Exeter, R I, died in Moravia, N Y, in 1856

Children

Joseph, born August 12, 1797.

Benjamin, born June 6, 1799 died in Moravia, N Y, 1868 He married Ann Eliza ——, March 16, 1819

Child, born March 20, 1800, died April 3, 1801.

Child, born Jan 13, 1801, died Jan 13, 1801

Teressa, born Dec 12, 1802; died July 9, 1809.

Lydia, born May 28, 1805, died Jan 31, 1838

Daniel W, born May 15, 1807, died 1879 He married Mary Kenyon Feb. 9, 1837

Child, born May 20, 1809, died May 20, 1809

Deborah, born Apr. 13, 1810, married William Parker, Dec 23, 1835

Nicholas P, born March 3, 1813, died June 3, 1813

Minerva P, born March 3, 1813, died in Moravia, N Y, 1876 Married Cyreneus Sanford, March 8, 1839

Harrison Grey Otis, born Feb 25, 1814, died April 28, 1894, married Elizabeth F Reynolds, July 17, 1841 Two children: Abbey, deceased, Millard

Child, born Oct 24, 1815, died Nov 20, 1815

Nabby Louisa, born March 28, 1817; died Aug 31, 1848, at Lyons, Ohio

Willet A, born Jan 1 1819, married Sally Sanford, March 8, 1839

Child, born Jan 1 1820

Nicholas S, born Dec 2, 1820, died 1882; married Sarah C Gardner July 4, 1842

ELCY GARDNER (6).

Capt Daniel (5), Sylvester (4), Nicholas (3), Nicholas (2), George (1).

Elcy Gardner, daughter of Capt Daniel and Christina (Hall) Gardner, was born December 29, 1796, died January 24, 1882, at Hancock, Mass Married Rodney Dawley, son of Job and Lois (Stafford) Dawley, August 10, 1814, at Hancock, Mass. They settled in Hancock Rodney died there December 18, 1880

Their children were

Lois C, born Sept 11, 1815, died in Hancock, Dec 5, 1865 married Anson Temple, June 7, 1860 No children

Silas G, born 1819, died Apr 20, 1887, married Mary Eldridge.

James Edward born May 2, 1826, living

Charlotte O, born Mar 28, 1828, died Aug. 20, 1886, at Hancock, Mass

SALLY GARDNER (6)

Capt Daniel (5), Sylvester (4), Nicholas (3), Nicholas (2), George (1).

Sally Gardner, daughter of Capt Daniel and Christina (Hall) Gardner, was born November 25, 1799, died June 23, 1871, married Gardner Smith, son of Daniel and Eunice (Gardner) Smith, January 28, 1821 He was born May 16, 1797, died June 18, 1849

Their children were.

Infant, born Nov 3, 1821, died same date

Artalissa, born Dec 17, 1822, died May 5 1854

Daniel G, born 1824, died June 2, 1830.

Aucelia M born May 15, 1827, died Oct, 1903

Minerva S, died Mar 23, 1868

Caroline, died Dec 25, 1831

Mary C, born Dec 26, 1831, living at Smyrna, N Y, married Mortimer Gardner

Dwight, born Oct. 20, 1836 died Nov. 20-3, 1870

Delbert, born 1839, died Aug 20, 1841

PALMER GARDNER (7)

Sylvester (6), Palmer (5), Sylvester (4), Nicholas (3), Nicholas (2), George (1).

Palmer Gardner, son of Sylvester and Sarah (Cogswell) Gardner, was born at Hancock, Mass, Feb 23, 1803 Died Jan 19, 1888, at Burlington, Racine County, Wis Married Margaret Williams of Manlius, Feb 14, 1844 She died May 19, 1871, aged 49 years He married (2) Mrs Leontine E Dezotell, April 21, 1872, who survived him till 1898 Mr Gardner was educated at Troy Polytechnic, and was Civil engineer on the Welland canal

He had one child by his first wife

Lucretia May, born Nov 24 1844, died Jan 19, 1865 She was educated at Rockford College in Illinois

In 1840 he acquired a farm at Burlington, Wisconsin, where he spent his days

Mr Gardner was a man of liberal belief, yet always as liberal in his gifts to the churches of Burlington Down to old age he retained his fondness for the higher mathematics and also his memory of long passages from the British poets

HANNAH GARDNER (7).

Sylvester (6), Palmer (5), Sylvester (4), Nicholas (3), Nicholas (2), George (1).

Hannah, daughter of Sylvester and Sarah (Cogswell) Gardner, was born at Hancock, Mass, Sept 13, 1806; died Oct 31, 1881 She married Evelyn Hart Porter, M D, of Williamstown, Mass, Feb 1, 1826 He was born July 11, 1801 died Oct 22, 1875 Resided at Skaneateles, N Y

Children were

Mortimer Gardner, born Oct 26, 1826, died Nov 24, 1863 He married Anna E Tallman of Jersey City, N J, April 22, 1858

Sarah Maria, born Aug 11, 1828, died June 9, 1895

William, born Aug 29, 1830, died 1884-5 He married Julia Isabella Williams of East Hartford, Conn, Nov. 20, 1862. He was a physician, employed at the Retreat for Insane at Hartford, and the Institution for the Deaf and Dumb at Washington Heights, New York City One son William Evelyn Porter of New York City

Isabella, born June 2, 1833, died May 28, 1868 She married William Porter Rhoades, Feb 27, 1867 One daughter Emma Belle, born May 27, 1868 Resides in California

Georges Geddes, born Feb 12, 1835, died July 23, 1893 He married Mary G Gifford of New Bedford, Mass, Oct 17, 1866 Mr Porter was a druggist and latterly proprietor of an iron foundry

James Sanford, born Dec 19, 1837, died June 3, 1868 He was a physician and army surgeon

Mary Eliza, born May 1, 1840, died May 20, 1888, was instructor upon the piano and organ, and organist of St James church, Skaneateles

Edward Evelyn, born Sept 25, 1842, died Oct 26, 1872, in Orange, N J He married Mary F Lyon of Utica, N Y, Oct 18, 1872 He was a physician and army surgeon

Emma Joanna, born Sept 25, 1842, died Dec 26, 1862

Henry Herbert, born Apr 23, 1845, died Feb 5, 1846

A son, born Mar 11, 1847, died Mar, 1847

Hannah (Gardner) Porter was a woman of queenly presence and rare endowments of mind and heart, a devoted wife and mother, a royal hostess and a devout church woman The high esteem in which she was held locally is witnessed in the following poem by Miss Mary Elizabeth Beauchamp of Skaneateles

In Memoriam
Hannah Gardner Porter
Oct 31, 1881

'Tis Hallowe'en and the trees are gay
With the gorgeous beauty of decay,
And the air is full of misty light
That soothes and charms the languid sight

Beneath our feet and above our heads
The golden drapery waves and spreads
And full and ripe, like the Autumn day
Is the life that is passing from earth away

With grace and beauty and culture blessed
The richest gift of each state possessed
As Christian, as wife, as mother, as friend
How brilliant the tints and how soft they blend!

Blest are the dead who die in the Lord,
They rest in peace, saith the mighty Word,
But even there, in their places of rest
Their works do follow the peaceful blest;

And the good she has been and the good she has done
Shall add to the bliss of the home she has won.

SYLVESTER COGSWELL GARDNER (7).

Sylvester (6), Palmer (5), Sylvester (4), Nicholas (3), Nicholas (2), George (1).

Sylvester C Gardner, son of Sylvester and Sarah (Cogswell) Gardner, was born March 24, 1811, at Manlius, N Y Died Sept 7, 1869 Married Caroline Collin, daughter of David and Anna (Smith) Collin, of Fayetteville, N Y, Sept. 25, 1838 She was born December 26, 1818 Died Sept 17, 1869 Both are buried at Fayetteville, N Y

Their children were

Edmund born June 20, 1840, died the same day

Caroline, born Jan 16, 1842, died Aug 14, 1903

Sylvester, born Nov 18, 1844 graduated from Hamilton College, Clinton, N Y, in 1870, unmarried Resides at Alameda, Cal

Sarah, born Jan 21, 1849

Anna, born Dec. 11, 1850, died Aug 31, 1869

Miriam, born Sept 6, 1852

William, born March 26, 1861

After his father's death Sylvester C bought out the interest of the other heirs in the Gardner homestead in Eagle Village, married, and settled upon a farm which was given to his wife by her father and was located near Fayetteville Later he doubled the acreage of this by purchase He was an industrious thrifty and successful farmer Though reared in the Episcopal church at Manlius, in 1855 he united with the Presbyterian church at Fayetteville, of which Mrs Gardner was a member and in the organization of which her father had been a prime mover

In his religion as in his business transactions he combined honesty and generosity He maintained a family altar and defined his religious experiences as "the joy of working from instead of toward the cross"

Politically he was a Republican from the inception of the party Only by age limit was he restrained from enlisting as a volunteer to aid in maintaining the Union Loyalty was a fundamental trait in the man Affection ruled his household Himself trained at Manlius and Cortland academies he gave his children good educational advantages, and instructed them to "stand by the minister and the school-master"

In address and reference he was accorded respect in the home and in the community Abhorring chicanery and pretense he was straightforward and to the point in his speech His manner was genial, his laugh was hearty and his regard open and direct Clear in judgment he formed just estimates of character Personal inclination would have taken him to Milwaukee in the 30's, filial and domestic duty held him in the east

Caroline Collin awakened his admiration while she was yet his pupil their wedded life was a response which she never had occasion to qualify or recall and they reached life's bourne together

Mrs Gardner's father was great-grandson of David Collin a French Huguenot ship owner who settled in Milford, Conn Her mother, Anna Smith, was a descendant of Elder William Brewster of the Mayflower. At the age of eleven she was the pupil of her future husband.

WILLIAM NICHOLS GARDNER (7).

Sylvester (6), Palmer (5), Sylvester (4), Nicholas (3), Nicholas (2), George (1)

William N., son of Sylvester and Sarah (Cogswell) Gardner, was born at Manlius, N. Y., July 22, 1813, died Aug 24, 1839, of prairie fever. He married Maria Sheldon at Milwaukee, Wis., Oct 12, 1837 She was the daughter of William B and Anna Sheldon of Delhi N Y, and was born 1821, died at Hyde Park, Chicago, 1901 Mr Gardner had located in Milwaukee in 1835 Through fidelity to a business engagement he drove fifteen miles across the country only to be disappointed by the other party to the appointment and returning the same night eager to see his mother and sister Sarah who had just arrived from the east to pay him a visit he contracted prairie fever and died Aug. 24, 1839, leaving his wife and one child

William Sheldon, born at Milwaukee, Mar 22, 1839, died Oct 29, 1859, and is buried beside his father in Oakwoods cemetery, Chicago

After Mr Gardner's death his widow married (2) Thomas Wright to whom she bore one son

Frank

She married (3) Hon Jonathan Young Scammon, Esq., of Chicago, founder of the Interocean, pioneer, Judge, posesssor of large real estate interest in that city and liberal donor to the old University of Chicago

SARAH ANN GARDNER (7).

Sylvester (6), Palmer (5), Sylvester (4), Nicholas (3), Nicholas (2), George (1).

Sarah Ann, daughter of Sylvester and Sarah (Cogswell) Gardner, was born at Manlius, N Y, Feb 6, 1815, died Jan 3, 1894, at New York City. She married Rev Samuel G Appleton, Sept 30. 1839 He was the son of Gen James and Sarah (Fuller) Appleton, and was born Nov. 5, 1808, at Gloucester, Mass, died Nov 29, 1873, at Morrisania, N Y. He graduated at Amherst College in 1830, and studied Theology at Andover and General Theological Seminary in New York Ordained 1836, and was rector at Hanover Mass, 1836, Manlius, N Y, 1838, Avon, N Y, 1840, Richfield Springs, N Y 1847, Delhi, N Y, 1850, Ansonia, Conn, 1854, and Morrisania, N Y, 1858-68

Children were

William Gardner, born Apr 17, 1843, at Avon, N Y

James Samuel, born 1848, at Richfield Springs, N. Y. died 1866, at Morrisania, N Y

HORACE DYER (7).

Abigail Gardner (6), Palmer (5) Sylvester (4), Nicholas (3), Nicholas (2), George (1).

Horace, son of Samuel and Abigail (Gardner) Dyer, married Mrs Sarah Julia (Sherrill) Baldwin, of New Hartford, N Y, 1835 She was born March 12, 1813, in New Hartford, died May 11, 1894, in Sherbrooke, Prov Quebec She married (1) Fowler Baldwin who died 1832 After her marriage to Mr Dyer, resided in Marcy, N Y He died 1861

Children were

Sherrill, born 1837, died in infancy

Sarah, born 1839, died 1905 She married (1) Dr Frederick Henderson Two daughters Mary, and Helen Spriggs, who married Archibald Valentine of Chicago and died some years ago Sarah married (2) John H McAvoy of Chicago

Horace Samuel, born June 9, 1844, died 1876 Served in the 146th N Y regiment during the Civil war, also on the staff of Gen Girard

Louisa born 1847 died in infancy

Lily Louisa, born 1852, married Samuel Foote Morey of Sherbrooke, P Q, died about 1904, survived by her husband and one daughter Louise

SARAH DYER (7).

Abigail Gardner (6), Palmer (5), Sylvester (4), Nicholas (3), Nicholas (2), George (1)

Sarah Nichols, daughter of Samuel and Abigail (Gardner) Dyer, was born ——, died about 1838 She married Andrew Tilman, of Geneva, N Y

Three children

Samuel, married a Miss Dielson of Albany, N Y, died long ago No children

Caroline, died 1882 in Geneva, N Y Married Dr O P. Laird in 1842

Louise, died in infancy

MILTON DYER (7).

Abigail Gardner (6), Palmer (5), Sylvester (4), Nicholas (3), Nicholas (2), George (1)

Milton, son of Samuel and Abigail (Gardner) Dyer, married and lived at Whitestown, N Y Had two sons and a daughter

Caroline, married (1) Dr May (2) Mr Beecher of Canastota N Y (3) Rev J W Whitfield of Utica who died about 1902 Milton Dyer died in Canastota at the home of his daughter who was then Mrs. Beecher We have no record of the two sons

GARDNER TOWNSEND (7).

Dorcas (6), Palmer (5), Sylvester (4), Nicholas (3), Nicholas (2), George (1)

Gardner, son of Nathan and Dorcas (Gardner) Townsend was born Aug 26, 1786, died May 2, 1869 He married (1) Achsah Bradish Dec. 26 1811 She died July 27, 1831 (2) Eunice Douglas

Children:

Orin G, born Oct 14, 1812 died Feb 12, 1834

Horace D, born Sept 16, 1814, died May 14, 1833

James B, born Dec 22, 1816, died July 17 1882 He was an attorney in San Francisco, Cal A son Clarence

Ingham D, born Feb 27, 1840, married Alma J Higby, May 6, 1866 No children Resided at East Martinsburg, N Y

Dorcas E, born Dec 17, 1842, married Albert B Wells, Sept. 15, 1864, died Feb 6, 1895 Children. D. Alberta, born June 13, 1865, died Oct 30, 1887 Gardner T, born Apr 18, 1871, died Aug 30, 1895 Ira G, born July 27, 1873, a dentist at Holland Patent, N Y

Gardner Townsend was four times married Ingham D and Dorcas E were the children of Eunice Douglas, his second wife

WILLIAM TOWNSEND (7).

Dorcas (6), Palmer (5), Sylvester (4), Nicholas (3), Nicholas (2), George (1)

William Townsend, son of Nathan and Dorcas (Gardner) Townsend, was born about 1788, died Sept 29, 1868, married Sallie Foster of Hancock She died May 6, 1864

Mr. Townsend cultivated the home farm of his father, Nathan, and bequeathed his acres and palatial residence to his only child

Sarah Ann, born Apr 9, 1816 Died July 4, 1902

RHODA TOWNSEND (7).

Dorcas Gardner (6), Palmer (5), Sylvester (4), Nicholas (3), Nicholas (2), George (1).

Rhoda, daughter of Nathan and Dorcas (Gardner) Townsend, was born Mar 5, 1797, died Jan 26, 1865 She married John McViccar, son of Archibald and Elizabeth McViccar, Jan, 1821, and resided in Fayetteville, N Y Previous to their marriage Mr McViccar taught school at Eagle Village, N Y, and it was during a visit to her uncle Sylvester, that Rhoda Townsend made his acquaintance

Children were·

Twins, born Oct 16, 1825, died in infancy.

John T, born 1827, died Mar 7 1854 He graduated at Hamilton College in 1849, Psi Upsilon fraternity. Married Miss Fiske of Fayetteville Harriet W, daughter of Aaron and Sallie Fletcher Fiske was born in Templeton, Mass, June 2, 1828, married Oct 2, 1850, died Feb 27, 1881 Mr and Mrs John T McViccar are survived by a daughter, Hattie Townsend, who was born July 18, 1853, and resides in Fayetteville, N. Y

Louisa, born 1831; died in infancy

Elizabeth, born 1833, died in infancy.

PALMER TOWNSEND (7)

Dorcas Gardner (6), Palmer (5), Sylvester (4), Nicholas (3), Nicholas (2), George (1).

Palmer, son of Nathan and Dorcas (Gardner) Townsend, married Miss Bush of Lowville, N Y. He was at one time County Judge at

Lowville, Lewis County, N Y After 1844 he was in the wholesale hardware business in New York City He died in Brooklyn

Children of whom he have record were

Louise, married Lewis B Reed

William H, born 1826, died Apr 15, 1905 He married and resided in Brooklyn, N Y

Mary, married J Earnest Miller

Frances, died Mar, 1906

The following is from "The Brooklyn Eagle" Nov 14, 1904

"Mrs. Louise Townsend Reed, wife of Lewis Benedict Reed, who died yesterday at her home 172 Rensen St, was born at Lowville Lewis Co, N Y, in 1825 She was the eldest daughter of Palmer Townsend, once a county judge of Lewis County and afterwards a wholesale hardware merchant in New York City The family moved to Brooklyn about sixty years ago and Mrs. Reed was educated in Prof Greenleaf's Academy in Pierrepont St, and at Rutgers Female Institute in New York She was married in November, 1849 and her golden wedding was celebrated at 172 Remsen St, in 1899, and received full notice in the Eagle at the time. She spent several years in Paris and Italy in her middle life and became a fine linguist and familiar with the languages and literatures of France, Italy, and Spain and also acquired some knowledge of German She had an attractive personality and a large circle of loving friends in Brooklyn and abroad She was a member of the First Baptist Church of Brooklyn from early girlhood until a few years ago, when she became a member of the Church of the Pilgrims Her husband was formerly a practicing lawyer in this city and has for several years past filled a responsible position in the American Surety Company of New York Her final illness was of two years' duration, but she was always cheerful and patient She had one son, Palmer Townsend, who is a resident of California Another son, Frank T, died aged 4 years.

HALSEY TOWNSEND (7)

Dorcas Gardner (6), Palmer (5), Sylvester (4), Nicholas (3), Nicholas (2), George (1)

Halsey, son of Nathan and Dorcas (Gardner) Townsend, married Miss Roche of Mississippi He was a brilliant lawyer at Natchez Miss Died from pulmonary troubles, leaving no issue

INGHAM TOWNSEND (7)

Dorcas Gardner (6), Palmer (5), Sylvester (4), Nicholas (3), Nicholas (2), George (1).

Ingham son of Nathan and Dorcas (Gardner) Townsend, married Julia Fox He was a member of the State Legislature in 1857 Resided at Holland Patent and entertained royally parties of students from Hamilton College and Houghton Seminary at Clinton who passed through Holland Patent to visit Trenton Falls.

It was through the kind offices of Ingham Townsend and John McViccar that Grover Cleveland was enabled to obtain the education which placed him in prominence before his country

Mr and Mrs Townsend had three adopted children

Fannie, a niece of Mrs Townsend, married George Anderson A son and daughter

Ingham

Anna, married Mr. Wright of Rome.

BETSEY TOWNSEND (7).

Dorcas Gardner (6), Palmer (5), Sylvester (4), Nicholas (3), Nicholas (2), George (1).

Betsey, daughter of Nathan and Dorcas (Gardner) Townsend, married Mr Ward of Oneida Lake

Children

Sarah, married Mr. Stephens

Anna, married Isaac Pierce.

HANNAH TOWNSEND (7)

Dorcas Gardner (6), Palmer (5), Sylvester (4), Nicholas (3), Nicholas (2), George (1).

Hannah, daughter of Nathan and Dorcas (Gardner) Townsend married James B Olcott She died early in life leaving children.

NATHANIEL TOWNSEND (7).

Dorcas Gardner (6), Palmer (5), Sylvester (4), Nicholas (3), Nicholas (2), George (1).

Nathaniel, son of Nathan and Dorcas (Gardner) Townsend, was born June 24, 1804, died 1864 at Holland Patent, N Y He married (1) Miss Roche of Mississippi

Children were·

Nathaniel, served in the ranks of a Pennsylvania regiment and was shot through the head at the battle of Gettysburg and buried on the battlefield

Halsey Palmer, died before the war and is buried on the family lot in the cemetery at Austin, Texas

Maria, died at the age of sixteen years at the home of her uncle Ingham in Floyd township, Oneida County, N. Y

Benjamin,

Nathaniel Townsend, married (2) Angeline Louise, daughter of Jas Wanton Townsend of Warrick Co, Ind She was born Jan 25, 1822, at Princeton, Ind, died in Austin, Tex, 1889 Buried there James Wanton was son of Martin and Susanna (Allen) Townsend of Hancock, Nathan's brother Nathaniel and James Wanton were therefore cousins

After her father's death in Indiana, Angeline Louise was adopted by her father's brother Nathaniel, of Williamstown, Mass, whose wife Cynthia Marsh was a lineal descendant of Miles Standish and Henry Adams, ancestor of John and Samuel Adams Children by (2) marriage were

Anthony, died in infancy and is buried at Kenosha, Wis

Angeline Louise, born July 7, 1850, at Williamstown, Mass

Susan Marsh, born Aug 22, 1852 at Austin Texas

Pauline Spencer born Dec 3, 1855, at Austin, Texas

James Wanton, born Oct 6, 1857, at Austin, Texas

Palmer Gardner, born 1860, at Mendham, N J, married Cynthia Beaumont of Wallingford, Conn Child Angeline Louise, born Oct, 1892 Resides in California

Mr Gardner's first wife brought him slaves but at the time of the secession he sided with the North and was an ardent Unionist and freed his slaves In consequence he suffered much during the war, he came on to New York State and was helped by his Townsend relatives. He was a successful merchant and business man at Austin, Texas, where he settled while Mexico held sway there His daughter says of him

"My father came to Texas about 1834 and aided in establishing the Republic He was consul to New Orleans from the Republic of Texas for a good many years Just before the Civil war he took his family north and we did not return to Texas until a year after the close of the war and two years after his death in 1864 When Jefferson Davis issued his orders for all property owners to return or their property would be confiscated within forty days, my father's health was such that he could not return, so all of his estate was confiscated and sold to the Confederate Government It must have been a great trial to him to leave his family in such financial straits, but he had faith in God and the United States Government, that it would come out all right, and so it did His children shall never cease to cherish his memory"

Nathaniel Townsend's brother Martin of Hancock whose (1) wife was Susanna Allen, married (2) Annie (Niles) Gardner of South Kingstown, R I She bore him two children

Lauren, married Amanda Smith of Hancock and spent his life in Cayuga Co, N Y One of his grandsons, Rev Smith Delancy Townsend, was an Episcopal clergyman in New York in 1871 One of his sons Lauren M Townsend, lived in Syracuse, N Y

Lucy, married Hon Volney Richmond of Hoosick Had several children, all of whom died young

SAMUEL W. WILSON (7).

Mary (6), Palmer (5), Sylvester (4), Nicholas (3), Nicholas (2), George (1).

Samuel W son of John and Mary (Gardner) Wilson, married Sabrina Gardner (8), Perry Greene (7), Robert (6), Nathaniel (5), Joshua (4) Robert (3), George (2), George (1) They resided at Smyrna, N Y He died Aug 31 1874, she died June 13, 1840.

By this marriage he had one son:

Perry Gardner, married Avaline Wilcox of Smyrna, N Y, died Mar, 1888 No children

Mr Wilson married (2) Lois A Clark of Lebanon Springs One son William Clark married Kate Babcock of Norwich, N Y He died at Lebanon Springs, leaving a wife and one daughter.

MORENCY GARDNER (7)

Joseph N. (6), Palmer (5), Sylvester (4), Nicholas (3), Nicholas (2), George (1).

Morency Gardner, son of Joseph N and Deborah (Reynolds) Gardner, was born August 12, 1805, at Hancock Hill, Stanbridge, Province Quebec Died April 10, 1880 Married Delana Wilson, March 29, 1846. Children were.

Clarissa Deborah born June 15, 1847 Died December 19, 1863

Helen, born August 17, 1853 Married Gardner Gates Stanton, a farmer residing at Stanbridge, East, October 5, 1876 One child Arthur Gardner, born Aug 4, 1883, died June 15, 1898

Emma, born May 18, 1855 Married Louis McMahon of Burlington, Vt, August 2, 1880 No children

Arthur Morency, born May 14, 1859 Married Bertha Baker, January 23, 1895 Resides upon the old Joseph N Gardner homestead at Stanbridge, Quebec No children

Adelaide, born August 28, 1866 Millinery business at Montreal

James Wellington, born May 17, 1869 Resides with brother Arthur at Stanbridge

LESTER GARDNER (7)

Joseph N (6), Palmer (5), Sylvester (4), Nicholas (3), Nicholas (2), George (1)

Lester, son of Joseph N and Deborah (Reynolds) Gardner was born Feb 7, 1808, died April 5, 1890 He married Lucy Chandler, 1836 Children were

Deidamia, born Dec 28, 1837, died Sept 5, 1879 Unmarried

Cyril Sylvester, born 1840

John Dana, born 1843, died 1867

Magdalen, born March 15, 1846, married Edward Westover Reside Calgary, Alberta, Canada Child Marion

Hannah, born March 10, 1850, married H B Kemp, Stanbridge, East Children Fred, Harry.

Marion, born Feb 18, 1853, married G S Soules, M D, Stanbridge, East

Edna, born Jan 1, 1856, married A N Reynolds flour and feed merchant Stanbridge, P Q

Harriet, born Aug 12, 1859, married Frank Hibbard Civil Engineer, Quebec

Ernest, born July 6, 1862

JAMES PALMER GARDNER (7).

Joseph N (6), Palmer (5), Sylvester (4), Nicholas (3), Nicholas (2), George (1).

James Palmer, son of Joseph N and Deborah (Reynolds) Gardner, was born April 25, 1812, died March 21, 1868, from injuries received in a runaway He married Elizabeth Rykerd in 1837 When a lad James Palmer went to live with his grandmother Reynolds in St Armand and that town was always his home After his marriage this old Reynolds farm became his either by purchase or deed of gift

Their children were

Joseph Palmer, born Nov 20, 1838

James Herbert, born July 11, 1843

Orcelia, born Oct 8, 1845

Charles Osborne, born Feb 11, 1848

Almeda Deborah, born Apr 13, 1850

Eva, born Feb 26, 1853

Delbert Morency, born Sept 26, 1855

Emmet, born Jan 6, 1867, married Nellie Fish, Sept 15, 1892 Traveling salesman for dairy supply house Residence Enosburg Falls, Vt

EMILY GARDNER (7).

Joseph N. (6), Palmer (5), Sylvester (4), Nicholas (3), Nicholas (2), George (1)

Emily, daughter of Joseph N and Deborah (Reynolds) Gardner, was born Sept 7 1817; died Oct 9 1900 She married Rev D W Sornberger, an Adventist preacher Sept. 6, 1838 Resided in Stanbridge and late in Stanstead, P Q.

Children

Gardner, born 1842, married Maria Oliver, 1870 Residence Barnston, P Q Children Bernard, Minnie

Langdon Morency, born 1842· married Florence Oliver, 1870, Barnston, P Q

Emily Diana, born 1844, died 1898

Ibri, born 1848, died 1895

ORCELIA GARDNER (7).

Joseph N. (6) Palmer (5), Sylvester (4), Nicholas (3), Nicholas (2), George (1)

Orcelia, daughter of Joseph N and Deborah (Reynolds) Gardner, was born Sept 2, 1824, died Sept 23, 1878 She married Erastus Chandler, 1842

Children

George, born Nov 3, 1844 died Sept 10, 1862

Harriet, born July 10, 1846

Auriola, born June 20, 1848 married Harvy Beattie, 1872. Stanbridge, East, P Q Children Minnie, Harry

CALISTA GARDNER (7)

Joseph N. (6), Palmer (5), Sylvester (4), Nicholas (3), Nicholas (2), George (1).

Calista, daughter of Joseph N and Deborah (Reynolds) Gardner, was born Sept 2 1824, died Nov 9, 1873. She married Cyril Chandler, March 19, 1846

Children

Bertha, born Mar 10, 1853, married Harvard Briggs, 1875 Live at Stanbridge, P Q

Florence, born Nov 24 1858, married W H Russell, 1900 Live at Riceburg P Q

Magdaline, born July 5, 1861

HANNAH GARDNER (7).

Palmer (6), Palmer (5), Sylvester (4), Nicholas (3), Nicholas (2), George (1).

Hannah, daughter of Palmer and Rhoda (Greene) Gardner was born in Rhode Island, Nov 24, 1803, died in Syracuse, N Y, May 30, 1890 She married Horace Brown Gates, Feb 12, 1824, in Eagle Village, Onondaga Co N Y He was the son of Nehemiah Gates, born in Massachusetts, Aug 25, 1770, died in Jamesville, N Y, Aug 12, 1823, and Phebe (Keeler) Worden married Nov 23, 1790 Horace Brown Gates was born Jan 9 1805 died Feb 27, 1882 He was a farmer, mill owner and merchant in and near Syracuse

Children were

Caroline Elizabeth, born Jan 10, 1825, died May 20, 1852

William Gardner born May 22, 1830

Mr and Mrs Gates were married in Brooklyn, N Y Mr Gates joined the church in Onondaga Valley, at the age of sixteen years, and in 1848 he united with the Park Presbyterian church of Syracuse and served it for many years as a ruling elder. Of him the Syracuse Journal said

"Mr Gates was an excellent citizen, a man of unspotted integrity and ardent piety He was ever ready for every good word and work and his genial smile in his intercourse with friends always revealed the cordiality and warmth of his friendship He entered the portals of the unseen world with an unfaltering trust in the Redeemer When stricken with paralysis so that he could not speak he would indicate his feelings and his full hope of a joyous immortality by a smile of peace upon his countenance and a bright glance of the eye Most emphatically can his friends say of him, 'The righteous hath hope in his death'"

SARAH GARDNER (7)

Palmer (6), Palmer (5), Sylvester (4), Nicholas (3), Nicholas (2), George (1).

Sarah, daughter of Palmer and Rhoda (Greene) Gardner, was born at Hancock, Mass, Dec 25, 1805; died 1876. She married Rev S. W D

Chace, Oct. 1825. He was born in Fall River, Mass, October 24, 1803 Mr Chace was a Methodist minister and was master of all three professions, the ministry, law and medicine. His daughter Mrs Adams, says of him "He would have been eminent wherever he was placed The word mediocre was not for him Aunt Jones (Calsina) says my mother was the prettiest girl she ever saw I knew her for the best woman with whom I have ever come in contact"

Their children were

Emeline Amelia, born Sept 9, 1826, died 1904, married Mr Allen and lived at Washington, Ill

Delia Louise born at Clarence, Erie Co, N Y, June 11, 1828, died 1844

Sarah Gardner, born at Attica, N Y, 1831, died in Attica, Genesee Co, N Y, 1832

William T born 1833 died in Brockport, N Y, 1835

George Gardner D, born Mar 7, 1835. died 1855 near Helena, Arkansas, killed by accidental discharge of a gun while hunting

Palmer, born Dec 29, 1837, died 1847 at Washington, Ill

Maryette, born Mar 9, 1840, in Bloomington, Ill

Sarah P, born May 2, 1843, at Frankport, Ill, married Mr Franklin, resides at Lexington, Ill

Wintemoyeh, born Apr 14, 1846, at New Orleans, La, married Mr Perkins Resides in Hudson, Mich

PATIENCE CALSINA GARDNER (7).

Palmer (6), Palmer (5), Sylvester (4), Nicholas (3), Nicholas (2), George (1).

Patience Calsina, daughter of Palmer and Rhoda (Greene) Gardner, married Rev Charles Jones, Aug 29, 1840 Mr Jones was born in Ontario, Canada, Aug 1, 1809 His father was Israel Jones, son of Israel Jones, Esq, of Williamstown, Mass, who died in 1828 at the advanced age of 92 years Charles fitted for College at Hopkins Academy, Hadley, Mass, and took three years at Williams and his fourth year under President Nott at Union College He studied divinity at Auburn and New Haven Dr Nathaniel W Taylor was then at the height of his fame and efficiency as a theologian at Yale Ordained in 1833, Mr Jones wrought in the Christian ministry without interruption for forty-eight years, and preached occasionally even after that He died Sept 3, 1889, at North Abington, Mass., at the home of his son by a former marriage Mrs Jones died Dec 4, 1906, at Sioux City, Iowa, and was laid to rest beside her husband at Fayetteville, N Y She was next to the last among the cousins of her generation Her personal beauty, her gentle bearing and her tender care of her sister Hannah during the closing weeks of her life are memorable to one who beheld them

Children were:

Elvira Elizabeth, born at Lafargeville, N Y, Feb 14, 1841; died Aug 6, 1849

Emeline Alathea, born at Bergen, N Y, Nov 7, 1843, died Dec 19, 1876

Sarah Louise, born at Oswego, N Y , Apr 12, 1845

Horatio Gates, born Oswego, N. Y., Feb 18, 1847, died Aug 23, 1848

HANNAH GARDNER SMITH (7).

Amy Gardner (6), Palmer (5), Sylvester (4), Nicholas (3), Nicholas (2), George (1).

Hannah G, daughter of Willard and Amy (Gardner) Smith, was born Nov. 17, 1804-5, in Canada, died July 26, 1898, at Gordon Merrick's, Spring Prairie, Wis She was married to Jeremiah Sheffield in the spring of 1823 aged 18 years He was born Dec 1, 1801, died July 9, 1874 He was an only child and his father who came from Rhode Island was lost in Canada The fall of 1823 Hannah and Jeremiah removed to Mansville, N Y

Children were·

Oscar, born Feb 12, 1824

Cordelia, born April 9 1826, died aged two years

Martha Elizabeth, born June 7, 1828 Living with her son Charles

Hannah Janette, born May 30, 1830, died 1844.

Daniel Jeremiah, born March 1, 1833, married Elsie Smith, June 30, 1870 Lives in Springfield, Minn One son Francis, Jr

Celeste Annette, born Nov 1, 1839

WILLIAM WALKER SMITH (7)

Amy Gardner (6), Palmer (5). Sylvester (4), Nicholas (3), Nicholas (2), George (1).

William W , son of Willard and Amy (Gardner) Smith was born Jan 27, 1807, died Nov 28, 1867 He was married June 7, 1842 to Mary Theresa Stowe. She was born April 16, 1821, died March 4, 1898 She was the daughter of William B and Lucy (Moore) Stowe of Marlborough, Mass , and sister of the late Alfred M Stowe of Canandaigua, N. Y She died at the home of her son in Utica, N. Y.

Child

Brainard Gardner born Oct. 20, 1846

SYLVESTER GARDNER SMITH (7)

Amy Gardner (6), Palmer (5) Sylvester (4), Nicholas (3), Nicholas (2), George (1)

Sylvester G , son of Willard and Amy (Gardner) Smith, was born in Hancock, Mass , June 16, 1796, died in Troy Center, Wis , June 24-5, 1878-9 He married (1) Diana Ward of Manlius, N. Y , March, 1824 (2) Mrs Charity Pierce

Children

Caroline, born Mar 10 1826 in Manlius Living in Troy Center, Wis

Sarah, married Oscar Smith, son of John, a brother of Willard.

Addie, married Harrison Montague of Troy Center, Wis

Lindsay, married Helen Stewart He died Aug 17, 1905 Children Mary, Clara, Carroll, Harold, Osmer and Rollins, who is married and living in Ft Morgan, Colarado

POLLY SMITH (7).

Amy Gardner (6), Palmer (5), Sylvester (4), Nicholas (3), Nicholas (2), George (1).

Polly, daughter of Willard and Amy (Gardner) Smith, married Nichols Briggs of Rhode Island

Children were

Howard, married Margaret Lapham of Hancock, Mass

James, married Sophia Dean of Troy, Wis

Orlando, unmarried

Benjamin, unmarried

Harriet, married Mr Dexter Salisbury, has daughter Hattie, who lives at San Lorenzo, Cal

Mary Ann, married Perez Merrick of San Lorenzo, Cal Have one son Orlando Briggs, born May 21, 1852 married Ida Stebbins He died Aug 31, 1905 Two children Nellie, married Mr Bevoir, Orlando Briggs born 1891

Maria, daughter of Nichols and Polly Briggs, married Mr Williams

EZEKIEL BROWN SMITH (7).

Amy Gardner (6), Palmer (5), Sylvester (4), Nicholas (3), Nicholas (2), George (1).

Ezekiel B, son of Willard and Amy (Gardner) Smith was born in Huntsburg, Canada, Feb 17, 1809, died in Lafayette, Wis, March 10, 1882 He married Sophronia Allen at Ellisburg, N Y, April 9, 1840 She was born at that place June 6, 1812, died Jan 5, 1885, in Troy Center, Wis

Children were

Henry Kirk, born Feb 5, 1841, in Mannsville, N Y, died July 19, 1841

Frances Amy, born Mar 7, 1843 in Mannsville, died March 3 1853, in Lafayette, Wis

Willard Allen born Oct 17, 1844, in Lafayette, Wis, died Jan 10 1848

Harriet Amelia, born at Lafayette, Nov 1, 1847, died Feb 27, 1864

Mary Rebecca, born Aug 10, 1851, in Lafayette, Wis Resides in Elkhorn.

ANNE MARIA SMITH (7).

Amy Gardner (6), Palmer (5), Sylvester (4), Nicholas (3), Nicholas (2), George (1).

Anne Maria, daughter of Willard and Amy (Gardner) Smith, was born January 23, 1811 Died December 17, 1892 Married Dewitt

Clinton Sheldon of Stephentown, N. Y Removed to Reedsburg, Wisconsin.

Children were:

Ezekiel B,

Caroline,

Dwelton Melvin, married Mary Hood, of Racine, Wis Lives at Reedsburg No children.

Charles Fox,

Kirk, lives at Eddyville, Nebraska. Three children

Amy.

HARRIET NEWELL SMITH (7).

Amy Gardner (6), Palmer (5), Sylvester (4), Nicholas (3), Nicholas (2), George (1).

Harriet N, daughter of Willard and Amy (Gardner) Smith, was born Jan 27, 1815, at Hancock, Mass; died Sept. 22, 1900, at Macon, Mich She married Edmund Hand, son of Edmund and Sarah (Ely) Hand, March 3, 1836 He was born at Hancock, Mass, Aug, 1813 They removed to Lake Ridge, Mich, in the early pioneer days and settled on a farm Six children were born to them and all settled near the old home

Josephine S, born Mar 20, 1838, in Macon, Mich

Horace A, born Apr 12, 1841

Howard A, born Sept 20, 1846, married Cynthia Kidder of Saline, Mich A retired farmer and lives at Hudson

Hemon E, born June 10, 1849, in Macon Unmarried and resides in Tecumseh

Helen A, born June 10, 1849

Annette M., born Nov 24, 1858

CHARLOTTE E SMITH (7).

Amy Gardner (6), Palmer (5), Sylvester (4), Nicholas (3), Nicholas (2), George (1).

Charlotte E, daughter of Willard and Amy (Gardner) Smith, was born April 26, 1817, died Feb 22, 1893 She married Charles, son of James and Elizabeth (Moore) Wheeler, Nov 3, 1840 He was born July 1, 1819, died Oct 23, 1893, at Bangor Van Buren Co, Mich He was a merchant Between the twelfth and sixteenth years of her life Charlotte lived in New York State and after that in Blissfield, Lenawee Co, Mich She died in Bangor, Mich

Children were

Arthur James, born Sept 25, 1841.

Cornelia Alicia, born Aug. 10, 1845

George Sylvester, born May 25, 1850; died 1857

Charles Francis, born July 1 1855, died July 8, 1855

Charlotte twin of Charles F, born July 1, 1855, died same date.

Adaline born Aug 5, 1857, died April, 1858

SYLVESTER G. HENRY (7).

Hannah Gardner (6), Palmer (5), Sylvester (4), Nicholas (3), Nicholas (2), George (1).

Sylvester G., son of Robert and Hannah (Gardner) Henry, was born Dec 15, 1806, died Sept 17 1887 His wife was Julianne Scouten, daughter of his father's second wife by a former marriage To Sylvester and Julianne were born in Medina Co, Ohio, July 20, 1845, twin daughters, Virginia J and Vietta J

In 1855 the family moved to Waterloo, Wis, and thence after a year to Fond du Lac Co, Wis, where they resided till the spring of 1868 when they removed to Grundy Co, Iowa Here they remained till Mr Henry's death, in 1887

ISAAC R. HENRY (7).

Hannah Gardner (6), Palmer (5), Sylvester (4), Nicholas (3), Nicholas (2), George (1).

Isaac R, son of Robert and Hannah (Gardner) Henry, was born April 22, 1810 died 1862 at Olmstead, Cuyahoga Co, Ohio Was a Universalist minister He married Mary Ransom

Children
Lucy, deceased
Robert, deceased
Isabelle married Mr Reed Beaumont, Cuyahoga Co, Ohio
Arthur, lives in the Philippines
Emma, deceased
Norris deceased

MYRON H. HENRY (7)

Hannah Gardner (6), Palmer (5), Sylvester (4), Nicholas (3), Nicholas (2), George (1)

Myron H, son of Robert and Hannah (Gardner) Henry was born Aug. 16, 1812, died in the 60's Married Eliza King and lived and died in Racine, Wis Carpenter by trade

Children
Sarah deceased
Edwin, living at Oshkosh, Wis. Bears the title "Captain"
Charles, deceased
Emmet, deceased

JAMES HARVEY HENRY (7).

Hannah Gardner (6), Palmer (5), Sylvester (4), Nicholas (3), Nicholas (2), George (1).

J Harvey, son of Robert and Hannah (Gardner) Henry was born July 23, 1815, died April, 1884 His wife was Laura Tillotson They had three children.

Caroline M, born May 2, 1843

Millie E. (Philomel), born March 16, 1846, in Medina Co, Ohio, married Daniel Ickes in Nov, 1894. They reside at San Jose, California

Robert.

MILTON DYER HENRY (7).

Hannah Gardner (6), Palmer (5), Sylvester (4), Nicholas (3), Nicholas (2), George (1).

Milton D, son of Robert and Hannah (Gardner) Henry, was born Dec 23, 1817, died March 17, 1906 He married Mary A Boyd. She was born Feb 18, 1830 Resided in Iowa and latterly at Independence, Kans, where he died Was express agent and highly esteemed as a citizen and as a man

Children

Thomas Boyd, born Oct 24, 1854; unmarried.

Milton Davis, born Dec 26, 1856, unmarried Is secretary of the J. E Hutt Contracting Co, of Kansas City

HANNAH MARIA HENRY (7).

Hannah Gardner (6), Palmer (5), Sylvester (4), Nicholas (3), Nicholas (2), George (1).

Hannah Maria, daughter of Robert and Hannah (Gardner) Henry was born April 10, 1820, married Marcus Prentiss Ashley, Oct 15, 1840, and is living in Hawarden, Iowa, with her son James Alton, Marcus P Ashley died April 19, 1877

Children

Marcus Henry, born at Medina, Ohio. Aug 11, 1841, resides at Madison, Wis

James Alton, born at Medina, O, May 20, 1843, resides at Hawarden, Iowa He was thrice married (1) Eliza Ann White Children: Joe Alton, born Mar 13, 1874. Myrtie Cynthia, born June 5, 1875 He married (2) Lucy Hibbard, by whom he had four children, three of whom survive Lucy, Warren and James

Helen Maria, born at Medina, Ohio, Jan. 19, 1846, married Dacre Freeman.

Genevra Juliet, born at Marshall, Wis, April 6, 1856, married William Lane Lives at San Jose, Cal Has one daughter, Ethel

ARTALISSA SMITH (7).

Sally Gardner (6), Capt. Daniel (5), Sylvester (4), Nicholas (3), Nicholas (2), George (1).

Artalissa Smith, daughter of Gardner and Sally (Gardner) Smith, was born December 17, 1822, died May 5, 1853-4, married John J Gardner (8), Nathaniel (7), Robert (6), Nathaniel (5), Joshua (4), Robert

(3), George (2), George (1), January 23, 1844 at Hancock, Mass He was born June 22, 1820-1, died July 22, 1893 Their children were

Don Aurelius, born May 2, 1846 Married Leonella Moore, Nov 15, 1879

Sarah Adella, born Nov 22, 1849 Teacher at Hancock, Mass.

AUCELIA M. SMITH (7)

Sally Gardner (6), Capt. Daniel (5), Sylvester (4), Nicholas (3), Nicholas (2), George (1).

Aucelia M. Smith, daughter of Gardner and Sally (Gardner) Smith, was born May 15, 1827, died October, 1903, married Bishop W Carpenter and lived at Lebanon Springs She is survived by two daughters.

MINERVA S. SMITH (7).

Sally Gardner (6), Capt. Daniel (5). Sylvester (4), Nicholas (3), Nicholas (2), George (1).

Minerva S Smith, daughter of Gardner and Sally (Gardner) Smith, was born (no date of birth); died March 23, 1868 Married Henry Cranston, of Oneida, New York

DWIGHT SMITH (7).

Sally Gardner (6), Capt Daniel (5), Sylvester (4), Nicholas (3), Nicholas (2), George (1).

Dwight Smith, son of Gardner and Sally (Gardner) Smith, was born October 20, 1836, died November 20-3, 1870, married Emily Chapman They lived on the old homestead of Capt Daniel Gardner at North Hancock, Mass, and Mr Smith died there

Three children were born to them

J. Gardner, a prosperous physician in New York City

William A, a grocer at Westfield, Mass.

John D, a druggist in Springfield, Mass

PERRY GREEN GARDNER (7)

Robert (6), Nathaniel (5), Joshua (4), Robert (3), George (2), George (1).

Perry Green, son of Robert and Amy (Arnold) Gardner, was born May 28, 1787, at Hancock, Mass Died August 20, 1856 Married Esther Ely Jan. 10, 1810.

Children were·

Noah Ely, born in Hancock, Oct 27, 1824, died Nov 21, 1849, unmarried. He graduated at Williams College in 1848 and taught in his native town successfully for a few months

Sabrina, born May 26, 1811

An infant son, died very young.

NATHANIEL GARDNER (7)

Robert (6), Nathaniel (5), Joshua (4), Robert (3), George (2). George (1).

Nathaniel Gardner, son of Robert and Amy (Arnold) Gardner, was born October 23, 1793, at Hancock, Mass, died there January 17, 1874. Married Sarah Calkins Wilson, daughter of John, Jr, and Mary (Gardner) Wilson, February 11 1820, and settled in Hancock She was born July 10, 1795, died January 10, 1879 Their children were

John J., born June 22, 1820, died July 22, 1893, at Hancock, Mass

Robert Palmer, born Mar 19 1823, died Apr 9, 1884 at Stephentown N. Y

Mary Minerva, born Feb 21, 1828, living, unmarried

Mortimer Wilson, born Feb 21, 1828, died June 13, 1905

James V, born Oct 28, 1834, died Sept. 30, 1862

CLARK R. REYNOLDS (7)

Martha Gardner (6), Nathaniel (5), Joshua (4), Robert (3), George (2) George (1).

Clark R., son of Griffin and Martha (Gardner) Reynolds He married Almira Persons

Children were

Mary, married J Armitage

Martha,

Amanda, married O B Rudd

Almira, married E A Earl

Etta Clark

LYDIA LOUISA GARDNER (7)

Capt. Joshua (6), Nathaniel (5), Joshua (4), Robert (3), George (2), George (1).

Lydia L Gardner, daughter of Capt Joshua and Lydia (Gardner) Gardner, was born Jan 5, 1808, married Sylvester Millman, a farmer near Baldwinville, Onondaga Co, N Y

Children

Hortense, lives at Bradford, Pa

Edna, twice married, present husband a clergyman lives at Bradford, Pa

EUNICE MINERVA GARDNER (7)

Capt. Joshua (6), Nathaniel (5), Joshua (4), Robert (3), George (2), George (1)

Eunice Minerva Gardner, daughter of Capt Joshua and Lydia (Gardner) Gardner, was born at White Creek, Washington Co, N. Y,

February 10, 1811, died November 23, 1885, married Reuben Ely Gorton, son of Abel D and Lucretia (Ely) Gorton, October 25, 1837

Their children were

William Ely, born Oct 4, 1840, at Hancock, Mass., died Mar. 8, 1842.

Louise (Louie) Minerva, born Dec 23, 1842, at Hancock, Mass. Living.

Adelos, born April 14, 1848, at Watervliet, N. Y Living

Josephine (Josie) Delia, born Sept 8, 1850, at Watervliet, N. Y. Living

George Russell, born May 26, 1853, at Watervliet, N Y Died July 5, 1904

Reuben Ely Gorton was a farmer, merchant and postmaster at Hancock Druggist at Watervliet, N Y, and one of the organizers of the Methodist Episcopal Church there. Also a druggist at Saratoga Springs, where he built the first brick house there on Union Street From that place he removed to a farm near Clayton, Gloucester County, New Jersey, later he lived with his son, Adelos, in Philadelphia, Pa, where he died April 7, 1888. Eunice Minerva always wrote her name Minerva E.

SUSAN GARDNER (7).

Capt. Joshua (6), Nathaniel (5), Joshua (4), Robert (3), George (2), George (1)

Susan Gardner, daughter of Capt Joshua and Lydia (Gardner) Gardner, married George Russell, a native of White Creek, N Y He had woolen, saw and grist mills at East Salem, ten miles from White Creek

One child was born to them

Josephine Minerva, born Feb 24, 1834

ANN GARDNER (7)

Capt Joshua (6), Nathaniel (5), Joshua (4), Robert (3), George (2), George (1)

Ann, daughter of Capt Joshua and Lydia (Gardner) Gardner, was born at White Creek, Wash Co, N Y (No record of date of birth or death) She married Eliphalet Wells They kept the hotel at Middle Granville N Y

Children were

Hannah, died at the age of 28 from appendicitis

Gardner, married Sarah Brown of Brownville, Jefferson Co, Ill Three children Anna, deceased, was a fine singer Two sons in Warren, Pa.

ISHMAEL GARDNER (7).

Capt. Joshua (6), Nathaniel (5), Joshua (4), Robert (3), George (2), George (1).

Ishmael, son of Capt Joshua and Lydia (Gardner) Gardner, married Cynthia Dyer. Both are buried at Waite Corners

Their children were·
Palmer, settled in Illinois
Lydia, settled in Illinois
Ishmael, settled in Illinois
Joshua Earl, settled in Illinois
Ann Eliza,
A son

JOSHUA GARDNER (7).

Capt. Joshua (6), Nathaniel (5), Joshua (4), Robert (3), George (2), George (1)

Joshua, son of Capt. Joshua and Lydia (Gardner) Gardner, married Mary Russell at White Creek, N. Y

Three children:
A son, deceased.
Mary, married (1) Mr Adams, one child, Mabel. (2) Mr Topping, of New York
Helen, deceased, married Augustus Mapes

DELIA GARDNER (7).

Capt. Joshua (6), Nathaniel (5), Joshua (4), Robert (3), George (2), George (1)

Delia Gardner, daughter of Capt Joshua and Lydia (Gardner) Gardner, married John Alley

One child
Anna Louisa, deceased Was said to have been very beautiful.

Delia Alley, married (2) Christopher Snyder, a farmer at Pittston, Rensselaer County, N Y No children.

DANIEL GARDNER (7).

George (6), Othniel (5), Benony (4), Isaac (3), Benony (2), George (1).

Daniel Gardner, son of George and Louisa (Dawley) Gardner, was born 1799 Died 1863, at Troy, N Y Married Ann Terry, 1835, daughter of Judge Terry, of Hartford Conn, a direct descendant of Samuel Terry, of Enfield, Conn

He graduated at Union College, 1817, was recorder of the city of Troy from 1824-1834 Author of "Moral Laws of Nations, Tracts on Representative Government, Laws of Rebellion, Institutes of International Law"

Children were:

Elizabeth, born April 20, 1838, died April 15, 1841.

Eugene Terry, born Sept 26, 1840, educated at Williams College and the Columbia Law School

James Terry, born May 6, 1842, married Josephine Rogers, 1868 He was educated at the Polytechnic College, Troy, N Y., and at the Columbia Law School He was an engineer of skill, and was employed on many works by the U S Government in the Yosemite Valley in California

ANN GARDNER (7)

Benjamin (6), Nathaniel (5), Benjamin (4), Nathaniel (3), Benony (2), George (1)

Ann, daughter of Benjamin and Polly (Allen) Gardner, was born July 17, 1809, went as missionary to Burmah and there married Rev Elisha Abbott, a missionary Died in Burmah Children were

Willard, resides at 600 Prospect St, Cleveland, O

Frank Wayland, was an oculist and aurist in Buffalo, N Y, where he died a few years ago He married Julia Baker, of Buffalo One child Wayne Abbott, who is a clergyman in the Episcopal Church and is at present assistant priest in New York City

DEWITT GARDNER (7).

Benjamin (6) Nathaniel (5), Benjamin (4), Nathaniel (3), Benony (2), George (1)

Dewitt, son of Benjamin and Polly (Allen) Gardner, was born Mar 28, 1819, married Elizabeth G Simmons, of Fulton, N. Y, June 2, 1842 She was born Aug 14, 1819, died Aug 14, 1847

Mr Gardner was born at Cazenovia, Madison Co, N Y, and resided in Fulton from 1835 until his death in 1897 He was a merchant in Fulton for twelve years In 1855 he with others organized the First National Bank, of which he was cashier for twenty years, and President from 1875 until his death. He was senior partner in the milling firm of Gardner and Seymour, St Louis flour mills

His children were

Frances Eliza, born May 1, 1843, married Henry O Silkman, Oct 20, 1864. Resides at Maplewood, Wayne Co, Pa

Abbott Roswell, born May 2, 1844, died May, 1897, at Syracuse, N Y. He married Nellie Maynard, Oct 19, 1870

Dewitt Gardner married (2) Jane H Townsend, Feb. 13, 1849 She was born July 30, 1829, died Apr 19, 1852 One child

Charles Townsend, born May 5, 1851, died Apr 19 1892, at Oswego N Y Married Katherine Morrell Jan 2, 1873 One child Anna Elizabeth, born Aug 28, 1873, married Nov 19 1903, Henry Clay Van Note, of Atlantic Highlands, N J, where she resides Child William Henry, born Mar 19, 1906.

Dewitt Gardner married (3), Sarah Smith, of Middlefield, Mass She was born Oct 1, 1824, died April 11, 1906 One child

Alice May, born Dec 12, 1861, resides at Fulton, N Y

MARIA GARDNER (7).

Benjamin (6), Nathaniel (5), Benjamin (4), Nathaniel (3), Benony (2), George (1)

Maria, daughter of Benjamin and Polly (Allen) Gardner, was born June 2, 1806, married Frederick Seymour Feb 1 1826 He was born Sept 25, 1799, died Dec 25, 1883

Children were

Lucien C., born Feb 7, 1827, died Oct 29, 1903, married Mary Helen Mix, Sept 24, 1852 She was born June 2, 1830, died Apr. 12, 1894 Children were: Nellie A., born Nov 26, 1855, died Mar 22, 1885, Alfred Mix, born Nov 6, 1860, married Nov 1, 1888, to Anna Bell Calkins, who was born Nov 1, 1866 One child Helen Lucille, born Aug 31, 1891 Carrie Blanche, born Oct 2, 1865, Marie, born May 9, 1873, died Aug 25, 1873

Chloe Ann, born May 6, 1829; married Allan McLean Oct 8, 1857

Ascah Marion born Oct 28, 1831, died Jan 22, 1901, at Fulton, N. Y

Ludley A, born Sept 13, 1836, married Hapzibale Hewitt, Jan 9, 1861 She died June, 1906 Resided at Fulton, N Y Children Harry Templeton born June 16, 1862, married Eliza Foster, Mar 6, 1887 One child, Mabel May, born July 27, 1889 Willard Abbott, born May 27, 1867, married Dora Fish, Nov 21, 1894 Children Helen C, born Aug 27, 1895, Ralph Willard, born Feb 14, 1900

Francis Allison born in Fulton, N Y, Mar 23 1839, died at Buffalo, N Y, Oct 8, 1894

Frederick De Valois, born Oct 24, 1844, resides at Fulton, N Y

LYDIA WILSON (7).

Mary (6), Palmer (5), Sylvester (4), Nicholas (3), Nicholas (2), George (1)

Lydia, daughter of John and Mary (Gardner) Wilson, married Heman Hand, of Hancock, Mass Farm north of that of Stephen A Douglas's parents

Children were

Samuel Wilson, married Hannah Ostrander, died about 1900, leaving no issue

Frederick A, graduated from Williams College, studied theology at Andover, preached near Boston for two years, died at Pittsfield, Mass Unmarried.

Helen Sabrina, died aged ten months.

SILAS G. DAWLEY (7)

Alice Gardner (6), Capt. Daniel (5), Sylvester (4), Nicholas (3), Nicholas (2), George (1).

Silas G Dawley, son of Rodney and Alice (Gardner) Dawley, was born in 1819, died April 20, 1887, married Mary Eldridge

Two children

Delbert S, died Sept. 5, 1865, in his 23rd year, was a soldier in Civil war

Helen C, born June 5, 1843, died May 2, 1894.

JAMES EDWARD DAWLEY (7).

Alice Gardner (6), Capt. Daniel (5), Sylvester (4), Nicholas (3), Nicholas (2), George (1).

James Edward Dawley, son of Rodney and Alice (Gardner) Dawley, was born May 2, 1826, married Helen S Eldridge, Nov, 1859, at South Williamstown, Mass Living at Heber, Arkansas

Two sons were born to them

Guy H, died 1861.

Truman G, dead

CHARLOTTE O. DAWLEY (7)

Alice Gardner (6), Capt. Daniel (5), Sylvester (4), Nicholas (3), Nicholas (2), George (1).

Charlotte O Dawley, daughter of Rodney and Alice (Gardner) Dawley, was born March 28, 1828, died August 20, 1886, at Hancock, Mass. Married Daniel Whitman at Hancock, Mass

Three children were born to them

Elcy Jennie, born Oct 3, 1861, married Fred M Northup, Sept 28, 1882 Lives at Williamstown, Mass.

Catherine Louise, born Jan 6, 1864, died Sept 14 1887

Daniel J, born Nov. ——. Married Ella J Eldridge, Mar 6, 1895, Hancock

GEORGE W. GARDNER (7).

Abner (6), George (5), Ezekiel (4), Nicholas (3), Nicholas (2), George (1).

George W, son of Abner and Mary (Champlin) Gardner, was born 1817, married Mary, daughter of Daniel Husted

Children were

Melville G,

Hannah,

Charles,

Mary

ROWLAND J. GARDNER (7).

Abner (6), George (5), Ezekiel (4), Nicholas (3), Nicholas (2), George (1).

Rowland J, son of Abner and Mary (Champlin) Gardner, was born 1821, married (1) Lydia L, daughter of Henry Hunt (2) Emma (or Emily), daughter of Stephen Bennett Children were

Rowland J,
Jonathan J,
Mary L

ABNER GARDNER (7).

Abner (6), George (5), Ezekiel (4), Nicholas (3), Nicholas (2), George (1).

Abner, son of Abner and Mary (Champlin) Gardner, was born 1825, married Sarah, daughter of John Stone, of Milo, N Y

Children were
Rowland J,
Abner E.

WILLIAM D S. GARDNER (7)

John (6), Nathaniel (5), Job (4), Nathaniel (3), Benony (2), George (1)

William D S, son of John and Elizabeth (Smith) Gardner, was born Oct 13, 1839, at Stephentown, Rens Co, New York Married July 30, 1863, to Julia A Martin, daughter of Calvin and Roxanna (——) Martin

To them were born eight children:
Allen W, born Aug 27, 1864
Wesley N, born Sept 11, 1866, died Oct, 1867.
Charles E, born Mar 20, 1868, died Apr, 1870
Harry U, born Nov 18, 1871.
Lizzie A, born May 30, 1872, died May 8, 1894.
Frank E, born Aug 5, 1876
Gilbert H, born Dec 21, 1879
Leslie O, born Nov 11, 1887.

Mr Gardner's early life was passed upon a farm In 1864 he enlisted in Company C of the 42d Wis Volunteers and served until the close of the war Returning home he again engaged in agricultural work until the fall of 1900, he removed to Lodi, where he now resides, his son Frank remaining upon his farm

DESEVIGNIA STARKS GARDNER (7).

John (6), Nathaniel (5), Job (4), Nathaniel (3), Benony (2), George (1)

Desevignia S, son of John and Elizabeth (Smith) Gardner, was born at Stephentown, Rensselaer Co, New York, Nov 14, 1837 Married Mercy A Appler, Nov 2, 1864

To them were born four children
Clarence Herbert, born May 10, 1867, died 1890
Mabel I, born July 18, 1870.
Albert I, born March 23, 1872
John H, born July 6, 1874.

In 1856 Mr Gardner went to West Point, Wisconsin, where he engaged in farming until 1861, when he went to Waukon, Iowa, where he enlisted in the 27th Iowa Vol Inf and served three years He was wounded July 14, 1864, at Tupelo, Miss Was in a number of battles during his service, and was discharged at Clinton, Iowa After his discharge he again went to West Point, Wis, and remained in that vicinity until Sept, 1883, when he removed to Lawrence, Kansas, where he now resides

LUCY M GARDNER (7)

John (6), Nathaniel (5), Job (4), Nathaniel (3), Benony (2), George (1)

Lucy M, daughter of John and Elizabeth (Smith) Gardner, was born April 19, 1834, at Stephentown, Rensselaer Co, New York. He married at Lodi, Wis, Apr 12, 1857, to Stephen E Woodward, son of Isaac and Harriet (Boughton) Woodward.

To them were born six children
Harriet E Woodward, Jan 26, 1859
Homer S, Nov 28, 1862, died Oct 16, 1863
Elmer E, Jan 13, 1864 Lodi
Hiram N, June 3, 1867 Weaver Lodi
Walter E, July 29, 1870 Died Sept 11, 1878
Lena M, Feb 2, 1874 Lodi

Mr and Mrs Woodward are now living in the village of Lodi, Wis

FRANCES H. GARDNER (7)

John (6), Nathaniel (5), Job (4), Nathaniel (3), Benony (2), George (1)

Frances H, daughter of John and Elizabeth (Smith) Gardner, was born April 28 1831, at Stephentown, New York Married Nov 30, 1848, to J N Fellows, son of David and Chloe (Turner) Fellows of Stephentown, Wis

To them were born eight children
William, born Oct, 1849
Helen M, born Dec 4, 1851
Niles, April, 1854
Emma, Feb, 1856, died Aug., 1859
Viola E, Sept 1, 1858
Ellie J, Aug 2, 1860
Clara I, Dec 21, 1865
Alice A, Dec 23, 1872

In the spring of 1857 Mr and Mrs Fellows moved to Wisconsin, making themselves a home at West Point He died there Nov. 26, 1887.

AMANDA M. GARDNER (7)

John (6), Nathaniel (5), Job (4), Nathaniel (3), Benony (2), George (1)

Amanda M Gardner, daughter of John and Elizabeth (Smith) Gardner, was born July 24, 1829, at Stephentown, New York, died Aug 1903, married Feb 13, 1855, to David Harvey Fellows, son of David and Chloe (Turner) Fellows

Seven boys were born to them·

David H, born Nov 30, 1855, died July, 1856

Elbert G. born Nov 14, 1858

Frank E, born Sept 30, 1860, U S survey, Washington State

J Herbert, born July 20, 1862, died ——

George N, born July, 1864, died Mar, 1866

Sydney L., born Oct 13, 1866

Chester N, born Sept 28, 1869, died Nov, 1890

In the spring of 1857 Mrs Fellows removed to West Point Wis, where she made her home until her death, Nov 19, 1887 Mr Fellows died Aug, 1903

JOB GARDNER (7).

John (6), Nathaniel (5), Job (4), Nathaniel (3), Benony (2), George (1)

Job Gardner, son of John and Elizabeth (Smith) Gardner, was born March 27, 1827, at Stephentown, Rensselaer Co, New York Married Sarah A Sluyter, daughter of William and Patty (Waterman) Sluyter, Dec 31 1851

To them were born nine children

Charles F, April 16, 1854, died May 22, 1865

George B, April 10, 1855, died Nov 6, 1887

John W, Nov 28, 1856

Fred J, Dec 8, 1859.

Elmer, March 29, 1862, died Apr. 9, 1862

Arthur Eugene, March 4, 1864, died May 4, 1879

Martha E, Oct 18, 1866, died Apr 22, 1889

Albert, Aug 31, 1869, died June 20, 1886

Chester N, March 12, 1873

In February of 1855 Mr Gardner moved to Monroeville, Ohio, where he lived one year, and in the spring of 1856 he moved to Lodi, then to West Point, Wiss, where he followed the occupation of a farmer until the time of his death, June, 1906

NATHANIEL GARDNER (7).

John (6), Nathaniel (5), Job (4), Nathaniel (3), Benony (2), George (1)

Nathaniel Gardner, son of John and Elizabeth (Smith) Gardner, was born July 21, 1844, at Stephentown, New York. In 1856 he with his parents, went to West Point, Wis, where his early life was spent Married Frank B Becker, Mar 12, 1878 Mrs Gardner died March 16, 1879 Mr Gardner was engaged in teaching from 1865 until June, 1896, when ill health compelled him to resign his work Since that time he has resided at Lodi, Wis

JOHN SMITH GARDNER (7).

John (6), Nathaniel (5), Job (4), Nathaniel (3), Benony (2), George (1)

John Smith Gardner, son of John and Elizabeth (Smith) Gardner, was born June 12, 1825, at Stephentown, New York Married Mary E Rose, daughter of Rufus and Malvina (Gardner) Rose, Nov 15, 1849

The following children were born

Florence Ada, Aug 30, 1850

Clarence R, Jan 19, 1851

Katie Elizabeth ('Libbie'), Oct 3, 1853

Mr Gardner followed the life of a farmer living near the vicinity of his birthplace until the fall of 1856, when he removed to Lodi, Wisconsin, where he resided until his death, Jan 21, 1902 His wife died Dec 10, 1904

MARY E GARDNER (7)

John (6), Nathaniel (5), Job (4), Nathaniel (3), Benony (2), George (1).

Mary E, daughter of John and Elizabeth (Smith) Gardner, was born Aug. 17, 1847, at Stephentown, New York Married Jan. 1, 1868, to Talcott E Chrisler, son of William B and Betsy (Carncross) Chrisler

Six children

F Eugene born Oct 28, 1868

Son June 2, 1870, died Aug, 1870

Edith M Oct 20 1872, died Sept 17, 1873

Clarence, Oct 26 1874 died July 13, 1882

Claude G, May 5, 1880, died July 11, 1882

Chester F, born July 12, 1891

Mrs Chrisler now resides at Lodi, Wis

MINERVA B. GARDNER (7)

John L (6), Caleb (5), Benjamin (4), Nathaniel (3), Benony (2), George (1).

Minerva B, daughter of John and Lydia (Gardner) Gardner, was born November 14, 1800, died 1876, married Darius Mead, of Blissfield, Mich, son of Stephen Mead who was born in 1763 and died in 1858

Their children were.

John,
Minerva,
Helen M., born 1827
Daniel

DANIEL H. GARDNER (7).

John L. (6), Caleb (5), Benjamin (4), Nathaniel (3), Benony (2), George (1).

Daniel, son of John and Lydia (Gardner) Gardner, was born November 7, 1807, died September 8, 1875, married Joanna Sweet, October 19, 1831. She was born April 29, 1812, died January 9, 1889. Both are buried on the old homestead at Hancock, Mass.

Children:

Kirk E., born June 4, 1833.
John D., born June 8, 1835; died October 30, 1857, at Decatur, N. Y.
Helen M., born March 19, 1838.
Louisa M., born May 28, 1845, died March 6, 1868.

SILAS H. GARDNER (7).

John L. (6), Caleb (5), Benjamin (4), Nathaniel (3), Benony (2), George (1).

Silas H. Gardner, son of John and Lydia (Gardner) Gardner, was born at Hancock, Mass., January 17, 1803, died September 6, 1857, married Charlotte Cogswell. She was born February 9, 1809, died August 22, 1890. Both are buried at Hancock, Mass., on the farm now owned by Kirk E. Gardner.

Their children were:

Charles, born Aug. 20, 1837, living at 65 Grant Pl., Chicago, Ill.

Sarah M., died 1902, unmarried; was for some years a successful teacher at Maplewood in Pittsfield, Mass.

Mary L., married Hiram L. Lewis, living.

Silas H. Gardner graduated at Williams College and became a lawyer as well as a farmer, owning and occupying the farm next east of the old homestead. He died in 1857, greatly esteemed and greatly lamented, leaving a widow and three children.

LYDIA LOUISA GARDNER (7).

John L. (6), Caleb (5), Benjamin (4), Nathaniel (3), Benony (2), George (1).

Lydia Louisa, daughter of John L. and Lydia (Gardner) Gardner, was born April 30, 1810, died December 10, 1892; married Leonard Doty of Stephentown, N. Y., 1836. He was born March 2, 1812, died March 6, 1882.

Their children were:

Albert, born 1840, died Sept. 28, 1873, married Emily Mason. She died Oct. 6, 1866. No children.

Amy, born ——, died Nov. 27, 1871.

Elizabeth G., living at Hancock, Mass.

CALEB GARDNER, JR (7)

Caleb (6), Benjamin (5), Benjamin (4), Nathaniel (3), Benony (2), George (1).

Caleb Gardner, Jr, son of Caleb, Sr, and Eunice (Northup) Gardner, was born Oct 30, 1789, died Jan 9, 1861, married Lydia Sweet Tanner, daughter of Abel and Lydia (Sweet) Tanner, September 2, 1811 She was born March 29, 1790, died July 7, 1864

Children were

Julia, married Randall Brown, no children

Caroline, married Nathaniel Wylie, one child Emma Caroline, married Daniel Shepardson, no children

Eliza, married Michael Halpin, no children

Eunice, married Orlando Rose, no children

Lydia, born March 1, 1831, married Britton Madison; three children Louis B, Walter, Olive

Caleb T born March 1, 1831, died March 12, 1891, married Caroline Gorton

OLIVE GARDNER (7)

Caleb (6), Benjamin (5), Benjamin (4), Nathaniel (3), Benony (2), George (1)

Olive Gardner, daughter of Caleb, Sr, and Eunice (Northup) Gardner, was born March 23, 1792, died Aug 31, 1872, married Rensselaer Bly He died Apr 7, 1869

Their children were

Nancy,

Malvina,

Caleb,

Frederick

NICHOLAS GARDNER (7).

Caleb (6) Benjamin (5), Benjamin (4), Nathaniel (3), Benony (2), George (1).

Nicholas Gardner, son of Caleb, Sr, and Eunice (Northup) Gardner, married Jane Wylie Died Nov 16, 1872

Children were

Mary,

Wylie, living at Lawton, Michigan

FRANCIS GARDNER (7)

Caleb (6), Benjamin (5), Benjamin (4), Nathaniel (3), Benony (2), George (1)

Francis Gardner, son of Caleb and Eunice (Northup) Gardner, was born May 4, 1798, died November, 1877; married, first, Electa Vary, daughter of Simeon and Mary Vary, January 18, 1825 She was born January 18, 1800, died December 5, 1830 He married, second, Esther Vary, daughter of Simeon and Esther Vary, August 7, 1831 She was born June 6, 1797, died December 3, 1872.

Children were

Simeon V, born May 25, 1826, died February 14, 1899

Oris H., born July 2, 1830

Daughter, born August 7, 1832, died August 7, 1832

Frances, Jr, born July 30, 1837, died Oct 24, 1905

SYLVESTER GARDNER (7)

Caleb (6), Benjamin (5), Benjamin (4), Nathaniel (3), Benony (2), George (1).

Sylvester Gardner, son of Caleb, Sr, and Eunice (Northup) Gardner, was born March 10, 1801; died March 10, 1888, married Elma Russell

Children were·

Loretta, born December 13, 1828, living at South Berlin, N Y

Myra, born November 24, 1830 living at Stephentown, N Y

Lucy, born August 17, 1835, living at Stephentown, N Y

Sylvester Gardner owned and occupied a farm of one hundred and thirty-two acres, which was a part of his father's homestead He lived in the house erected by his father, where his three daughters were born Mr Gardner's life was a very active one He was not a member of any particular denomination of church, but it is said, was a very conscientious man Without exception before retiring he would very fervently pray to his God His wife was a member of the Christian Church They are both buried in the Baptist cemetery at Stephentown, N Y

GEORGE GARDNER (7).

Caleb (6), Benjamin (5), Benjamin (4), Nathaniel (3), Benony (2), George (1).

George Gardner, son of Caleb, Sr, and Eunice (Northup) Gardner, was born May 22, 1796, died Sept 1865, married Sarah Shaw about 1817 She was born at Stephentown, May 26, 1795, died Oct 17, 1846, in Rock Co, Wis

Their children were

George W, born Nov 26, 1819.

Olive,

Sarah A,

Lorenzo D,

Caleb J, unmarried

Jane A, died aged 21; not married

Burton H, born Sept 25, 1827, died March 7, 1857

Benjamin, went west at the age of 23, never heard from since

Mary Emily, born 1830, living at Denver, Colorado

Orlando, born March 4, 1832, died October 31, 1846

Eunice M, born April 12, 1836, died October 26, 1846

Oliver Perry, born 1834, died at three years of age.

George Gardner was born and reared in the Berkshire Hills where he remained until 1841 when he removed to western New York with his wife and seven youngest children In 1841 with his wife and five youngest children (leaving Caleb and Jane in New York) emigrated to the Territory of Wisconsin, going by lake to Milwaukee, thence across country west ninety miles to what is now Rock Co, Wis, where he entered government land on the west line of the County and built a cabin. In September of the same year, the country was visited by an epidemic of cholera and many of the settlers were taken Himself, wife and two youngest children were stricken The mother and two children were taken, the father recovered and removed with the remaindr of his family three miles to Decatur Village, Green Co, which was soon after organized, he being elected first Chairman of the Township and a member of the county board of Greene County Later he married again and removed to his farm in Rock Co, adjoining the city limits of the present city of Brodhead, where he resided till his death and is buried in Greenwood Cemetery, located on land entered by him in 1846 Of his numerous family none are known to be living except Mrs M. E Smith of Denver, Colo. The graves of the others are scattered from New York to California

CAROLINE GARDNER (8).

Sylvester Cogswell (7), Sylvester (6), Palmer (5), Sylvester (4), Nicholas (3), Nicholas (2), George (1)

Caroline, daughter of Sylvester C and Caroline (Collin) Gardner, was born Jan 16, 1842 She was educated at Homer, N Y, and Pittsfield, Mass, married Frederick Theodore Pierson, April 25, 1872 Mr Pierson died Jan 16, 1899, in his sixtieth year Mrs Pierson died Aug 14, 1903 They resided at Fayetteville and Syracuse and are survived by seven children, all of them graduates of Syracuse University

Frederick Theodore, Esq, of Syracuse, N Y, born May 23 1873, married Deetta Cecilia, daughter of W G Mitchell, of Rochester N Y, Oct 3, 1906

Robert Hamilton, M D born Aug 13, 1874, army surgeon at Ft Gibbon, Alaska

Horace Huntington, Esq, of New York, born Nov 30, 1875

Sarah, M D, of Rochester, N Y, born June 18, 1877

Herbert Varney, born Aug 13, 1879, electrician in New York

Caroline Emma, born March 7, 1881, Syracuse, N Y

Wallace Nelson, born Dec 27, 1882, divinity student in New York

SARAH GARDNER (8)

Sylvester Cogswell (7), Sylvester (6), Palmer (5), Sylvester (4), Nicholas (3), Nicholas (2), George (1)

Sarah, daughter of Sylvester Cogswell and Caroline (Collin) Gardner, was born January 21, 1849, graduated at Houghton Seminary, Clinton, N Y, 1869, valedictorian. Her services as Presbyterian missionary

SYLVESTER GARDNER (8).

Sylvester Cogswell (7), Sylvester (6), Palmer (5), Sylvester (4), Nicholas (3), Nicholas (2), George (1).

Sylvester, Esq., son of Sylvester Cogswell and Caroline (Collin) Gardner, was born at Fayetteville, N Y., November 18, 1844.

He was graduated in 1870, from Hamilton College, at Clinton, N. Y., where he was a member of the Delta Upsilon fraternity, won the Hawley Classical prize, and was elected to membership in the Phi Beta Kappa, to which his high scholarship entitled him.

After a course of law-study, he was admitted to the bar at Albany, N Y.

He has worked for many years, in lines connected with his profession, at San Francisco, Cal , and now (1908) resides at Modesto, Cal.

Omitted from p 244 Printer s erro

at Tokyo, Japan, for thirteen years from 1889 to 1902 deserves more than casual mention Her personal winsomeness captured the hearts of her pupils Her unstinted expenditure of time and vital force in ministering to their intellectual, moral and musical development was little short of a vicarious sacrifice, and so in their gratitude they regarded it And when at length after toiling at this rate unrelieved by recruits her strength collapsed and she was ordered home, her colleagues and pupils felt for a time as though the school had lost its main stay

Her influence and efforts reached beyond the school She taught on Sunday a large class of cadets from the naval academy at Tokyo. From independent sources comes the opinion that she was by reason of her deep spirituality a missionary to the missionaries themselves of whatever denomination, in a word that she contributed more inspiration to the work of evangelism in Japan than any other missionary there during the same period And what she was then she had been before in other spheres It has been a continuous story of self-forgetful devotion to the happiness and good of others

MIRIAM GARDNER, M D. (8).

Sylvester Cogswell (7), Sylvester (6), Palmer (5), Sylvester (4), Nicholas (3), Nicholas (2), George (1)

Miriam, daughter of Sylvester Cogswell and Caroline (Collin) Gardner was born Sept 6, 1852, graduated at Temple Grove Seminary, Saratoga Springs, 1874, M D, Ann Arbor, 1886, gynecologist at the Foster sanitarium Clifton Springs, N Y, for thirteen years and now holds similar position at the Walter Sanitarium, Pennsylvania In no degree inferior to that of her sister Sarah in either value or importance has been the service which Dr Miriam Gardner has rendered during an equal term of years within a different sphere Hers has been the work of healing the physical ills of womankind The patients to whom she has ministered and who acknowledge their indebtedness to her as beyond the range of pecuniary compensation are legion Among them were missionaries and teachers, many of whom are enabled by her to resume work and thereafter prosecute it with due conservation of energy Like Sarah's, her life has been one of unselfish toil for others

WILLIAM GARDNER (8).

Sylvester Cogswell (7). Sylvester (6), Palmer (5), Sylvester (4), Nicholas (3), Nicholas (2), George (1)

William, son of Sylvester C and Caroline (Collin) Gardner, was born at Fayetteville, N Y, March 26, 1861 He was graduated from Amherst College in 1884 and from Princeton Seminary in 1887 For the twenty years following he preached in Presbyterian and Congregational churches in the middle west He is now located in the State of Iowa.

He was married Sept 18, 1890, to Sarah Boardman, daughter of George B and Helen (Wing) Boardman of Chicago. She was born April 11 1866, at Saginaw, Mich.

Their children were

George Boardman, born at St Peter, Minn, Feb 18, 1892, died same day

Helen, born at Des Moines, Iowa, Feb. 22, 1893

SARAH ANN TOWNSEND (8)

William (7), Dorcas (6), Palmer (5), Sylvester (4), Nicholas (3), Nicholas (2), George (1)

Sarah A Townsend, daughter of William and Sallie (Foster) Townsend, was born Apr 9, 1816, at Floyd, N Y Died July 4, 1902, at Los Angeles, Cal She married Dr William Olmstead Laird in 1844. He was born at Lairdville, N Y, Nov 7, 1818, and died at Stittville, N. Y, March 24, 1897

Three children were born to them

William Townsend, born Aug 2, 1846, died Oct 7, 1899, in Watertown, N Y Married Minnie Raplee in June, 1878 No children He was a graduate of Hamilton College and a successful practitioner of the Hahnemann school of medicine

Mary Esther, born Feb 22, 1850, died Apr 20, 1852

Frank Foster, born Apr 15, 1856, died Aug 20, 1906

It was for Dr Laird's grandfather, Samuel, that Lairdville was named His great grandfather came to New England from Scotland Dr Laird was a dentist and when not occupied with his profession he worked the farm and garden connected with his hospitable and attractive residence at Stittville He was a brother of Dr Orville P Laird of Oneida Castle, the husband of Nancy Dyer and Caroline Tilman.

WILLIAM HALSEY TOWNSEND (8).

Palmer (7), Dorcas Gardner (6), Palmer (5), Sylvester (4), Nicholas (3), Nicholas (2), George (1)

William H, son of Palmer and —— (Bush) Townsend, married Frances Cornelia Bostwick, June 5, 1856 She was the daughter of Gerrit and Revera (Allen) Bostwick of Connecticut

Children were

Louise born May 22, 1858, married Daniel L Remsen Dec 20, 1882 Three children Allen Halsey, Frances Louise, Gerard Townsend

William Halsey, born Mar 1, 1860, married Josephine Gurley July 24, 1882.

Frank Le Grand, born June 21, 1862, married Gertrude Voorhees. Dec 12, 1899

Palmer Gardner, married Phoebe Josephine Eldredge, Oct 20, 1895 Three children. Atwood Halsey, Marjorie, Gerald

Gerard Bostwick, married Helen Bininger Houghton, June 5, 1901 Children Gerard Bostwick, Helen Mildred

All of the foregoing reside in Brooklyn A cousin characterized William Halsey Townsend as follows "A splendid good man, kind, generous, full of life and cheer and so unselfish, always thinking of others more than himself"

BENJAMIN TOWNSEND (8).

Nathaniel (7), Dorcas Gardner (6), Palmer (5), Sylvester (4), Nicholas (3), Nicholas (2), George (1)

Benjamin, son of Nathaniel and —— (Roche) Townsend, married Alice Merrican of Connecticut

Children were

Catherine, died in infancy

Frederick, married in Pennsylvania about 1903 and is in the insurance business at Meriden, Conn

Nathaniel, died in infancy

Edward Benjamin, student of Mining Engineering at Columbia College, New York

Alice, unmarried, is with her mother at Wallingford, Conn

Mr Townsend won great distinction as a Colonel in the Union service during the civil war After the war he engaged in farming in Texas and later resided in Wallingford, Conn In 1890 he invested in copper mines in the northwest and died there about 1903, interment at Wallingford

ANGELINE LOUISE TOWNSEND (8)

Nathaniel (7), Dorcas Gardner (6), Palmer (5). Sylvester (4), Nicholas (3), Nicholas (2), George (1)

Angeline L, daughter of Nathaniel and Angeline Louise (Townsend) Townsend, married William Alexander Blackburn in 1875 He was of Paris, Ill, and was born 1847, was all through the civil war with his father, who commanded an Illinois regiment of cavalry, until the father was killed in Mississippi during Grierson's raid. After the war William studied law in Chicago, went to Texas in 1871 and has attained eminence in his profession at Austin where he holds the position of Judge

Children are

Anna Louise, born Oct. 8, 1876, at Austin, Texas, died 1894

William Decatur, born Nov 2, 1878, at Austin Mining Engineer and Assayer in Mexico.

Nathaniel Townsend, born Mar 19, 1881 at Austin, has a government position as Civil Engineer at Galveston, Texas

Henry Paul, born Feb. 21, 1884 at Austin

Helen Elizabeth, born Sept. 1, 1890, at Short Beach, Conn

Alexander Louis, born June 5, 1893, at Austin

SUSAN MARSH TOWNSEND (8).

Nathaniel (7), Dorcas Gardner (6). Palmer (5), Sylvester (4), Nicholas (3), Nicholas (2), George (1)

Susan Marsh. daughter of Nathaniel and Angeline L (Townsend) Townsend, married James H. Robertson of Tennessee, in 1877 He is a very successful attorney and has held many prominent positions They reside in Austin, Texas

Children are

Warren Townsend, born Sept 3, 1878 at Austin, an attorney there.

Mary Louise, born at Round Rock, Texas, died in infancy.

John Benjamin, born July, 1882, an attorney in Austin

James Harvey, born 1884, died 1892

Margaret, born Nov 15, 1886, at school in Washington, D C.

Sue Lillian, born Oct 20, 1891.

PAULINE SPENCER TOWNSEND (8).

Nathaniel (7), Dorcas (6) Palmer (5), Sylvester (4), Nicholas (3), Nicholas (2), George (1)

Pauline Spencer, daughter of Nathaniel and Angeline L (Townsend) Townsend, married William J Culbertson of Paris, Ill, 1888; cousin of William Alexander Blackburn

Children are

Angeline Louise, born Aug 27, 1889, at Austin

A son, died in infancy

James William, born May 16, 1892, at Paris, Ill.

Mr Culbertson died in May 1903, at Paris, Ill, where he and his wife had made their home after their marriage Mrs. Culbertson now resides in Austin, Texas

JAMES WANTON TOWNSEND (8).

Nathaniel (7), Dorcas (6), Palmer (5), Sylvester (4), Nicholas (3), Nicholas (2), George (1)

James Wanton, son of Nathaniel and Angeline L (Townsend) Townsend, married Mattie Verlander of New Orleans He is a journalist at Houston Texas Mrs Townsend died in 1902, and the children who survive her live with their grandmother Verlander in New Orleans

Pauline Spencer, born June 20, 1887, in New Orleans

James Wanton, born May 3, 1892, in New Orleans

Martin Ingham, born April 26, 1895, in New Orleans

Nathaniel died in infancy

Elma Verlander, born July 3, 1897, in New Orleans

AMY DOTY (8).

Lydia Louisa (7), John L (6), Caleb (5), Benjamin (4), Nathaniel (3), Benony (2), George (1).

Amy, daughter of Leonard and Lydia Louisa (Gardner) Doty married George F Hull of New Lebanon, N Y, Oct 16, 1860

Children

Fred D., married, has daughter Lochellen.

Alice L, born June 30, 1862, married Henry A Whiting of Great Barrington, and has two children Amy, born Aug, 1890, Ruth, born 1892

ELIZABETH G. DOTY (8)

Lydia Louisa Gardner (7), John L (6), Caleb (5), Benjamin (4), Nathaniel (3), Benony (2), George (1)

Elizabeth G, daughter of Leonard and Lydia Louisa (Gardner) Doty, married Hiram A Carpenter, Apr 20, 1870 He was born Feb 25, 1843; died May 19, 1880

The following children were born

Mary Oakley, born June 10, 1872

Howard Doty, born Apr 20, 1874

C Lockwood, born Oct 17, 1877

CHARLES GARDNER (8)

Silas (7), John L (6), Caleb (5), Benjamin (4), Nathaniel (3), Benony (2), George (1).

Charles Gardner, son of Silas H and Charlotte (Cogswell) Gardner was born August 20, 1837; married Louise M Crapo, daughter of Seth and Mary (Merchant) Crapo at Albany New York She was born October 23, 1833 Her father was a leading merchant of Albany and her mother was a native of Nassau, New York She died at Stillwater, New York, September, 1875

Two boys were born to them

Lewis Crapo, born November 17, 1866, in Hancock, Mass.

Harry Gilson born March 16, 1869, Chicago, Ill

Charles Gardner, married second, Emma August Schute, June 23, 1877 She was born May, 1848, in Dover, New Hampshire, died June 11, 1878

One son was born to them.

Walter Allport, living at Chicago, Ill, unmarried

Charles Gardner, married, third, Jessie Louisa Stewart March 29, 1888 She was the daughter of John Russell and Mary (Howe) Stewart

Mr. Gardner enjoyed the advantages that came to the better homes of the Berkshire gentlemen His father a college graduate, attorney, and country gentleman, gave to this son opportunities that prepared him for a successful college man He received the degree of A M from Williams College and graduated from the Harvard Law School Taught in the public schools of Massachusetts Principal and assistant superintendent of the state reformatory at Waukesha, Wis Five years in the University of Chicago in charge of the Greek department collegiate and preparatory, the old original University of Chicago

Aside from business he has for about thirty years made Biblical translations and criticism his specialty Mr Gardner has lived about forty years in the city of Chicago

MARY L. GARDNER (8).

Silas (7), John L (6), Caleb (5), Benjamin (4), Nathaniel (3), Benony (2), George (1).

Mary L Gardner daughter of Silas H and Charlotte (Cogswell) Gardner, married Hiram Lamont Lewis He was born Sept 17, 1829, died March 20, 1900

Two children were born to them

Ann Charlotte died Jan 4, 1883, aged 11 years, 21 days

Arthur, living

Mr Hiram Lamont Lewis was a graduate of Williams College and made his mark and fortune as a successful lawyer in Chicago

Mrs Lewis and son Arthur now own and occupy the Silas Gardner place as a summer residence

HELEN M. MEAD (8).

Minerva B Gardner (7), John L. (6), Caleb (5), Benjamin (4), Nathaniel (3), Benony (2), George (1).

Helen M. daughter of Darius and Minerva B (Gardner) Mead, was born in 1827, married to Frederick L Eaton in 1862. He was born 1836 and died 1901.

Two children·

Louise, who in 1887 married Fred Buck, formerly of Adrian, Michigan. They have one child Helen, born 1888

Frederick L, born in 1869, unmarried

JOHN MEAD (8).

Minerva B Gardner (7), John L (6), Caleb (5), Benjamin (4), Nathaniel (3), Benony (2), George (1).

John Mead, son of Darius and Minerva B (Gardner) Mead, married Lydia Ely, who after John's death married a Mr Van De Warker by whom she became the mother of Dr E E. Van De Warker, who married Louisa M, daughter of Daniel and Joanna (Sweet) Gardner. See record of Louisa M Gardner (8)

KIRK E. GARDNER (8)

Daniel (7), John L (6), Caleb (5), Benjamin (4), Nathaniel (3), Benony (2), George (1)

Kirk E Gardner, son of Daniel and Joanna (Sweet) Gardner, was born June 4, 1833 married Helen M Hadsell, December 24, 1853 She was born August 25, 1832

Children

Minnie Joanna. born August 12, 1856, living

John Daniel, born April 19, 1860, living

Helen Louise, born December 12, 1867, a teacher at Pittsfield, Mass

Kirk E Gardner is the present owner and occupant of the old homestead purchased by Caleb B Gardner, and has lived upon this property all of his long and useful life He is a man of great force and personality, and has been a very useful man in the course of his long life He represented the Berkshire County district in the State Legislature in 1873

He is one of those very careful farmers The traits characteristic of this family is also of the subject of this article

The house in which he lives was erected in 1795 and is a frame structure and is in as good a state of preservation at this writing as many houses are that have been built in the last decade The care of the property for many years has been given to Mr Gardner The entire farm is a model of beauty and exactness It is said to be the best kept farm in Western Massachusetts and has been awarded the first prize as such It is a large colonial structure and has a spacious lawn, and Mr Gardner takes great pleasure in the care of this beautiful property. It is no better situated than most properties, but has the care of one of the best men

He is a strong man intellectually and is a very fine conversationalist, a man of strong convictions and not afraid to assert himself and is usually found on the right side of the subject

We have great reverence of this man in his religious views He was reared a Baptist and is a devout adherent of the doctrines of that particular denomination

HELEN M GARDNER (8)

Daniel (7), John L (6), Caleb (5), Benjamin (4), Nathaniel (3), Benony (2), George (1)

Helen M Gardner daughter of Daniel and Joanna (Sweet) Gardner, was born March 19, 1838, married Charles Frederick Shumway, March 31, 1863 Living at Hancock, Mass

Children are

Mary Joanna, born July 26, 1866, living at Hancock, Mass

Nellie H, born September 24, 1868, living at Hancock, Mass

Daniel Gardner, born July 3 1874, living at Troy N Y

LOUISA M. GARDNER (8).

Daniel (7), John L (6), Caleb (5), Benjamin (4), Nathaniel (3) Benony (2), George (1)

Louisa M Gardner daughter of Daniel and Joanna (Sweet) Gardner, was born May 28, 1845, died March 6, 1868, married Doctor Edward Ely Van de Warker To them was born one child, Maude, who married Walter Barker January, 1897 To them was born one son, George Ely Barker, born March 14, 1902 Maude (Van de Warker) Barker died May 1, 1902.

GEORGE W. GARDNER (8)

George (7), Caleb (6), Benjamin (5), Benjamin (4), Nathaniel (3), Benony (2), George (1).

George W., son of George and Sarah (Shaw) Gardner, was born Nov 26, 1819, at Stephentown, N Y Married Aucelia A. Rose, daughter of Rufus and Amanda (Gardner) Rose, Jan 14, 1843 She was born Aug 27, 1825, died March 3, 1877 Buried at Brodhead, Wis, cemetery.

Their children were as follows

Infant daughter born Oct 15, 1844, died age six months

Burton J, born Feb 3, 1849

Charles F, born Apr 2, 1853

John W, born Oct 6, 1855.

In 1856 George W Gardner removed with his family to Brodhead, Wis In 1859 he went to Texas, his family remaining in Wisconsin He was not heard from after the beginning of the civil war of 1861.

BURTON H GARDNER (8)

George (7), Caleb (6), Benjamin (5), Benjamin (4), Nathaniel (3), Benony (2), George (1).

Burton H Gardner son of George W and Sarah (Shaw) Gardner, was born at Stephentown, N Y, Sept 25, 1827, died in San Jose, Cal, Mar 7, 1905 He married Harriet E Lampson, of Decatur, Wis., June 9, 1857

Children

Frank B,

Harley W,

Charles O,

Edith A,

Mattie D.,

Ernest L

Burton H. Gardner was born at Stephentown, New York, and had the disposition of the sturdy emigrant With his father he emigrated to Wisconsin where he married in 1857 and resided until 1862. While living in Wisconsin the first three children were born He removed to Waverly, Iowa, where he resided until 1889 and where the last three children were born In 1889 he removed to San Jose California He died and is buried at San Jose His family, with the exceptions of Harley W and Edith A (Mrs. S L. Riese), live at San Jose

MARY EMILY GARDNER (8).

George (7), Caleb (6). Benjamin (5), Benjamin (4). Nathaniel (3), Benony (2), George (1).

Mary Emily, daughter of George W and Sarah (Shaw) Gardner, was born in 1830 married to Roderick M Smith of Springvalley, Wis, Nov. 25, 1847

One child

Nettie C, born Jan 13, 1851, living at Denver, Colo.

Mary Emily (Gardner) Smith was the tenth child of her parents Early in her life she accompanied her parents to the new wilderness home of Wisconsin Her father was one of the first emigrants to settle in that western home He possessed all of the traits of the colonial pioneer and this large family encountered the difficulties and experiences of the many families of this name who had the courage to make their home in an unbroken wilderness of the west Mr Gardner saw service in the war of 1812, being a fifer He lived to the ripe old age of three score and ten

The subject of this article assisted to plow the first furrows on the old Wisconsin homestead The writer calls attention of the reader to the group of four in the second volume of this work, a hale, rugged constitution at the age of seventy-six, perfect health and bids fair to live to see the addition of the fifth generation of which she is the head

CALEB T. GARDNER (8)

Caleb, Jr (7), Caleb, Sr (6), Benjamin (5), Benjamin (4), Nathaniel (3), Benony (2), George (1)

Caleb T Gardner, son of Caleb, Jr, and Lydia S. (Tanner) Gardner, was born March 1, 1831, died March 12, 1891, married Caroline Gorton

Their children were:

John C, born July 21, 1859, married Clara B. Sweet, Jan 11, 1898, no children

Reno E, born July 25, 1862, married Edith Briggs, who was born May 17, 1874, no children

Eulis M, born Feb 3, 1865, married Bee Sweet, one child Clara J, born Dec 4 1893

Fred G, born July 20, 1868, married Adelaide Wood who was born Feb 11, 1870 Two children Helen M born Apr 11, 1898, Fred E, born Sept 5, 1901

Carrie L, born Oct 18, 1870, married Dr Clarence Chaloner Two children Mary A, born Jan 10, 1897, Reginald Gardner, born Aug 28 1899

Jessie M, born Dec 17, 1883, married William K. Hatch No children

SIMEON V. GARDNER (8)

Francis (7), Caleb (6), Benjamin (5), Benjamin (4), Nathaniel (3), Benony (2), George (1)

Simeon V Gardner, son of Francis and Electa (Vary) Gardner was born May 25, 1826, died February 14, 1899, married Susan Wilson, March 8, 1848

Children

Vila, born October 13, 1853

Ida O, born April 28, 1855 married Seward F Harper, living at Battle Creek, Mich One child William

FRANCIS GARDNER, JR (8).

Francis (7), Caleb (6), Benjamin (5), Benjamin (4), Nathaniel (3), Benony (2), George (1)

Francis Gardner, Jr, son of Francis, Sr, and Esther (Vary) Gardner, was born July 30, 1837, married Nancy Vantiflin, January 15, 1861

Children

Esther H born October 25 1861 Living

Belle born September 17, 1863 Living

Olive, born June 9, 1880 Living

LORETTA GARDNER (8)

Sylvester (7), Caleb (6), Benjamin (5), Benjamin (4), Nathaniel (3), Benony (2), George (1).

Loretta Gardner, daughter of Sylvester and Elma (Russell) Gardner, was born Dec 13, 1828, married Rynaldo Shaw, Oct 20, 1847

Children

Dwight, born July 13 1849

James, born Nov 2, 1851, married Ella Weight of Petersburg, N Y one child Clayton

Elton, born Sept, 1856, married Flora Armsby, two children, died young

Elma, born ——, married Edwin D Matteson. No children

MYRA GARDNER (8)

Sylvester (7), Caleb (6), Benjamin (5), Benjamin (4), Nathaniel (3), Benony (2), George (1).

Myra Gardner, daughter of Sylvester and Elma (Russell) Gardner, was born November 24, 1830, married Ralph Bull, Oct 20, 1849

Children:

Frank J, born Nov 9, 1850

Ida Belle, born Apr 20, 1854, married William Cranston, daughter Clara Louise, born Feb 14 1875

LUCY GARDNER (8).

Sylvester (7), Caleb (6), Benjamin (5), Benjamin (4), Nathaniel (3), Benony (2), George (1).

Lucy Gardner, daughter of Sylvester and Elma (Russell) Gardner was born August 17, 1835, married John J Moffitt, Aug. 10, 1853.

Their children were:

Charles J, born June 2 1856, died Dec 24, 1892

Ora E, born June 12, 1858; died Nov 23, 1882

MORTIMER WILSON GARDNER (8)

Sarah (or Sally) C (7), Mary Gardner (6), Palmer (5), Sylvester (4), Nicholas (3), Nicholas (2), George (1)

Mortimer W, son of Nathaniel and Sarah C (Wilson) Gardner, was born Feb 21, 1828, died June 13, 1905 He married Mary C Smith Dec 22, 1852, daughter of Gardner and Sally (Gardner) Smith Mortimer W Gardner was a farmer and lived near Smyrna, N Y, and was a member, trustee and liberal supporter of the Baptist church at that place

Children were

Kate M, born June 13, 1856, married George P Pudney of Smyrna, Mar. 10 1880 Children Bessie Minerva, born May 10, 1884, Gardner Walstein born Oct 11, 1888, died Mar 2, 1898

Frank Smith, born Dec 19, 1860, married Julia B Wells, Dec 17, 1897 One child Mary Louise, born Dec 1, 1902

Walter Vander, born Dec 26 1864, married Margaret Monagle, Mar 18, 1891 Children are Robert Mortimer, born Dec 20, 1891 died 1901, Homer Vander, born July 26, 1893, Edmund Sidney, born Sept 9, 1895, Grace Emily, born Feb 7, 1898, Walter Wilson, born June 23, 1903

Minnie Louise, born Apr 23, 1869 Teacher in Baldwinsville, N Y

Anna Sabrina, born Apr 7, 1869, Sherburne, N Y

Mary Grace, born Mar 22, 1872 died July 14, 1886

Nathaniel Dwight, born Sept 7 1876, died Dec. 7, 1900

CLARENCE R GARDNER (8)

John S. (7), John (6), Nathaniel (5), Job (4), Nathaniel (3), Benony (2), George (1)

Clarence R Gardner, son of John S. and Mary E (Rose) Gardner, was born Jan 19, 1851, at Stephentown, New York Married Lucy Tyler, of Sabetha, Kansas

Two children were born to them:

Dora, Feb, 1885

Florence, 1890

Mr Gardner's early life was passed upon a farm His present home is Seattle, Wash, where he is engaged in the boot and shoe business

KATIE E. GARDNER (8).

John S. (7), John (6) Nathaniel (5) Job (4), Nathaniel (3), Benony (2), George (1)

Katie E Gardner, daughter of John Smith and Mary E (Rose) Gardner, was born Oct 3, 1853, at Stephentown New York When but three years old she, with her parents, went to Lodi, Wis, where she now resides Married Dwight Narracong May 5, 1874, son of Jonas and Sallie (Hunt) Narracong Mrs Narracong now resides at Lodi, Wis (1907)

FLORENCE ADA GARDNER (8)

John S. (7), John (6), Nathaniel (5), Job (4), Nathaniel (3), Benony (2), George (1)

Florence Ada, daughter of John S and Mary E (Rose) Gardner, was born Aug 30, 1850, at Stephentown, New York In the fall of 1856 she went with her parents to Lodi, Wis Married Charles Flanders, son of Samuel and Hannah (Thomas) Flanders

To them were born two children

Clarence G, born Nov 2 1875

Lola L, born Oct 7, 1882

Mrs Flanders resided upon a farm in West Point, Wis, until Sept, 1897, when, with her family, she removed to Lodi where she now lives, in order to give her children better educational advantages

CHESTER N. GARDNER (8)

Job (7) John (6), Nathaniel (5), Job (4), Nathaniel (3), Benony (2), George (1).

Chester N Gardner, son of Job and Sarah A (Sluyter) Gardner, was born March 12, 1873, at West Point, Wisconsin Married Daisy Holdridge, Oct 1895

Five children

Opal,

Evelyn

Elsie,

Gordon,

Royal

Mr Gardner now resides at Waunakee, Wis

JOHN W GARDNER (8)

Job (7), John (6), Nathaniel (5), Job (4), Nathaniel (3), Benony (2), George (1)

John W Gardner, son of Job and Sarah A (Sluyter) Gardner, was born Nov 28, 1856, at Lodi, Wis Married Dec 15, 1883 to Emma Horton daughter of Elijah and Anna (Summers) Horton

One son

Gilbert H, born Sept, 1886

Mr Gardner is a tiller of the soil His home is in West Point, Wis

FRED J GARDNER (8)

Job (7), John (6), Nathaniel (5), Job (4), Nathaniel (3), Benony (2), George (1)

Fred J Gardner, son of Job and Sarah A (Sluyter) Gardner, was born Dec 8, 1859 Married Sara A Plentz 1885 Mr Gardner lives upon the homestead in West Point and is considered a first-class agriculturalist

GEORGE B GARDNER (8)

Job (7), John (6), Nathaniel (5), Job (4), Nathaniel (3), Benony (2), George (1)

George B Gardner, son of Job and Sarah A. (Sluyter) Gardner) was born Sept 10, 1855, at Monroeville, Ohio Married Jan, 1878, to Florence Chrisler, daughter of John W and Julia A.(Passage) Chrisler

Three children

Martha E M, born March 6, 1880; married John Compton, August 1903, and resides at Milwaukee

Ida M, born Aug 10, 1881, died Sept 6, 1897

Charles B, born Apr 2, 1883

Mrs. Gardner, died April 9, 1883

Mr Gardner was a successful teacher from 1878 until his death, Nov 6, 1887.

ELBERT G FELLOWS (8).

Amanda Gardner (7), John (6), Nathaniel (5), Job (4), Nathaniel (3), Benony (2), George (1).

Elbert G Fellows son of David H and Amanda M (Gardner) Fellows, was born Nov 14, 1858, at West Point, Wis Married Nov 29, 1882, Matilda Sanderson, daughter of Allan and —— (Travis) Sanderson

Children

Avis A, born July 8, 1887.

Kenneth E, born Nov. 18, 1888

David Clayton, born July 25, 1889

Mr Fellows is a successful farmer, living upon the homestead at West Point

SYDNEY L. FELLOWS (8)

Amanda Gardner (7), John (6), Nathaniel (5), Job (4), Nathaniel (3), Benony (2), George (1).

Sydney L Fellows, son of David Harvey and Amanda M (Gardner) Fellows was born Oct 13 1866, at West Point, Wis Married Jan 8 1892, to Nellie M Bartholomew, daughter of R N and Priscilla (Eells) Bartholomew, of Lodi, Wis

Four sons and two daughters

Harry Leith, born Jan 11, 1893

Frank C, born March 14, 1895

Joseph Smith Dewey, born May 15, 1898

Gilbert Claire born Nov 26, 1900

Amanda P, born June 16, 1903

Dorcas E, April 17, 1905

Mr Fellows lives at West Point, Wis

Mrs. Fellows died Sept 13, 1905

ELLIE J FELLOWS (8).

Frances H (7), John (6), Nathaniel (5), Job (4), Nathaniel (3), Benony (2), George (1)

Ellie J, daughter of J N and Frances H (Gardner) Fellows was born Aug 2, 1860, at Lodi Wis Married Dec, 1889 to Durward Waffle, son of Byron and Donna (Wheeler) Waffle Mrs Waffle resides at Pendleton, Oregon

VIOLA E FELLOWS (8)

Frances H (7), John (6), Nathaniel (5), Job (4), Nathaniel (3), Benony (2), George (1)

Viola E, daughter of J N and Frances H (Gardner) Fellows, was born Sept 1, 1858 at Lodi Wis Married Aug 7, 1883, to Dr S F Verbeck, son of C C and Sarah (Knight) Verbeck, of West Point, Wis

One son and three daughters

Vivian E, born Nov 2 1884

Norma I born Sept 8, 1886

Carleton F, Aug 5, 1888

Frances Lucile born Dec 2, 1902

Dr and Mrs Verbeck live at Lodi, Wis

CLARA J FELLOWS (8)

Frances H (7), John (6), Nathaniel (5), Job (4), Nathaniel (3), Benony (2), George (1)

Clara J, daughter of J N and Frances H (Gardner) Fellows, was born Dec 21, 1865 at West Point, Wis Married Dec 23, 1888, to Frank O Sisson, son of Frank O and Zilpha (Lyman) Sisson

Two children

Helen, born Dec 30, 1889

Lisle, born Apr 2, 1892

Mr Sisson died May, 1894

Mrs Sisson and daughters have a beautiful home at Prairie du Sac Wis

NILES FELLOWS (8)

Frances H (7), John (6), Nathaniel (5), Job (4), Nathaniel (3), Benony (2), George (1)

Niles, son of J N and Frances H (Gardner) Fellows, was born April 12, 1854 at Stephentown Rensselaer Co, New York Married June 20 1885, to Mary L Hesselgrave daughter of David and —— (Armor) Hesselgrave of West Point Wis

One son

Raymond N, born Sept 17, 1887, at West Point, Wis

Mr Fellows is a painter and resides at Madison, Wis

ALICE A FELLOWS (8).

Frances H (7), John (6), Nathaniel (5), Job (4), Nathaniel (3), Benony (2), George (1)

Alice A, daughter of J N and Frances H (Gardner) Fellows, was born Dec 23, 1872, at West Point, Wis. Married Nov 24, 1892 to Charles Verbeck son of C C and Sarah (Knight) Verbeck

One daughter

Frances Elizabeth, born July 12, 1906

Mrs Verbeck is now (1907) living at Madison, Wis

WILLIAM FELLOWS (8).

Frances H (7), John (6), Nathaniel (5), Job (4), Nathaniel (3), Benony (2), George (1)

William, son of J N and Frances H (Gardner) Fellows, was born Oct —, 1849, at Stephentown New York Married Sept 7, 1878, to Isabella Rapp

One son and two daughters

Nellie E, born July 4, 1881

Harry, born Nov 25, 1885

Abbie, born May 5, 1890

Mr Fellows is a farmer.

HELEN M. FELLOWS (8).

Frances H (7), John (6), Nathaniel (5), Job (4), Nathaniel (3), Benony (2), George (1)

Helen M daughter of J N and Frances H (Gardner) Fellows, was born Dec 4, 1851, at Stephentown Rensselaer Co, New York Married Dec 7, 1875, to Charles L Nott son of Geo W and Maria (Nutting) Nott of West Point, Wis

Two children

Jessie L, Aug 2, 1883

Ethel M, June 14, 1890

In Sept, 1898, Mr and Mrs Nott removed to Lodi, Wis

HARRIET E. WOODWARD (8)

Lucy M Gardner (7) John (6), Nathaniel (5), Job (4), Nathaniel (3), Benony (2), George (1)

Harriet E, daughter of Stephen E and Lucy M (Gardner) Woodward, was born at Lodi, Wis, Jan 26, 1859 Married Dec 6, 1893, Reuben S Brown, son of Joseph and Emeline (Newberry) Brown of Lodi Wis

Five children

Myrtle M., born Aug 13, 1894, died Mch 25, 1902
Baby boy, born June 19, 1896, died July 7, 1896
Walter W., born June 20, 1899
Arthur M, born Nov. 13, 1902
Mildred M, born May 29, 1906
Mr and Mrs Brown live at the old homestead near the village of Lodi

MABEL I GARDNER (8)

Desevignia (7), John (6), Nathaniel (5), Job (4), Nathaniel (3), Benony (2), George (1)

Mabel I daughter of Desevignia S and Mercy A (Appler) Gardner, was born July 18, 1870 at Lodi, Wis Married Aug. 7, 1888, to Edward W S Houston of Lawrence, Kansas

Children
Nellie E, born Feb 13, 1890
Mercy M, born Nov 21, 1891.
George A born June 1, 1893.
Warren A, born July 19, 1894
Clarence H born March 30, 1896
Bayard T, born July 29, 1902
Chester O, born July 20, 1904
Albert E, born Sept 15, 1906
Mr and Mrs Houston reside at Lawrence, Kansas

ALBERT J. GARDNER (8)

Desevignia (7), John (6), Nathaniel (5), Job (4), Nathaniel (3), Benony (2), George (1).

Albert J son of Desevignia S and Mercy A (Appler) Gardner, was born March 23, 1872 Married Oct 28, 1892, to Amy O Whipple of Lawrence, Kan

To them were born five children
Alfred C, born March 22 1894
Albert Ray, born Oct 13, 1895
Marjorie B, born Apr 27, 1899
Helen P, born Jan 8, 1904
Mabel M, born Aug 11, 1906
Mr Gardner resides at Spokane, Wash

JOHN H GARDNER (8)

Desevignia (7), John (6), Nathaniel (5), Job (4), Nathaniel (3), Benony (2), George (1)

John H, son of Desevignia S and Mercy A (Appler) Gardner was born July 6, 1874 Married to Rosa Vaughn, April 2, 1901

One child
Eunice Elizabeth, born June 4, 1902
Mr Gardner lives at or near Lawrence, Kan.

ALLEN W GARDNER (8).

William D. S (7), John (6), Nathaniel (5), Job (4), Nathaniel (3), Benony (2), George (1)

Allen W, son of William D S and Julia A (Martin) Gardner, was born Aug. 27, 1864, at West Point, Wis Married Hattie Davis, Nov. 11, 1887

Three boys

Hazen L, born Apr 8, 1889

Lawrence, born Jan 19, 1891.

Wayne, born Apr 17, 1896

Mr Gardner now lives in the Dominion of Canada where he owns and tills a large farm.

HARRY U GARDNER (8)

William D. S (7), John (6), Nathaniel (5), Job (4), Nathaniel (3), Benony (2), George (1)

Harry U, son of William D S and Julia A (Martin) Gardner, was born Nov 18, 1871 Married Rose Kernerzer, Apr 25, 1900

Two children

Floyd born June 25, 1901

Julia S, born July 31, 1904.

Mr. Gardner follows farming for a living, working his father's farm

GILBERT H GARDNER (8).

William D. S (7), John (6), Nathaniel (5), Job (4), Nathaniel (3), Benony (2) George (1)

Gilbert H, son of William D S and Julia A (Martin) Gardner, was born Dec 21, 1879, at West Point, Wis Married Eleanor Vlivian, Dec 24, 1902 Mr Gardner now lives at Durango, Colo, following his his occupation of painting.

F. EUGENE CHRISLER (8).

Mary E Gardner (7), John (6), Nathaniel (5), Job (4), Nathaniel (3), Benony (2), George (1)

F Eugene, son of Wallcott E and Mary E (Gardner) Chrisler, was born at West Point, Wis, Oct 28, 1868 Married June —, 1892, to Myrtie A. Todd, daughter of Miles G and Helen (Parker) Todd

Two children

Elmer Todd, born June 27, 1897

Helen M, born June 23, 1899

Mr Chrisler is a merchant at Albert Lea, Minn.

CHARLES C GARDNER (8).

William (7), Job (6), Job (5), Benjamin (4), Nathaniel (3), Benony (2), George (1)

Charles C Gardner, son of William Gardner, the son of Job, married but we have no record of it

Children were

Elida, married Sidney Regen of Crisfield, Md.

Ella, married William Greenhart of Rensselaer County, N Y

Nelson, resides at Schenectady, N Y.

Arthur, resides at Sunnyside, Va

EDWARD N GARDNER (8)

William (7), Job (6), Job (5), Benjamin (4), Nathaniel (3), Benony (2), George (1)

Edward N Gardner, son of William, the son of Job, was born December 27, 1832 Married Martha Ballershall of Chatham, N Y

Their children were

William E, married Ella Pary

Henry C, resides at Miles, Indian Territory

Edward H., married Hattie Pettil

WILLIAM H GARDNER (8)

William (7), Job (6), Job (5) Benjamin (4), Nathaniel (3), Benony (2), George (1)

William H Gardner, son of William, the son of Job, married Jane Flagler.

Children were

Leisler, deceased

Westfall May,

John Milton,

William H.,

Horatio N,

Caroline, deceased

Sarah, deceased.

CYRIL SYLVESTER GARDNER (8).

Lester (7), Joseph N (6), Palmer (5), Sylvester (4), Nicholas (3), Nicholas (2), George (1).

Cyril S, son of Lester and Lucy (Chandler) Gardner, was born 1840, married Catherine Casey, living at Stanbridge, East, P Q

Children were

Lucy Alice, born July 19, 1861, married Albert Laraway, June 25, 1888 Reside at Stanbridge, East

Deborah Catherine, born Jan 16, 1863, married William Beattie, Nov 19, 1881, has three children Beulah, born Apr 19, 1885, died 1885, Jennie Katherine, born Aug. 29, 1882, Ruby Deborah, born Nov 30, 1888 Mr. Beattie died Aug 4, 1906, at Everett, Mass

Pruella Gladys, born April 12, 1867, married Henry Connor, Apr 11, 1888 Residence, Bedford, P Q

Dana Cyril, born Mar 3, 1870, married Hattie Johnson, Oct 3 1890 Residence Stanbridge, P Q

Ethel Irene, born Sept 19, 1874, married M Allen Cornell, Sept 25, 1895 He is with the Ogilvie Milling Co, Fort William, Ont

John Chandler, born Oct 5, 1876, married Annie Eagen, May 30, 1906 Residence Hartford, Conn

ERNEST L GARDNER (8)

Lester (7), Joseph N (6), Palmer (5), Sylvester (4), Nicholas (3), Nicholas (2), George (1).

Ernest L, son of Lester and Lucy (Chandler) Gardner, was born July 6, 1862, married Josephine Borden and resides at 455 Pine Street, Manchester, N H

Children·

George Lester, born Dec 7, 1882

Gertrude Ernestine, born Feb. 5, 1885; died June, 1886

Dwight Reginald, born June 4, 1890.

JOSEPH PALMER GARDNER (8).

James P. (7), Joseph N (6) Palmer (5), Sylvester (4), Nicholas (3), Nicholas (2), George (1).

Joseph Palmer, son of James Palmer and Elizabeth (Rykerd) Gardner, was born Nov 20, 1838, died Aug 10. 1887 He married Mary Martindale, Feb 9, 1863

One son

Byron, born Aug 22, 1867, married Edna Crellor, Sept 15, 1892 One child· Aileen, born Nov 2, 1898

After the death of Joseph Palmer his widow married Johnson Rhicard Residence Pigeon Hill, P Q

JAMES HERBERT GARDNER (8).

James P. (7). Joseph N (6), Palmer (5), Sylvester (4), Nicholas (3), Nicholas (2), George (1).

James Herbert, son of James Palmer and Elizabeth (Rykerd) Gardner, was born July 11, 1843, died Jan 21, 1890 He married Nancy Hall in 1870 After his death she married (2) E C Burt, reside at Enosburg Falls, Vt

One son

Clifford, born 1884, resides at Boston, Mass

ORCELIA GARDNER (8).

James P. (7), Joseph N (6), Palmer (5), Sylvester (4), Nicholas (3), Nicholas (2), George (1).

Orcelia, daughter of James Palmer and Elizabeth (Rykerd) Gardner, was born Oct 8, 1845, died 1871 She married J W Martindale, March 15, 1863 He died some years ago

One child

Jennie, born May 5, 1865, died Dec 31, 1897; married M E Stanton, Apr, 1884 Child Birney, born Aug 15, 1885

CHARLES OSBORNE GARDNER (8).

James P. (7), Joseph N (6), Palmer (5), Sylvester (4), Nicholas (3), Nicholas (2), George (1).

Charles Osborne, son of James Palmer and Elizabeth (Rykerd) Gardner, was born Feb 11, 1848, married Eva Preston in 1880 Lives at Santa Ynez, Santa Barbara Co, California

Children

Three daughters died young

James, born 1893

ALMEDA DEBORAH GARDNER (8)

James P (7), Joseph N (6), Palmer (5), Sylvester (4), Nicholas (3), Nicholas (2), George (1).

Almeda Deborah, daughter of James Palmer and Elizabeth (Rykerd) Gardner, was born April 13, 1850, died Aug. 19, 1905 She married Eli Martindale in 1874, Stanbridge, East, P Q

Children

Ethel, born Dec, 1875

James Curtis, born Aug, 1878

Grace born 1880

Merritt, born 1887

EVA GARDNER (8)

James P. (7), Joseph N (6), Palmer (5), Sylvester (4), Nicholas (3), Nicholas (2), George (1).

Eva, daughter of James Palmer and Elizabeth (Rykerd) Gardner, was born Feb 26, 1853, married Prof H S Hubbard, musician, Apr 2, 1877 Resides in Sherbrooke, P Q

Children

Mary, born Nov 3, 1878

Idell, born Nov 5, 1884

DELBERT MORENCY GARDNER (8)

James P. (7), Joseph N (6), Palmer (5), Sylvester (4), Nicholas (3), Nicholas (2), George (1).

Delbert Morency, son of James Palmer and Elizabeth (Rykerd) Gardner, was born Sept 26, 1855, married Annette Lawrence in 1877 Residence, Enosburg Falls, Vt.

Children

Glenna Maria, born Sept 13, 1877, married Robert Mears, has one son, Edward Gardner, born Oct 7, 1901. Lives at Enosburg Falls, Vt

Dwight Merritt, born June 26 1882

William Lawrence, born May 13, 1886.

WILLIAM GARDNER APPLETON (8).

Sarah Ann (7), Sylvester (6), Palmer (5), Sylvester (4), Nicholas (3), Nicholas (2), George (1).

William Gardner Appleton, son of Rev Samuel G and Sarah Ann (Gardner) Appleton, was born April 17, 1843, at Avon, N Y Married Katherine Ritter, of New York, Oct 5, 1870 She was born Aug 21, 1846, at New York City

Children are

Floyd, born Aug. 20, 1871

Daniel Fuller, born July 16, 1873, at Morisania, N Y

Madelaine, born Aug 31, 1876, married J R Gleason One child Rosalind, born 1900, died

Edith Cushman, born Apr 29, 1878, married Kenneth Ives, Oct 30, 1901 Two children Kenneth Appleton, born Dec 30, 1902, Philip, born Aug 8 1904

Osgood, born May 6, 1884, died Nov 19, 1892

MAGDALINE CHANDLER (8)

Calista Gardner (7), Joseph N (6), Palmer (5), Sylvester (4), Nicholas (3), Nicholas (2), George (1).

Magdaline daughter of Cyril and Calista (Gardner) Chandler, was born July 5, 1861, married Montague Rice, October 23, 1884

Children are

Glenna Chandler, born Oct 16, 1886

Florence Leora, born Mar. 9, 1890

Bertha Magdalen, born Dec 29, 1892

Cyril Montague born May 3 1895

Evelyn Calista Vincent, born Sept 28, 1898.

EMELINE ALATHEA JONES (8).

Patience Calsina Gardner (7), Palmer (6), Palmer (5), Sylvester (4), Nicholas (3), Nicholas (2), George (1).

Emeline A, daughter of Rev Charles and Patience Calsina (Gardner) Jones married (1) George P Deshon, Jan 1, 1863

One son

George D, born Aug. 5, 1864, at Brookline, Mass, A B Dartmouth College, 1883, West Point, 1886, M D Bellevue Medical College, 1890, and University of Pennsylvania, 1893, Major-Surgeon U S Army, stationed at Fort Des Moines, Iowa He married Susie Howard Copeland, July 7, 1886 Two children: Marjorie, born Apr 14, 1888, at Ft Wayne, Detroit, Mich, Percy, born July 12, 1889, at South Somerset, Mass

Emeline A (Jones) Deshon, married (2) Dr George S Eddy of Fall River, Mass, Nov 7, 1870 One son George Stetson, born Aug 9, 1873, died Oct 27, 1897

SARAH LOUISE JONES (8)

Patience Calsina Gardner (7), Palmer (6), Palmer (5), Sylvester (4), Nicholas (3), Nicholas (2), George (1).

Sarah Louise, daughter of Rev Charles and Patience Calsina (Gardner) Jones, married David Boal Wilson, Sept 27, 1870 He was the son of John F. and Agnes Sawyer (Boal) Wilson and was born March 12, 1838, graduated at Jefferson College, Washington, Pa., in 1860, served as volunteer from Aug. 18, 1862, till Sept 29, 1865, entered the Regular Army July 28, 1866, retired March 12, 1902, with the rank of Lieutenant-Colonel, retired April 23, 1904, with the rank of Colonel Residence 1721 Rebecca St, Sioux City, Iowa

Children

Percy, born Jan 10, 1872, at Ft Clark, Texas, A B Princeton College, 1892, Ann Arbor Law School, 1894, Attorney at law Silver City, New Mexico, married Violette Bertha Caruthers, nee Ashenpelter, Dec 25, 1900

Guy, born Nov 19, 1873, at Saxonville, Mass., A B Princeton College, 1894, Cashier Farmers' State Bank, Laurel Nebraska

CAROLINE ELIZABETH GATES (8).

Hannah Gardner (7), Palmer (6), Palmer (5), Sylvester (4), Nicholas (3), Nicholas (2), George (1).

Caroline E, daughter of Horace Brown and Hannah (Gardner) Gates was born in Jamesville N Y, July 10, 1829, married Thaddeus Mason Wood in Jamesville, Feb 18, 1845 She died in Syracuse, N Y, May 20, 1852 Thaddeus Wood was born Aug 22, 1822, died at Syracuse, N. Y, Aug 19, 1865

One child was born to them:

William Theodore, born in Syracuse, May 21, 1848, married Georgiana Durney, January 26, 1902 No children They reside in Syracuse and during the summer conduct a hotel at Inlet, Hamilton Co , N Y.

WILLIAM GARDNER GATES (8)

Hannah Gardner (7), Palmer (6), Palmer (5). Sylvester (4), Nicholas (3), Nicholas (2), George (1).

William G , son of Horace B and Hannah (Gardner) Gates was born at Jamesville, N Y , May 22, 1830, married Mary Elizabeth Warner Brown, Oct 27, 1853, in Syracuse, N Y She was born at St Catherines, Canada, Oct 15, 1835, and was the daughter of Johnson Butler Brown, son of Peter and Mary (Hare) Brown, born at Port Dalhousie. Ont, Jan 10, 1810, died Feb 28, 1892, at St Paul, Minn , and Mary Elizabeth Warner, born in Brooklyn. N. Y , April 13, 1798, died in Rochester, N Y , 1842, daughter of Harvey Warner

William G Gates went to Minnesota in 1857 and in 1862 settled permanently in St Paul He was in the grain and elevator business through the state until about 1895 and for the past ten years he has been statistician for the Chamber of Commerce of St Paul though not in active business

Children

Horace Butler, born May 10, 1856, in Syracuse; married Jessie Hackett May 10, 1882 She was born in Lake City, Minn , Aug 27, 1858, daughter of Chas W Hackett and Mary Holt He is president of the Hackett, Walther, Gates Wholesale Hardware Company of St. Paul, Minn Children Lewis Harold, born in St Paul, May 1, 1885 Sophomore at Cornell University Frederic Hackett, born Apr 25, 1892

Carolyn Anna, born in St Paul, Nov 16, 1866, married in St Paul, Minn, Paris, son of Albert A and Delia (Murray) Fletcher of Vermont, June 19, 1889 No children

Mary Brown, born June 18, 1869, died Feb 27, 1871, in St Paul, Minn

Willard Frederic, born Dec 23, 1870, in St Paul, married Katheryn Dubois, Feb 19, 1895 She was daughter of Joseph Oliver and Ann (Cody) Dubois He is city salesman for Hackett, Walther, Gates Hardware Co One child Carolyn Fletcher, born Dec 20, 1896

Gardner Brown, born in St Paul, Minn , July 6, 1872, shipping clerk for French, Finch & Henry, Wholesale Boots and Shoes, St Paul Unmarried

SARAH MARIA PORTER (8)

Hannah Gardner (7), Sylvester (6), Palmer (5) Sylvester (4), Nicholas (3), Nicholas (2), George (1)

Sarah Maria, daughter of Evelyn H and Hannah (Gardner) Porter married Lewis Sanford Thomas July 2 1849 He was the son of Nathaniel Gardner Thomas Mr L S Thomas was an attorney in New York and resided in Orange, N. J

Children:

Clara Mortimer, born July 2, 1850, married Rev John W. Craig, graduate of Harvard University and some time rector of St John's School, Manlius, N Y Children Edith, born Oct 11, 1880, married Minot Lester Wallace. children Eleanor Woodworth, born Nov 11, 1883, Dorothy Mayhew, born Mar 10, 1885

Gardner, born May 25, 1854, died Apr 14, 1880

Mary Evelyn, born Mar 13, 1861, living at Skaneateles, N. Y

Frederic Mayhew, born Mar 11, 1863, married Caroline Lucas, of Hagerstown Md, died June 10, 1906 Civil Engineer

WILLIAM PORTER (8).

Hannah Gardner (7), Sylvester (6), Palmer (5), Sylvester (4), Nicholas (3), Nicholas (2), George (1).

William, son of Evelyn H and Hannah (Gardner) Porter, was born Aug 29, 1830, died Nov 9 1884 He married Julia Isabella daughter of Horace and Mary Ann (Robertson) Williams of East Hartford, Conn She was born Sept 10, 1839, died May 19, 1877

Children

William Evelyn Porter, born June 16, 1866

Kate Isabella, born June 26, 1869, died Aug 10, 1869

Mary, born May 1 1877, died May 1, 1877

MARYETTE CHACE (8).

Sarah Gardner (7), Palmer (6), Palmer (5), Sylvester (4), Nicholas (3), Nicholas (2), George (1)

Maryette, daughter of Rev S E D. and Sarah (Gardner) Chace, was born March 9, 1840, in Bloomington, Ill married Dr Jesse L Waughop, December 28, 1865 He died Feb 5, 1867 She married (2) Francis Adams, Esq, of Chicago, Ill, August 26, 1875 Mr Adams has served seventeen years as Judge, first of the Circuit Court and since three terms on the Appellate bench

Children were

Fred, died at the age of 28 years

John, died at the age of 20 months

Frances Emeline died at the age of 13 months

Two infants unnamed

Florence born 1876, married Mr Dobson and has an infant daughter, Maryette Chace Mr and Mrs Dobson reside with her mother in Chicago caring for her in her all but total blindness

Francis, graduated from Amherst College and has now about completed his law course at the Northwestern Law School in Chicago

EMILY DIANA SORNBERGER (8).

Emily Gardner (7), Joseph N. (6), Palmer (5), Sylvester (4), Nicholas (3), Nicholas (2), George (1).

Emily Diana daughter of Rev D W and Emily (Gardner) Sornberger, was born 1844, died 1898. She married David Peebles.

Children
Florence,
Jennie, married Howard Sells. Lives in Minnesota.
Ora,
Wellington
Susan.
Last three live in Boston, Mass

WINTEMOYEH CHACE (8)

Sarah Gardner (7), Palmer (6), Palmer (5), Sylvester (4), Nicholas (3) Nicholas (2), George (1).

Wintemoyeh, son of Rev S W D and Sarah (Gardner) Chase, married Galusha James Perkins, at Washington, Ill, Oct 8, 1867 He was born at Hannibalville, N Y, Mar 31, 1846 They reside at Hudson, Mich

Children

Clarence De Forest, born Oct 15, 1869, died July, 1886.

Bessie Margaret born Mar 3, 1873, died Feb 9, 1882

Harry Le Roy, born Apr 8, 1875, married Harriet Jane Osborne, daughter of Joseph W and Helen A (Hand) Osborne Children are Helen Osborne, born May 7, 1898, Margaret Jane, born May 3 1900, Robert Le Roy, born June 11, 1905

Robert Martin, born June 10, 1877

Bernice Chace, born Aug 19, 1880 married Francis Joseph McClue, Jan 9, 1906 He was born Mar 11, 1873, at Mt Pleasant, Mich

Eloise Wintemoyeh, born May 19, 1884.

SARAH P CHACE (8)

Sarah Gardner (7), Palmer (6), Palmer (5), Sylvester (4), Nicholas (3), Nicholas (2), George (1).

Sarah P, daughter of Rev S W D and Sarah (Gardner) Chace, married James N Franklin, Dec 24, 1862 Resides at Lexington, Ill

Children are

Maud Franklin, born July 10, 1864, married to Dr H P Perry, Oct 17, 1890 Two children Ralph Franklin, born Nov 3, 1891, Elvira, born 1899

John Herbert, born Oct 25, 1868, married Florence Cameron, Nov. 28, 1897 Two children Donald, born 1899 Ruth, born 1901

George L, born Mar 12 1871, married Genevieve Wiggins, June 23, 1897 Two children Beatrice, born 1898, Jack, born 1900

Irwin Chace, born Apr 23, 1875, married Lucretia Mott Smith, Oct. 14, 1902 One child Sarah Chace, born Oct 6, 1906

Wintemoyeh born Oct 28, 1878, married L B Strayer, Oct 29 1901

James Russell, born Oct 5, 1880 Single

Edward Lynn, born Feb 28, 1885 Single

OSCAR SHEFFIELD (8).

Hannah G Smith (7), Amy Gardner (6), Palmer (5), Sylvester (4), Nicholas (3), Nicholas (2), George (1).

Oscar son of Jeremiah and Hannah G (Smith) Sheffield, was born Feb 12, 1824, married Adeline Chamberlin, Feb 12, 1851 She was born Nov. 30, 1833 at Mannsville, N Y.

Children

Alice Louise, born Nov. 5, 1851, at Mannsville, N Y, married Joseph Hilton Vaughn, Jan. 20, 1875, at Spring Prairie, Wis He was born at Spring Prairie, Jan 20, 1850, and died there June 20, 1896 Children Olive Allign, born June 13. 1883, married George James Allen, Oct 5 1904 He was born Sept 13, 1880 Reside in Chicago, Ill

Nettie Lillian, born in New York June 23, 1853, married (1) Richard J McDonald, Jan 6, 1880 One child Willis Leigh, born July 6, 1882 She married (2) George Allen Gunther, Feb, 1894 No children Live at Columbus, Wis

Nellie Bly, born at Lafayette, Wis, Aug. 6, 1856, died Aug 12, 1905 at Spring Prairie, Wis She married George J Jewell, Mar. 31, 1875 He was born May, 1851 Lived at Duluth, Minn

Willist, born May 23, 1858, married and lives at Chicago Three children

Minnie, born at Spring Prairie, Jan 28, 1860, married Henry Vaughn, July, 1896 He was born Oct 30, 1836 Live at Elkhorn, Wis One son Glenn Henry, born Aug 21, 1897

Harriet Julia, born Apr 14, 1862, at Spring Prairie Resides in Elkhorn, Wis

Cora Belle, born Oct 15, 1875, died Apr 19, 1878

MARTHA E SHEFFIELD (8)

Hannah G Smith (7), Amy Gardner (6), Palmer (5), Sylvester (4), Nicholas (3) Nicholas (2), George (1).

Martha E, daughter of Jeremiah and Hannah G (Smith) Sheffield, was born June 7, 1830 married John Middleton at Mannsville, Jefferson County, N Y, Jan 1, 1854

Six children, four of whom are living

Frederick W, born Aug 26, 1856, resides at Edmonton Unmarried

Jeanette born Dec 13, 1859 married Hartwell Benson, of Oswego, N Y Lives in Syracuse, N Y Four children of whom the eldest daughter is Mrs George Porter of Seattle, Wash, mother of two children

John J, born Apr 13, 1861, married Mina Avery of Lyons Co, Minn, Nov, 1886 Three sons have been born to them of whom the second, a boy of fourteen years, was killed by the accidental discharge of his gun while hunting

Charles H, born Nov 19, 1863, married Martha Loser of Oswego Co, N Y., Feb 17, 1890

Children
May L., born Dec. 11, 1892
Glen C., born Feb. 16, 1893
Elsie M., born Dec. 24, 1895
John F., born Apr. 24, 1899

The three sons of Martha E. (Sheffield) Middleton are farmers and stock raisers, all of them owning and running well tilled farms.

CELESTE ANNETTE SHEFFIELD (8).

Hannah G. Smith (7), Amy Gardner (6), Palmer (5), Sylvester (4), Nicholas (3), Nicholas (2), George (1).

Celeste Annette, daughter of Jeremiah and Hannah G. (Smith) Sheffield, was born November 1, 1839. Married Gordon Merrick, Dec., 1864, and lives in Spring Prairie, Walworth County, Wisconsin. He was born Apr. 5, 1836. Cousin of Perez Merrick.

Children were:

Lucretia May Gardner, born August 22, 1866. Married Frank E. Harry, June 4, 1893. Children: Ray, Roy, Willard, Leonard.

Edith, born December 21, 1868. Kindergarten Teacher at Fond du Lac, Wisconsin.

George Gates, born July 9, 1871. Died February 7, 1891.

Eugene Roderick, born August 31, 1878, married Mae Katzman, Jan. 26, 1898. No children.

BRAINARD GARDNER SMITH (8)

William W. Smith (7), Amy Gardner (6), Palmer (5), Sylvester (4), Nicholas (3), Nicholas (2), George (1).

Brainard G., son of William W. and Mary Theresa (Stowe) Smith, was born Oct. 20, 1846, married Mary Cornelia Bevier, Sept. 27, 1876. She was born Feb. 21, 1853, a descendant of an old Huguenot family, the Beviers of Ulster County, where she was born and married. They live in New Jersey.

Children

Bevier, born July 30, 1877.
Amy Gardner, born Mar. 31, 1882, died Aug. 10, 1883.
Helen Brainard, born Jan. 29, 1886.

EZEKIEL B. SHELDON (8)

Anne Maria Smith (7), Amy Gardner (6), Palmer (5), Sylvester (4), Nicholas (3), Nicholas (2), George (1).

Ezekiel B., son of Dewitt C. and Anne Maria (Smith) Sheldon, married Alzada Flagg of Sauk County, Wis., 1860. They settled in Alzada, Montana.

They had seven sons, six of whom were
Jay,
Cutler,
Elmer,
George,
Oscar,
Ray

CAROLINE SHELDON (8).

Anne Maria Smith (7), Amy Gardner (6), Palmer (5), Sylvester (4), Nicholas (3), Nicholas (2), George (1).

Caroline, daughter of Dewitt C and Anne Maria (Smith) Sheldon, died 1897 She married Charles R Ingalls of Minneapolis, Minn

Children were
James,
Hattie, married Mr Beaudreau, live at Caron, Assiniboia
Fred, lives at Caron, Assiniboia
Herbert,
Frank,
Arthur,
Pearl

CHARLES FOX SHELDON(8)

Anne Maria Smith (7), Amy Gardner (6), Palmer (5), Sylvester (4), Nicholas (3), Nicholas (2), George (1).

Charles F, son of Dewitt C and Anne Maria (Smith) Sheldon married Belle Hood of Racine, Wis, sister of Mary Lives at Reedsburg, where Mr Sheldon is postmaster

Children

Walter Dewitt, married June 2, 1906, Byrd Hunter of Eau Claire, Wis She was born Oct 1, 1872 He completed his medical studies at Vienna and is at present consulting physician at Minneapolis

Mabel, graduated at State University at Madison, Wis Is now teaching at Reedsburg

AMY SHELDON (8).

Anne Maria Smith (7), Amy Gardner (6), Palmer (5), Sylvester (4), Nicholas (3), Nicholas (2) George (1).

Amy, daughter of Dewitt C and Anne Maria (Smith) Sheldon, married Rev James S Thomas, M D, and was Presbyterian missionary in Siam Fright and general nervous tension during an outbreak of persecution, together with la grippe brought on paralysis After a year or more of rest and treatment at Clifton Springs she was largely restored to health Their present address is Fairoaks, Sacramento Co, Cal, where the Dr is in general practice

JOSEPHINE S. HAND (8).

Harriet N Smith (7), Amy Gardner (6), Palmer (5), Sylvester (4), Nicholas (3), Nicholas (2), George (1).

Josephine S, daughter of Edmund and Harriet N (Smith) Hand, married in Macon, Mich, to William W Osgood, May 4, 1859. He was the son of John and Martha Osgood of Ridgeway, Mich They reside on the farm where they settled forty-two years ago

Four children were born to them:

Edmund Hand, born Jan 26, 1862, in Hillsdale, Mich, married Estelle M Miller of Macon, May 27, 1886 Reside in St Johns, Mich Two children William H, born May 27, 1888; George E, born Feb 16, 1893

Harriet M, born Oct 30, 1865, in Macon, married Revilo G Sage, a farmer of Macon, Mar 16, 1893 Child Edmund Osgood, born Feb 10, 1896

Willard W, born Aug 13, 1869, died Aug 16, 1869

May E, born May 16, 1872, married Percy K Morgan, a farmer of Macon, Oct 3, 1893 Children Henrietta J, born Nov 20, 1895, Helen M, born Sept 23, 1901, Marjorie, born Feb 19, 1907

HORACE A. HAND (8).

Harriet N Smith (7), Amy Gardner (6), Palmer (5), Sylvester (4), Nicholas (3), Nicholas (2), George (1).

Horace A, son of Edmund and Harriet N (Smith) Hand, married Abbie Green of Hancock, Mass, settled on a farm near Ridgeway, Mich, where they still (1907) reside

Children

Harriet, died in childhood

Ella, married Fred Aten and resides in Ridgeway Three children. Leota, Harriet, Gertrude

Gertrude, married Alonzo Sisson of Macon Children LeMar, Truman, Rosella

Truman, died in childhood

Josephine, married Arthur Phillips of Ashfield, Mass, Sept, 1901

HELEN A. HAND (8).

Harriet N Smith (7), Amy Gardner (6), Palmer (5), Sylvester (4), Nicholas (3), Nicholas (2), George (1)

Helen A, daughter of Edmund and Harriet N (Smith) Hand was born June 10, 1849, married Joseph W Osborne, Feb 8, 1871 He is a farmer at Macon, Mich

Two daughters

Anna M, born July 11, 1872 She is instructor in music in the Higbee school at Memphis, Tenn

Harriet J, born Nov 28, 1876, married Harry Perkins, a merchant in Hudson, Mich, Aug, 1897 Children Helen, born May 6, 1898, Margaret, born Aug 6 1901, Robert, born June 11, 1905

Mr. Perkins is a great grandson of Palmer (6), Amy's brother

ANNETTE M. HAND (8)

Harriet N. Smith (7), Amy Gardner (6), Palmer (5), Sylvester (4), Nicholas (3), Nicholas (2) George (1).

Annette M, daughter of Edmund and Harriet N (Smith) Hand, married Charles C Hendershot, Dec 20, 1877 They own the old Edmund Hand homestead

One child

Lilah, born March 18, 1889

ARTHUR JAMES WHEELER (8).

Charlotte E. Smith (7), Amy Gardner (6), Palmer (5), Sylvester (4), Nicholas (3), Nicholas (2), George (1).

Arthur J, son of Charles and Charlotte E (Smith) Wheeler was born Sept 25, 1841 married Dorlisca J, daughter of Alvin and Ann (Harris) Adams A B Northwestern University, 1866, Pres of the Eau Claire Wesleyan Seminary, Eau Claire, Wis 1866-7, B D Garrett Biblical Institution, 1870 A M Northwestern University, Ph D McKindree College, 1899 He has had one pastoral charge in Wisconsin and seventeen in Michigan during the thirty-eight years of his ministry He resides in Marcellus, Mich

One child

Florence, died Sept 3, 1889

CORNELIA ALICIA WHEELER (8)

Charlotte E. Smith (7), Amy Gardner (6), Palmer (5), Sylvester (4), Nicholas (3), Nicholas (2), George (1)

Cornelia A, daughter of Charles and Charlotte E (Smith) Wheeler, was born Aug 10, 1845, married Charles Holyoke of Chicago, Ill, Oct 1875 His parents were Mr and Mrs Christopher of Nova Scotia He was legally adopted by Dr and Mrs Edward Holyoke of Chicago Dr Holyoke was of an old Colonial family Mrs Holyoke was Maria Ballard of Mass His family came to Quincy, Ill, and during the Civil war the old homestead was a well known station on the "underground railroad" Charles was a student at Oberlin and prepared himself for an elocutionist He died Oct, 1893

Children were:

Charles Edward born Aug 29, 1876; married Eva L, daughter of C G Chamberlin, of Lockport, Ill Two children Edward, born Dec 20, 1902 Virginia Delight, born Nov 18 1904.

Eleanor Mary, born Nov 27, 1878

Mrs Holyoke resides at 1808 Van Camp Avenue, Omaha, Neb.

VIRGINIA J. HENRY (8).

Sylvester G. (7), Hannah Gardner (6). Palmer (5), Sylvester (4), Nicholas (3), Nicholas (2), George (1).

Virginia J, daughter of Sylvester G and Juliana (Scouten) Henry, was married Feb 22, 1866, to Adin Gibson at Fond du Lac, Wis Since 1868 their residence has been Grundy Co, Iowa

Adin Gibson was born April 13, 1841, in Summit County, Ohio In 1854 with his parents he removed to Fond du Lac County, Wis From Sept 11, 1861, till Oct 9, 1865, he served in the Federal army, Company H, 14th Wis Infantry

They have one child

Alma Geneva, born July 14, 1867

VIETTA J HENRY (8).

Sylvester G (7), Hannah Gardner (6), Palmer (5), Sylvester (4), Nicholas (3) Nicholas (2), George (1).

Vietta J, daughter of Sylvester G and Julianna (Scouten) Henry, was married March 12, 1871, to Alfred Cheesman in Grundy Co, Iowa

Children:

Llewelyn, born Sept 11, 1872, died Feb 15, 1879

Clarence, born Sept 30, 1876

Frederick, born April 8, 1880, died Jan. 30, 1881.

Elmer, born March 31, 1882

Bertha, born Dec 6, 1883

CAROLINE M HENRY (8)

J. Harvey (7), Hannah Gardner (6), Palmer (5), Sylvester (4), Nicholas (3), Nicholas (2), George (1)

Caroline M, daughter of J Harvey and Laura (Tillotson) Henry, was born May 2, 1843, in Medina Co, Ohio She was married Jan. 19, 1866, at Fond du Lac, Wis, to Charles W Gibson From 1869 till Mr. Gibson's death, Jan 16, 1884, they resided in Grundy Co, Iowa

They had two children

Lola E, born Feb 6, 1871; married March 16, 1892, to Francis C Erickson

Mr and Mrs Erickson reside in Grant Township, Grundy Co They have three children· Theron, born Nov 21, 1896 Milton Kenneth, born March 30, 1898, died March, 1901 Lawrence, born Apr 27, 1902

Lucie E, born April 2, 1873.

MARCUS HENRY ASHLEY (8)

Hannah M. Henry (7), Hannah Gardner (6), Palmer (5), Sylvester (4), Nicholas (3), Nicholas (2), George (1)

Marcus H, son of Marcus P and Hannah M (Henry) Ashley, was born Aug 11, 1841, living at Madison, Wis He married Laura Helen Mooney, of Windsor, Wis, who died Jan, 18, 1884

Children

William Prentiss, born in Grant Township, Grundy County, Iowa, March 16, 1868, died Mar 5, 1906, at Milwaukee, married Ann Koehler. One child William Henry, born 1900

Maude Emma, born in Grundy County, Iowa, Mar 3, 1876, married June 29 1899, George Edwin Leech, veterinary surgeon of Winona, Minn

Madge Laura, born at Madison, Wis, Dec 26, 1883 Resides at Windsor, Wis

JOHN J. GARDNER (8).

Nathaniel (7), Robert (6), Nathaniel (5,) Joshua (4), Robert (3), George (2), George (1)

John J son of Nathaniel and Sarah Calkins (Wilson) Gardner, was born June 22, 1820, died July 22 1893 at Hancock, Mass, married Artalissa Smith, daughter of Gardner and Sally (Gardner) Smith, January 23, 1844, at Hancock, Mass She was born Dec. 17, 1822, died May 5 1853-4.

Their children were

Don Aurelius, born May 2, 1846

Sarah Adella, born Nov 22, 1849, unmarried

John J Gardner, married (2) Abbie S Smith daughter of Augustus and Susan (Cranston) Smith, January 4, 1859 She died October 28, 1899 One child:

William Augustus, born May 30, 1861, at South Williamstown, Mass

Abigail S (Smith) Gardner, was the granddaughter of Daniel and Eunice (Gardner) Smith

ROBERT PALMER GARDNER (8).

Nathaniel (7), Robert (6), Nathaniel (5,) Joshua (4), Robert (3), George (2), George (1)

Robert P Gardner, son of Nathaniel and Sarah Calkins (Wilson) Gardner was born Mar 19, 1823 Died April 9, 1884, at Stephentown, N Y Married Caroline Sweet, Nov 19, 1851 She was born Aug 28, 1823 Died Apr 15, 1900 They lived at Stephentown, N Y

They had two children

Noah E, born Nov 21, 1854 Married Elizabeth Moore, Feb 22, 1877 No children

John H., born August 26, 1856 Married Caroline E Sweet

MORTIMER WILSON GARDNER (8.)

Nathaniel (7), Robert (6), Nathaniel (5) Joshua (4), Robert (3), George (2), George (1)

Mortimer Wilson Gardner, son of Nathaniel and Sarah Calkins (Wilson) Gardner, was born Feb. 21, 1828, at Hancock, Mass Died

June 13, 1905 Married Mary C, daughter of Gardner and Sally (Gardner) Smith, December 22, 1852, and settled on a farm in Sherburne, N Y, where he died. His widow lives at Smyrna, N. Y

Children

Kate M, born June 13, 1856, married C P Pudney, Smyrna, N Y
Frank Smith, born Dec 19, 1860 A druggist at Baldwinsville, N Y
Walter Vander, born Dec 26 1864 Living at Smyrna, N Y.
Minnie Louise, born Apr. 23, 1867 Teacher at Baldwinsville, N Y
Anna Sabrina, born Apr 7, 1869, Sherburune, N Y
Mary Grace, born Mar 22, 1872, deceased.
Nathaniel Dwight, born Sept 7, 1876, deceased

SABRINA GARDNER (8)

Perry G. (7), Robert (6), Nathaniel (5), Joshua (4). Robert (3), George (2), George (1)

Sabrina Gardner, daughter of Perry Green and Esther (Ely) Gardner, was born May 26, 1811, died June 13, 1840, married Samuel Washburn Wilson son of John, Jr, and Mary (Gardner) Wilson, April, 1838. He was born January 25, 1792, died August 31 1874 They settled in Smyrna, N Y, and died there He was for many years a prominent citizen of that place

One son

Gardner P born June 5, 1840, died several years ago in Minneapolis, Minn, childless

LOUIE MINERVA GORTON (8)

Eunice Minerva (7), Capt. Joshua (6), Nathaniel (5), Joshua (4), Robert (3), George (2), George (1).

Louie Minerva Gardner, daughter of Reuben E and Eunice Minerva (Gardner) Gorton, was born December 23, 1842, married (1) William Shires at Saratoga Springs, N Y, Sept 10, 1861 After his decease she married (2) William C Silver, June 8, 1876 They live at Paulsboro, Gloucester Co N J, where he has served as Magistrate

Children of first marriage.

Gorton, born Sept 27, 1862, married Mary Early and have two sons Gorton, Jr, and Willie

Estella, born May 6, 1864; married Chas L Le Cato, two children Gladys and Charles B

Child of second marriage:

Nellie, born June 7, 1877; unmarried.

ADELOS GORTON (8).

Eunice Minerva (7), Capt Joshua (6), Nathaniel (5), Joshua (4), Robert (3), George (2), George (1).

Adelos Gorton, son of Reuben E and Eunice Minerva (Gardner) Gorton, was born at Watervliet, Albany County, N Y, April 14, 1848

Married (1) Eunice Fanning Barringer, daughter of Albert P and Elizabeth (Fanning) Barringer, of Troy N Y, April 23, 1891 She died November 19 1892 Mr Gorton married (2) Alice E Potter, daughter of Joseph Kinnecut and Almira Warner (Cooper) Potter, of Germantown, Pa, December 4, 1895

One child

Adelos Jr, born Sept 30, 1896, in Philadelphia, Pa

Mr Gorton is an old Philadelphia book publisher and has printed, bound and sold many thousands of copies of Teachers and Family Bibles and other books He is an editor and writer and has recently published a book entitled "Life and Times of Samuel Gorton," a Colonial History of Rhode Island He is a member of the American Academy and various societies He resides at 4345 Paul Street, Philadelphia, Pa

JOSIE DELIA GORTON (8)

Eunice Minerva (7). Capt. Joshua (6), Nathaniel (5), Joshua (4), Robert (3), George (2), George (1).

Josie Delia Gorton, daughter of Reuben and Eunice Minerva (Gardner) Gorton, was born September 8, 1850, at Watervliet, Albany County, N Y Married Dr James A Wamsley, son of John B and Judith (Burroughs) Wamsley of Mullica Hill, Gloucester Co, N J, December 26, 1869 Dr Wamsley is a graduate of Jefferson Medical College, and was City Physician for many years Now of Philadelphia He is the author of Arabian Degree Klan and other rituals

Their children were

James Winter, born Jan 22, 1873 married Ann C Meeley

Clair Armenia, born May 23, 1880, married Elizabeth T Anderson.

GEORGE RUSSELL GORTON (8).

Eunice Minerva (7). Capt. Joshua (6), Nathaniel (5), Joshua (4), Robert (3), George (2), George (1)

George Russell Gorton, son of Reuben E and Eunice Minerva (Gardner) Groton, was born May 26, 1853, at Watervliet, Albany County, N Y Married Lena Hopf, Saturday, August 29, 1896 She died December 2, 1902 He died July 5, 1904

Their children are

Carl Russell, born Jan 16, 1898, in Philadelphia, Pa

Alfred Hopf, born May 16, 1901, in Philadelphia, Pa

Willie, born Apr 3, 1902, died Mar 27, 1903

Harry, born April 3, 1902, died Feb 18, 1904

George R Gorton was in the book publishing business with his brother in Philadelphia for many years He was killed in a collision of trains on the suburban railway while going from his home to his business in the center of the city

JOSEPHINE MINERVA RUSSELL (8).

Susan (7), Capt Joshua (6), Nathaniel (5), Joshua (4), Robert (3), George (2), George (1)

Josephine Minerva Russell, daughter of George and Susan (Gardner) Russell, was born February 24, 1834 Married Cornelius Stewart Master, January 6, 1857, at East Salem, N Y He died at Charleston, West Virginia, June 8, 1906.

Three children

Anna Susan,

Helen Marguerite,

Mary Emila, kindergarten teacher, Rochester, N Y.

Mr Masters was a civil engineer They lived at Beloit, Wis, Milwaukee, Wis, Chicago, Ill, and Cambridge, N Y., before the war He was four years in the war, after which they lived in Cambridge eleven years, in Rochester, N Y, three years, in Moberly, Mo., ten years, in Phoenix, Arizona, ten years, and in Charleston, W Va

While working on the Maricopa & Proenix Ry, Mr Masters' health failed. A flood carried away his bridge and trestle and he was stricken with nervous prostration For the past fourteen years he has been an invalid with locomotor ataxia and mental collapse.

ANN ELIZA GARDNER (8).

Ishmael (7), Capt Joshua (6), Nathaniel (5), Joshua (4), Robert (3), George (2), George (1)

Ann Eliza Gardner, daughter of Ishmael and Cynthia (Dyer) Gardner, married a Mr Moore and lived in Beloit, Wis

Four children were born to them·

Henry, lives at Devil's Lake, Wis

Ransom, lives at Owatonna, Minn

Hattie, married Major Myrick Deceased

Helen married Gen Ruger Two daughters, one is living at Easton, Pa.

FRANK FOSTER LAIRD (9).

Sarah A Townsend (8), Gardner Townsend (7), Dorcas Gardner (6), Palmer (5), Sylvester (4) Nicholas (3), Nicholas (2), George (1).

Frank F Laird, son of Dr William O and Sarah A (Townsend) Laird, was born April 15, 1856 Died in Atlantic City, N J, Aug 20, 1906 He married (1) Annie Cole Taylor, of Utica, N Y, May 30, 1883 She died May 20, 1895 Her parents were the Hon William B. and Eliza Ann (Fairbanks) Taylor of Utica N Y. He married (2) Mary Ella Pixlee June 23, 1896 She was the daughter of William Franklin and Sarah Jane (Price) Pixlee, of Seattle Wash

His children were both by his first wife

Frank Townsend, born Oct. 3, 1885, at Utica, N Y

Mary Louise, born May 12, 1890, at Utica, N. Y.

Dr F F Laird was graduated from Hamilton College in 1877, excelling in every department of study during his course, but taking especial delight in oratory In this he was given a start by his cousin, Horace Samuel Dyer of Whitestown In his senior year he carried off the prize at the intercollegiate oratorical contest at the Academy of Music in New York city He was class orator at graduation He studied medicine and graduated valedictorian of his class at the Hahnemann Medical College in Philadelphia From 1881 to 1900 he practiced his profession in Utica, and met with great success in his calling Gradually, however, asthma got the better of him so that he was obliged to remove to the milder climate of Los Angeles There with surprising rapidity he built up a splendid practice but in 1904 he had to give up the fight. He returned to Utica and there resumed his residence the remaining two years of his life

The Utica Daily Press says of him.

There are hundreds still living hereabouts who remember Frank Laird as one of the brightest boys of Whitestown Seminary and at Hamilton College They remember him as a brilliant scholar, an eloquent speaker and a popular and much beloved associate His course in school and college set the pace and gave promise, of the professional success which he achieved in after years It was easy for him to lead in his studies and he did it always It seemed likewise easy for him to succeed in his profession He had not been very long in practice here before he drew around him a large circle of acquaintances who became patients and patients who became friends It falls to the fortune of but few physicians to have either a better or a better class of practice than Dr Laird had in Utica

"Intellectually bright and keen, of genial, kindly disposition, he had those qualities and attributes in a large measure which go to make up a successful physician

'Those familiar with the facts have realized the little likelihood there was that he could regain his health and realize his ambitions about returning to his practice, but even to these the news of his death comes as a severe shock and a heavy sorrow"

MAY HENDERSON (9)

Sarah (8), Horace Dyer (7), Abigail Gardner (6), Palmer (5), Sylvester (4), Nicholas (3) Nicholas (2), George (1).

May, daughter of Dr Frederick and Sarah (Dyer) Henderson, married Francis Stuyvesant Peabody of Chicago.

Two children

Stuyvesant,

May Henderson.

The following is from the Chicago Record-Herald of Nov 28, 1906

"Mrs Francis S Peabody, wife of F S Peabody, president of the Peabody Coal Company, died yesterday at Nice, France after a brief illness of typhoid fever Mrs Peabody left Chicago Oct 1, last in the company of Miss Florence Clark of this city for a tour of Europe. They first visited Naples, and a week ago, just after their arrival in Nice, Mrs

Peabody was stricken with typhoid fever She was Miss May Henderson, daughter of a leading business man of Utica, N Y, and was married to Mr Peabody in 1887 She leaves two children, May and Stuyvesant, both of whom are in the East attending school Her mother, who by a second marriage became Mrs John H McAvoy died about a year ago Mrs Peabody was forty-one years old. The body will be brought to Chicago for burial."

FLOYD APPLETON (9).

William G. Appleton (8), Sarah Ann Gardner (7), Sylvester (6), Palmer (5), Sylvester (4), Nicholas (3), Nicholas (2), George (1)

Floyd, son of William G and Katherine (Ritter) Appleton, was born Aug 20, 1871, at Morrisania, N Y After graduating from Grammar school No 61 he studied at the College of the City of New York, where he was Prize Speaker in 1891-2 In this latter year he entered Columbia University and received the degree of Bachelor of Arts in the Class of 1893

He graduated from the General Theological Seminary in 1896, being Seymour Prizeman (for extempore speaking) that same year and was ordered Deacon by the Bishop of New York, May 31st, 1896 After serving as Chaplain of the City Prison and Ludlow Street Jail, New York, for about six months, he became Curate of Grace Church, Plainfield, New Jersey, where he was ordained Priest by the Bishop of New Jersey, April 24th, 1898 At the Fourth Lambeth Conference he served as Chaplain to the Bishop of Texas in 1897, and in the summer of 1900 was in residence at the Oxford House, London A sermon entitled "The Verdict of Mankind on the Facts Found in the Trial of Jesus of Nazareth," preached in the University Chapel at Bonn, was printed by request in 1900 During the years 1893-4 and again from 1897 to 1900 he was in residence as a graduate student at Columbia University, and received the degree of Doctor of Philosophy in 1906

He took charge of the Mission Chapel of St Luke's Church, Brooklyn, New York, in 1901, and the following year became Assistant to the Rector of Christ Church, Brooklyn In 1904 he assumed the Rectorship of St Clements Church, in the same place

ALMA GENEVRA GIBSON (9)

Virginia J. Henry (8), Sylvester G (7), Hannah Gardner (6), Palmer (5), Sylvester (4), Nicholas (3), Nicholas (2), George (1).

Alma G, daughter of Adin and Virginia J (Henry) Gibson, was born July 14, 1867, and married Dec 19, 1894, to Francis M Merrick She died May 21, 1902, at Reinbeck, Iowa, survived by three children

Floyd G, born Dec 16, 1895

Ruth G, born March 2, 1898

Marwin P, born Sept 8, 1900

DON AURELIUS GARDNER (9).

Artalissa (7), Sally (6), Capt. Daniel (5), Sylvester (4), Nicholas (3), Nicholas (2), George (1).

John J (8), Nathaniel (7), Robert (6) Nathaniel (5), Joshua (4), Robert (3), George (2), George (1)

Don Aurelius, son of John J and Artalissa (Smith) Gardner, was born May 2, 1846, married Leonella Moore, November 15, 1879

Their children are

Maude Adella, born May 31, 1881, at Hancock, Mass.

Howard J born Sept. 10, 1891, at Hancock, Mass

WILLIAM AUGUSTUS GARDNER (9).

John J (8), Nathaniel (7), Robert (6), Nathaniel (5), Joshua (4). Robert (3), George (2), George (1)

William A , son of John J. and Abbie S (Smith) Gardner, was born May 30, 1861, at South Williamstown, Mass Married Jennie Elizabeth Fillmore, daughter of William H and Ella J Fillmore, November 14-15, 1895, at Hancock, Mass She was born Nov 11, 1878

Their children were

Jay Hammond born Nov 16, 1897.

Ray Bishop, born June 28, 1900

Mary Minerva, born Oct 18, 1902

Ruby, born Dec 12, 1905, died Dec 13, 1905

Ruth, born Dec 12, 1905 died Dec 22, 1905

William A Gardner lives on the farm settled by his great, great-grandfather, Nathaniel (5)

ANNA SUSAN MASTERS (9)

Josephine M (8), Susan (7), Capt Joshua (6), Nathaniel (5), Joshua (4), Robert (3), George (2), George (1)

Anna Susan Masters, daughter of Cornelius S and Josephine M (Russell) Masters, married her cousin, Wilmer Russell Estill, at Catlettsburg, Ky He is a printer They reside at Charleston, W Va

They have four children

Davis Hudson,

Josephine May,

Anna Masters,

Cornelius Masters

HELEN MARGUERITE MASTERS

Josephine M (8), Susan (7), Capt Joshua (6), Nathaniel (5), Joshua (4), Robert (3), George (2), George (1)

Helen M. Masters, daughter of Cornelius S and Josephine M (Russell) Masters, married Clare Latimore Montgomery, of Rochester, N Y.

Three children:

Gardner Masters,

Russell Francis,

Robert Carter

WILLIAM EVELYN PORTER (9).

William (8), Hannah Gardner (7), Sylvester (6), Palmer (5), Sylvester (4), Nicholas (3), Nicholas (2), George (1).

William Evelyn, son of William and Julia I (Williams) Porter, was born June 16, 1860 Is a physician in general practice at 149 West 37th Street, New York City, and ranks high in his profession He married Mary Rossiter daughter of John Rossiter and Mary Elizabeth (Wilkes) Redfield, July 8, 1885

Children:

William Redfield. born July 29, 1886 A law student in Columbia University, Valedictorian of the class of 1906

Edward Evelyn, born June 5, 1888. Student in Columbia University, pursuing at the same time preparation for the medical profession.

CLARENCE G. FLANDERS (9).

Florence A. Gardner (8), John S (7), John (6), Nathaniel (5), Job (4), Nathaniel (3), Benony (2), George (1)

Clarence G Flanders, son of Charles S and Florence A (Gardner) Flanders, was born Nov 2, 1875, at West Point, Wis, where he enjoyed the pleasures of a farmer's life Married Dec 23. 1903, to Susan Wallace, and now lives at Lodi Wis Occupation at present (1907) Tonsorial Artist

LOLA L. FLANDERS (9)

Florence A. Gardner (8), John S (7), John (6), Nathaniel (5), Job (4), Nathaniel (3), Benony (2), George (1)

Lola L Flanders, daughter of Chas. S and Florence A (Gardner) Flanders, was born Oct. 7, 1882, at West Point Wis Married Feb 12, 1907, to Elmer E Mills, son of Job and Amanda (Dye) Mills. Mrs Mills resides at Madison Wis, where her husband is engaged in mercantile business.

FRANCIS JEREMIAH SHEFFIELD (9)

Daniel J. Sheffield (8), Hannah Smith (7), Amy Gardner (6), Palmer (5), Sylvester (4), Nicholas (3), Nicholas (2), George (1).

Francis J, son of Daniel J and Hannah (Smith) Sheffield, was born April 20, 1874, at Spring Prairie, Walworth Co, Wis; married Berdine Estelle Hamilton, Nov 26, 1903 He is a farmer and resides at Springfield, Minn No children.

ELEANOR MARY HOLYOKE (9).

Cornelia A. Wheeler (8), Charlotte E. Smith (7), Amy Gardner (6), Palmer (5) Sylvester (4), Nicholas (3), Nicholas (2), George (1).

Eleanor Mary, daughter of Charles and Cornelia A (Wheeler) Holyoke, married Melvin Barker, or Barber, of Chicago Children are.
Ethel Mary, born July 19, 1899
Alice, born June 11, 1903
Twin boys, died at birth
Bertha Alice, born July 16, 1882

WESTFALL MAY GARDNER (9).

William H (8), William (7), Job (6), Job (5), Benjamin (4), Nathaniel (3), Benony (2) George (1)

Westfall May Gardner son of William H and Jane (Flagler) Gardner Married Margaret ——
Their children are
Lillie,
John W,
Adelaide,
Norah,
Caroline,
Ruth,
William H,
Andrew Jackson

JOHN MILTON GARDNER (9).

William H (8), William (7), Job (6), Job (5), Benjamin (4), Nathaniel (3), Benony (2), George (1)

John Milton Gardner, son of William H and Jane (Flagler) Gardner married Eugenia Northup No children

John M Gardner was born the 30th day of June, 1858, at Edenville, Orange County, New York He is the third son of William H Gardner His father for many years was a teacher and principal in the public schools and academies of various places in Orange and Ulster counties and was a man who possessed varied learning.

Mr. Gardner received special instruction and tutorage from his father and completed his studies preparatory to entering college with his father, but at the age of nineteen he entered the law office of E A Van Sickle, Esq , a prominent member of the OrangeCounty bar, as a student at law and studied until he was admitted to the bar, May, 1881, settling at Broadabin, Fulton County New York

Mr Gardner had a lucrative practice, acting as attorney, among other clients, for the Mutual Life Insurance Company of New York, in then what was known as the eighteenth progressive district, combining the counties of Montgomery, Fulton and Saratoga He married Virginia, the daughter of Mr Leonard S Northrup, one of the most prominent manufacturers and citizens of Fulton County, and immediately after completing an extensive European trip, settled at Newburgh, New York in Orange County, where he continued the practice of law At the Orange County bar he acquired immediate prominence in successfully prosecuting several cases of importance, one among which gave him reputation as a trial lawyer, in his professional work, to wit, the settlement of Mowatt vs Mowatt, in which he recovered nearly $1,000,-000 for his client, whereas when he started he had an almost hopeless case

After practicing in Newburgh for about ten years, he moved to New York in 1895 where ever since he has been a member of the New York bar, identified with many important litigations Mr Gardner is also the editor of the American Negligence Report, the most extensive and best known work on that subject.

WILLIAM H. GARDNER, JR (9).

William H (8), William (7), Job (6), Job (5), Benjamin (4), Nathaniel (3), Benony (2), George (1)

William H Gardner, Jr , son of William H Sr , and Jane (Flagler) Gardner married Mary Stout

Children were:
John N.,
Ianthe M ,
Gladys E

HORATIO N GARDNER (9)

William H (8), William (7), Job (6), Job (5), Benjamin (4), Nathaniel (3), Benony (2), George (1)

Horatio N Gardner, son of William H Sr , and Jane (Flagler) Gardner, married Margaret A Heckmann, daughter of William Heckmann, of Archbald, Pa

Children were
Horatio Forest born Feb 11, 1891
Pearl Jeanette, born April 28, 1895
Eugena Margaret, born the 20th of Nov , 1896
John Milton, born the 20th of Oct , 1898

BURTON JAY GARDNER (9)

George W (8), George (7), Caleb (6), Benjamin (5), Benjamin (4), Nathaniel (3), Benony (2), George (1)

Burton J Gardner, son of George W and Aucelia A (Rose) Gardner, was born February 3, 1849, at Stephentown, N Y, removed with his parents to Green Co, N Y, married Virginia M Putnam, daughter of John J and Magdalene Putnam, Nov. 22, 1874. She was born Jan 26, 1852 No children

Mr Gardner experienced the early days of Wisconsin, having removed there in 1884 and was engaged as a farmer and a dealer in lumber until 1890 His latter years have been occupied in banking and telephone interests

CHARLES F. GARDNER (9)

George W (8), George (7), Caleb (6), Benjamin (5), Benjamin (4), Nathaniel (3), Benony (2), George (1).

Charles F Gardner, son of George W and Aucelia A (Rose) Gardner, was born April 2 1853, at Stephentown, N Y, married Mary L Davis, daughter of John U Davis, of Monroe, Wis She was born March 11, 1852

Children

Maud A, born July 24, 1883

Nellie E, born March 12, 1885

Charles F Gardner was but three years of age when taken to the forest home of Wisconsin where he was reared and has devoted his life to agricultural pursuits He is a retired farmer, enjoying the accumulations of his life

JOHN W GARDNER (9)

George W (8), George (7), Caleb (6), Benjamin (5), Benjamin (4), Nathaniel (3), Benony (2), George (1).

John W Gardner, son of George W and Aucelia A (Rose) Gardner was born Oct 6 1855 at Stephentown, N Y, married Dorothy E Springsted of Brodhead Wis, 1875

Children

Harry W, born November 29, 1877

John F, born October 20, 1879

Sadie A, born November 10, 1883

John W Gardner was an infant when his parents removed to Brodhead, Wis, and by recollection knows nothing of the place of his birth Reared and educated in the new western home he made for himself the opportunities His life was spent largely upon his farm He served as sheriff of his county and is at present a retired farmer His son, Harry W Gardner, is Professor of Civil Engineering of the Illinois State University, Champaign, Illinois His son, John F Gardner, is bookkeeper in a bank at Larimore, North Dakota

NETTIE C SMITH (9)

Mary Emily (8) George (7), Caleb (6), Benjamin (5), Benjamin (4), Nathaniel (3), Benony (3), George (1)

Nettie C Smith, daughter of Roderick M and Mary Emily (Gardner) Smith, was born January 13, 1851, married Enos Warren Persons of Brodhead Wis, Dec 16, 1873

Children

Ray, born April 12, 1877, died October 6, 1877
Nellie Haines, born August 13, 1880
Myron Bowen, born October 24, 1888

BELLE GARDNER (9)

Francis, Jr (8), Frances (7), Caleb (6), Benjamin (5), Benjamin (4). Nathaniel (3), Benony (3), George (1)

Belle Gardner, daughter of Francis, Jr, and Nancy (Vantiflin) Gardner, was born September 17, 1863 Married George H Vailance, April 18, 1892

One son has been born to them

Frank Gardner, born September 26, 1894

IDA O GARDNER (9).

Simeon V (8), Frances (7), Caleb (6), Benjamin (5), Benjamin (4), Nathaniel (3), Benony (3), George (1).

Ida O Gardner daughter of Simeon V. and Susan (Wilson) Gardner, was born April 28, 1855, married Seward F Harper, Dec 3, 1879

Children

An infant, born and died April, 1882
William Gardner born May 12, 1887

DWIGHT SHAW (9)

Loretta (8), Sylvester (7), Caleb (6), Benjamin (5) Benjamin (4). Nathaniel (3), Benony (3), George (1)

Dwight Shaw, son of Rinaldo and Loretta (Gardner) Shaw, married Harriet Cranston

Children:

Byron,
Mabel,
Phoebe

FRANK J. BULL (9).

Myra (8), Sylvester (7), Caleb (6), Benjamin (5), Benjamin (4), Nathaniel (3), Benony (2), George (1)

Frank J Bull, son of Ralph and Myra (Gardner) Bull, was born November 9, 1850 Married Flora Cranston

Their children were

Josephine, born September 11, 1874

Harry born April 14, 1879

Edwina, born May 20, 1891

ORA E MOFFITT (9)

Lucy (8), Sylvester (7), Caleb (6), Benjamin (5), Benjamin (4), Nathaniel (3), Benony (2) George (1)

Ora E Moffitt, daughter of John J and Lucy (Gardner) Moffitt, was born June 12, 1858, died Nov 25, 1882, married Charles W Ford of North Adams, New York

One child

Charles Moffitt, born November 12, 1882

MINNIE JOANNA GARDNER (9)

Kirk E. (8), Daniel (7), John (6), Caleb (5), Benjamin (4), Nathaniel (3), Benony (2), George (1).

Minnie Joanna Gardner, daughter of Kirk E and Helen M (Hadsell) Gardner, was born August 12, 1856, married Fern Eldridge September 28, 1875

Children are

Mabel Grace, born March 18 1878 Living at Pittsfield, Mass

Alice L., born March 8, 1880 Living at Pittsfield, Mass

JOHN DANIEL GARDNER (9)

Kirk E. (8), Daniel (7), John (6) Caleb (5), Benjamin (4), Nathaniel (3), Benony (2), George (1).

John Daniel, son of Kirk E and Helen M (Hadsell) Gardner, was born April 19 1860, married Ida C Whitman

One daughter

Dora K., born October 9, 1883 Living at Hancock Mass

Mr Gardner is a man of no small talent and usefulness He remained upon the old homestead of his grandsires till a short time since, when he purchased a property and removed from the farm

He represented Berkshire County in the State Legislature in 1903

DANIEL GARDNER SHUMWAY (9).

Helen M Gardner (8), Daniel (7), John (6), Caleb (5), Benjamin (4), Nathaniel (3), Benony (2), George (1).

Daniel Gardner Shumway, son of Charles Frederick and Helen M (Gardner) Shumway, was born July 3, 1874, at Lebanon Springs, N Y ; married to Candace Rebecca Varnum October 15, 1902. She was born at Cropsey, Illinois March 22, 1879

One child has been born to them

Helen Madeline, born June 16, 1903, at St. Paul, Minn

LEWIS CRAPO GARDNER (9).

Charles (8) Silas (7), John (6), Caleb (5), Benjamin (4), Nathaniel (3), Benony (2), George (1).

Lewis Crapo Gardner, son of Charles and Louise M (Crapo) Gardner, was born November 17, 1866 at Hancock Mass , married Annie Leake, of Albemarle County, Va

They have four children, two boys and two girls, but we have no record of their birth Mr Gardner lives at Louisville, Ky.

HARRY GILSON GARDNER (9).

Charles (8), Silas (7), John (6), Caleb (5), Benjamin (4), Nathaniel (3), Benony (2), George (1).

Harry Gilson Gardner, son of Charles and Louise M (Crapo) Gardner, married Matilda Hall, daughter of Frederick Hall, editorial writer of the Chicago Tribune Mr Gardner lives in Washington, D. C , and is staff correspondent for many papers No children

WALTER ALLPORT GARDNER (9)

Charles (8), Silas (7). John (6), Caleb (5), Benjamin (4), Nathaniel (3), Benony (2), George (1).

Walter Allport Gardner, son of Charles and Emma A (Schute) Gardner, is unmarried and lives at Chicago. Ill. He is associated with the Marshall Field Co , and other large corporations

MARY OAKLEY CARPENTER (9).

Elizabeth G Doty (8), L. Louisa Gardner (7), John (6) Caleb (5), Benjamin (4) Nathaniel (3), Benony (2), George (1)

Mary Oakley, daughter of Hiram A and Elizdabeth G ((Doty) Carpenter, married I S F Dodd of Pittsfield, Mass . Sept 20, 1892

Their children are

Elizabeth Carpenter, born Feb 14, 1894

Spencer S , born May 17, 1896.

C LOCKWOOD CARPENTER (9)

Elizabeth G Doty (8), L. Louisa Gardner (7), John (6), Caleb (5), Benjamin (4), Nathaniel (3), Benony (2), George (1)

C. Lockwood, son of Hiram A and Elizabeth G (Doty) Carpenter, married L Amanda Clark, November 18, 1902

Their children are

C Whitney, born June 28, 1903

Margaret Louisa, born March 31, 1906

NELLIE HAINES PERSONS (10)

Nettie C (9), Mary Emily (8), George (7), Caleb (6), Benjamin (5), Benjamin (4), Nathaniel (3), Benony (2), George (1)

Nellie Haines Persons, daughter of Enos Warren and Nettie C (Smith) Persons, was born Aug 13, 1880 Married Jasper Curtis Wasson, of Depere, Wis, Nov. 13, 1899

Children.

Reid Persons, born September 7, 1900.

Marion Nellie, born October 8, 1903

Gunter Curtis, born March 5, 1906

JOSEPHINE BULL (10).

Frank (9), Myra Gardner (8), Sylvester (7), Caleb (6), Benjamin (5), Benjamin (4), Nathaniel (3), Benony (2), George (1)

Josephine Bull, daughter of Frank J and Flora (Cranston) Bull, was born September 11, 1874, married Charles Budlong.

Children

Ruth, born Dec 11, 1897

Flora, born Apr 28, 1899

Mettie, born June 16, 1903

HARRY BULL (10).

Frank (9), Myra Gardner (8), Sylvester (7), Caleb (6), Benjamin (5), Benjamin (4), Nathaniel (3), Benony (2), George (1).

Harry Bull, son of Frank J and Flora (Cranston) Bull, was born April 14, 1879, married Frances Fowler

Children

Dorothy, born May 13, 1901

Doris, born Nov, 1902

CHARLES MOFFITT FORD (10)

Ora (9), Lucy Gardner (8), Sylvester ,7), Caleb (6), Benjamin (5), Benjamin (4). Nathaniel (3), Benony (2), George (1)

Charles Moffitt Ford, son of Charles W and Ora E (Moffitt) Ford, was born Nov 12, 1882, married Hattie Reynolds

Children

Ora Madeline, born June 26, 1904

Edward Moffitt, born February 15, 1906.

OHIO.

BENJAMIN GARDNER (6).

Benjamin (5), Benjamin (4), Nathaniel (3), Benony (2), George (1).

Benjamin Gardner, son of Benjamin and Elizabeth (Olin) Gardner, was born September 13, 1760, at Exeter, Washington County, Rhode Island We have not the record of his first wife His second was Lucy Hawks, born in Connecticut and probably emigrated to New York with her parents. No date of their marriage secured As near as we can determine, and the record is not complete, the following were their children

Charlotte, born June 19, 1785, died November 28, 1853, married James Teller, Mar. 24, 1807

Phineas

Simeon, married Phebe Precher, Dec 15, 1808

Rodman, married Polly Worstell, Jan 19, 1809

Clarissa, married Joseph Wright.

Matthew, born December 5, 1790

Seth, born 1792

Lucy, born September 29, 1793

William,

Henry,

Clarissa,

Abraham, born 1802

Benjamin, born 1804

From Autibiography of Elder Matthew Gardner

When he was but ten years old, which was about the year 1770, his father moved to the State of New York When about seventeen years of age he went into the Revolutionary army He enlisted and served in Captain James Dennison's Company, 4th Regiment (1776-1781), New York militia, commanded by Colonel Killian van Rensselaer After independence was gained and peace was secured, he returned home and settled on thirty acres of land

Being a house carpenter by trade he devoted little time to the cultivation of his land, but supported his family principally by his trade

When about forty years of age, and having a large family, he determined to go west The territory, now called Ohio, was first settled in 1788 At the close of the Revolution 243 officers of the army, mostly New England men, solicited Congress, through General Washington, to secure lands for them between the Ohio River and Lake Erie. In 1783 General Putnam said, "the country between the Ohio and Lake

Erie will be filled with inhabitants, and thereby free the western territory from falling under the dominion of a foreign power " This was desirable, for, having no strong general government, foreign commanders kept defiant possession of forts on the very soil, now Ohio The first settlers, formed under the grant of Congress, were led by General Rufus Putnam from Massachusetts and Connecticut and laid the foundation of the State of Ohio at the Muskingum River, now Marrietta, on the seventh day of April 1788

Cincinnati started in 1789, the same year the Constitution of the United States was adopted

Then the lands from the Ohio river to the Pacific ocean were inhabited by Indians and wild beasts, excepting a very few distant forts and French posts or settlements in the valley of the Mississippi

In 1800 Mr Gardner sold his lease hold and started with his family for the northern territory of Ohio This was two years before Ohio became a State It was a beautiful morning on the first of September, 1800, when they started It was regarded by many as impossible to succeed in such a journey with such a large family of small children, especially with his limited means He had but one small wagon with three horses and other means correspondingly limited The country they had never seen, the route was new, and unknown till they approached it There was then little communication with the wilderness west Not only railroads and steamboats but turnpikes were unknown

When they started many came to bid them farewell, and stood looking after them with tearful eyes until they passed beyond their view, while others accompanied them on horseback for miles before turning back (None of this family ever returned to visit, except Matthew Gardner, and none of the Stephentown relatives ever again saw any of them save this one)

The mountains were difficult to climb, the streams were dangerous to ford, the undertaking was hazardous, and the journey was long The weather was pleasant and the journey as prosperous as could be expected They reached Pittsburg on the Ohio river by the first of October, just one month from the time they started Pittsburg was a small village They waited two weeks before they found a boat going down the river They embarked on a flat-boat, the boats then used, with four other families, furniture, wagons, horses and all, crowded on one small flat-boat The river was low, the progress was slow, sometimes they floated rapidly and sometimes they were long aground

They were nearly four weeks going down to Limestone, a little village on the Kentucky side of the river It had but few houses then Limestone is now called Maysville The reader will note the comparison of time required from Stephentown to Pittsburg, the route being over the mountains, with the time occupied to drift with the current a much less distance

At Limestone Henry Hughes, a land trader, came to the boat to sell them land in Ohio Mr Gardner went with him to see the land He liked it and traded him two horses for one hundred acres He returned to Limestone and with his family proceeded on with the boat down the river, about twelve miles at a landing two miles below where Ripley now stands They disembarked and the boat and its passengers went on down the river There was no town then where Ripley now stands They landed within a few miles of the property and soon reached their future home where everything was new and strange They were all in good health except one son and daughter who had slight attacks of fever and ague which soon disappeared Mr Gardner rented a cabin to move into while he and the oldest boys built a cabin on their own land The weather continued fine until after Christmas

Having completed their new house, they moved into it about the first of January, 1801 The fine weather continued that year, there being no weather to prevent outdoor work

What a contrast between this forest home where could be heard only the howling of wolves, the scream of panthers and the hooting of owls, with their former home in a thickly settled country, surrounded by friends! There were only two cabins within two or three miles of them There was no ground to rent There was none of the land cleared Provisions were scarce and only to be procured at any price from a very great distance His money was about all expended The land was covered with heavy forest principally with beach and poplar, which must be immediately cleared for crops to prevent starvation the coming year All who were large enough commenced work By spring they had nearly five acres cleared which was planted in corn and potatoes which sustained them the coming year One of the greatest difficulties was to procure those things which the land would not produce Salt cost from three to four dollars for a bushel of fifty pounds and other merchandise was proportionately high They were forced to study economy and compelled to practice it This laid the foundation of discipline that became characteristic of all the members of that family

It was difficult to procure money to purchase a little and they were taught the lesson to make a little do

Wild beasts were in abundance Bears, deer and wild turkey supplied the table with meat till domestic animals were reared Sheep and wool were not to be had, so the clothing was made of flax and hemp Suits of these served for all seasons, summer and winter The material was prepared by the father and boys and the mother and daughters manufactured the cloth, and made the garments No shoes or boots were worn, but moccasins made of deer-skins, for they could get no leather. The deer-skin being spongy, absorbed the water from the ground and snow, so wet feet were a frequent occurrence. Yet they were stout and healthy

Corn prevailed as the staple article of food, they preferred it They did not eat wheat, it was called "sick-wheat," making those sick who ate it They went on clearing, and in a few years the heavy timber gave place to orchard trees, and the wilderness to fruitful fields The wants for food and clothing were plentifully supplied, but there were other wants They had now passed the crisis for food and raiment and began to feel sadly the want of school and churches There was no teaching, no preaching, no schools, no religious meetings Mr and Mrs Gardner, while in New York, had united with the Free Will Baptist Church, but, it is said, on moving west Mr Gardner had neglected his religion though Mrs. Gardner retained her piety, so that, though they were without church or school the children were encouraged by their mother's pious example Mr Gardner possessed many good traits of character He was frugal and industrious He kept each tool and farming implement in its place He was kind to strangers and to the poor His intellectual capacity was above the ordinary, and his memory was perfect He was punctual and honest in business

All of the family as they grew up professed religion which made the home pleasant Mr Gardner's intellect was of high order, and being a fair speaker he often opened and led the religious meetings, till the latter part of the summer of 1811 Then a difficulty arose between Elder Alexander (who had organized a church), and Mr Gardner The preacher did not like Mr Gardner very well, for he was hard to please, and often called in question the things Mr Alexander preached Mr Alexander's parents were Presbyterians The Presbyterians were very particular to "remember the Sabbath day to keep it holy" Mr Gardner made cheese, sometimes hours would be spent at this on Sunday mornings, the same as on other days It was considered necessary to take care of the milk on Sunday Mr Alexander considered this a violation of the fourth commandment and considered Mr Gardner responsible for it The consequence of the hasty movement of Mr Alexander was, that the church suffered a severe injury Mr Gardner was a man of determination and manifested much resentment

The home of Mr Gardner was well located and ideal The writer spent some time in studying the place where the first cabin was erected, which gave way to a more commodious structure This second building was erected about 1810 The timbers in this house are all hewn, and with the exception of the sills, doors and windows, are all there as Mr Gardner placed them with his own hands

It was the age of fireplaces, and every room has a good large fireplace The house was erected with a basement, in this basement was built a large oven, used for baking for this large family The crane is still in the fireplace on which hung the kettle that boiled and roasted the bear, deer and turkey The house was intended to be a frame structure, but the timbers are so large they present the appearance of hewn logs weather boarded and cased The stone and brick walls of the basement and chimneys are in as good state of preservation as when erected

One can not but contrast this building with the comforts it brought to the family, with that of the forest hut hastily erected to shelter the large family, that, but so recently floated down the Ohio river

The record from which the preceding statements have been gathered closes when the subject was about fifty years of age, except what may be found on file at the office of Probate Court, Georgetown, Ohio

Mr Gardner made a will and appointed his son Matthew executor and administrator We had hopes of finding a complete list of names of the children The only records there, were an appraisement of the chattels and a few receipts given by Matthew Gardner as administrator, one of which is for a payment of the stone mason who built the stone work on the grave of the father In the closing remarks in connection with his father's estate, Matthew Gardner says "I closed all the business without difficulty with any of the heirs though there was then twelve children living"

The next record was secured from a grandson John W Gardner of Ripley, Ohio, who visited his grandfather at his home Mr Gardner stated that his grandfather was totally blind and confined to his bed

There came to the State of Ohio ten children, and there were born in Ohio two, of whom we have record.

This large family was most peculiarly separated While some of them only lived a short distance from Brown County they were as effectually lost to each other as if they had gone to another continent

The writer could scarcely believe that there could live in an adjacent county one branch of the family and not be known to the others

Such was the condition When Abraham Gardner removed to what was then Allen County, Ohio (now Auglaize County, having been organized since 1835), there was no communication that informed the family in Brown County There seem to have been three groups of the children Seth, Rodney, Clarissa and Lucy, living near Russellville, Brown County, Ohio They associated and visited Benjamin and Henry lived in the western part of Brown County, and near Feesburg. Matthew Gardner lived several miles south of the old homestead There was evidently no communication or visiting between these three branches of the family for we have been unable to learn anything of the families of the different groups one from the other

Each group seem to have been a law unto themselves Each of the older members of the family possessed a knowledge of the location of the others, but did not impart it to their children that it could come down to the following generations This has made the work of securing the information in connection with the children of this Benjamin Gardner a very difficult task

The writer has no doubt but some of the families of this name in the western States are the descendants of the older boys of the family

The records of this family are not complete and only by conversing with old settlers who personally knew them are we able to close the account of the life of this colonial pioneer

Located about three hundred yards south of the northeast corner of the farm, about two miles south of Russellville, Brown County, Ohio, on the west side of the road is the little cemetery where rests the body of Benjamin Gardner Two graves of the old English style of erecting, stone vaults, are the evidences of two honest lives On the stone of the southgrave is inscribed

In memory of Benjamin Gardner,
A soldier of the Revolution of 1776,
Who departed this life March 1, 1840
Aged 79 years, 5 months and 17 days.

Inscribed on the stone of the north grave is

Lucy Gardner
Consort of Benjamin Gardner
Who departed this life January 12 1846
Aged 83 years, 3 months and 14 days.

Lucy Hawks Gardner, wife of Benjamin Gardner, was born in Connecticut, September 29, 1762

She was Benjamin Gardner's second wife It is said of her that she was a very devout Christian woman, and all of her children loved her

We are always sorry not to be able to say more about the useful life of these good mothers. We cannot but recall the hardships and solicitude of a mother while rearing such a large family under the difficulties and deprivations of the early days and remember the reverence due them and their memory.

ALBON CROCKER GARDNER (6)

George (5), Ezekiel (4), Nicholas (3), Nicholas (2), George (1)

Albon Crocker Gardner, son of George and Mary (Reynolds) Gardner, was born April 12, 1799 Married Saloma Bancroft, who was born March 13, 1803

Their children were

Telottsey, born August 31, 1818

Hannah, born February 20, 1820 Died April 23, 1865.

Jane S, born March 13, 1822 Died September, 1900

Thomas, born July 17 1824 Died July 16, 1825

Albon Bancroft, born June 1, 1826 Died December 15, 1903

Caroline, born September 20, 1828 Died September 26, 1861.

Cornelia S, born February 24, 1831 Died June, 1903

Eliza, born July 5, 1836 Died October 5, 1836

Albon Crocker Gardner removed from Wayne County, New York, to Ohio near Parkman, and settled on government land, where he built a green log house in the dense forest Mrs Telottsey (Gardner) Cutler was a nursing infant when they came to Ohio, which was the winter of 1818-19 Unlike our modern advantages for travel they came from central-northern New York on a boat sled drawn by a yoke of cattle Led behind this sled was a cow Except the cow and yoke of cattle all their earthly possessions were on the sled Mr Gardner started with seven dollars in money and had it all when he reached Ohio In those days the people would not accept any money as a charge for entertainment of emigrants, neither could he persuade them to take it

As provision en route, they had a roast pig, a bag of corn meal, a very meager supply of quilts and woolen sheets, a straw tick, a feather bed, a pair of feather pillows, and a few cooking utensils Mr Gardner had an axe, a long handled shovel, a hoe, a pickaxe, a crow-bar, two saws, a log chain, two pails, and three augers One saw was a cross-cut saw and the other a hand saw

When they had selected the place destined to be their new home the neighbors agreed to exchange work and assist to build a log house This house proved to be one of a single room without anything for a floor and the woolen sheets became the windows

The house was completed and they moved into it one cold night, Thanksgiving eve, about nine o'clock They had a good fire in the big fireplace with a big back log that would last

They laid two poles across the room and bored holes in the poles and placed sticks in the holes for legs, and this made the old fashioned high bed, which they made up and slept in that night. They had a bond-fire in front of the house to frighten away the wolves, wildcats and panthers. They had to get up each hour during the night and fire off the old musket to assist to frighten away the wolves.

Their nearest neighbor was a mile and a quarter distant, and their next nearest neighbor four miles. The spring from which they carried water was a quarter of a mile away.

Mr. Gardner was nineteen years of age and Mrs. Gardner fourteen when they were married. She weighed seventy-two pounds the day on which they were married. Mr. Gardner not being of age, purchased his time of his father for thirty-five dollars, borrowing the money with which to make the payment.

The reader will observe the first child was born to them when the father was twenty and the mother fifteen years of age.

Mr. Gardner became a man of wonderful ability both physical and mental. His stature developed into full six feet in his stocking feet and he was a giant in strength. His mental capacity was no less than his physical. He was endowed by nature with a wonderful memory. We should say here his school work did not exceed three months. He could read three pages of a large book and repeat word for work and seldom, when tested, ever made an error.

In his business life whatever he gave his attention to turned into wealth. As a result when he died he was in possession of a very large fortune. He was a generous liver. He always gave more than any of his neighbors or associates to worthy causes.

Before he came to Ohio he was a member of the Quaker church. After they arrived in their wilderness home they became identified with the Methodist Episcopal church. Mr. Gardner was not only a member of the church, but an active participant in all the means of grace and was one of the largest contributors to the support of the one where he lived, besides rendering great assistance in the building of new churches elsewhere.

It is recorded elsewhere in this book that his daughters nearly all married Methodist Preachers.

It is with great pleasure the children and grandchildren look back upon the Christian life which was even and tempered with grace to guide him during the years he was rearing that large family and accumulating a fortune. He used his wealth for the advancement of the cause he advocated.

His political life was not uneventful as he was a man of the most scrupulous character and would have everything open to the light and to inspection. He was elected to the Ohio State Legislature and when his term closed he declined to engage any further in politics. He declared he never would accept any further relations with any political work because of the corruption in it.

His judgment was exceptionally good and his advice was sought by all who knew him. He possessed a wonderful faculty of saying what he desired and his language was always well selected.

His mind was of a mathematical cast. He was a reasoner and never decided the merits of a proposition without debating the subject.

As a result he became the foremost man of the country in which he lived He was the leader and directed all things He was counseled with and his advice was taken It was before the days of banks He kept a general store at Chagrin Falls and the farmers and inhabitants of the town placed their money in his safe for protection and security

These deposits grew to enormous proportions, frequently amounting to hundreds of thousands of dollars at a given time The confidence of these people was not misplaced, for every dollar was sacredly returned to its owner

He belonged to the "under-ground railway service" He was a Whig, free soiler and republican He was a man of temperate habits and very devoted to his family

After a long and useful life at his trade and in his store he removed to Cleveland, Ohio, where he lived until his death

He died March 3, 1875. Aged 75 years, 10 months, 9 days He is buried in Lake View Cemetery, Cleveland, Ohio, at the east side of the drive near the main entrance A granite shaft marks his final resting place

Mrs Gardner died September 30, 1885 Aged 82 years, 6 months, 18 days She is buried beside her husband

His was a long life, well spent and eminently useful, during which he enjoyed the implicit confidence of his friends and never betrayed them He served God to the best of his understanding and has gone to his reward leaving a record which will prove an inspiration and example to his posterity

REV. MATTHEW GARDNER (7).

Benjamin (6), Benjamin (5), Benjamin (4), Nathaniel (3), Benony (2), George (1).

Matthew Gardner, son of Benjamin and Lucy (Hawks) Gardner, was born in Stephentown, New York, December 5 1790 He married Sally Beasley, daughter of Jeptha and Sally Beasley, on May 20, 1813

To them were born the following children

Barton Beasley, born March 27, 1814
Sally, born December 5 1815
George Washington, born January 30, 1819
Jeptha Monroe, born April 10, 1820
Lucinda Eliza, born March 28, 1823
Louisa Maria, born September 15, 1825
Julia Elmira, born April 1, 1828
James Alexander, born November 13, 1830
Mary Jane, born July 23, 1833
John Wicklif born April 17, 1836
Elnathan Matthew, born September 12, 1839, died Sept, 1906.

Why We Devote So Much Space to Elder Matthew Gardner.

The following pages are extracts from the autobiography of Elder Matthew Gardner, and we will use them in preference to any matter that we might write We have given a great amount of space to Elder

Gardner's writings, as they set forth a great many features which so predominate in the Gardner family, as well as the early history of the Ohio branch

EXTRACTS OF AUTOBIOGRAPHY

I was born in Stephentown, N Y, on the fifth of December, A D, 1790 My father moved from there to Ohio, A D, 1800 and I visited the place after that, first in May of 1851, and again in August of 1854, and in August of 1857, during which visit I made particular inquiries respecting the ancestors of our family I will then give you a true narrative of my own eventful life The Gardners, who were our forefathers, came from England to America, and settled in Rhode Island

My father was born in Rhode Island, on the 13th day of August, A D 1759 My mother was born in Connecticut on the 29th day of September, A D 1762 Her maiden name was Lucy Hawks

My father being about forty years old, and vigorous and strong, and having a large family, he determined to go west

In 1800 my father sold his leasehold, and we all started for the northwestern territory of Ohio I was in my tenth year when we left Stephentown, and well do I remember those scenes of my childhood It was a beautiful morning, on the first of September

When we arrived in the wilderness west, the duty assigned to me was the care of the cattle We had no fenced fields and while they roamed in the forest for food it was my care to seek them, and keep them from straying far away and being lost While in this care I received my first religious impressions In those lonely hours the good spirit often strove with me and renewed the impressions of my early childhood While laboring under conviction, my mind was impressed with the duty of preaching the gospel of Christ, which for me seemed impossible

When I was perhaps in my fourteenth year, during February or March, my older brothers concluded to improve their evenings by hunting raccoons in order to sell the skins for the fur, and secure some money I desired to share the peril and the profits to which they would not consent I then offered to go for the twentieth skin to which they consented The twentieth one happened to be a large fine one, and when the purchaser came, I showed it to him, and said, "What is this skin worth?" He answered, "A quarter of a dollar" This was the highest price for the very best skins

When I got the money I felt a little proud It was more money than I remember having had before in my life I could perhaps get a pocket knife, which I needed very much, I finally decided

My father went, from time to time, to Limestone village, now Maysville, Kentucky, a distance of about sixteen miles, to purchase stores for the family I sent my "quarter" with him, and bought "Webster's Spelling Book" The price of this book was twenty-five cents, so I gave all my newly acquired fortune for a book There being no schools where we lived, I had so far forgotten what I learned when six or seven years old, in New York, that I knew little more than the alphabet, I concluded, however, that education was worth more to me than any thing else and I now think that the best purchase of my life For that twenty-five cents profited me more than a thousand dollars would have done, laid out in any other way, had I neglected my education

After this my spare hours at night were spent in study; and by diligence, I soon learned to read After some years, an eastern man took board at our house during the winter instructing us in the long evenings At this night school I learned to write, improving my hand afterward by practice

I could read and I could write a little, but I knew nothing of arithmetic I began with the beginning and the teacher seeing my diligence, gave me all the assistance he could in justice to the other children

The first church that I organized was Union Church, in the western part of Brown County, two miles from Higginsport, on the Ohio river, and sixteen miles from my home It was organized in 1818, soon after my ordination No other Christian minister had preached there, consequently they were unacquainted with our views previous to my preaching there The additions were rapid The preaching was in the woods in warm weather The people came from far around, and the congregations were very large Such was the work in 1818, the first year of my ordination I also made beginnings in some new places Also that year I hired help, and put up a new house By working night and day I got it under roof and enclosed and had two rooms finished ready to move into by the last of December, 1818 We moved on the first day of January, 1819 I finished the house as time and circumstances permitted During all this time, though my work was so urgent both on the house and farm, I attended all my appointments, giving to them two or three days of a week beside Lord's day.

December 5th, 1830 I entered upon the forty-first year of my life with a family of eight children to educate and provide for We kept them in school as much of the time as circumstances would justify, and also endeavored to teach them to work and the importance of making their living by honest industry Our eldest sons were able nearly to do the work of men Our little farm—one hundred acres—not being large enough to afford them full employment, and having saved a little money, in March 1831, I purchased another small farm of one hundred and thirty acres

Our two oldest sons having become of age, needed homes of their own So about the year 1835 I purchased nearly four hundred acres of excellent land for which I paid at that time, nearly four thousand dollars

A great part of the land was cleared and under cultivation So I told my two oldest sons that if they would go on the land and in their own time pay me beck one-half of the purchase money without interest, I would make them deeds In eight years—they paid me and got their deeds

I have pursued the same course with all my sons They till the land and make a part of the value, or price of the farm, and pay it back to me before I make them a deed

In the spring of 1851 I had made arrangements to visit the place of my birth in New York. I also desired to spend some time in various eastern cities, and to visit some other places of interest I started soon after the middle of May I went to Cincinnati by boat, from there to

Cleveland by railroad, and from there over Lake Erie, to Buffalo, New York, by steamboat, then took the cars to Albany, and from there by stage-coach to Stephentown, the place of my birth Though only nine years and not quite nine months old when my father moved from Stephentown and I had not seen the place for over fifty years, when I saw everything pertaining to the face of the country, it appeared familiar as when we left there, the mountains and valleys, the brooks and pathways, looked as they did when seen in my childhood The houses looked time worn I went to the house which we moved out of on the first day of September, A D 1800, which brought sweet memories of days long, long gone by, when I loved to be with my mother How mournfully dear to my heart were the recollections There was a great change observable in the people we left there in 1800, and those found there in 1851 Very few of those we left could be found Death had called away many, and others had moved to other parts I found many relations (the Gardners), but only two or three of those we left remained The nearest relations I found were first and second cousins All my uncles and aunts were gone I tarried at Stephentown a short time I preached a few times near the place where I was born The Christians have a good chapel there, but I was sorry to find the church in a low state, with little interest

After spending a few days in New Bedford, I went to Fall River This is a thriving manufacturing city Here I found a large prosperous Christian church, with a good pastor I preached on the Lord's day, and a number of times before leaving I was kindly received and was pleased with my visit I now left Massachusetts for Rhode Island, the first home in America of my forefathers In Providence, Rhode Island, there are two Christian churches To one of them I preached twice at night, as I could not tarry over the Lord's day From Providence, I proceeded to Stonington, Connecticut, where I took an ocean steamer for New York city We had a stormy night, but morning brought us safely to New York, a few days before the fourth Lord's day in June, 1850 I remained in New York over Lord's day and preached for the Christian church there twice

Being nearly "three score and ten" years old, I desired relief from worldly care Our youngest son now being of age, I made a sale on the 18th of October of all my personal property, such as cattle, horses, farming utensils, etc, retaining only my own riding horse and one belonging to my wife The household goods I left entirely to the disposal of my wife I was now relieved of much care that old men generally retain

I had observed the condition of the old man generally It is about as follows In his declining years he gives up the control of his property, others come in to take care of the old folks The youngest son, or whoever it may be, gives little or no attention to the old utensils which the old man had labored to obtain When he uses them they are not returned to their places When broken they are not repaired Those who now use them did not purchase them They will not labor to preserve what they did not labor to obtain They regard them as of little worth, and prefer them out of the way, that the young man may procure others of later style and fashion The dear old man sees his tools out of place and gathers them up and puts them back He next finds them broken, and goes upon his staff and carefully gathers up the pieces of the old implements, and takes them to the shop, and has them repaired, and puts them back in their place again. This he repeats from time to time, from year to year, all the time fretting and worrying. His untimely care and unnecessary anxiety makes him and all about him miserable, not considering that the time has passed when he has any use for them, or that they do not want them. He thus makes the evening of his life, when he needs rest, a time of toil and care, instead of repose and quiet, he has torment and vexation. Having seen this, I determined, with the Lord's help, to avoid it, and sold everything off for what it would bring.

The farm contained three hundred and forty acres, and was a little over one mile long and a half mile wide. The original one hundred acres we had moved onto January 1st, 1814, and still live there in 1865. I had bought other farms and added to it, all joining it, except about ten acres, one and one-half miles distant. The lands I now divided equally between our two youngest sons, John Wickliffe Gardner and Elnathan Matthew Gardner, binding them to pay to me or to my estate a sum defined and understood, which will make their portion about equal to the other children.

I thus, almost in a single day, freed myself from the great burden and care which had so long been upon me. After doing this, I felt, for a time, almost like a stranger to myself and my surroundings, as if I had entered into something like a new state of existence, perhaps something like a slave feels when he has obtained his freedom. It was but a short time until those cares began to seem repugnant, and it seemed to me that no earthly reward could induce me to take such a burden of cares upon me again.

Twenty-two churches have been organized by my labors. Having not kept a particular account of all those who embraced religion under my ministry, I can only state the result of subsequent calculations, which is as follows. About five thousand have been received into the church under my preaching. Of this number over one thousand were received into the Union Church as shown by the records, during my first twenty-eight years' pastorate, not including those received into other churches where I labored.

Into the Bethlehem church, during my pastorate of over forty years, upward of thirteen hundred members were received. This leaves only one-half of the five thousand to be made up from the numbers received into the twenty other churches raised from my labors, and elsewhere. Therefore, it is certain that the number exceeds five thousand.

During my forty years' pastorate of the Bethlehem church, I have made but two disappointments. One occurred when I was sick, the other when high water rendered the streams impassable, before bridges were built.

Having begun the world comparatively poor, I was under the necessity of adopting a system of rigid economy and frugality, which became so habitual as to be like a second nature to me. Consequently, when I had accumulated property it seemed impossible to depart from my old habits, even in regard to time and apparel. In taking care of my clothing and shoes, being careful to make everything last and do service as long as possible. I have now a pair of old coarse leather shoes which

I have worn more or less every year for twenty years Five or six years they were the only shoes I wore at all when about home I wear them yet when in the house at times, but not out doors as for several years past they could not keep out the water I have thought of throwing them aside, but am unwilling, and feel almost sorry to part with them It seems like parting with old friends I have had but four pairs of shoes in twenty years and no boots at all These four pairs of shoes—two pairs of coarse leather and two pairs of calf-skin—have lasted me, and are lasting yet

The coarse pair first named are about worn out The second pair are about two-thirds worn The first calf-skin pair are about three-fourths worn, while the other pair are not yet quite half worn out

I wear shoes all the time, both summer and winter I never wore out but one pair of boots in my life When our grandsons—now young men—one after another come to see us, I show them these four pairs of shoes particularly the twenty year old pair, and inquire the cost of their boots and shoes during one year None give the cost less than from fifteen to twenty dollars One said, "Twenty-five dollars a year" Said I, "The whole cost of my shoes has not been more than from ten to twelve dollars in twenty years, while yours, at the rate you say, must cost you five hundred dollars for the same time" Then I tell them it was the aforesaid economy and frugality that enabled me to give anything to their parents or to them I do this to teach them that economy is the road to wealth, while extravagance is the road to ruin My clothing of all kinds, including shoes, etc, has not cost me more than ten or twelve dollars per year The old overcoat I now have, though I have traveled much, is the only one that I have had or worn during twenty years It was a remarkable piece of cloth, and has never been wet through though I have worn it in many heavy rains It is not yet half worn out My other clothing has lasted about as proportionately long

These facts may seem strange to some in the present age of extravagance and pride, yet they are true

I have in my pocket now a small, two bladed pocket knife, which I have carried more than thirty-five years The first blade I wore out and got another put in which I broke, and then had another put in, which is in use now, and not very much worn. The small blade that was in it when I bought it is in it yet.

When a boy there was hardly an article which I prized more than a pocket knife It was hard for me to get one They were high in price, and there were none near for sale, and I had little money to buy with, if I lost my knife, which was seldom, I was so greatly troubled that I could hardly sleep at night I finally adopted the plan, that when I used my knife never to lay it down, but put it carefully into my pocket, and if I lent it, to keep my eye upon the person till he was done with it and if he did not think to return it, remind him of it So I have not lost my knife in either of these ways, since I have adopted said plan Another part of the system is to be always certain that my pocket has no hole in it Thus I have kept one and the same knife thirty-five years Why could not every man do the same if careful? The buck horn handle of this knife is now nearly worn off It may be said that a pocket knife is of too little value to keep with such care—to preserve so long

I reply The same care that will prevent its loss a month, will a year, ten years, and so on, till the knife is worn out Is not this true? Let it be borne in mind that small savings have made great estates and that the old adage is true "Take care of the pennies and the pounds will take care of themselves"

I have an umbrella that I have carried for more than twenty-five years It has sheltered me in many storms of rain and hail and snow When the first cover was worn out I had a new one put on and it is nearly worn out

It was this rigid system of economy that enabled me, without salary from the churches, and dependent almost wholly upon my own resources to spend half of all my time in traveling and preaching during fifty-eight years, up to this time, and to support my family, and to give hundreds upon hundreds of dollars to aid in building Christian chapels, and to sustain the cause of religion in Southern Ohio and elsewhere and to give a great deal to the needy, and to give eleven hundred dollars to the endowment of Union Christian College

I have given to all our children, eleven in number, dividing it equally among them, sixty thousand dollars, while I have nearly that amount left My own wisdom and economy could not accomplish all this. It has been done through and by the mercies of my Heavenly Father

June 27, 1871 Having written my will, and made all necessary arrangements for the trip, I this day started, for the sixth visit to my native state I went down the river to Cincinnati on the steam-boat, and then by railway, and reached Stephentown on the 30th of June, thanking God for his protecting care over me, and my safe arrival

The journey or change of living improved my health But death has been here, and although the mountains, brooks and valleys look just as they did when my father left here for the West, seventy-two years ago, the inhabitants have changed Year by year my relatives have dropped off, till few even of my cousins remain

The following is from the Christian Herald Published in Newburyport, Massachusetts, September 3 1872 Elder D P Pike Editor "We have had the rich pleasure of a visit from this venerable minister of Jesus Christ He came to us with the blessing of the gospel of Christ Brother Gardner experienced religion August 10, 1810, at the age of nineteen He was born in the State of New York, moved to the State of Ohio in 1800 He commenced preaching immediately after his conversion, presenting Christ as the sinner's friend He was baptized by Archibald Alexander and was ordained in 1815 He has had a successful ministry Between six and seven thousand have professed the religion of Christ under his ministry He was one of the first ministers who formed the Southern Ohio Christian Conference, in 1820, and has not missed a session of that Conference since, and is, at the present time, president of that body It is composed of about thirty ministers, and between four and five thousand members He is now in his eighty-second year, and of course his ministry extends over sixty years It spans two generations His health is good, his mind active, his powers strong and vigorous He is an able minister of the new testament, evangelical and orthodox in his doctrine, true to the preciousness of Jesus, holding forth his equality with the father, and his power to save repenting sinners. It is encouraging to meet with those ministers who have not been carried about by every wind of doctrine He has walked by the same rule, and attended to the duties of the same gospel He gave Court Street Church, in this city, a sermon, August 29, in the afternoon, from Luke VII, 22 It was an impressive sermon, received with devout attention, and will be long remembered His introduction was appropriate and truthful The anxiety of John the Baptist, and the kindliness of Jesus was feelingly presented The miracles of Christ were ably set forth admitted and defended, the gospel correctly defined, and the mission work of Jesus earnestly commended. 'To the poor the gospel is preached' Our people will not soon forget Brother Gardner nor his sermon Many manifested their faith in Christ, showing that they rejoiced in the pardoning mercy of Jesus Christ God bless Grother Gardner, making his last days his best and crowning his sunset with a glorious immortality He left us August 26th, on his return West Safely may he reach his home, blessed with improved health and increased encouragement to trust the master, and honor his own blessed work in saving souls"

After parting with kind friends at Newburyport, I took the cars for Boston, where, after tarrying two days, I left for North Stephentown, where I arrived on the 29th, at two P M, there I remained and visited a little more than two weeks I preached on the Lord's day, September 15, to a Presbyterian congregation, by the request of their preacher They were all well pleased On the 16th inst I bade farewell to my dear friends and relatives, and started for home, where I arrived on the 19th, about three P M, with my health much improved

November 12, 1872 On this day I started on my return to the land of my birth, to spend the winter I had a pleasant journey and reached my intended home in safety on the fourteenth day of November in good health, for a man of my age I found my relatives in good health generally

On March 10th, 1873, I bade farewell to my dear cousin Rose and his kind companion, and left that pleasant home for Ohio Cousin took me to the depot, three-fourths of a mile, to take the 6 30 A M train and I was soon on my way I arrived home on the 14th of March.

July 26th, 1873 From this date the aged pilgrim's bark was visibly turned toward worlds eternal, and pressed hard for the distant shore Elder A W Coan wrote "The numerous friends of the venerable Matthew Gardner, of Ripley, Ohio will learn with much regret that he is now prostrate at his room at the hotel, on the camp-ground near Hyannis, Massachusetts, from the effects of a fall from the steps of a hotel on the grounds He fell on Saturday evening July 29th, breaking the thigh bone at the hip-joint He is remarkably patient and appears to suffer as little as could be expected It is not probable that he will ever be able to walk"—(Herald of Gospel Liberty)

The veranda was broad, without front safety of banister balustrade The steps extended but a portion of the way across the broad front, and in the dark the aged minister missed the steps and walked off, falling about three feet It is supposed that the sure-footed old man came down upon his feet, the weight of his body, by the fall, bursting the socket of his thigh.

His son and grandson, John W. and James F. Gardner, go and bring him home to the house of his son-in-law, S H Hopkins, arriving August 15th He writes from Bentonville as follows 'I am now staying, in my affliction, at Bentonville, Adams County, Ohio, which is about twelve miles east of my old home I reached here on the 15th of August, having left the camp-ground on the 12th of August. We came day and night, making our connections without detention My friends told me that I would stop at the first station after starting, but, by more than human strength from the Lord, I was enabled to stand the journey through, though very feeble indeed I am at the house of my daughter, Julia C Hopkins and all is done that can be in reason for my welfare

M GARDNER"

Elder A R Heath wrote 'He stood the trip home well The route was by Fall River boat to New York, thence by broad gauge railroad to Cincinnati, and by Ohio river boat to Manchester landing, and thense by spring wagon to Bentonville unto the house of his daughter, Sister Hopkins He will be kindly and well cared for Let Brethren address him at Bentonville with words of cheer "

September 27, 1873 Elder Gardner writes "It is now over two months since I received the injury at Hyannis, namely, on the 26th of July, and how I have been able to endure the suffering is truly a mystery to myself Not the injury itself gave much pain, but the being confined upon my back for four weeks, during which I traveled from Hyannis, Cape Cod, Massachusetts, to this place My health is as good as could be expected under the circumstances I move about the house on crutches, my leg seems to be slowly mending

M GARDNER"

The Southern Ohio Christian Conference will meet, in its fifty-fourth annual session, on Saturday, October 4, 1873, at ten o'clock A M, at the Bethlehem Christian Chapel, Brown County, Ohio The chapel is about one mile from the Ohio river

Saturday morning Elder Matthew Gardner rode, seated in a large chair, in a spring wagon and was thus conveyed ten miles, to the conference by his son-in-law, S H Hopkins and thus he returned in the evening to his home, that is, to the house of his son-in-law, where he made his home after his return from the East On Tuesday, October 7, his son-in-law, conveyed him for the second time, to conference This was the last conference that he would ever attend, and he went to preach his farewell sermon He was conveyed as before in a spring wagon, sitting in a large arm chair It was ten miles—a long ride, but he was inured to hardship

The hour has come Here is the church which he had organized half a century before, and of which he had been pastor forty-five years, and was yet a member Here are the representatives of the churches, many of which he had organized, and to all of which he had preached statedly or at intervals for many years The aged patriarch could not stand but sat in his large chair It was a sermon directed chiefly to the ministers

Text.—"Preach unto it the preaching that I bid thee.' Jonah III, 2 Elder Gardner said "I believe that the Lord has spared me to preach this sermon" He said, "This is the last conference that I ever expect to attend" He then alluded to the conference in its rise and history, and of his early labors in the region of country and elsewhere, and said "I desired to be at this conference and the Lord has granted my request'

He exhorted the preachers to faithfulness, and spoke of the opposition which he had encountered, the persecution which he had endured, and the long labor which he had performed and said "Be faithful Never preach a doctrine that cannot be stated in the exact words of the Scriptures My success in a ministry of over sixty years I attribute to my strict adherence to the word of God I have preached the preaching that God bids me to preach This is the last conference that I ever expect to attend Remember the word, 'preach the preaching that I bid thee' And now farewell! farewell!"

Report of Elder Rush, the Editor—"We made good time to Maysville Landing there we ferried the river to Aberdeen It was now eleven o'clock A. M, and the conference nearly two miles away We heard Father Gardner was to preach at eleven. So learning, we hastened to a livery stable, determined to hear at least a part of what we feared would be the dear old man's dying discourse And so it proved! He preached with strength and emphasis, told them it was his last sermon, went home, and two days afterwards died, after thirty minutes sickness.

After Elder Gardner's discourse there came a season of farewell handshaking! The crippled and helpless old veteran sat in the chair from which he had preached his sermon The large congregation came forward, and one by one bid him a final farewell Ah, who that had tears could not have shed them then? Strong men wept, and from many, many eyes, came those overflowings of grief It seemed like a funeral of the living, and such in a sense it proved to be It was Father Gardner's dying farewell to the people for whom he had been pastor forty years, it was his final farewell to his brethren of the ministry, who shall see his face no more in the flesh"

Elder J P Daugherty says· "He gave his last solemn charge to his brethren in the ministry, in the fifty-fourth session of the Southern Ohio Christian Conference, he himself never failed in a single instance to meet the conference in any of its sittings Every heart was full and every face bathed in tears, as he bade the conference an affectionate farewell"

The Maysville at which Elder Rush landed on his way to Bethlehem, over a mile distant, to hear Elder Gardner preach, was the "Limestone" village in the fall of 1800, just seventy-three years before, at which Matthew Gardner landed then a little boy, on his first voyage down the Ohio How little the boy thought, when standing on the shore in 1800 that in seventy-three years he would be preaching his final farewell to a weeping congregation, within about a mile of where the boy then stood, and that editors and ministers would be hastening over that same Limestone landing to hear him! How little we know of the future! The meeting has closed The pilgrim has bidden farewell to his brethren, the church and the conference, and under the shadows of the great hills which border the eastern shore of the Ohio River, the aged minister sitting in the spring wagon is for the last time returning to his earthly home, then only ten miles, but he will be far, far away in two or three days

He said to his son-in-law, on his way home from the conference, "I am now released from the affairs of this life, and will never again be entangled therein"

The morning before his death he had a talk of about two hours with his daughter, Mrs Hopkins in which he said, "If I die soon, all is well, the will of the Lord be done All I need here is a place to stay a little while"

He was well and hearty the last night He ate heartily at supper, and retired as well as usual.

He began to complain soon after half past one o'clock in the morning He was perfectly sane, but said nothing about dying, except the words, 'I fear that I shall not live till morning" His mental powers continued strong to the very last, and his utterance was clear and distinct

His son-in-law Samuel H Hopkins, wrote, 'I was holding him in my arms, when he said 'Lay me down He lived but a few minutes afterwards A more devoted man I have never seen end his days than Father Gardner '

The immediate cause of his death was supposed to have been 'valvular disease of the heart" He had often prayed, 'Lord, give me a tranquil hour in which to die," and the hour was there The prayer was answered, and he said, 'Lay me down" And all the days of Matthew Gardner were eighty and two years, ten months and five days, and he died

October 11th, his body was conveyed by land, thirty-two miles, for interment, as he had directed them to bury him in the burying ground of the "Union Church,' the first church organized by him, in his early ministry, and now commonly called "Shinkle's Ridge,' near Higginsport the body was interred October 12th, after which a funeral discourse was preached by Elder J P Daugherty, on the words of Saint Paul (II Timothy IV 6-8 ' For I am now ready to be offered, and the time of my departing is at hand I have fought a good fight, I have finished my course I have kept the faith, henceforth there is laid up for me a crown of righteousness, which the Lord, the righteous Judge, shall give me at that day, and not to me only, but unto all them also that love his appearing" While the minister was proceeding from one to another of the parallels between the deceased and the great apostle, in perseverence, energy, devotion, labor, persecution, suffering and success the audience, largely composed of the most prominent citizens and statesmen of the four consecutive counties was bathed in tears The preacher said As a minister of the gospel, and indeed in every relation in life he was most scrupulously exact and punctual in his promises, both in regard to the time and the thing promised When he announced preaching at eleven o'clock, he never meant ten minutes after He was a textual preacher, carefully stating his points in the exact language of the Bible

Though not a learned man in the common acceptance of the term, yet his knowledge of the Bible and of men made him successful in many thelogical discussions He was practically educated He was a man of prompt decision, and seldom, if ever, had occasion to change his first impressions He was an excellent financier, and by his industry and economy accumulated a large estate His large compass of mental vision, and far-reaching judgment, enabled him to succeed in almost everything he undertook His moral courage enabled him to stand where most men would have fallen Having determined his course, he was unmoved by flattery or reproach, hence, while he had many warm friends, he also had some bitter enemies These he at last won, and died, so far as I know, without a personal enemy He was a profound judge of human nature and hence was seldom deceived in men He was emphatically the man for the time and place of his ministry, and though it lasted sixty-three years, yet he kept pace with the world's advancement in thought, hence his congregations were large and attentive till the close of his ministry He was a strong, lion-hearted man—victorious over fear, gathering strength and animation from danger, and bound the faster to duty by its hardships and privations He was a man of great firmness—his countenance at times wearing the stern decision of unyielding principle Uninfluenced by numbers, popularity or power, he seemed almost too tenacious for his own convictions His heroism had its origin and life in reason, in the sense of justice, and in the disinterested principles of Christianity, which recognizes the right of every man

He had great respect for minds which had been trained in simple habits, and amidst the toils of industrious life He despised indolence and lack of economy almost beyond expression With whatever faults he had, he was a great and good man His greatness as a minister was immeasurably above the arts by which inferior minds thrust themselves into notice

Surrendering himself wholly to the cause of God and salvation of men, he labored to that end with unfaltering zeal till Jesus called him to his immortal home

Having timely made his will, and properly adjusted all his earthly business he now seemed to have nothing to do but to fall asleep in Jesus, hence he calmly sank into the repose of death without a struggle

"But what shall I say more? The time would fail me to speak of all the interest of so long and eventful a life as that of Elder Matthew Gardner! What I have here said is but the plucking of a little fruit here and there from the wide-spreading branches of a life tree, bowing under the fullness of more than three score years We are only satisfied to pause here and await the production of some abler pen, and in the expectation that we shall soon be favored with the autobiography of his long and eventful life.

His remains were interred in the cemetery at Shinkle's Ridge, on the 12th of October, 1873, after which a sermon was delivered with reference to the deceased, by the writer, in the presence of a large and weeping audience The Lord sanctify this dispensation of his providence to the good of all concerned

Georgetown, Ohio, October 18, 1873

J P DAUGHERTY

(Epitaph Written by Himself)

Elder Matthew Gardner,
A Christian Minister
Born in the State of New York, December 5, 1790
Died in the State of Ohio, October 10, 1873
"He claimed no merits of his own,
His trust was all in Christ alone"
He preached the Gospel Sixty-three Years

SETH GARDNER.

Benjamin (6), Benjamin (5), Benjamin (4), Nathaniel (3), Benony (2), George (1)

Seth Gardner, son of Benjamin and Lucy (Hawks) Gardner, was born at Stephentown, N Y, March 5, 1782 Married Betsey Wright, Feb 7, 1815

To them was born one child

Benjamin Wright born December 4, 1815

In December, 1818, Betsey (Wright) Gardner died at the age of 22 years, two months and five days She was buried on the old homestead of Benjamin Gardner July 18, 1827, Seth Gardner married Elma Sands Barrere, daughter of George W Barrere, of New Market, Highland County, Ohio

To them were born three sons as follows.

George B, born May 2, 1828

Mills T, born Jan 30 1830

Thomas F, born Feb 18, 1832

Seth Gardner was the fifth child of Benjamin Gardner and experienced that long western trip of his parents from Stephentown, N. Y His early boyhood days were spent on the sunny slopes of the western Berkshire Hills amidst Eastern New York scenery He was reared on his father's farm from eight years of age until he reached his estate It is unfortunate that we are unable to learn more of the early life of so many members of this family His brother, Matthew Gardner, casually states in his book, "that we got along very well on the farm" This is all we know of the early life of Seth Gardner

It is fair to assume that the oldest brothers left the farm as soon as they became of age and the duties of the farm fell upon the next older brothers of which Matthew was the older, and Seth the next younger When Mr Gardner was but 20 years old he enlisted as a soldier of the war of 1812, and was a captain We have not been able to determine the amount of service rendered in this war.

On his return and marriage he lived on his father's farm where his first wife died and is buried in the family burying ground

Mr Gardner learned the trade of a cabinet maker and later in life, or about the time of his marriage to Elma Sands Barrere engaged in business and occupied his time with his trade at Russellville, Brown County, Ohio Later in life he became a merchant and proprietor of a hotel

Mr Gardner, like all of the other Gardners, had his peculiar traits of character and eccentricities There was a time in the life of this man fixed unalterably for everything, and that service was required punctually without any variation or modification. His son, Judge George B. Gardner, said of him, 'that rigid discipline to which everything and everybody was subject, as demanded by all of the early families frequently became burdensome and not infrequently almost unbearable" Reader, there was a reason for this Do you see this strong character, a man of powerful energy, reared as he was a youth of the forest inured to all the hardships of an early pioneer life Sacrifice, without the comforts of life, required to practice the most rigid economy during his early life This established for him a habit which was never changed That constant application from early morning until late at night, service was exacted from every one with whom he was associated.

He had a place for everything and no one was suffered to remove any article when he had placed it where he desired it, without first obtaining his consent Seth Gardner was fourteen years older than his last wife He lived to a ripe old age, and the blessed influences of a religious life tempered and influenced the life of this great man in his last days It was true with every member of this family to which he belonged, that as they approached the last years of their lives, that rigidness softened into obedience and childlike simplicity He died August 20, 1873 Age 81 years five months and fifteen days

ELMA SANDS (BARRERE) GARDNER.

Elma Sands, daughter of George W and Abbe Mills Barrere was born in New Market, Highland County, Ohio on the Fourth of July, 1806, and died in Washington C H, Ohio, on the thirteenth day of July, 1891 She was married in 1827 to Seth Gardner, of Brown County Ohio She had three sons, all of whom survive her, namely, George B Gardner, of Hillsboro, Ohio, and Mills and Thomas F Gardner, of Washington C H, Ohio She resided in Highland and Brown counties until May, 1850, at which time she removed to Washington C H residing there until her death

Her father, George W Barrere was born at Wheeling, W Va, then a government fort, March 17, 1770, emigrated to Kentucky, married there, and removed to Highland County Ohio, the year following the admission of the State into the Union His family was large, of whom five sons and three daughters lived to the respective ages of 70, 74 75, 77, 80, 81 85 and 86 years, an average life of 78½ years, a longevity of which few families in this country can boast

Mrs Gardner who had completed her four-score and five years, was the last of this remarkably long-lived family to succumb to the superior power of that last enemy we call death, with which we too shall grapple, and to whose greater strength sooner or later we shall all be compelled to yield

Our dear old friend was endowed with great mental and physical strength and vigor, and gave evidence all through her long and useful life of a superior wisdom and judgment One of the common infirmities incident to old age is dotage or mental imbecility, or childishness, as it is sometimes called And perhaps of all the afflictions which fall upon man with the weight of years, there is nothing more pitiable than this The spectacle of a once strong and healthy and vigorous mind falling into a hopeless ruin in the merciless grasp of an enfeebling senility, is indeed most distressing

But, thank God, this is not always the price of long life There are conspicuous exceptions to this distressing rule, and Mrs Gardner was one of them Up to the moment in which, without a struggle, or any perceptible hesitancy, she surrendered her spirit to the God who had given it, she retained her mental powers in all their fullness, strength and vigor

She never lost interest in social and public affairs, but, to the last, as in all the years of her life, she kept herself informed upon subjects of general interest, keeping abreast with the current of public opinion by extensive reading, intelligent conversation and a healthy and thorough digestion of the things she read and heard

She had a strong predilection for the society of the young, and always manifested a lively and loving interest in their welfare Is it then any wonder that young people who had the pleasure of living within the bright circle of her acquaintance, loved, confided in and were devoted to her, or that they found in her society a delight, a joy, that grew as their knowledge of her character increased?

In the best and noblest sense of the phrase Mrs Gardner was a strong-minded woman She had not only her convictions as to right and wrong, good and evil, the true and the false, the honest and the dishonest, but she had also the courage of her convictions

Hypocrisy stood abashed in her presence, or slunk away, unable to meet her honest gaze Everything that smacked of meanness or cupidity or sordid selfishness she adbored, and was not afraid to denounce

When stricken down with her last illness she was fully persuaded that she would not survive it, yet she did not shrink, nor murmur She had out-lived every other member of her father's large family, she had gone far beyond the milestone which limits the allotted age of man, and could see no good reason why she should wish to continue a journey which had already carried her so far from the time and scenes of her childhood, and so, with Christian courage, confidence and hope, she turned her face toward the dawn and like as a child, weary with its play, lays its head in its mother's lap and sweetly falls asleep, she breathed out her life in sweet, calm and undisturbed repose, and peacefully entered into everlasting rest

Mrs Gardner did not live unto herself Her three sons, themselves on the western slope of the hill of time, were all there to bid an affectionate farewell to the brave old mother whose self-sacrificing devotion to them, and to theirs and whose untiring and laborious toil in poverty, and often doubtless in suffering for their support and education they remember with tenderest emotions, but shall never perhaps be able fully to appreciate, and shall ever be powerless of course to describe.

But others beside these mourning sons have been given abundant reasons to cherish in grateful hearts the loving deeds of this good woman

LUCY GARDNER (7).

Benjamin (6), Benjamin (5), Benjamin (4), Nathaniel (3), Benony (2), George (1).

Lucy, daughter of Benjamin and Lucy (Hawks) Gardner, was born at Stephentown, N Y., Sept 29, 1793 She married (1) Phillip Jolly (2) —— Ellis, (3) George D Moody

Children by first marriage were

Alexander,

Charlotte,

Clara,

Benjamin Gardner,

Lucinda,

One child by second marriage

America.

HENRY GARDNER (7).

Benjamin (6), Benjamin (5), Benjamin (4), Nathaniel (3), Benony (2), George (1).

Henry Gardner, son of Benjamin and Lucy (Hawks) Gardner, married Rachael Newlands, March 1, 1821, in Brown County, Ohio License is recorded in Book A, No 1, Page 88 The following children were born to them of whom we have record

John Wesley Went west but no record of when or where

Matthew,

Thomas Lives at Ripley, Ohio

Clarke Went to Indiana about 1855

Martha

Amanda Married Timothy Poole, who died, she went to Kentucky and married again No further record

Claretta

RODMAN GARDNER (7)

Benjamin (6), Benjamin (5), Benjamin (4), Nathaniel (3), Benony (2), George (1).

Rodman Gardner was probably the eighth child of Benjamin and Lucy (Hawks) Gardner As this family had no family record we are unable to determine anything relative to him except the record of his marriage in Adams County, Ohio He married Polly Worstell, Jan 19, 1809

ABRAHAM GARDNER, SR. (7).

Benjamin (6), Benjamin (5), Benjamin (4), Nathaniel (3), Benony (2), George (1).

Abraham Gardner, son of Benjamin and Lucy (Hawks) Gardner, was born February 13, 1802 He married Sarah Purcell, November 10, 1823 She was born January 18, 1804

To them were born the following children

Elizabeth Jane, born 1824

Lucy, born November 19, 1826

Benjamin, born June 22, 1829

Marinda, born June 22 1829 Died Feb 16, 1861

Sarah, born August 5, 1832

Ursula, born 1834

The above children were born on the old homestead near Russellville Brown Co, Ohio The following children were born on the Gardner homestead, near Wapakoneta

Abraham, born March 21, 1836

Clarissa, born March 21, 1836

Caroline, born September 8, 1838

Elizabeth, born 1840

Abraham Gardner son of Benjamin and Lucy (Hawks) Gardner, was born and reared on the old homestead near Russellville, Brown County, Ohio As with the other children of this family we know but little about him until he became of age and married On November 10, 1823, he married Sarah Purcell The marriage license is recorded in Book C, No 3, Page 13, office of the Probate Court, at Georgetown, Brown County Ohio This is the first written record obtainable of Abraham and Sarah (Purcell) Gardner

Sarah Purcell Gardner was born Jan 18, 1804 Her father was of sturdy Irish descent. They lived upon the old homestead until about the year 1835 when he, with his family, removed to what was then Allen Co, for the purpose of procuring land. An Indian reservation was about to be opened, and to avail himself of the opportunity, he located on what was then known as Muchinippe Creek, Logan County, where he raised one crop Within the year 1835 he purchased 160 acres of very excellent land at the junction of Blackhoof Creek and the Auglaize River About January 1, 1836, he removed his family to a log cabin on what was then known as the Williams farm, until he could complete his own cabin on the newly acquired farm This was finished and ready for occupancy about March 1, 1836

The aggressive, hard work now began, to clear away a heavy growth of black walnut, burr oak and hard maple Having no use for the timber it was cut, logged and burned in order to remove it from the land The first spring found about five acres ready for planting, and then began the cultivation of the new farm

This family, unlike the average family, with two exceptions were girls The son Benjamin was only seven years of age, and of very little help to his father, consequently the heavy, hard work fell upon the father

He was a rugged man and inured to hardship and hard labor He soon had a sufficient amount of land cleared so that the products of the land exceeded the necessities of the family Not content with the profits from his own farm he became a trader in the products of his neighbors farms Mr Gardner's farm became the central point for the gathering of animal and vegetable life to be taken to the nearest market

When he first located on this land his nearest market where he was compelled to go for supplies was Sandusky, Ohio Soon after locating here the Miami Canal was completed which afforded and built up a market at St Marys, Ohio, which place developed into a very important trading center Produce was brought here and shipped to Toledo, Ohio, where it was reloaded on lake boats and sent to New York via Buffalo

A plank toll road was built from St Marys to Wapakoneta, which was then as great an improvement over the mud road as the steam road was over the turn-pike of later years

Mr Gardner lived about sixteen miles from St Marys and it required three days to take a drove of hogs to St Marys and return Hundreds of hogs were driven over these soft, muddy roads

A wooden scale was erected for the purpose of determining the weight of the animals Usually two hogs were taken at a time to weigh

An old professor of the writer used to say: 'I could close my eyes and guess the weight of a hog more nearly than one of these scales would weigh"

Amidst the strivings to maintain a large family of ten children, Mr Gardner did not neglect their early training and education There was erected a round log school house on the same site where now stands a commodious brick building, which school district, for so many years, has been known as the "Parlett school'

The first building was a typical colonial house, puncheon floors, logs split, with sticks placed in holes for legs The flat side was used for seats and desks The older boys would chop wood at the noon hour for fire which was kept in a large fire-place in the end of the room. It was only a few years until a hewed loghouse appeared Only about three months each year was there school, but the children learned rapidly Geography and grammar were taught by singing The master supplied the tune It would begin

Maine Au—gus—ta on the Ken—e—bec riv—er,
New Hamp—shire Con—cord on the Mer—ri—mac riv—er

The same was true of grammar in its various parts The school soon learned by this method, from the oldest to the youngest The writer has frequently heard his father singing as above

Mr Gardner was, during all his life, a very devout man He was a leader in his community in all things The early pioneer preacher made his home at his house He was an adherent of the doctrine taught by Alexander Campbell.

While Mr Gardner was clearing away the large trees to cultivate his land he was also saving the choice trees to build new buildings

Quite soon a large commodious hewn log house replaced the crude one first erected The logs were hewn with such exactness that no marks of heavy scoring appear. That very exact, careful nature is evidenced, and although nearly seventy-five years have passed since these timbers were hewn, the careful life-work of this man is apparent

A large barn was ercted with a great threshing floor All cereals were flailed or tramped out The neighbors used this until more barns were erected.

Mr Gardner being a religious man, would have preachers use the new barn for religious services, and as this religious denomination is accustomed to do, the new convert would be taken to the stream near by (Blackhoof creek) and immersed

The Rev Mr Lister was a favorite of Mr Gardner s and often preached in the new barn He preached the sermon at Mr Gardner's funeral

The church erected at Uniopolis (the old one) was at the direction and with the assistance of two of its first advocates and members, Mr and Mrs Gardner

Wapakoneta became the county seat of Auglaize County, the new railroad had been built, and this brought the old pioneer within four and one-half miles of a new commercial center The town flourished A tide of fraternalism moved over the land and he connected himself with the Independent Order of Odd Fellows at Wapakoneta, and became a regular and devoted attendant It is said that in this connection he was as zealous as he was particular in all other affairs

The "world s fair" at New York was of interest to him, and he went there via Miami Canal to Toledo, Ohio, thence by rail to New York

There he had a very excellent daguerreotype taken The half-tone used in the second volume is a copy of same The daguerreotype is now the property of his grandson, Charles M Gardner

Mr Gardner prospered and in 1853 erected a new house The bricks were made on the farm The boards were made from the fine walnut trees of the farm Eight large rooms are in the house He declared he would build a house that would last one hundred years It is in a very excellent state of preservation

Abraham Gardner enjoyed his wealth He was not miserly or narrow, but used and enjoyed his accumulation No article of clothing was too good for him What he had for himself he provided for his family

The writer desires to say that the first coat he had was made from a broadcloth coat of this man

His demands upon his family were very much the same as the other members of the Gardner family He had no idle hours No one was permitted around him who did not work He was eccentric, but kind He was industrious and charitable His neighbors regarded him as an honest, Christian man He demanded every penny due him, and as scrupulously paid

It is said he paid his help every night, allowing no indebtedness for labor.

The family had grown up, a pleasant comfortable home had been established He was trimming his apple orchard in the spring of 1855, contracted a cold and in a few weeks died, evidently with pneumonia

In the midst of a useful life he was taken away

At his request, selected by himself before he died, a grave was prepared upon his own farm where he was buried on a beautiful May day with the rites of the Independent Order of Odd Fellows

The short history of the life of Abraham Gardner is not complete without the life of his good wife Until her death, July 29, 1879 aged 75 years, 7 months and 11 days, after her husband's death, she lived with her children She had a very kindly disposition, always doing something for some one She was never idle, the stockings, trousers and coast always bore evidence of grandma having visited the home We all loved her After an illness of three days she departed this life and was buried beside her husband who had preceded her nearly twenty-five years

She was a sister of Squire Purcell of Sardinia Ohio, and an aunt of Dr J T Purcell of St Joseph, Illinois

BENJAMIN H. GARDNER (7).

Benjamin (6), Benjamin (5), Benjamin (4), Nathaniel (3), Benony (2), George (1).

Benjamin H, the youngest son of Benjamin and Lucy (Hawks) Gardner, was born about 1804 He was married twice His second wife was Matilda Howells Several children were born to them The writer has been unable to secure the record of the family further than a son, William, who resided in Clermont Co where he reared a family

There are several descendants of this Benjamin Gardner in Clermont Co but they have not responded to inquiries as to their whereabouts and history

ALBON BANCROFT GARDNER (7).

Albon C. (6), George (5), Ezekiel (4), Nicholas (3), Nicholas (2), George (1).

Albon Bancroft Gardner, son of Albon Crocker and Saloma (Bancroft) Gardner, was born June 1, 1826, at Parkman, Ohio He married Sarah White, daughter of Deacon Hervey White, June 1, 1846

Their children were

Albon Luther,
Roscoe Gaylord,
Austin Harvey,
Sarah Saloma
Charles Herbert,
Mary Wales,
Lizzie Lincoln

Albon Bancroft Gardner began his life under more favorable circumstances than did his father When this young man discontinued his public school work his father had removed to Chagrin Falls, Ohio, and was engaged in the dry goods business This son his only son, was his young clerk

In the year 1845 he was married to Sarah White, daughter of Deacon Hervy White The ceremony was performed by Rev Alvin Nash.

Seven children were born to them, six of whom survived them Soon after his marriage his father desired him to accept the farm in Bainbridge, which he did, and when several of his children were born, he left the farm and became a partner in the milling business with his father. He became an insurance agent representing several companies

He inherited the traits characteristic of his father He was a strong man of the physique of his father.

The social life of this young man was a very brilliant one, as he was in possession of an estate that few boys possessed at that time

While he did not have to undergo the deprivations of his father's early days there was not the extravagance that is so frequently noticeable in young men when the father is wealthy

He entered into business relations with his father and amassed a very comfortable fortune before he died

His home life was a great part and place for him After the children had grown to maturity the father would engage in the amusements of the home with them The recollection of the games of the home are still fresh in the minds of these sons and daughters that have reached and passed the half-century mark in life

The sacred memories that cluster around the homes and the reiteration of them to the children make life the more worth living

With Albon Bancroft Gardner the making of money was not the first consideration The assiting to make some one happy and to make more out of life was his ideal

He was for many years Justice of the Peace in the township and when parties came to him to begin suit he would almost always bring the parties together and have a mutual adjustment of the difficulties and thus avoid a suit and for his services make no charges He was termed "the peacemaker of Chagrin Falls"

When parties came to have suit brought leading up toward divorce proceedings he would have the parties understand one another and they would go home happy

Albon Bancroft Gardner spent his life doing good to those that needed wise counsel and guidance instead of plunging them into suits in courts

He was a member of the Methodist Episcopal Church and served in this connection all of his long and useful life

The first Ohio father directed the course and the children followed, and the children's children and so on down to the last generation

A career such as Albon Crocker Gardner's followed by that of Albon Bancroft Gardner is sufficient for the enlightenment of all the families that have sprung from them

The life of this man was not entirely his own moulding He entered into marriage relations with a lady who had had similar parental guidance Deacon Hervey White was a man of more than ordinary ability in every degree

SARAH (WHITE) GARDNER.

This branch of the Gardner family would not be complete without a record and history of this mother and her ancestors

Her grandfather was Nehemiah White, born in Williamsburgh, Massachusetts, 1756, who is in the line of descent of Peregrine White, who was the first child born after the pilgrims landed at Plymouth Rock

The father of Mrs Gardner was one of the early Ohio pioneers and conducted a large axe factory from which place Ohio was largely supplied with edged tools He amassed quite a fortune and was a very liberal man He had a large family and was very devoted to them He was a member of the Congregational church and for many years was the leader of the choir He was a natural musician as was each of his eight children With small exceptions he built and furnished the Congregational church

He was of tall, noble figure He was in his glory with his family about him at home or church He had a beautiful home with plenty, sharing his income with his God and his neighbors

As he was broad in his philanthropy he was broad in his nature and in his interpretation of the Scriptures He was dominated by a love as broad as humanity He gave of his time and money to the cause of the slave He was a staunch member of the "underground railway system"

Unselfish in every respect he was greatly loved by his family and especially by his grandchildren One of his grandsons has said

"In memory I have gone back to the years of my childhood to the 'old home on the hill,'—a barefoot boy, there again I met his gracious smile and welcome as he extended the liberty of the town, as such it was, with the numerous buildings and business that his genius had wrought While his time was engrossed with a large business enterprise which required his entire time, his great heart never allowed him to neglect his grandchildren He would tell us where we could go in swimming with safety, and tell us to help ourselves to the walnuts and butternuts in the garret He would tell grandma to spread a whole piece of bread with butter and honey and she should put the honey on thick, and superintend the spreading of the first piece, and exact a promise from her to spread them all as the first one. She always kept her promise He was always ever mindful of his grandchildren and there was quite a crowd of us"

He had a choir of his own and on Sabbath morning his children, the melodeon and a variety of instruments would be brought down from his house in the old-fashioned spring wagon drawn by their old family horse, "Cubb" for a number of years his own family composed the choir

On the north was the White industry On the south was the Gardner mills and store On the north was the leader of the Congregational church On the south was the leader of the Methodist Episcopal Not much difference in polity and none in doctrine The interests of these two families became general They were thrown so closely together that they were inseparable

It is needless to say that the interests became broad and they both amassed great fortunes They were both blessed with all of this world's goods that could be desired

Mr White had his own village and lived one of the contented happy lives Mr Gardner had his farms and about a mile below the business port of town erected a large brick building that for years was the wonder of the surrounding country For many years this was the home of Albon Crocker Gardner and his family One son was all he had The daughters nearly all married Methodist Episcopal preachers The reason can clearly be seen This was the home of Methodism The young preachers came there and as long as there was a Gardner girl they were to be considered eligible for a preacher's wife

Albon Bancroft Gardner was reared under these influences He saw the life of his father spent for the accumulation of property and laying the foundation of this section of the country and the making of character for the hundreds of employees and citizens

It is natural that the life of this man would diverge from that of his father to the extent of providing the means of retaining that which his father had established. This mission was performed by this only son

There is a lesson to be drawn from the life of Albon Bancroft Gardner that we do not want the reader to fail to secure His father was in possession then of what would make him a multi-millionaire at this day

This son did not demonstrate the disposition to consume in revelry, neither did he manifest a disposition of hoarding He spent his life where his father had spent his by "doing good unto all men," and chose the place of the good samaritan As his father before him was counselor in all matters so was the son He became the advisor and in his official relation as Justice of Peace occupied the place in its true sense a Justice of Peace His principles were to be at peace with all men Chagrin Falls has had its Whites and Gardners and as the birthplace is so sacred to the memory of each of the children of this branch of the family so it is to all of the citizens of this town.

ELIZA JANE GARDNER (8).

Abraham (7), Benjamin (6), Benjamin (5), Benjamin (4), Nathaniel (3), Benony (2), George (1)

Eliza Jane Gardner was the eldest child of Abraham, Sr, and Sarah (Purcell) Gardner Born in Brown County in 1821 She married Andrew Brentlinger

To them were born children as follows

John,
Peter,
Abraham.
Sarah Ann,
Cordelia,
Mary,
Caroline,
Susie,
Elizabeth,

The family has become so scattered it was a difficult matter to obtain this limited information

URSULA GARDNER (8).

Abraham (7), Benjamin (6), Benjamin (5), Benjamin (4), Nathaniel (3), Benony (2), George (1).

Fifth child of Abraham, Sr, and Sarah (Purcell) Gardner, was born in Brown County, Ohio, in the year 1834 She married Daniel Brentlinger, July 8, 1852 They were married by George B Bennet, Justice of the Peace Unable to secure record of children

LUCY GARDNER (8).

Abraham (7), Benjamin (6), Benjamin (5), Benjamin (4), Nathaniel (3), Benony (2), George (1).

Lucy Gardner, daughter of Abraham, Sr, and Sarah (Purcell) Gardner, was born November 19 1826 Married Samuel Carter, March 8, 1849. He was born January 19, 1819 To them were born the following children

Sarah Elizabeth, born February 19, 1850
John, born November 16, 1852
Charles H, born September 1, 1854, died Nov 10, 1855
William S, born April 25, 1855

BENJAMIN GARDNER (8).

Abraham (7), Benjamin (6), Benjamin (5), Benjamin (4), Nathaniel (3), Benony (2), George (1).

Benjamin Gardner, son of Abraham and Sarah (Purcell) Gardner, was born June 22, 1829, on the old homestead in Brown County, Ohio He married, first, Susan Vaughn, to whom children were born One reached womanhood, Susan He married, second, Catherine Orr, July 21, 1853 Married by R D Oldfield, Minister To them were born children, two of whom died early and are buried in the family cemetery on the old homestead in Auglaize County, Ohio One daughter, who reachd womanhood

Katherine, born October 5, 1860

Mr Gardner married, third, Rachel Groff, of Wapakoneta, Ohio.

There was born to them the following children.

Milo,
Ella,
Sarah,
Millie,

Benjamin Gardner was the first son born to the parents, and was given the family name of Benjamin, which had marked the record for several generations He had a twin sister Marinda. He was about six years of age when his father came to the wilderness of Allen County, Ohio, (now Auglaize County), and began a pioneer life with his large family.

Young Benjamin, being the only boy until 1836, when his only brother Abraham, Jr, was born, it can readily be understood the very difficult part this young boy and man played in the clearing up and improvement of the new home.

The writer, having never seen any member of this family, must depend upon the history of the life of Mr Gardner from incidents related by Abraham, Jr., and letters from the daughters From the record of the death of the father of Benjamin, it will be seen that the care of the younger members of the family largely fell upon this son He remained at home and with his brother tilled the farm and preserved the home until the children had all reached their estate

In 1861 Benjamin Gardner, having sold his interest in the homestead, concluded to make a home for himself and little family in the west He had the spirit of his forefathers, and departed overland, driving over the prairies and through the forests to the state of Iowa, locating in West Union, Fayette County He did not remain there long until he resumed his search for a home and finally located at Chester, Jefferson County, Kansas He continued there some time, and sold his property and removed to Bunker Hill, Russell Co, Kansas, in 1876

He continued to live at Bunker Hill until a few years before his death, when he sold his property and removed to Rossville, Kansas and from there to Dennison, Kansas, where he lived until the time of his death, which occurred Sept 9, 1904 He was buried at Dennison, Kansas The widow and youngest daughter reside at Dennison, Kansas

Mr Gardner's entire life was of the strenuous character. During his boyhood days in the assistance to clear up a forest home, and, early after his marriage, began his life with his family in the unbroken and unsettled west

Mr Gardner became a prosperous farmer and enjoyed the advantages that accrue with the increase of valuation of property He was very much of the disposition and temperament of his father He had received good common school education He was a man devoted to his church, and enjoyed the blessings of a religious life

MARINDA GARDNER (8).

Abraham (7), Benjamin (6), Benjamin (5), Benjamin (4), Nathaniel (3), Benony (2), George (1).

Marinda Gardner, daughter of Abraham, Sr, and Sarah (Purcell) Gardner, was born June 22, 1829; married William Brentlinger, Jr, March 29, 1849 She died February 16, 1861. William Brentlinger was born April 15, 1824, died July 19, 1879

To them were born the following children

Abram E, born December 15, 1849
Charles, born March 9, 1851
William T, born January 4, 1853, died January 13, 1854
Sarah Elizabeth, born November 23, 1854
Levi James, born November 23, 1854
Samuel, born November 22, 1856, died February 10, 1862
Andrew T, born November 24, 1858
John Henry, born February 5, 1861, died March 11, 1861

SARAH GARDNER (8).

Abraham (7), Benjamin (6), Benjamin (5), Benjamin (4), Nathaniel (3), Benony (2), George (1).

Sarah Gardner, daughter of Abraham, Sr., and Sarah (Purcell) Gardner, was born in Brown County, Ohio, August 5, 1832 She married, first, David Kent, who died No children. She married, second, David Butler, January 3, 1856 Mr Butler was born March 3, 1835.

To them were born children as follows

Twins—Albert and Alice, born May 12, 1857

Florence born Feb 20, 1860. Died young

Lewis, born July 9, 1863

Cora, born December 20, 1865 Died young

Robert, born February 20, 1868

Mrs Butler was the fifth child of her parents and was a very small girl when her father settled in Auglaize County The early pioneer life is familiar to her

Mr Butler enlisted from Auglaize County, Ohio, January 27, 1864, and was mustered into U S. service as a private of Company I, 34th Regiment, O V I, under Captain Underwood and Colonel F R Franklin, to serve three years or during the war He was captured at Beverly, W Va, January 10, 1865, and confined in Libby Prison until March 5, 1865, then paroled

He was honorably discharged July 27, 1865, at Wheeling, W Va., on account of close of the war

The regiment was assigned to Johnson's brigade, Dural's Division, 8th Corps, Army of W Va, and participated in many of the important engagements His health was very materially impaired and for the last few years of his life he was blind He died Feb. 3, 1897.

Mrs Butler resides at her own home at Uniopolis, Ohio.

CLARISSA GARDNER (8)

Abraham (7), Benjamin (6), Benjamin (5), Benjamin (4), Nathaniel (3), Benony (2), George (1).

Clarissa Gardner, daughter of Abraham Gardner, Sr., and Sarah (Purcell) Gardner, was born on the old homestead, Auglaize County, Ohio, March 23, 1836 Married George Fairfield, January 21, 1856

To them were born the following children

Horace, born Aug. 1, 1857

Lewis William, born October 15, 1858

As written in the history of Abraham, Jr, she was born soon after the removal to the new home in what is now known as Auglaize County, Ohio

Being one of the younger children, and a girl, she did not have the discomforts of the older children, for the log hut soon gave place to a very comfortable home and before her marriage, the palatial brick, erected by her father The home was luxuriously furnished for the home of an early farmer While so situated there lived on the farm south, another family that had encountered the hardships of a pioneer life

In that home was a stalwart young man of excellent character

Frequently these young people visited and family greetings would be exchanged Exchange of labor was the custom of those days This brought the young man to whom we refer to this home

George Fairfield, the husband of Clarissa Gardner, lived a distance from the old homestead Mr Fairfield was a member of the Church of Christ and preached the doctrine advocated by Alexander Campbell He preached much and was not in touch with the other branches of the family, consequently his early life was not as familiar to the writer as other members of the family

They removed to Paulding, Paulding County, Ohio, and have resided there on a farm, owning quite a large tract of land. He has been a very devout, religious man and careful in his transactions. With pleasure we listened to him recount the experiences of a pioneer life, when a boy living near the farm of Abraham Gardner, Sr The Fairfields are very tall and slender Mr Fairfield is more than six feel tall, and has a son Lewis who is six feet and four inches tall and weighs usually about one hundred and sixty pounds

ABRAHAM GARDNER, JR (8).

Abraham (7) Benjamin (6), Benjamin (5), Benjamin (4), Nathaniel (3), Benony (2), George (1).

Abraham Gardner, Jr, youngest son of Abraham, Sr, and Sarah (Purcell) Gardner, was born in Auglaize County, Ohio, March 21, 1836 Died at Berkeley, California, January 21, 1905 Aged 68 years, 10 months and 6 days

In the year 1857 he married Mary Jane Northup, who died November 28 1860

To them were born two children

Horace W, born March 15, 1858

An infant daughter Died November 23, 1860

Abraham Gardner, Jr, married, second, Harriett Brentlinger, 1861, daughter of William Brentlinger, Sr

To them were born three children

Walter Scott, born February 3, 1862

Charles Morris, born July 25, 1863

Mary Jane (Jennie), born September 2, 1865

Mr Gardner was the twin brother of Clarissa, and they were the first children born to the parents after coming to the new wilderness home in what is now Auglaize County, Ohio

What is peculiar to early pioneer life of the father of this boy was true of him Only a small patch of land had been cleared on the new farm when he was born

The writer well remembers the long evenings of winter being occupied with the telling of the incidents peculiar to the early life in the wilderness Deer were so plentiful that they made themselves troublesome and were destructive to the growing crops

Wild hogs were plentiful, and small game abounded Blackhoof Creek, just west of the house, was the fishing creek for young Abraham, and so abundant was the finny tribe that they experienced no difficulty in securing a large catch Quite a portion of the farm had been cleared when young Abraham was old enough to take his part in the work His father procured for him a light-weight axe with which to assist in chopping timber He also procured for him a short scythe, and young Abraham took his place in mowing the field, but he has said he was always victorious in the rivalry to maintain his place, and never permitted a man to mow around him

His father had purchased additional farms and there was a large area of land to be tilled, which was done by the two boys His father being one of those diligent men, not knowing what it was to have idle time, they accumulated a large amount of property and erected large buildings upon the same Young Abraham became an expert in the use of the axe and adz Many of the heavy timbers that are in the large barn were hewn by him The writer has seen him fell a large tree and in a very short time, have it transformed into a stick ready for the position intended

A large sugar camp occupied the north part of the farm This camp gave employment for the early weeks of spring It fell upon young Abraham to gather the sap, his brother Benjamin to chop the wood and keep the fire, while their father attended to the "stirring off"

An experience that the children of Abraham, Jr, would frequently call for was the story of the run-away horse He had, what was always regarded, a very docile, trusty old horse There came a good run of sap and every effort was taxed to care for it A sled had been prepared with a large barrel fastened upon it with which to gather the sap and convey it to the kettles Everybody had grown weary and wished the sap would quit flowing, but as the product was a source of revenue, it must not be neglected Even the old horse gave evidence of becoming weary of the strenuous hours and resolved to break away from it, as the boys wished they could do When the barrel was about full of sap the old horse concluded to break the monotony and for the first time in his life went cantering off with the sled and load of sap Turned over the sled, spilled the sap, took a circuitous route, returning to his driver In the meantime the young driver had cut a large whip to punish the horse, but he said, "the old horse looked so innocent I threw away the whip and took him to the barn" Each year hundreds of pounds of maple sugar would be made, the family using this as well as the syrup

Young Abraham was given the advantages that the schools then afforded, and became more than an ordinary scholar Practical lessons were taught

The writer remembers one problem in the arithmetic used by young Abraham The terms in use then and propositions were of a practical, everyday occurrence The picture of a tree with a squirrel in the top was said to be seventy-five feet high The man with a gun could see the squirrel when standing fifty feet from the tree What was the distance the ball from the gun would have to travel to hit the squirrel?

Nearly all the problems in that old arithmetic were based upon propositions with which they were familiar.

When he reached early manhood he enjoyed the advantages of a good home with plenty of comforts. Their father did not deprive them of the enjoyments when they had the means, but by example encouraged it

His father dying when he was about nineteen years of age the care of the farm and the duties thereof fell upon him and his older brother

These brothers proceeded to purchase the interests of the eight sisters This proved to be a greater effort than they were able to carry through, and the farm was sold to George Kelsey, of St Marys, Ohio

The balance due was paid to the sisters and the difference retained by the brothers. This occurred at the close of the year 1861

The interests of the two brothers then separated, and Abraham took possession of a farm a short distance west of Wapakoneta, which for many years was known as the Burke farm, situated on the Glynwood pike, where the writer was born

Mr. Gardner continued to live near Wapakoneta until 1879, when he concluded to go west He stopped for a short time at Springfield, Mo.

He did not like the prairie land and pushed on farther west until he reached California His attention here was given largely to ranches, and with the McPherson Brothers planted large vineyards in Arizona and California. He spent a great portion of his time at the following places: Los Angeles, Santa Ana, Hanford, Anaheim, having financial interests with different ranches.

Mr Gardner was a practical, honest man. Making no great profession, but was a believer in the Christian principles and higher life He died January 21, 1905

He is buried on the family lot of his son Charles M Gardner, Woodlawn cemetery, Toledo, Ohio

CAROLINE GARDNER (8).

Abraham (7), Benjamin (6), Benjamin (5), Benjamin (4), Nathaniel (3), Benony (2), George (1).

Caroline Gardner, daughter of Abraham and Sarah(Purcell) Gardner, was born September 8, 1838. Married George W Harshbarger January 15, 1860.

Three children were born and died in infancy. The following lived to maturity

Charles, born December 12, 1866

Enos,born August 12, 1872

Ida, born August 12, 1872

George W. Harshbarger was born in Rockingham County, Virginia, October 6, 1835 Moved with his parents and grandparents to Licking County, Ohio, in 1838, and from there to Auglaize County in 1852, where he now resides. In the fall of 1862 he enlisted in the service of his country and served in Company K O V I He was with General Grant in the western division in many of the heavy engagements He has enjoyed a quiet life and has been one of Auglaize County's prosperous farmers.

ELIZABETH GARDNER (8).

Abraham (7), Benjamin (6), Benjamin (5), Benjamin (4), Nathaniel (3), Benony (2), George (1).

Elizabeth Gardner, youngest daughter of Abraham, Sr, and Sarah (Purcell) Gardner, was born in the year 1840, married John W Fairfield, November 6, 1859 They were married by J D Williams, Justice of the Peace, Auglaize County, Ohio.

Their children were

Elizabeth, born December 18, 1860.

Thomas, born October 7, 1862

Mrs Fairfield, after a very brief illness, died April 1, 1863 leaving these two small children. In the fall of 1865 Mr Fairfield removed to Livingston County, Ill In 1870, he removed to Champaign County, Ill He died October 3, 1879

JUDGE GEORGE B. GARDNER (8).

Seth (7), Benjamin (6), Benjamin (5), Benjamin (4), Nathaniel (3), Benony (2), George (1).

George B Gardner, son of Seth and Elma Sands (Barrere) Gardner, was born in Russellville, Brown County, Ohio, May 12, 1828. He was married May 3, 1853, to Maria Amanda Robinson of Fayette County, Ohio

Two children were born to them as follows·

Carey, died in infancy

Grace G, born March 3, 1854.

His father, Seth Gardner, was a cabinet maker, also a merchant and hotel keeper He was an active participant in the war of 1812

His mother was a native of Highland County, Ohio, a daughter of Judge George W Barrere, a prominent pioneer of the last named county

His paternal grandfather was Benjamin Gardner, a soldier in the army of the American Revolution

George B Gardner in his early boyhood days worked on a farm during the summer and attended school in the winter. At the age of twelve he was placed as an apprentice in the printing office of "The Practical Examiner" at Georgetown, Brown County, Ohio, where he remained for four and a half years He afterwards went to Ripley, Ohio, and worked in the office of the Ripley Bee," a weekly paper at that place Here he attended the select school at Ripley, Ohio, for about two years

He remained in Ripley as printer and student until 1848, when he spent a few months in the law office with his uncle, Nelson Barrere, of Hillsboro, Ohio He then removed to Washington C H, Ohio, where he purchased the "Fayette New Era" He edited and published this paper until June, 1856 In 1855 he was admitted to the bar From 1856 until the fall of 1861 he was in practice of law at Washington C. H, Ohio

In 1861 he accompanied the 60th Regiment, Ohio Volunteer Infantry, as Captain of Company C, to the seat of the war of the Rebellion in Virginia, and served with his Company, and as Acting Assistant Adjutant General of brigade until the surrender of Harper's Ferry, where his regiment was one of the bodies captured It was then immediately paroled and sent to Camp Douglas, at Chicago, Illinois, and there remained until the expiration of its term of service

In November, 1862, he returned to Washington C H, Ohio, and in the winter of 1862-3 served as Deputy Assessor of the United States for Internal Revenue. In April, 1863, he was appointed Commissioner of Enrollment of the Sixth Congressional Ohio district with headquarters at Hillsboro, Ohio, and continued in that office till the close of the war.

In 1865 he opened a law office in Hillsboro, Ohio, where he yet remains in the practice of law He has been Justice of the Peace, Mayor and Probate Judge

Politically he was a Whig Upon the breaking out of the war of 1861 he joined the Union party and then became and is at present a Republican.

Mr Gardner has been a very strong man in the moulding of the political and social life of Hillsboro He is one of those resolute, strong personalities He has been a clean-cut professional man and enjoyed the full confidence of the people

HON. MILLS T. GARDNER (8).

Seth (7), Benjamin (6), Benjamin (5), Benjamin (4), Nathaniel (3), Benony (2), George (1).

Hon Mills T Gardner, son of Seth and Elma Sands (Barrere) Gardner, was born at Russellville, Brown County, Ohio, Jan 30, 1830 He married Margaret Morrow of Highland County, Ohio, in 1857 To them the following children were born who are still living Mr and Mrs Gardner had five children older than the two mentioned, all of whom died within one week of diphtheria.

Gertrude,

Edith Hortense

Hon Mills T Gardner, son of Seth and Elma Sands (Barrere) Gardner, received his early preliminary education at the common schools, and afterwards went to an academy taught by the Rev John Rankin, Ripley, Ohio, where he remained until fourteen years of age, when he entered a dry goods store as clerk, and sold goods until 1855

While employed in the mercantile business he was also studying law under the supervision of his uncle, the Hon Nelson Barrere, of Hillsboro, Ohio

In 1855 Mr Gardner became a resident of Fayette County, and in 1855 was admitted to the bar, and has been continuously engaged in the active work of his profession

He has been a very strong factor in the political history of the Republican party of his State.

We might insert at this place that his uncle, Hon Nelson Barrere, of Hillsboro, Ohio, was the last Whig candidate for governor of Ohio His grandfather, George W Barrere, was also a very prominent political factor in the early history of the State

In 1855 Mr Gardner was elected prosecuting attorney of Fayette County, and re-elected to the same office, serving four years.

He was a member of the Ohio State Senate in 1862-3, during that memorable and historic period

In 1864 he was presidential elector from his congressional district and voted for Abraham Lincoln in the Electoral College

He enjoys the distinction of having voted three times for Abraham Lincoln for President, twice as a citizen, and once as the chosen representative of the people in the Electoral College of 1864

He was a member of the Ohio State House of Representatives 1866-7.

In 1872 he was elected to the Constitutional Convention of the State, and served during its sessions of 1872-3

In 1876 he was elected a member to the Forty-fifth Congress from the Third District of Ohio, and the same year was a member of the National Republican Convention, which nominated Rutherford B Hayes for President

Mr Gardner s seat while in Congress was between that of the two martyred Presidents, James A Garfield and William McKinley, and they were very warm friends

He has been a very devout member of the Methodist Episcopal Church, having united with this church very early in his life.

He has been a leader in this denomination, not only in his home town has his influence been felt but throughout the State He has been abundantly blessed with this world's goods and has been a liberal contributor to his church

Washington C H, Ohio, his home, has one of the most beautiful M E Churches in the denomination, and great credit is due Mr Gardner for the erection and financing this project.

His business career has been a long and successful one He is president of a National Bank, and interested in a great many of the financial institutions of his county.

He owns a large tract of real estate adjacent to the town and has one of the most beautiful residences there

The history of the home of Hon Mills T Gardner is not complete without gracious mention of these two very excellent daughters who are the comfort and consolation of Mr Gardner in his advancing years The good wife of this home has gone to her reward some nine years Cultured and self-sacrificing are both these daughters Because they have remained at home and made this home agreeably pleasant, they are never going to grow old so there will always be two young ladies at the home of Hon Mills Gardner Miss Edith spent several years abroad studying with the masters in vocal art

The great success of Washington C H Methodist Episcopal church is due largely to the musical ability of Miss Edith Gardner.

THOMAS F. GARDNER (8).

Seth (7), Benjamin (6), Benjamin (5), Benjamin (4), Nathaniel (3), Benony (2), George (1).

Thomas F Gardner, youngest son of Seth and Elma Sands (Barrere) Gardner, wah born in Highland County, Ohio, February 18, 1832

Three children, two of whom are living, the other having died in infancy

Charles F

Nanny

Mr Gardner early in life learned the trade of printer, and devoted his life to this work He was the editor and proprietor of the Republic, a paper of Washington C H, and performed a great service to his political party as an editor He was one of those keen, witty writers.

The reader will observe the traits characteristic of the Gardner family in that punctual exactness. This is true of Thomas Gardner He has every trait of the Gardner ancestry He owns a fine property in Washington C H, which receives personal care He has been termed the Burbank of Ohio His lawn, which is his constant pride and care, is the most beautiful in his town

LUCINDA JOLLY (8).

Lucy (7), Benjamin (6), Benjamin (5), Benjamin (4), Nathaniel (3), Benony (2), George (1).

Lucinda, daughter of Phillip and Lucy (Gardner) Jolly, was born in southern Ohio She married Soloman Thompson

Children

Mary,

Amanda,

George W,

Sarah Ann,

Isabella,

Francis M.

BARTON BEASLEY GARDNER (8).

Matthew (7), Benjamin (6), Benjamin (5), Benjamin (4), Nathaniel (3), Benony (2), George (1).

Barton Beasley Gardner, oldest child of Elder Matthew and Sally (Beasley) Gardner, was born March 27, 1814 Died March 5, 1889

October 20 1836, he married Susanna Elliot. There were no children born to them He was a prominent business man in his day, from 1852 to 1878, when he quit business and went to his farm which was located about two miles north of Higginsport He met several heavy business reverses from the last of which he never rallied

SALLY GARDNER (8).

Matthew (7), Benjamin (6), Benjamin (5), Benjamin (4), Nathaniel (3), Benony (2), George (1).

Sally, oldest daughter of Matthew and Sally (Beasley) Gardner, was born December 5th, 1815 Died October 25, 1891 Married Michael Shinkle, December 1st, 1836 He was born March 6th, 1815 Died February 15th, 1900

To them were born the following children:

Walter L, born September 13, 1837

John G born May 23rd, 1840

Barton B, born about 1843, records not clear.

Thomas C, born 1845

Matthew Hale, born 1848

Sarah Josephine, born about 1852, and died young.

Michael E, born 1854

George Washington, born 1857 and died young

Six members of this family grew to manhood and reared families

Mrs Shinkle was a very devout member of the 'Union Church," which her father organized in 1818, and continued in that relation for more than fifty years

Mr Shinkle was a member of the same church with his wife, being one of the leaders and served as trustee about thirty years He was a prosperous farmer and for a number of years was prominent in business.

He was a man of plain habits, but noted for his sterling worth in his community Prompt in all his business transactions, one of the best of neighbors, always prompt in attendance in illness in the community

GEORGE WASHINGTON GARDNER (8)

Matthew (7), Benjamin (6), Benjamin (5), Benjamin (4), Nathaniel (3), Benony (2), George (1).

George W, son of Matthew and Sally (Beasley) Gardner, was born Jan 30, 1818; died May 7, 1868 He married Eliza Slack, Dec 30, 1841, at Logan's Gap, Ohio They settled on a farm near Oak Grove, Ohio, which is about three miles north of Higginspirt They resided there until Mr Gardner's death

Children

Martha Anna born Jan 14, 1843, married Henry Kinney, Mar 16, 1866 Children Hattie, Maud, Belle, George

Sarah Ellen, born May 17, 1844, married John Franklin Shinkle, April 17, 1861 Six children were born to them, but we have not their names.

John Franklin born May 13, 1846, married Adaline Elliot, and had three children, of whom Frank, the youngest, is the only survivor

William Matthew, born Jan 21, 1848, married Sarah Belle Bartlow

George Washington born March 23, 1850, married Lucy London, and lives at Higginsport, Ohio

Barton Beasley, born March 4, 1852, died in infancy.

James Dillaway, born Dec 27, 1854, married Jennie Lind Hite, daughter of James M Hite, one child. Lela, married Mr Blair

Wesley Beacher, born Sept 27, 1856, married Lulu Bertz Children· Pearl, Lottie.

Emma Maria, born Nov 27, 1859, married Jesse Dugan Hite, June 23, 1885 Children Albert, Leona, married —— Biltz

Mary, born May 28, 1862, died in infancy

Of this large family only the mother and two sons, William Matthew and George Washington, survive The mother at the advanced age of 81 has a clear mind and pursues her household duties unaided

JEPTHA MONROE GARDNER (8).

Matthew (7), Benjamin (6), Benjamin (5), Benjamin (4), Nathaniel (3), Benony (2), George (1).

Jeptha Monroe Gardner, son of Elder Matthew and Sally (Beasley) Gardner, was born April 10, 1820. Died February, 1906 Married Marguerite Dalton, December 9, 1842

There were born to them six children as follows

John D, born April 4, 1843, died 1907

George F, born September 22 1846

Sarah M, born April 30, 1848

Elnathan M, born April 2, 1850

Mary C, born September 13, 1851-2

Thomas H (known as "Doc"), born July 7, 1853

Jeptha M Gardner being one of the older sons of the preacher, had the experiences that but few of the older people realized

In connection with this man's life we would call attention to the history of the life of his father Very many more pages have been devoted to Matthew Gardner because it narrates events and conditions that touch the life of his entire family Early in the second dacade of the nineteenth century his father began preaching on what is known as "Shinkle Ridge"

The father had an eye to business as well as to preaching, and he purchased several tracts of very excellent land on this ridge

By this means Jeptha Gardner took up a home in the western part of Brown County, some sixteen miles from his father's home This farm is located about midway between Higginsport and Georgetown on the west pike

Soon after locating he erected a large commodious house, where he continued to live until his death Mr Gardner had inherited the traits of character so peculiar to the Gardner family He was diligent and by close application amassed a large fortune His eldest son John D Gardner, was the main support of the farm He served his father as few sons do

Mr Gardner lived to a ripe old age, reaching the age of eighty-six We have learned there was none in the family that lived to be older than he He retained his mental faculties until his death

By reason of his age and his home being open, his family possessed more valuable information of the family record than any place the writer visited. We were sorry not to have seen this aged man Soon after he passed away a peculiar accident occurred Many valuable records belonging to his father which affected the disposition of the property and estate of Benjamin Gardner the early settler of Ohio, were consumed by fire

Mr Gardner was very eccentric. During his long life he never had one dollar of fire insurance, but fortunately never suffered any loss

When he died his property passed into the hands of an administrator, who insured the buildings, and only three weeks elapsed till nearly every building except the barn was destroyed by fire.

Mrs Gardner died several years before he did and he remained a widower till his death

LUCINDA ELIZA GARDNER (8).

Matthew (7), Benjamin (6), Benjamin (5), Benjamin (4), Nathaniel (3), Benony (2), George (1).

Lucinda Eliza Gardner, daughter of Elder Matthew and Sally (Beasley) Gardner, was born in Brown County, Ohio, March 28, 1823 Died January 12, 1888 She married William Johnson Lindsey, May 2, 1842 He was born in Kentucky October 14, 1821 Died at Manchester Ohio May 15 1898 The following children were born to them

Sarah Bell, born August 7, 1847, at Maysville, Kentucky Married Amos W Hamer and live at Manchester, Adams County, Ohio

Mary Maria, born February 22, 1850, in Brown County, Ohio Married Nathan M Foster and lives at Clarence, Ford County, Ill

Barton Beasley, born April 8, 1853, in Brown County, Ohio Married Tamer Eldred and lives at Portsmouth, Ohio

John Gardner, born December 28, 1854, in Brown County, Ohio Married Dora Amelia Holmes, March 25, 1880, and resides at Columbus, Ohio

George William, born December 8, 1856, in Brown County, Ohio Married first, Margarette Perry, who died He married, second, Dora Ploughman, who also died His place of residence is unknown

Charles Oscar born December 20 1859, in Adams County, Ohio Married Ella Ashenhust, December, 1881 He died July 25, 1896 at Manchester, Ohio Mrs Gardner died December 25 1895

Franklin Sherman, born February 6, 1865, in Adams County, Ohio Married Belle Parker and resides at Cincinnati, Ohio.

LOUISA M GARDNER (8).

Matthew (7), Benjamin (6), Benjamin (5), Benjamin (4), Nathaniel (3), Benony (2), George (1).

Louisa M Gardner, daughter of Elder Matthew and Sally (Beasley) Gardner, was born September 15, 1825 Married Abner DeVore, March 5, 1846

Abner DeVore was born May 12, 1824 There was born as the issue of this union:

Benjamin F, March 20, 1847
Julia B, November 27, 1848
John W, February 14, 1850.
Louis G, November 28, 1851
George W, February 19, 1854, died June 3, 1882.
Carey M, January 17, 1856
Charles P, January 2, 1858
Mrs DeVore died December 6, 1860

JULIA ELMIRA GARDNER (8).

Matthew (7), Benjamin (6), Benjamin (5), Benjamin (4), Nathaniel (3), Benony (2), George (1).

Julia Elmira Gardner, daughter of Elder Matthew and Sally (Beasley) Gardner, was born April 7, 1828 Married Samuel H Hopkins

Samuel H Hopkins was born January 22, 1826 The following children were born to them

James Marion, born October 2, 1849 Never married

Sarah Ruth, born April 17, 1851

Edward Elnathan, born April 29, 1859 Never married

Mr Hopkins has been one of the prosperous farmers of Adams Co, Ohio He is living at this writing at a ripe old age and one of the honored citizens of his county

JAMES ALEXANDER GARDNER (8).

Matthew (7), Benjamin (6), Benjamin (5), Benjamin (4), Nathaniel (3), Benony (2), George (1).

James Alexander Gardner, son of Elder Matthew and Sally (Beasley) Gardner, was born November 13 1830 Married Mary Toner, January 14, 1850

The following is a statement recorded by his father "In July, 1851, our fourth son, James Alexander, died of 'bloody-flux' This was the first death in my family He was almost twenty-one years of age. He lived some five miles from us, and left a wife and one child He was a young man of excellent constitution I had baptized him and his wife a few months previous to his death. Shortly before he died he said 'The spring of life is the time to prepare for death' "

He is buried beside his mother in the Beasley cemetery just south of the Matthew Gardner homestead

JOHN WICKLIFFE GARDNER (8).

Matthew (7), Benjamin (6), Benjamin (5), Benjamin (4), Nathaniel (3), Benony (2), George (1).

John Wickliffe Gardner, son of Elder Matthew and Sally (Beasley) Gardner, was born April 17, 1836 Married Nancy Jane Boggs, April 23, 1857

Eight children were born to them as follows.
Charles Walter, born August 7, 1859
Louis Oscar, born October 18, 1860
Malinda Alice, born September 5, 1862
George Washington, born September 2, 1866
William Matthew, born September 18, 1869
Stacy Emerson, born September 11, 1870
Hattie May, born April 24, 1872
Frederick Eugene, born March 21, 1874 Drowned winter 1906-7

Mr. Gardner was one of the sons who remained on his father's homestead The rest of the children, with the exception of Elnathan M., had been placed upon farms in the eastern or western part of the county Mr Gardner has been a farmer during his entire life, remaining upon this farm, enjoying a quiet life with his large family He has not been a rugged man, and would have been better adapted to almost any other vocation Early in life his desire was for a college education He expressed his wishes to his father and evidenced a desire to enter the work of the ministry It may seem strange to the reader when he remembers that his father was one of the most earnest, self-sacrificing preachers, that he would not permit his son to attend school as he desired The young man agreed to repay the money with interest, and to serve his father for the same period of time consumed while in college His father would not comply with the young man's wishes, consequently John W Gardner has spent his life upon his farm He has been very successful in the conduct of his farm, and has a very pleasant, comfortable, country home He is a man of broad experience and fine intellect, being a good conversationalist and pleasing in address

ALBON LUTHER GARDNER (8)

Albon B. (7), Albon C. (6), George (5), Ezekiel (4), Nicholas (3), Nicholas (2), George (1).

Albon Luther Gardner, son of Albon Bancroft and Sarah (White) Gardner, was born September 18, 1847, at Chagrin Falls, Ohio He married Kate Maria Doolittle, eldest daughter of Mark R. and Alta (Persons) Doolittle, November 6, 1872

To them were born two children as follows
George Albon, born March 13, 1874.
Kate Saloma, born November 7, 1880 Married Broy Canfield, October 19, 1904 One child was born to them Sarah Jeanette

Albon Luther Gardner, the oldest son of Albon Bancroft Gardner, was born at Chagrin Falls, Ohio in what was then the rear of the Post Office He was reared on the farm one mile south of Chagrin Falls from his tenth till his sixteenth year When eighteen years of age he entered the dry goods store of his uncle, B. Williams, where he remained one year While engaged in this occupation he was also preparing for his medical course under the direction of Dr H W Curtis. He entered the office of the Doctor and continued his studies with him until he had graduated from the Western Reserve Medical College, Cleveland Ohio, in the spring following his reaching his majority He then entered into a partnership with Dr Nathan Schneider professor of surgery, Cleveland, Ohio, and the following year graduated from the Cleveland Homoeopathic Hospital College of Cleveland, Ohio The partnership was then extended admitting Dr H F Bigger both of whom became distinguished surgeons He has been continuously in the practice of his profesion since 1871, and it has proved an exceptionally lucrative practice

ROSCOE GAYLORD GARDNER (8).

Albon B. (7), Albon C. (6), George (5), Ezekiel (4), Nicholas (3), Nicholas (2), George (1).

Roscoe Gaylord Gardner, son of Albon and Sarah (White) Gardner, was born April 16, 1849, at Chagrin Falls, Ohio, a short distance from Cleveland

He had the advantages of a home with a sufficiency of means and a good school education and when seventeen years old attended Commercial College at Cleveland, Ohio After completing his course he became bookkeeper for his uncle, Benjamin Williams, a dry goods merchant of Chagrin Falls, Ohio This was in the year 1867 Three years later October 12, 1870, he married Miss Florence Eveline Clover, of Greenville, Pennsylvania.

In 1871 he became bookkeeper for Elisha B Platt, who was a banker at Chagrin Falls, Ohio He remained with Mr Platt fourteen months after which he removed to Cleveland, Ohio, and became the individual bookkeeper for Everett Weddell and Company, bankers, which position he held from December 15, 1872, till April 1, 1883

April 6, 1883, he removed to Peoria, Illinois, where he became a member of the firm of Donnemyer, Gardner and Gates Ten years later this firm changed to Donnemyer, Gardner and Company.

Mr Gardner has been a very successful business man and his milling company is known all over the great central section of the United States

As is characteristic of this Gardner family, he has been a member of the Methodist Episcopal Church for about forty years

That strong personality of the father and grandfather is prominent in Mr Gardner In all his business, social and religious life, he is a man of sterling qualities and character

He is a man of his own convictions and when his mind is settled on a matter it is not to be changed In doing this he has gained for himself the reputation of being resolute and firm

That very excellent trait of life and character is the cardinal feature of this man He has the experience of being a man of fifty-seven years of age without having ever taken a glass of any spirituous liquors of any character nor has he ever used tobacco in any form

A business man cannot say he is obliged to do any one of these in order to succeed, for there is no better business man, no cleaner man socially nor a more conscientious Christian gentleman than our friend, R G Gardner

Mr Gardner is a man who enjoys his accumulations with his family and has a beautiful, commodious home

To Mr and Mrs Gardner was born one child, Cora Lee, born November 21, 1873

AUSTIN HARVEY GARDNER (8).

Albon B. (7), Albon C. (6), George (5), Ezekiel (4), Nicholas (3), Nicholas (2), George (1).

Austin Harvey Gardner, son of Albon Bancroft Gardner, and Sarah (White) Gardner, was born at Chagrin Falls, Ohio, December 23, 1850 Married Nellie Ford, of Chagrin Falls, Ohio, October 14, 1873

To them has been born one child

Charles Ford, born December 20th, 1875.

Nellie (Ford) Gardner died at Kansas City Jan 7th, 1897 Austin H Gardner was again married at Kansas City to Miss Ella Elliott, of Kansas City, October 4th, 1905

Austin Harvey Gardner, the subject of this sketch, was employed on his father's farm and attended school until 1870, when he accepted a position as cashier and bookkeeper for the Chagrin Falls Paper Mill, remaining there for one year, resigning to accept a position with the dry goods firm of Williams and Gates, Chagrin Falls, Ohio, which he held for one year He then entered the insurance field, engaging at Youngstown, Ohio, where he remained for three years Owing to the continued strikes at rolling mills, blast furnaces, and manufactories in that section, he disposed of his interests and returned to Chagrin Falls, and engaged in the sewing machine business At the expiration of one year he accepted a position as bookkeeper with Adams & Co, paper mills, of Chagrin Falls At the end of the year the mill and factory was placed in his charge as manager This position he held for 11½ years, resigning much against the wishes of the company to accept a position as cashier of the Excelsior Refining Co, Cleveland, Ohio, which position he held for one year, resigning to take position with the Continental Oil Co (Standard Oil Co), Denver, Colorado First had charge of the bookkeeping department, then credits, later charge of all their stations Held this position for four years, resigning much against their wishes to take the management of The National Oil Co, at Kansas City, Missouri, which position he has held for the past fifteen years, and occupying same position at the present time, having never yet asked for a position, the position having always sought him

SARAH SALOMA GARDNER (8).

Albon B (7), Albon C (6), George (5), Ezekiel (4), Nicholas (3), Nicholas (2), George (1).

Sarah Saloma Gardner, daughter of Albon Bancroft and Sarah (White) Gardner, was born July 14, 1853, at Chagrin Falls, Ohio Married Rev Alfred G Wilson, May 18, 1881.

Their children were:

Royal Gardner, born March 4, 1882

Florence Bell, born January 27, 1884

Edna Saloma, born December 16, 1886

Rev Wilson was born at Clarion, Pennsylvania, May 18, 1850, and is the son of Rev William S Wilson He is a graduate of Mt Union College, Alliance Ohio, and Drew Theological Seminary He was a minister in the Methodist Episcopal Church until 1890, when he identified himself with the Congregational Church The children have inherited the musical qualities of the grandparents of the mother and are identified with musical colleges

CHARLES HERBERT GARDNER (8).

Albon B. (7), Albon C. (6), George (5), Ezekiel (4), Nicholas (3), Nicholas (2), George (1).

Charles Herbert Gardner, son of Albon Bancroft and Sarah (White) Gardner, was born August 26, 1855, at Chagrin Falls, Ohio He married Hattie Elizabeth Vaughn, of Greenville, Pa born May 5, 1858

To them has been born the following children

Laurence V, October 6th, 1886

Eugene R, August 5th, 1889

Grace, March 2nd, 1892

Marjorie, May 30th, 1894

Charles H Gardner bears all the qualifications and strains of character of both parents and their ancestors In business he has been successful

Early in life he began what has proven to be one of the most successful business careers A number of years since he purchased property in the extreme eastern part of the city of Cleveland, Ohio, where he has enjoyed the increase of valuation He has erected and enjoys the comforts of one of the palatial residences of Euclid Avenue

Mr Gardner with each member of his family are natural musicians and in his home can be found an orchestra as well as a choir He is a man of strong convictions and asserts same He is a member of the Methodist church, not only a member, but a leader, and Methodism in the great city of Cleveland has profited very materially by his assistance and practical work His entire family are co-workers with him His sterling qualities have been augmented by the very excellent wife he has been fortunate to possess

MARY WALES GARDNER (8).

Albon B. (7), Albon C. (6), George (5), Ezekiel (4), Nicholas (3), Nicholas (2), George (1)

Mary W. daughter of Albon Bancroft and Sarah (White) Gardner, was born Oct 12, 1858, living at Chagrin Falls, Ohio She married Sheridan P Harris, of Chagrin Falls, Oct 8, 1889

Children are·

Madeline Gardner, born Aug 2, 1890

Carlyle Sheridan born July 6, 1895

Mrs Harris was educated at Oberlin and Vassar She was a teacher in the publics chools for ten years Mr Harris is Chagrin Falls' most prominent business man He is occupying the offices of trust as the choice of the people of his town Mr Harris is one of the most active fraternal men, having reached the highest degree in Masonry

JOHN D. GARDNER (9).

Jeptha M. (8), Matthew (7), Benjamin (6), Benjamin (5), Benjamin (4), Nathaniel (3), Benony (2), George (1).

John D Gardner, son of Jeptha Monroe and Marguerite (Dalton) Gardner, was born September 4, 1843 Married Sarah M Grimes January 1 1868

To them was born one child which died before reaching her estate

The mother also died and he married Bettie Willet, April 19, 1877, who died about 1889 He married Nannie Willet, sister of second wife

The following children were born by second wife

Belle W, born May 14, 1878.

Charles W M, born February 7, 1880

Elmer C, born September 2, 1882.

Lulu M, born February 13, 1884

Nannie L, born September 4, 1886

M Florence, born September 13, 1888

GEORGE F. GARDNER (9).

Jeptha M (8), Matthew (7), Benjamin (6), Benjamin (5), Benjamin (4), Nathaniel (3), Benony (2), George (1)

George F Gardner, son of Jeptha Monroe and Marguerite (Dalton) Gardner, was born September 22, 1846 He married Caroline Waterfield, April 20, 1871 There were no children

SARAH M. GARDNER (9)

Jeptha M (8), Matthew (7), Benjamin (6), Benjamin (5), Benjamin (4), Nathaniel (3), Benony (2), George (1).

Sarah M Gardner, daughter of Jeptha Monroe and Marguerite (Dalton) Gardner, was born April 30, 1848 Married William Grimes, October, 1872

Two children were born to them

Simeon Grimes, who lives at Feesburg, Brown County, Ohio

Carrie, who married Mr Stall and lives at Middle Branch, Ohio

ELNATHAN MATTHEW GARDNER (9).

Jeptha M. (8), Matthew (7), Benjamin (6), Benjamin (5), Benjamin (4), Nathaniel (3), Benony (2), George (1).

Elnathan Matthew Gardner, son of Jeptha Monroe and Marguerite (Dalton) Gardner, was born April 2, 1850 Married Mollie Griffith about December, 1870

There was born to them one son

Lowell F, who lives at Felicity Clermont County, Ohio

MARY C. GARDNER (9).

Jeptha M. (8), Matthew (7), Benjamin (6), Benjamin (5), Benjamin (4), Nathaniel (3), Benony (2), George (1).

Mary C Gardner, daughter of Jeptha Monroe and Marguerite (Dalton) Gardner, was born September 13, 1851-2 Married Charles Wood, July, 1883

One child was born to them

Marguerite Woods, born April 20, 1887 They live on a farm about one-half mile west of the old homestead Her father's homestead was recently sold by the administrator Mrs Woods had always been desirous of owning the farm and purchased it at this sale

THOMAS H GARDNER (9).

Jeptha M. (8), Matthew (7), Benjamin (6), Benjamin (5), Benjamin (4), Nathaniel (3), Benony (2), George (1)

Thomas H Gardner, son of Jeptha Monroe and Marguerite (Dalton) Gardner, was born July 7, 1853, and we have no further record of him

WILLIAM MATTHEW GARDNER (9).

George W (8), Matthew (7), Benjamin (6), Benjamin (5), Benjamin (4), Nathaniel (3), Benony (2), George (1)

William Matthew Gardner, son of George Washington Gardner, married Sarah Belle Bartlow.

The following children

Jesse J., born February 19, 1873

Grace Ann, born October 17, 1874

Osa Lee, born October 8 1876 Married George Jennings.

Louis Carl, born February 4 1883

Nina Bell, born September 7, 1887

MARY MARIA LINDSEY (9).

Lucinda E. Gardner (8), Matthew (7), Benjamin (6), Benjamin (5), Benjamin (4), Nathaniel (3), Benony (2), George (1)

Mary Maria Lindsey, daughter of William J and Lucinda (Gardner) Lindsey, was born February 28, 1850 Married to Nathan M Foster, October 5

Their children were born as follows

William Jesse, born Wednesday, August 12, 1874 Married Mary Boyer, of Ohio, and have two children. They live at Cameron, Mo

Charles Alexander, born Thursday, December 14, 1875 Married Edith Adell Hanks, February 22 1904 One child, Bernice Maud, born July 16, 1905 Live at Tilden, Nebraska

John Edward, born Thursday, February 21, 1878 Married Julia Jurden and have one child Live at Clarence, Ill

Bertha Belle, born Friday, July 30, 1880. Married Henderson Flannery and has one child Live at Paxton, Ill

Flora E., born Tuesday, July 31, 1883 Died 1889

Dexter Marshall, born Tuesday, August 31, 1886 Lives at Clarence, Ill

Albert Franklin born Sunday, September 1, 1889. Lives at Tilden, Nebraska

Cary Alford, born Sunday, September 1, 1889 Lives at Clarence, Ill

Ida Myrtle, born Friday, January 20, 1893 Died 1893

Clarence Marion, born Thursday, July 12, 1894 Lives at Clarence, Ill

SARAH BELLE LINDSEY (9)

Lucinda E. Gardner (8), Matthew (7), Benjamin (6), Benjamin (5), Benjamin (4), Nathaniel (3), Benony (2), George (1)

Sarah B., daughter of William Johnson and Lucinda Eliza (Gardner) Lindsey, was born Aug 7, 1847, at Maysville, Kentucky Married Amos W Hamer and lives at Manchester, Adams County, Ohio

Children.
Nancy Eliza,
William S,
Thomas B,
Matthew G,
Lorenzo D.,
James C.,
Besse M,
Susan Elmira

WALTER L. SHINKLE (9)

Sally (8), Matthew (7), Benjamin (6), Benjamin (5), Benjamin (4), Nathaniel (3), Benony (2), George (1).

Oldest child of Michael J and Sally (Gardner) Shinkle, married November 30, 1858, Miss Nancy E Nowlin To them were born five children She was a resident of Dearborn County, Indiana Mr Shinkle lives near "Union Church," in Brown County, Ohio He has been a deacon in the church where his father served and which his grandfather organized, for many years

He is a very devout man well respected by his neighbors

He rendered very valuable assistance to the writer in compiling the records in that port of the state

JOHN G. SHINKLE (9).

Sally (8), Matthew (7), Benjamin (6), Benjamin (5), Benjamin (4), Nathaniel (3), Benony (2), George (1).

John G. Shinkle was the second son of Michael J and Sally (Gardner) Shinkle, died March 17th, 1884 Was married to Mary F Nowlin, September 6th, 1864 Mrs Shinkle was a sister of the wife of Walter L. Shinkle.

BARTON B. SHINKLE (9).

Sally (8), Matthew (7), Benjamin (6), Benjamin (5), Benjamin (4), Nathaniel (3), Benony (2), George (1).

Barton B., third child of Michael J and Sally (Gardner) Shinkle Married Eliza Mefford, January, 1868 The daughter of Elder G. M Mefford, who was the assistant pastor of "Union Church" in the year 1861, during the last pastorate of Elder Matthew Gardner

THOMAS C. SHINKLE (9).

Sally (8), Matthew (7), Benjamin (6), Benjamin (5), Benjamin (4), Nathaniel (3), Benony (2), George (1).

Thomas C., son of Michael J and Sally (Gardner) Shinkle Married Jane Grimes, October, 1869 Mr Shinkle owns a very beautiful farm about midway between Georgetown and Higginsport, on the west pike He is one of the very prosperous farmers, a large land owner and dealer in tobacco

MATTHEW HALE SHINKLE (9)

Sally (8), Matthew (7), Benjamin (6), Benjamin (5), Benjamin (4), Nathaniel (3), Benony (2), George (1).

Matthew H., son of Michael J and Sally (Gardner) Shinkle, married Josephine Park, December 6th, 1876. Mr Shinkle owns a fine farm on what is known as Shinkle Ridge, near where he was born He is engaged in banking as cashier of the bank in Higginsport, Ohio

MICHAEL E. SHINKLE (9)

Sally (8), Matthew (7), Benjamin (6), Benjamin (5), Benjamin (4), Nathaniel (3), Benony (2), George (1).

Michael E., youngest son of Michael J and Sally (Gardner) Shinkle, married Sally B Marsh, October 25, 1876 Mr Shinkle owns the home farm and is proprietor of the "Dennison House," of Cincinnati, Ohio.

SARAH RUTH HOPKINS (9).

Julia Elmira (8), Matthew (7), Benjamin (6), Benjamin (5), Benjamin (4), Nathaniel (3), Benony (2), George (1).

Sarah Ruth Hopkins, daughter of Samuel H and Julia Elmira (Gardner) Hopkins, was born April 17, 1851 Married John P Leedom, November 25 1869 He was born December 20, 1847

Their children were

Eva L born June 24, 1871 Married W E Bundy, May 8, 1890 One son William Sanford

Effie B, born August 27, 1872 Died November 5, 1891 Married to Jesse H Dugan, October 27 1890 One son Paul

Wilbur H, born March 8, 1877 Married April 20, 1892 One son, John Oliver Leedom

WILLIAM A GARDNER (9).

James Alexander (8), Matthew (7), Benjamin (6), Benjamin (5), Benjamin (4), Nathaniel (3), Benony (2), George (1).

William A Gardner, son of James Alexander and Mary (Toner) Gardner, was born in Brown County, Ohio, November, 1850 Married September, 1871, to Isabella McGofney, who was born December, 1849

Three children have been born to them as follows

Wesley E, born June, 1872 Died September, 1898

Carry C, born September, 1874

Wilbur R, born December, 1876

Mr Gardner resides at Cherry Fork, Adams County, Ohio

BENJAMIN F. DE VORE (9)

Louisa M (8), Matthew (7), Benjamin (6), Benjamin (5), Benjamin (4), Nathaniel (3), Benony (2), George (1).

Banjamin F De Vore, son of Abner and Louisa M (Gardner) De Vore, married Sarah L Richards, November 27, 1867

To them was born the following children

Louisa M, who married F W Wall and lives near Georgetown, Ohio

Henry A, who married Gertrude Elmer and resides at Fostoria, Ohio

Joseph L, died November, 1875

Lillie F, whose address is Georgetown, Ohio

Bertha, who married C C Meranda and resides at Georgetown, Ohio

Edward C, who married Lillie Kinkade and resides at Georgetown, Ohio

Charles R, married Daisy McDonald and resides at Columbus, Ohio

Nellie, Catherine, and Crawford, each of whom together with Lillie, reside with their parents near Georgetown, Ohio

JULIA B DE VORE (9).

Louisa M. (8), Matthew (7), Benjamin (6), Benjamin (5), Benjamin (4), Nathaniel (3), Benony (2), George (1).

Julia B De Vore, daughter of Abner and Louisa M (Gardner) De Vore, married Rev Samuel Godfrey about 1870, and resides at Chicago, Illinois

To them were born two children, Marie and Jessie, each of whom married, but we have not secured their names or addresses.

JOHN W DE VORE (9).

Louisa M. (8), Matthew (7), Benjamin (6), Benjamin (5), Benjamin (4), Nathaniel (3), Benony (2), George (1).

John W De Vore, son of Abner and Louisa M (Gardner) De Vore, married Samantha Dean, March 3, 1872, and resides at Chilo, Clermont County, Ohio

To them were born the following children.

Eva, who married James Neal, whose address is Sardinia, Ohio

William, who married Mattie Cahill, their address is Higginsport, Ohio

Cora, who married Harry Hatfield, whose address is Higginsport, Ohio

Samuel, who married Anna Smith, whose address is Chilo, Ohio.

Addie, who married Jessie Utter, whose address is Georgetown, Ohio

Lewis, who married Stella Shaw and resides at Chilo, Ohio

LOUIS G. DE VORE (9).

Louisa M. (8), Matthew (7), Benjamin (6), Benjamin (5), Benjamin (4), Nathaniel (3), Benony (2), George (1).

Louis G De Vore, son of Abner and Louisa M (Gardner) De Vore, married Lucy A Richards, February 18, 1875

To them were born the following children

William C, who died October 1, 1878

Steven M, who died August 3, 1880

Ada B, born December 29, 1881

M Ethel January 5, 1883, who married C A Lieberman, November, 1904, and resides in Georgetown, Ohio

George R, October 8, 1886

Lucy A De Vore, died June 23, 1889, and Mr. De Vore married Tina Lawwill, October 14, 1891, and to them was born one child Stanley Ray, born May 1, 1895

CAREY M. DE VORE (9).

Louisa M. (8), Matthew (7), Benjamin (6), Benjamin (5), Benjamin (4), Nathaniel (3), Benony (2), George (1).

Carey M De Vore, son of Abner and Louisa M (Gardner) De Vore married India A Smith, February 6, 1879, and resides at Howard, Mason County Kentucky

To them were born two daughters as follows

Ora S, born February 6, 1881, married Clarence Nowers and resides at Dover Kentucky

Mary Oma, born June 8, 1889

CHARLES P. DE VORE (9).

Louisa M. (8), Matthew (7), Benjamin (6), Benjamin (5), Benjamin (4), Nathaniel (3), Benony (2), George (1).

Charles P. De Vore, son of Abner and Louisa M (Gardner) De Vore, married Emma B Bowers, February 6, 1877. Their address is Winchester, Ohio.

To them were born the following children

Joe W, born November 27 1877, married Dora Kendall, November 18, 1903, and live at Winchester, Ohio

Laura E, born June 12, 1879, died November 9, 1900

Alice N, born July 27, 1881, married Jesse A West, Nov 19, 1903

Mollie D, born July 12, 1883, married Earl A Wilson, October 4, 1905 Resides at Winchester, Ohio

Lela E, born January 24, 1886

Wilbur C, born May 25, 1887

Harry E., October 9, 1891.

Minnie L, born August 18, 1893

John E, born October 5, 1896

Maymie M, born March 10, 1900.

JAMES D GARDNER (9).

George Washington (8), Matthew (7), Benjamin (6), Benjamin (5), Benjamin (4), Nathaniel (3), Benony (2), George (1).

James D, son of George Washington Gardner, married and lived at Ripley, Ohio, until his death, which occurred about 1900 He was postmaster at Ripley and was held in high esteem by his fellow-citizens

He had one child, Lela, who married Mr James Blair and resides at Cincinnati, Ohio

CHARLES WALTER GARDNER (9).

John W. (8), Matthew (7), Benjamin (6), Benjamin (5), Benjamin (4), Nathaniel (3), Benony (2), George (1).

Charles Walter Gardner, eldest son of John W and Nancy (Boggs) Gardner, was born August 7, 1859 Married Alice Gray, December 27, 1883 She was born December 3, 1861

To them have been born children as follows

Walter Gray, born June 29, 1885

Eugene Myron, born September 9 1894

Mr Gardner lives in the historic town of Aberdeen Ohio He has enjoyed the advantages of a careful farmer and the result is an accumulation and a prosperous life Mrs Gardner comes from one of the leading families and possesses an estate in her own right We mention a part of this historic property.

Prior to 1870 there was built a very substantial house on the north bank of the Ohio River by one of the sturdy stock and eccentric characters, "Massa Beasley," who was elected a Justice of the Peace, who served between the years of 1870 and 1892, the time of his death This house and man have made Aberdeen famous the world over, and it has earned the title, "Gretna Green of America," and has been frequently the basis of magazine and newspaper articles

The "Squire" and house are described in James Lane Allen's novel, "Summer in Arcady" The property came into possession of Mrs Gardner's mother, February, 1900, by purchase, and later to Mrs Gardner, by inheritance

In this house from 1870 to 1892 were celebrated, according to the records, no less than four thousand four hundred and twenty-seven marriages, records of which are on file in this house and were made by Mr Beasley

LOUIS O. GARDNER (9).

John W (8), Matthew (7), Benjamin (6), Benjamin (5), Benjamin (4), Nathaniel (3), Benony (2), George (1).

Louis O Gardner, son of John W. and Nancy (Boggs) Gardner, was born October 18, 1860 Was married to Jeannette M Buchanan, October 21, 1884, by the Rev H D Rice, Georgetown, Ohio She was born September 13, 1860

To them were born the following children

Stacy Earl, born October 23, 1885

Thomas B born August 12, 1887

Frank S, born July 10, 1889 Died August 27, 1892

Charles H, born April 29, 1892

Mr Gardner owns and lives on a farm about two miles south of where he was reared He is a prosperous farmer and has taken great interest in the education of his boys The two oldest have graduated from the Ripley schools

GEORGE W. GARDNER (9).

John W. (8), Matthew (7), Benjamin (6), Benjamin (5), Benjamin (4), Nathaniel (3), Benony (2), George (1).

George W Gardner, son of John W and Nancy (Boggs) Gardner, was born September 2 1866 Married Elizabeth Smith, daughter of Samuel and Mary Smith, February 17, 1892 She died a few years later Elizabeth (Smith) Gardner was born in England in 1863

To them were born the following children

Wilbert Samuel, born May 20, 1893

Viola Florence born June 16, 1895

Mr Gardner married, second, Emma Jane Eyler, daughter of John W and Nancy Eyler, February 17, 1906

WILLIAM MATTHEW GARDNER (9).

John W (8), Matthew (7), Benjamin (6), Benjamin (5), Benjamin (4), Nathaniel (3), Benony (2), George (1).

William Matthew Gardner, son of John W and Nancy (Boggs) Gardner, was born September 18, 1868 Married Agnes Stevenson, December 7, 1904 No children have been born to them

In the study of the character of the Gardners we have found none that came more nearly filling our ideal of a young man than did William Matthew Gardner He and his brother Stacy Emerson Gardner, who is no less a model man, own and farm the greater portion of the old homestead By industry and frugality they have acquired this property

GRACE G. GARDNER (9).

George B. (8), Seth (7), Benjamin (6), Benjamin (5), Benjamin (4), Nathaniel (3), Benony (2), George (1).

Grace G Gardner, daughter of George B and Amanda (Robinson) Gardner, of Hillsboro, Ohio, was born March 3, 1854, in Washington C H, Ohio In her early childhood her parents removed to Hillsboro, Ohio, where she was educated in the Hillsboro Female College, and the Highland Institute, graduating from the Highland Institute while the renowned Miss Emily Grand Girard was principal Her social career was a brilliant one Her father, a successful lawyer, her mother a charming hostess, gave this only child every advantage, but her church, the Methodist Episcopal, and her studies, music, French, German, and her interest in literary clubs, all have their place in her life She was President for several years of the many Alumnae of the Highland Institute, honorary member of the Hillsboro Female College Alumnae held prominent offices in her church organizations was secretary of the first society of Hillsboro, Ohio, for "prevention of cruelty to animals," established the first Flower Mission, and was President of the first Home Missionary Society in her town

She showed a talent for music at a remarkably early age. The college town in which she lived afforded fine advantages along these lines Later she studied at the Cincinnati College of Music, winning a diploma in vocal art and musical education She also lived two years in Europe studying with some of the finest masters in Italy Germany and England

In concert, oratorio, and church singing she has won fame in both Europe and America She was a great favorite in her tours through England and Ireland

After returning to America she established her studio in New York, where she is now singing and teaching

In the music world she is a recognized authority of the highest standing in her branch of the profession

Her studio at 36 West 25th street is an interesting center From it she has sent and is sending artists into grand opera, light opera, concert and finest church choir positions

She has attracted to her a large circle of friends from the musical, literary, art and social world She is now prominent in "Daughters of Ohio in New York," being chairman of the music and entertainment committee, the presidency of this society having also been urged upon her, but because of her busy life in the music world it was necessary to decline the honor

Lately she is becoming known as a composer, writing the music for her songs

SARAH A CHARLES (9)

Lucinda (8), Lucy (7), Benjamin (6), Benjamin (5), Benjamin (4), Nathaniel (3), Benony (2), George (1)

Sarah A Charles is granddaughter of Lucy (Gardner) Jolly We have not the family record of same The line of descent is established and record may be made

CHARLES F. GARDNER (9).

Thomas (8), Seth (7), Benjamin (6), Benjamin (5), Benjamin (4), Nathaniel (3), Benony (2), George (1).

Charles F Gardner, son of Thomas F., was born April 25, 1855 Married Jane A Hathaway, Feb 21, 1882 She was born Jan 28, 1854 No children

SUSAN GARDNER (9).

Benjamin (8), Abraham (7), Benjamin (6), Benjamin (5), Benjamin (4), Nathaniel (3), Benony (2), George (1).

Susan Gardner, daughter of Benjamin and Susan (Vaughn) Gardner, was born on the Gardner homestead, Auglaize County, Ohio She married Leslie Stoddard There were born to them the following children

May,
Pearl,
Benjamin,
Effie,
Maud,
Henry,
A boy, name not known

KATHERINE GARDNER (9)

Benjamin (8), Abraham (7), Benjamin (6), Benjamin (5), Benjamin (4), Nathaniel (3), Benony (2), George (1).

Katherine Gardner, daughter of Benjamin and Catherine (Orr) Gardner, was born Oct 5, 1860, at the old homestead of her grandfather She married Daniel Gross, of Bunker Hill, Kansas, Aug 29, 1879 Mr

Gross was born April 30, 1858 The following children were born to them

Walter Augustus, born March 25, 1884
Helen May, born November 11, 1887
Ethel Estell, born March 8, 1895.

When Mrs Gross was a very small child she was taken by her father to the western home, as described in the life of Benjamin Gardner, son of Abraham, Sr Only those who have experienced an early childhood in the sparsely settled prairie country can appreciate the early life of this daughter At Bunker Hill Kansas, she married Mr Gross, after which her home was in Bunker Hill

Mr Gross has a general merchandise store which he has conducted successfully for more than 25 years

NELLIE C. GARDNER (9).

Benjamin (8), Abraham (7), Benjamin (6), Benjamin (5), Benjamin (4), Nathaniel (3), Benony (2), George (1).

Nellie C Gardner, daughter of Benjamin and Rachel (Groff) Gardner, was born ——, died June 23, 1903 Married Rufus L Davis in the spring of 1890 Five children were born to them as follows

Carlton Gardner, born October 12, 1891
Howard Irvil, born October 17, 1893
Rufus Percival, born August 19, 1895
Edith Irene, born January 7 1897
Leslie Manard, born July 21, 1899

ELLA J. GARDNER (9)

Benjamin (8), Abraham (7), Benjamin (6), Benjamin (5), Benjamin (4), Nathaniel (3), Benony (2), George (1).

Ella J Gardner, daughter of Benjamin and Rachel (Groff) Gardner, was born in the state of Kansas, May 22, 1863 Married Frank H McClellan, October 16, 1882

The following children were born to them

George Baynard born November 19, 1885
Daphne Vivian, born October 30, 1887, died April 23, 1900
Herbert Norman, born October 10, 1890
Benjamin born October 15, 1895, died February 22, 1896
Ruth Louise, born December 28 1896

MILO GARDNER (9).

Benjamin (8), Abraham (7), Benjamin (6), Benjamin (5), Benjamin (4), Nathaniel (3), Benony (2), George (1).

Milo Gardner, son of Benjamin and Rachel (Groff) Gardner, was born 1867 Living at Holton, Kansas Married Eva McClarren, 1899. She was born 1875.

To them has been born one child

Jeannette G, born 1901

ABRAM E BRENTLINGER (9).

Marinda (8), Abraham (7), Benjamin (6), Benjamin (5), Benjamin (4), Nathaniel (3), Benony (2), George (1).

Abram E Brentlinger, son of William and Marinda (Gardner) Brentlinger, was born December 15, 1849, married Lucy Ann Shaw, March 23, 1873 She was born October 13, 1850

To them were born the following children.

Alvin Amoor, born June 2, 1874

Herman Andrew, born May 4 1877 Died August 22, 1879

Clarence William, born September 12, 1879

Ada Gustava, born November 2, 1882 Married to William Carter, September, 1906

Waldo D, born February 16, 1886

CHARLES BRENTLINGER (9)

Marinda (8), Abraham (7), Benjamin (6), Benjamin (5), Benjamin (4), Nathaniel (3), Benony (2), George (1).

Charles Brentlinger, son of William, Jr, and Marinda (Gardner) Brentlinger, was born March 9 1851 Married Louisa Lovina Holtzapple, February 19, 1879 No children

SARAH ELIZABETH BRENTLINGER (9).

Marinda (8), Abraham (7), Benjamin (6), Benjamin (5), Benjamin (4), Nathaniel (3), Benony (2), George (1).

Sarah Elizabeth Brentlinger, daughter of William, Jr, and Marinda (Gardner) Brentlinger, was born June 16, 1856 She married John M Shaw, February 4, 1877 He was born June 16, 1856

To them were born the following children

Lawrence E born August 6, 1878

Harvey M, born February 5, 1884

Homer M, born July 19, 1886

Charles M, born October 11, 1887

LEVI JAMES BRENTLINGER (9).

Marinda (8), Abraham (7), Benjamin (6), Benjamin (5), Benjamin (4), Nathaniel (3), Benony (2), George (1).

Levi James Brentlinger, son of William, Jr, and Marinda (Gardner) Brentlinger, was born November 23, 1854 Married Sarah Elizabeth Golden, January 28, 1878 She was born August 6, 1858

To them were born the following children

Thomas Elbert, March 31, 1879, died March 14, 1882

Charles Elmer, October 5, 1882

Harley Ellsworth August 30, 1885, died January 8, 1887

Clarence Edward, October 10, 1889, died October 2, 1890

Virgil Ray, September 20, 1891

ANDREW T. BRENTLINGER (9).

Marinda (8), Abraham (7), Benjamin (6), Benjamin (5), Benjamin (4), Nathaniel (3), Benony (2), George (1).

Andrew T Brentlinger, son of William, Jr, and Marinda (Gardner) Brentlinger, was born November 24, 1858 Married Oral E Gierhart on July 24, 1881. She was born in Fairfield County, Ohio, on September 3, 1863

To them was born one child:

Irvil C December 29, 1884

SARAH ELIZABETH CARTER (9).

Lucy (8), Abraham (7), Benjamin (6), Benjamin (5), Benjamin (4), Nathaniel (3), Benony (2), George (1).

Sarah Elizabeth Carter, daughter of Samuel and Lucy (Gardner) Carter, was born February 19, 1850 Married Jacob W Logan, March 1, 1868

To them were born the following children

Melville, born May 7, 1869, died May 26, 1904
Blanche, born January 1, 1871, died December 11, 1890.
Flora, born January 23, 1874
Emma, born January 3 1876 died March 18, 1892
Cathryn, born August 9, 1877
Charles E, born July 14 1879
Sylvia, born September 25, 1881
Jacob, Jr, born November 11 1884
Grover C born November 28, 1886, died Sept 14, 1887
Callie, born November 28, 1886 Died April 21, 1887
Bond W, born February 22, 1888
Velma, born July 19, 1891, died May 3, 1892
Vint H, born January 10, 1894

JOHN CARTER (9)

Lucy (8), Abraham (7), Benjamin (6), Benjamin (5), Benjamin (4), Nathaniel (3), Benony (2), George (1).

John Carter, son of Samuel and Lucy (Gardner) Carter was born November 16, 1852 Was married to Mary Cummins, January 9, 1872

Their children were

Floyd, born November 3, 1872
Florence I, born August 8 1874 died Nov 27, 1881
William A born July 9, 1876
Pearl M, born Nov 2, 1883

Mary (Cummins) Carter died November 21 1883 John Carter was married to Louisa Myers, October 1, 1885 No children born to them

WILLIAM S. CARTER (9).

Lucy (8), Abraham (7), Benjamin (6), Benjamin (5), Benjamin (4), Nathaniel (3), Benony (2), George (1).

William S Carter, son of Samuel and Lucy (Gardner) Carter, was born April 25, 1855 He married Orlinda Harshbarger, July 6, 1879

To them were born the following children

Jennie M., born May 20, 1880, died January 5, 1884

Eliza, born May 7, 1882, died Oct 2, 1903

Bernard, born May 8, 1884

Charles H, born November 19, 1885

Joseph H, born Aug 25, 1887

Roy, born March 23, 1891, died Nov 16, 1905

Florence, born Sept 30, 1893

Cora born May 14, 1897, died Sept 28, 1899

Iva, born March 1, 1900

Infant, died Aug 25, 1901

ALBERT BUTLER (9).

Sarah (8), Abraham (7), Benjamin (6), Benjamin (5), Benjamin (4), Nathaniel (3), Benony (2), George (1)

Albert Butler, son of David and Sarah (Gardner) Butler, was born May 12, 1857 Married Jane Heston about 1876

To them were born two sons

John, born December 1st, 1877

Oliver, have no date of birth furnished

Mr Butler died October 1st, 1887.

LEWIS BUTLER (9)

Sarah (8), Abraham (7), Benjamin (6), Benjamin (5), Benjamin (4), Nathaniel (3), Benony (2), George (1).

Lewis Butler, son of David and Sarah (Gardner) Butler was born July 9, 1863 Married Sarah I Harruff, May 7, 1887 She was born June 6, 1869

To them were born the following children, who are at present living others having died in infancy

Ester D., born March 15, 1890

Gracie E, born June 17, 1892

Raleigh P, born Jan 24, 1894

Gladys I, born Oct. 26, 1897

Frederick O, born Oct 1, 1899

Mrs Butler died August 21, 1905

ROBERT BUTLER (9).

Sarah (8), Abraham (7), Benjamin (6), Benjamin (5), Benjamin (4), Nathaniel (3), Benony (2), George (1).

Robert Butler, son of David and Sarah (Gardner) Butler, was born February 20, 1868 Married Minnie Lowry, September 12, 1895

To them have been born five children, three of whom are living as follows:

Nellie Marie, born July 9, 1897

Mabel Irene, born Oct 2, 1903.

Howard Lee, born March 12, 1905

This young man owns and lives on the homestead of his parents He is one of the exemplary young men, industrious and frugal His personal attention is given to the care of his mother, which commands the respect of all who know him

HORACE WELLS GARDNER (9).

Abraham, Jr. (8), Abraham, Sr. (7), Benjamin (6), Benjamin (5), Benjamin (4), Nathaniel (3), Benony (2), George (1).

Horace Wells Gardner, son of Abraham, Jr., and Mary Jane (Northop) Gardner, was born March 15, 1858 Married 1884.

Children were

Audrey, born about 1885

Maida, born 1892

Roger, born 1894

Horace, born 1897.

Horace W Gardner was born on the old homestead near Wapakoneta, Auglaize County, Ohio He was educated in the public schools, such as the rural districts then afforded Completing the course here he attended the high school at Wapakoneta

In 1876 he went to the State of Kansas, where he remained for a short time, where he became engaged as a lineman for the Western Union Telegraph Company He continued in this relation and was changed from place to place, State to State, until he was finally located in charge of the lines of a small road from St Paul to Duluth, Minn It was not long until he was appointed Superintendent of construction of a portion of the Northern Pacific Railroad

In October, 1903, he removed to Topeka, Kansas, and assumed charge as superintendent of the electrical department of the Santa Fe Railway system

We have been unable to get any reply to our request for his family record and the above is given from our knowledge of the family.

WALTER SCOTT GARDNER (9).

Abraham, Jr. (8), Abraham, Sr (7), Benjamin (6), Benjamin (5), Benjamin (4), Nathaniel (3), Benony (2), George (1).

Walter Scott Gardner, son of Abraham, Jr., and Harriet (Brentlinger) Gardner, was born February 3, 1862 Married Alice Cowan of Anna, Shelby County, Ohio, November, 1882

To them was born one child

Harry Willis

Walter Scott Gardner was educated in the rural district schools of Auglaize County, Ohio After completing the district schools attended the high school at Wapakoneta, Ohio

After his marriage he went to St Paul, Minn., where he engaged with his brother, Horace W Gardner in the electrical department of the railroads with which he was connected It was not long before he was assigned a division of the Northern Pacific Railroad in charge of the electrical department.

CHARLES MORRIS GARDNER (9).

Abraham, Jr (8), Abraham (7), Benjamin (6), Benjamin (5), Benjamin (4), Nathaniel (3), Benony (2), George (1).

Charles Morris Gardner, son of Abraham, Jr., and Harriet (Brentlinger) Gardner, was born July 25, 1863, near Wapakoneta, Ohio

He married, first, Clara Lambert of Anna, Shelby County, Ohio, on January 13, 1883

To them were born the following children:

Bonnie Loretta, born December 16, 1883

Amy Marguerite, born March 13, 1891, died May 16, 1892 She is buried in the family lot in Woodlawn Cemetery, at Toledo, Ohio

Charles Abram, born April 13, 1893

His second wife was Lillian May Stickney Married March 31, 1904.

Charles Morris Gardner remained with his parents on the farm till 1879, when they went west He continued on the farm in Ohio, not desiring to go west He obtained employment in this manner until he had sufficient funds to pay his expenses in college After preparing himself, he devoted several years to school work, after which he returned to college, spending some four years more at the Ohio Northern and Ohio Wesleyan Universities

Later he entered the field work of life insurance He has spent some eighteen years traveling in this capacity, which has called him to many of the important places of the United States Mr Gardner has never used tobacco in any form or liquors, being a total abstainer in every respect He is a member of Lake Shore Lodge, No 718 Heneosis Adelphon Encampment, No 42, and Canton Erie, No 12, of the Independent Order of Odd Fellows of Pennsylvania. He is also a member of Erie Lodge, No 327, the Knight of Pythias

CLARA (LAMBERT) GARDNER.

Clara (Lambert) Gardner, the first wife of Charles Morris Gardner, was the youngest daughter of Gabriel and Nancy (Imes) Lambert Mr. Lambert was born March 20, 1825 Mrs Lambert was born November 13, 1826.

Mr Lambert is buried in the cemetery one mile north and one mile west of Anna, Shelby County, Ohio Mrs Lambert is buried in the cemetery two miles south of Anna The home farm of the Lamberts' is two miles north and one mile west of Anna, Shelby County, Ohio.

The father and grandfather of Mr Lambert were early pioneer Methodist Episcopal preachers, in the days when horse-back riding was the custom, and it required several weeks to itinerate on those large circuits Both of the grandparents lived to be very aged men, having devoted their lives to the Christian ministry The writer never met Mr Lambert, as he died before he became acquainted with the family.

The writer desires to say that of all elderly people with whom he has become acquainted, he has not met one of more kindly disposition or even temper than Mrs Lambert Having reared a large family and experienced the trials and usual hardships, and having been left a widow before the family had reached their estate, she constantly grew into a lovely disposition and character The entire family were members of and close adherents of the doctrine of the Methodist Episcopal church.

LILLIAN MAY (STICKNEY) GARDNER

Lillian May (Stickney) Gardner, daughter of A McCall and Caroline C (Lathrop) Stickney, was born at Fargo, Genesee County, New York, January 6, 1878 She was educated in the schools of her county, after which she went to Buffalo, N Y She remained in Buffalo for some five years, when she went to Ohio, where she met Charles Morris Gardner, to whom she was married March 31, 1904 No children have been born to them Mrs Gardner comes of the family of Lathrop, whose line of descent will follow this article, which we record for the following reasons

In tracing the Gardner and Lathrop genealogy we found in several instances where the families had intermarried in early colonial times. The Rhode Island and Connecticut branches of these two families were closely connected and lived in the same town some two hundred years before the subject of this article was born

It is indeed strange how families will diverge for centuries and then return and again intermarry as has been the case in this particular instance, following a lapse of some two hundred years We frequently say "We are not related in any manner," but without the knowledge have a much closer relation than it is possible to suspect. The earlier settlers of these States were all intermarried and from them have come the families that become the study of this work

ONE LINE OF LATHROP GENEALOGY.

The Lowthorpe—Lothropp—Lathrop Family of England.

Lowthorpe is a small parish in the wapentake of Dickering, in the East Riding of York, four and one-half miles northeast from Great Driffield, having about one hundred and fifty inhabitants It is a perpetual curacy in the archdeaconry of York 'The church, which was dedicated to St Martin, and had for one of its chaplains, in the reign of Richard the Second, Robert de Louthorp, is now partly ruinated, the tower and chancel being almost entirely overgrown with ivy It was a collegiate church from 1333, and from the style of its architecture, must have been built about the time of Edward III

There has been no institution to it since 1579 The church consists of a nave, chancel, and tower at the west end, the latter finished with brick and clumsy pinnacles It was formerly a very handsome structure, the windows being lofty, of three lights with trefoil heads, and three quaterfoils in the sweep of the arch The portion of the church now used for divine service is the nave, the chancel having been desecrated for a considerable period In this part of the church are two large ash trees and some curious monuments, one of which is a brass tablet rendered illegible through the weather Affixed to the north side of the nave is the following historical tablet in bad repair

"The collegiate church of Lowthorpe was an ancient rectory, dedicated to St Martin

"A D 1333, it was endowed by Sir John de Haslerton, who founded in it six perpetual chantries

"A D 1364, Sir Thomas de Haslerton added another chantry for the souls of himself and Alice his wife He endowed the church with the manor Lowthorpe and the mansion house

"A D 1776, the inhabitants of the township of Lowthorpe repaired the roof of the church"

'A D. 1777, the church was paved, and the chancel contracted and painted by Sir William St Quintin, Bart, lord of the manor and patron of the living, descended from the family of Haslertons."

In 1789 the south side of the chancel was entirely rebuilt, leaving, however, the tower and chancel as they have stood for many generations The church is a perpetual curacy

Our pedigree of that branch of the old Lowthorpe family which had its earliest known English seat in Lowthorpe, wapentake of Dickreing Fast Riding of York, begins in John Lowthorpe, gr-grandfather, to Rev John Lothropp, the American pioneer Early in the sixteenth century he was living in Cherry Burton, a parish about four miles from Lowthorpe He was, though belonging to a junior branch of the family, a gentleman of quite extensive landed estates both in Cherry Burton and in various parts of the county In the 37th year of Henry VIII (1545), he appears on a Yorkshire subsidy roll, assessed twice as much as any other inhabitant of the parish His son Robert succeeded to the estates of his father in Cherry Burton, and during his lifetime made considerable additions to them.

Thomas, son of the above mentioned Robert, was born in Cherry Burton, England, and was the father of John, baptized in Eton, Dec. 20, 1584, and who became the pioneer and founder of the Lothrop—Lathrop family in America

John Lothropp, for this is the form in which he wrote his name, was baptized as English records show, in Etton, Yorkshire, Dec 20, 1584 He was educated in Queens College, Cambridge, where he was matriculated in 1601, graduated B A. in 1605, and M A in 1609

He labored as a minister of the English church as long as his judgment could approve the ritual and government of the church But when he could no longer do this, we find him conscientiously renouncing his orders and asserting the right of still fulfilling a ministry to which his heart and his conscience had called him Accordingly, 1623, his decision is made He bids adieu to the church of his youth, and with no misgivings, subscribes with a firm hand to the doctrines, and espouses with a courageous heart the cause of the independents. Henceforth his lot is with conventicle men in his mother land, and with the exiled founders of a great nation in a new world.

The congregation of dissenters to which he ministered had no place of public worship, their worship itself being illegal Only such as could meet the obliquy and risk of danger of worshiping God in violation of human statute, were likely to be found in that secret gathering Yet in goodly numbers, in such places in South Wark as they could stealthily occupy, they held together and were exhorted and instructed by the minister of their choice For not less than eight years they so worshiped No threats of vengeance deterred, and no vigilance of officious ministers of the violated law detected them More watchful grew the minions of the law Keen-scented church hounds traversed all the narrow ways of the city whose most secret nooks could by any possibility admit even a small company of the outlaws One of the wiliest of these pursuivants of the Bishop tracked Mr Lothropp and his followers to their retreat They had met for worship as had been their wont, little thinking that it would be their last gathering with their beloved minister Their private sanctuary, a room in the house of Mr Humphrey Barnett, a Brewer's clerk in Black Friars, is suddenly invaded Tomlinson and his ruffian band, with a show of power above their resistance, seize forty-two of their number, allowing only eighteen of them to escape, make that 22d day of April, 1632, forever memorable to those suffering Christians by handing them over in fetters to the executioners of the law which was made for godly men to break In the old Clink prison in Newgate, and in the Gatehouse, all made for felons, these men, "of whom the world was not worthy," lingered for months. During these months a fatal sickness was preying upon his wife, and bringing her fast toward the end of which illness she died, he procured liberty of the Bishop to visit his wife before her death, and commended her to God by prayer On his return to prison, his poor children, being many, repaired to the Bishop of Lambeth, and made known to him their miserable condition, by reason of their good father's being continued in close durance who commisserated their condition so far as to grant him liberty, he soon after coming over into New England.

On reaching Boston with that portion of his London flock who had accompanied him, he found already the preparations begun to welcome him to a new home in Scituate. The last nine pioneers had built their houses in that new settlement and to it, with such of his people as were ready to accompany him, he repaired September 27, 1634 Something near the end of September he makes an entry in the private Journal to preserve the names of those pioneers who had so prepared the way before him Their names, Hatherly,, Cudworth, Gilson, Anniball, Rowlyes, Turner, Cobbes, Hewes, Foster, show them to have been mainly London and Kent men, and would suggest that they had known of Mr Lothropp's previous career and had called him to come among them as their minister.

The church, the walls of which were made of poles filled between with stones and clay, the roof thatched, the chimney to the mantle of rough stone, and above of cobble work, the windows of oiled paper, and the floors of hand sawed planks"

The following record, preserved in the handwriting of the Scituate pioneer, is perhaps the only record extant regarding his call and settlement in the ministry at Scituate

"Jann 19, 1634, att my house, uppon wch day I was chosen Pastour and invested into office"

Mrs Gardner's great grandfather was Samuel Lathrop; his wife was Lucy Pendleton They removed from Bozrah, Conn, to New York State, settling in Genesee County, where he lived and died on what is now known as the "Young" farm, located on the line between the townships of Darien and Alexander Her grandfather was Anson Lathrop, a prosperous farmer, who lived near Attica, N Y. in Wyoming County He was born in Bozrah, Conn, in 1803, and removed with his parents to New York State One of his sons, Samuel, served in a New York regiment during the civil war, was taken prisoner and died of starvation in Libby prison Another son, Henry, served in a Pennsylvania regiment and was killed at the battle of Gettysburg Burr, another son, was also killed in the war Of her father's family, back of her grandfather, Mrs Gardner knows but little, save that they were among the early settlers of New England and that her grandfather, Jonas Stickney, was one of the early settlers of Erie County, N Y, removed to Genesee County, where he was a prosperous farmer, owning a large farm in the township of Darien

HORACE FAIRFIELD (9).

Clarissa (8), Abraham (7), Benjamin (6), Benjamin (5), Benjamin (4), Nathaniel (3), Benony (2), George (1).

Horace Fairfield, son of George and Clarissa (Gardner) Fairfield, was born Aug 1, 1857 Married Mary E Hamilton, who was born November 5, 1858

To them were born the following children

Richard O, born Feb 18, 1882

Evelyn, born October 2, 1883

Minnie D, born Sept. 30, 1886.

Ruth M., born June 6, 1893.

Paul C born April 18, 1896

Horace Fairfield has been actively engaged as traveling salesman for farming implements for some twenty years He owns and lives upon a very large farm located near Paulding, Paulding County, Ohio

LEWIS W. FAIRFIELD (9).

Clarissa (8), Abraham (7), Benjamin (6), Benjamin (5), Benjamin (4), Nathaniel (3), Benony (2), George (1).

Lewis W Fairfield, son of George and Clarissa (Gardner) Fairfield was born October 15, 1858, near Uniopolis, Auglaize County, Ohio Married Ina Maud Howe, of Mt. Victory, Ohio, July 2, 1884

To them were born the following children

Rachel, born June 19, 1885.

George Howe, born June 18, 1887

Roger, born May 28, 1888

Ina Maud (Howe) Fairfield, died July 3, 1888, and Mr Fairfield married, second, Marie L Almond, June 25, 1891

To them four children have been born

Almond Crockett, born March 1, 1893.

Thomas Gardner born May 9, 1895

Myra Olivia, born August 31, 1898

Frances Helen, born October 31, 1904

Lewis W Fairfield has spent his entire life in school work. Educated at the Ohio Northern University he became associated with Prof L M Sniff, who was one of the leaders of that institution When Prof Sniff severed his relation with the O N U it was to establish the Tri-State Normal University at Angola, Ind Prof Lewis W Fairfield, who had always been one of the advanced students of the O N U, was selected as his associate in this new enterprise Mr Fairfield has been a success in all his work He is a devout Christian gentleman

CHARLES HARSHBARGER (9).

Caroline (8), Abraham (7), Benjamin (6), Benjamin (5), Benjamin (4), Nathaniel (3), Benony (2), George (1).

Charles Harshbarger, son of George W and Caroline (Gardner) Harshbarger, was born December 12, 1866 Married Wannettie Naumburg, September 14, 1890

To them has been born two children:

Ada,

Dewey

IDA HARSHBARGER (9).

Caroline (8), Abraham (7), Benjamin (6), Benjamin (5), Benjamin (4), Nathaniel (3), Benony (2), George (1).

Ida Harshbarger, daughter of George W and Caroline (Gardner) Harshbarger, was born August 12, 1872 Married Frank M. Baker

To them was born one child.

Ida May.

The mother died when the babe was about one week old. The grandparents, parents of the mother, adopted Ida May as their own child, giving the name of the grandparents.

SARAH ELIZABETH FAIRFIELD (9).

Elizabeth (8), Abraham (7), Benjamin (6), Benjamin (5), Benjamin (4), Nathaniel (3), Benony (2), George (1).

Sarah Elizabeth Fairfield, daughter of John W and Elizabeth (Gardner) Fairfield, was born December 18, 1860. Married James B. Naylor, who was born February 14, 1858

The following children were born to them

Ora Emery, born April 30, 1884

Iona Ann, born January 19, 1886.

James Thomas, born March 18, 1892

Straut Wade, born January 11, 1898

THOMAS FAIRFIELD (9).

Elizabeth (8), Abraham (7), Benjamin (6), Benjamin (5), Benjamin (4), Nathaniel (3), Benony (2), George (1).

Thomas Fairfield, son of John W. and Elizabeth (Gardner) Fairfield, was born Oct. 7, 1862 He married Leanna Moore, December 8, 1886 She was born October 15, 1865

To them were born two children, the first dying in infancy, the second was

Ora Guy, born April, 1889

Mr Fairfield is a very prosperous farmer, owning a large farm in the prairie district, near Mahomet, Ill.

CHARLES F. GARDNER (9).

Austin H. (8), Albon B. (7), Albon C. (6), George (5), Ezekiel (4), Nicholas (3), Nicholas (2), George (1).

Charles F Gardner, son of Austin H. and Nellie (Ford) Gardner, was born December 20th, 1875. Married Ollie De Ford of Kansas City. Mo, in 1899, and located upon his father's stock farm at Markuette, Kan.

CORA LEE GARDNER (9).

Roscoe G. (8), Albon B (7), Albon C (6), George (5), Ezekiel (4), Nicholas (3), Nicholas (2), George (1)

Cora Lee Gardner, daughter of Roscoe Gaylord and Florence Eveline (Clover) Gardner, was born November 21, 1873 On March 25, 1899, she married Ira Barton Penniman Mrs. (Gardner) Penniman was educated in the schools of Cleveland, Ohio, and Peoria, Illinois Graduating from the public schools she attended college for two years at Oberlin, Ohio, then entered the "Woman's College of Baltimore, from which she graduated in 1897 Mr Ira B Penniman is a graduate from both college and conservatory at Oberlin He is a musician of very extraordinary ability, and gives his entire time and attention to music.

SARAH ANN THOMPSON (9).

Lucinda Jolly (8), Lucy Gardner (7), Benjamin (6), Benjamin (5), Benjamin (4), Nathaniel (3), Benony (2), George (1).

Sarah Ann, daughter of Solomon and Lucinda (Jolly) Thompson, married Samuel B Charles

Children:
Ada,
Lucinda,
Bertha Lee,
Corliss D.,
David M.

EVA LEEDOM (10).

Sarah Ruth (9), Julia Elmira (8), Matthew (7), Benjamin (6), Benjamin (5), Benjamin (4), Nathaniel (3), Benony (2), George (1).

Eva Leedom, daughter of John P. and Sarah Ruth (Hopkins) Leedom, was born June 24, 1871 Married W E. Bundy of Cincinnati, O

One child
William Sanford

Mrs Bundy was educated in the schools at Washington, D C, and enjoyed a brilliant social career

NANCY ELIZA HAMER (10).

Sarah B. Linsey (9), Lucinda E. Gardner (8), Matthew (7), Benjamin (6), Benjamin (5), Benjamin (4), Nathaniel (3), Benony (2), George (1).

Nancy E., daughter of Amos W and Sarah B (Linsey) Hamer married James R Bowman

Children
Harry Glenn,
Walter Myers,
Elizabeth Belle,
Marjorie

MELVILLE LOGAN (10)

Sarah Elizabeth (9), Lucy (8), Abraham (7), Benjamin (6), Benjamin (5), Benjamin (4), Nathaniel (3), Benony (2), George (1).

Melville Logan son of Jacob W and Sarah Elizabeth (Carter) Logan, was born May 7, 1869, died May 26, 1904

The following children

Mamie G., born January 19, 1892

Eva V, born August 1, 1896

FLORA LOGAN (10).

Sarah Elizabeth (9), Lucy (8), Abraham (7), Benjamin (6), Benjamin (5), Benjamin (4), Nathaniel (3), Benony (2), George (1)

Flora Logan, daughter of Jacob W and Sarah Elizabeth (Carter) Logan, was born January 23, 1874 Was married to C W Beere, February 25, 1893

To them were born the following children

Ward, born August 29, 1894.

Don J, born Sept 29, 1897

Marguerite, born Nov 4, 1899

Two girls, unnamed, died infants

CATHERINE LOGAN (10)

Sarah Elizabeth (9), Lucy (8), Abraham (7), Benjamin (6), Benjamin (5), Benjamin (4), Nathaniel (3), Benony (2), George (1).

Catherine Logan, daughter of Jacob W and Sarah Elizabeth (Carter) Logan, was born August 9, 1877. Married to V E. Burden, May 29, 1897.

To them was born

Fariel, born March 24, 1898

CHARLES E LOGAN (10).

Sarah Elizabeth (9), Lucy (8), Abraham (7), Benjamin (6), Benjamin (5), Benjamin (4), Nathaniel (3), Benony (2), George (1).

Charles E Logan, son of Jacob W and Sarah Elizabeth (Carter) Logan, was born July 14, 1879 Was married to Anna Sneary, August 11, 1900

Their children are

Murlin, born September 12, 1901.

Reba V., born September 9, 1903.

SYLVIA LOGAN (10).

Sarah Elizabeth (9), Lucy (8), Abraham (7), Benjamin (6), Benjamin (5), Benjamin (4), Nathaniel (3), Benony (2), George (1).

Sylvia Logan, daughter of Jacob W and Sarah Elizabeth (Carter) Lagon, was born September 25, 1881 Married Otto Burden, December 12, 1900

Their children were
Lela, born March 2, 1901
Geraldine, born February 24, 1903.
Ruth, born March 3, 1906.

FLOYD CARTER (10).

John (9), Lucy (8), Abraham (7), Benjamin (6), Benjamin (5), Benjamin (4), Nathaniel (3), Benony (2), George (1).

Floyd Carter, son of John and Mary (Cummins) Carter was born November 3, 1872 Married Louisa B Burden, April 7, 1895.

Their children were
Orvilla N, born May 31, 1896
Rodger L, born Ocotber 6, 1897.
Harold D, born August 15, 1904
Daughter, born August, 1907

WILLIAM CARTER (10).

John (9), Lucy (8), Abraham (7), Benjamin (6), Benjamin (5), Benjamin (4), Nathaniel (3), Benony (2), George (1).

William Carter, son of John and Mary (Cummins) Carter, was born July 9, 1876 Married Almeda Buffenbarger, February 1 1896

Their children were
Nellie M, born November 24, 1897
Richard D, born May 9, 1899

PEARL CARTER (10).

John (9), Lucy (8), Abraham (7), Benjamin (6), Benjamin (5), Benjamin (4), Nathaniel (3), Benony (2), George (1).

Pearl Carter, daughter of John and Mary (Cummins) Carter, was born November 2, 1883 Married Charles W Jenkins, July 3, 1903.

Children
Marguerite M, born May 2, 1904
Donald W, born November 3, 1905, died February 9, 1906

IONA ANN NAYLOR (10).

Sarah Elizabeth (9), Elizabeth (8), Abraham (7), Benjamin (6), Benjamin (5), Benjamin (4), Nathaniel (3), Benony (2), George (1).

Iona Ann Naylor, daughter of James B and Sarah Elizabeth (Fairfield) Naylor, was born January 19, 1886. She married Frank Layman, of Matthew, Mo, July 12, 1905.

BONNIE LORETTA GARDNER (10).

Charles Morris (9), Abraham (8), Abraham (7), Benjamin (6), Benjamin (5), Benjamin (4), Nathaniel (3), Benony (2), George (1).

Bonnie Loretta Gardner, daughter of Charles Morris and Clara (Lambert) Gardner, was born at Sidney, Shelby County, Ohio, December 16, 1883.

She married Lawrence Henry Gautz, December 24, 1903 Mr Gautz was born May 25, 1881, in Raisinville township, Monroe Co, Mich.

To them has been born one son:

Charles Wilber David, born November 2, 1905

CHARLES ABRAM GARDNER (10).

Charles Morris (9), Abraham (8), Abraham (7), Benjamin (6), Benjamin (5), Benjamin (4), Nathaniel (3), Benony (2), George (1).

Charles Abram Gardner, the only son of Charles Morris and Clara (Lambert) Gardner, was born at Toledo, Ohio, on the 13th day of April, 1893.

This son has been a great student and has accomplished more in a few years than most boys do in their entire school work. Books and libraries are his constant companions.

CHAGRIN FALLS OHIO.

Chagrin Falls is a little town located about an hour's ride by trolley from Cleveland, Ohio The country surrounding this village is broken and affords scenery that would please the most critical eye

A small stream of water meanders through the hills and affords the watering facilities for the town As is characteristic of several of the streams in northern Ohio, there is a rapids at this place from which the town takes its name of Falls We were not advised how the first part of the name became attached as we could not see any evidence of chagrin while we were there

At the northeast of the town the valley is narrow and beyond this is a broad valley Following this narrow valley the stream makes very rapid descent, which affords one of the most advantageous water powers

Early in the nineteenth century this water power was appropriated by two of Ohio's early pioneers.

Deacon Hervey White came to this location and threw a dam across the narrow place in the stream and created a very large lake on the low grounds back of the dam Only a few feet of race was required till the water was upon the wheel of the large manufacturing plant he erected. Hervey White was an axe maker He erected here a mill and pursued his occupation and enlarged till he possessed a very large plant Surrounding him was a veritable village known as Whitesville

The location was nearly a mile from the falls in the stream At these falls there was erected another industry Another dam was thrown across the stream and retained the supply for another of the pioneers.

Albon Crocker Gardner erected here a flouring, carding and woolen mill Two separate industries by two different characters and dispositions in men Mr Gardner had come to this place later in life than Mr White, as Mr Gardner had lived in Parkman prior to this where he had conducted a trade similar to that which he opened here

From both these mills went the products all over the State of Ohio and the town became the central point for trade and sale

Thus you see the lives of two men, the leaders of this little place who had the employment of all the people of this town and upon whom the responsibility of the place depended

They were to do more than purchase the raw material and convert it into the product of their factories They were to mould and frame the minds and character of the entire town The children were to be educated, churches were to be maintained. Families were to be supported Competencies for the future of the families was of vital importance

In the providence of God this town was supplied with the material to accomplish this work

Back in the mother country were families that believed in the worship of God according to the dictates of one's own conscience

The Mayflower brought to this country a family by the name of White, and while laying in anchor after landing on the shore of the new country, there was born to this family a son who was to be the first American born child of this noble family

From this has come this family of which Deacon Hervey White was a descendant

About the time of the landing of this family there was another that came to this new world, not as an infant in his mother's arms, but a strong man, ready to battle with the conflicts of life in a wilderness home Landing as they did at the same place we follow the two families to Ohio George Gardner not remaining in Massachusetts because of the religious freedom of Rhode Island, went to the island of Rhode Island Here began the line of descent of Albon Crocker Gardner and the lines are to be followed Trace the descent to 1800 and the reader finds the branch to which Mr Gardner belongs inherited the early teaching of the Quakers, which form of religion it is said Mr Gardner had embraced and was a member of that denomination when he came to Ohio.

Quiet, unassuming and honest were the principles of these two men, and in those lives we have those traits of character

Deacon Hervey White with the strains of Puritan blood from a descent of more than a century and a half of the influence of Massachusetts, and Albon Crocker Gardner were the two men who were to guide the future and lay the foundation for the village of Chagrin Falls

Is it any wonder the place succeeded? We have written a sketch of the life of these two characters under the family title and with the study of these lives with the town the reader can readily understand why Chagrin Falls has been the peaceful little village it is

INDEX.

RHODE ISLAND.

A

B

RHODE ISLAND—Continued

C

RHODE ISLAND—Continued.

RHODE ISLAND—Continued

RHODE ISLAND—Continued

SIXTH GENERATION

SEVENTH GENERATION

RHODE ISLAND—Continued

EIGHTH GENERATION

RHODE ISLAND—Continued

RHODE ISLAND—Continued

RHODE ISLAND—Continued

RHODE ISLAND—Continued

RHODE ISLAND—Continued

RHODE ISLAND—Continued

T

RHODE ISLAND—Continued

RHODE ISLAND—Continued

CONNECTICUT.

CONNECTICUT—Continued

CONNECTICUT—Continued

CONNECTICUT—Continued

MAINE.

MAINE—Continued

MAINE—Continued

NEW YORK AND MASSACHUSETTS.

NEW YORK AND MASSACHUSETTS—Continued.

NEW YORK AND MASSACHUSETTS—Continued

NEW YORK AND MASSACHUSETTS—Continued

G

THIRD GENERATION

FOURTH GENERATION

FIFTH GENERATION

SIXTH GENERATION

NEW YORK AND MASSACHUSETTS—Continued

SEVENTH GENERATION.

EIGHTH GENERATION

NEW YORK AND MASSACHUSETTS—Continued

NINTH GENERATION

NEW YORK AND MASSACHUSETTS—Continued

TENTH GENERATION

MISCELLANEOUS

NEW YORK AND MASSACHUSETTS—Continued

NEW YORK AND MASSACHUSETTS—Continued

NEW YORK AND MASSACHUSETTS—Continued

NEW YORK AND MASSACHUSETTS—Continued

NEW YORK AND MASSACHUSETTS—Continued

NEW YORK AND MASSACHUSETTS—Continued

NEW YORK AND MASSACHUSETTS—Continued

NEW YORK AND MASSACHUSETTS—Continued

OHIO.

OHIO—Continued

OHIO—Continued

OHIO—Continued

OHIO—Continued

OHIO—Continued.

ERRATA

Original spelling of words has been retained in all legal documents copied herein

Page 68—The letter e in Antis is superfluous
Page 105—Should read as follows Dorcas, daughter of Caleb
Page 109—The word Conenticut should read Connecticut
Page 151—The word Presreve should be Preserve
Page 124—The word HANAH should be HANNAH
Page 163—The word linquist should be linguist
Page 173—The word Muad should be Maud
Page 174—The word Duramesq should be Dumaresq
Page 177—The word marritd should be married
Page 189—The word yau should be you
Page 208—The word crildren should be children
Page 238—He married at Jodi should read, She married at Lodi
Page 291—Clarissa appearing second time is superfluous
Page 310—SETH GARDNER (7)
Page 314—Elizabeth Jane should read Eliza Jane

ADDENDA

I.

According to another source than that which is followed in the text Polly Tamplin was the mother of William Smith Senior, of Hancock, and his wife was Mary Walker There was thus but one William Walker Smith, and he was the grandson of this couple and the son of Willard and Amy (Gardner) Smith William Smith Senior fought in the battle of Bunker Hill His mother, Polly Tamplin was the daughter of an Irish nobleman

II

Hannah Maria (Henry) Ashley (7), Hannah Gardner (6), Palmer (5) Sylvester (4), Nicholas (3) Nicholas (2), George (1) the last of the seventh generation, died of pleuro-pneumonia April 28 1907 at the home of her son, James Alton Ashley at Hawarden Iowa, at the age of 87 years and 18 days Bereft of her mother at the age of five, she made her home at her uncle, Sylvester (6), at Eagle Village, Manlius, N Y, until her fifteenth year, when she joined the other members of her family at Medina Ohio There she married, and at Marshall, Wis and at Grundy Co, Iowa experienced the rigors of pioneer life She was a woman of godly and lovable character, a lifelong member of the M E Church "Grandma Ashley" was a household term in the homes of the entire community in which were passed her declining years She retained her mental powers unimpaired to the last Just a month before her death she wrote, without the aid of spectacles, a page of names and dates for this work Cut off her lifelong from an acquaintance with her cousins, she eagerly awaited the publication of the book, that she might learn their whereabouts and fortunes as hers' and her brothers' had by dint of diligent search been found just in time to be given a place in this History and Genealogy The loss and late recovery of these Henry cousins to the knowledge of their kin forcibly demonstrate the value and necessity of such a work as this, if families are to be kept together in acquaintance and sympathy.

CPSIA information can be obtained
at www.ICGtesting.com
Printed in the USA
BVHW050032060320
574203BV00003B/78